Māori
Boy

Māori Boy

a memoir of childhood

WITI IHIMAERA

VINTAGE

 The assistance of Creative New Zealand is
gratefully acknowledged by the publisher.

A VINTAGE BOOK published by Random House New Zealand, 18 Poland Road,
Glenfield, Auckland, New Zealand

For more information about our titles go to www.randomhouse.co.nz

A catalogue record for this book is available from the National Library
of New Zealand

Random House New Zealand is part of the Random House Group
New York   London   Sydney   Auckland   Delhi   Johannesburg

First published 2014

ISBN 978 1 86979 726 3
eISBN 978 1 86979 727 0

Design: Megan van Staden
Cover illustration: Teria with the author

Printed in New Zealand by Printlink

This publication is printed on paper pulp sourced from sustainably grown
and managed forests, using Elemental Chlorine Free (ECF) bleaching, and
printed with 100% vegetable-based inks.

For the mokopuna,
so that they know

Contents

A GLIMPSE THROUGH SEVEN GENERATIONS OF THE WHAKAPAPA

HOANA'S WHAKAPAPA

Harete Awatea *was espoused to* ?
they were the parents of
Mere Karaka Tiritapu *who married* George Babbington (aka Hōri Paputene)
they were the parents of
Hone (John) Hikurangi Babbington *who married* Mere Arahi Pōtae
they were the parents of
Rēnata (Len) Tūpara Babbington *who married* Matepe Tautau
they were the parents of
Hoana Putiputi (Flowers) Babbington, Mōkena (Romio) Babbington and Hātea Rangi Babbington
(Hoana was raised by her grand-uncle, Moana Tautau, and his wife, Wharerautawa)

Hoana Putiputi (Flowers) Babbington *married* Kereama (Graham) Hātarei Keelan

KEREAMA'S WHAKAPAPA

Tatai O Te Rangi *was espoused to* Ngauru
they were the parents of

Rīria Te Rau Mawhai *who was espoused to* Hopa Te Ari   Rāwiri Tangaroa *was espoused to* Tarati Angiangi
they were the parents of   *they were the parents of*

Rihara Mahemahe *who was espoused to* Erana Te O Kore   Hana Konewa *who was married to* William Thomas Keelan
they were the parents of   *they were the parents of*

Turuhira Mahemahe *who married* Wī Koka Keelan
they were the parents of

Kereama (Graham), Lena, Tiorare (Joe), Rūtene, Hana Konewa, Hera (Sarah), Karauria, Dick,
Hone (John), Ngāi Te Wai Motu, Kopa, Thomas William and Mary

Kereama (Graham) Hātarei Keelan *married* Hoana Putiputi (Flowers) Babbington

TERIA'S WHAKAPAPA

Ngarangi Ka Piere *was espoused to* Ihukauki Parakau
they were the parents of
Rīria Mauaranui *who married* Thomas Halbert
they were the parents of
Wī Pere Halbert *who was married to* Arapera Tautahi O Te Rangi
they were the parents of
Mirianata Pere, Hani Pere, Mana Pere Edwards, Tūruki Pere, Teria Pere Smiler, Hiraina Pere Whaanga,
Mahanga Pere, Mafeking Pere, Mere Tahatū Horsefall, Charles Taare Pere, Parakau Bella Pere,
Waioriwa Pere Baker *and* Te Kani Pere

Teria Pere *married* Pera Punahāmoa Ihimaera (Smiler)

PERA PUNAHĀMOA'S WHAKAPAPA

Hēmi Te Uri *was espoused to* Tauiwa
they were the parents of
Ruihi *who was married to* Wikiriwhi Uenuku
they were the parents of
Te Rina Parewhai *who married* Hamiora Parahi
they were the parents of

Wī Tamahi Hānene *was espoused to* Ripeka Tahere Manuwai
they were the parents of
Te Iraia Te Hānene *who was espoused to* Rāwinia Torere
they were the parents of
Te Teira Ringarore Te Hānene *who married* Turuhira Tāmaku
they were the parents of

Hine Te Ariki Pera (or Taniwha Parawhai) *who married* Ihimaera Te Teira Te Hānene (The Honey Gatherer)
they were the parents of
Pera Punahāmoa Ihimaera (Smiler) *and* Te Raukura
(*after The Honey Gatherer's death* Hine Te Ariki *married* Manu Tāwhiorangi *and they
were the parents of* Nani Mini Tāwhiorangi Tūpara)

Pera Punahāmoa Ihimaera (Smiler) *married* Teria Pere

WHAKAPAPA OF WITI
AND HIS SISTERS AND BROTHERS

Hoana Putiputi Babbington *and* Kereama Hātarei Keelan
were the parents of
Rangiora, Molly, Hiro, Nacy, Polly, Api, Turi-teretimana
(Julia), Dinah, Violet, BoyBoy and Brownie (a half-sister
was my beloved Aunty Mate). One child died in infancy

Teria Pere *and* Pera Punahāmoa Ihimaera Smiler
were the parents of
Te Haa-o-Rūhia (Tom Jnr), Win, Mike, Mary, Puku,
Mafe, Joey, Danny, Hani, Sid and Alice. Two children
did not reach adulthood. Maioha was Teria's
first child from her previous relationship

Turi-teretimana (Julia) Keelan *married* Te Haa-o-Rūhia (Tom) Ihimaera Smiler Jnr
they were the parents of
Witi, Kararaina, Thomas, Tāwhi, Viki, Derek, Gay and Neil
Dad's son, of whom we are so proud, is Puke Peawini

(Apologies to whānau for any misspellings, errors, incorrect sequencing of siblings or any other
misinterpretations, as sometimes handwriting in the whakapapa is hard to read)

PART ONE

TĪPUNA
ANCESTORS

Chapter One

Ka Awatea Dawn

THE FIRST MEMORY I have is of people chanting.

The chanting arises out of complete and utter darkness. Then comes a whistling wind and the sound of flax seed pods, rattling. From somewhere arises a faint glow of red. Next moment the blackness streaks with crimson, and the voices ring out: 'He mea hanga nā te Atua i te tīmatanga te rangi me te whenua.'

I awake to a red sky, my heart beating with fear. My mother is there, her profile silhouetted against the blood of the dawn. She has been sitting next to me, watching me as I sleep, and because I am frightened she smiles to reassure me. 'Don't be afraid, son,' she says. 'It is only the old people and they are at their morning prayers.'

This element of the sacerdotal, of the sound of karakia and the ceremonials that went with it, was the unvarying constant of my boyhood. I was always surrounded by people at prayer. They shouted their greetings to the day, to the land, to the sky: 'Ko Ranginui kei runga, ko Papatūānuku kei raro.' When they planted seed in the earth they prayed. When they went fishing, they prayed. If ever they were about to embark on a journey, they prayed. They said thanksgiving prayers when they were happy. They prayed when they were sad.

The first words I heard in the morning were the prayers at dawn. Throughout the day, karakia kept the structures of the world safe and everything in its place, the sky above, the earth below. The prayers were invocations and entreaties, and I often thought that without them, why, the world might not appear at all. I would cross my fingers and close my eyes, because for a long time I was very afraid of the dark and feared that all humankind would forever have to wander in the blackness.

The people also prayed when whānau were ill so that they would become well. They prayed for good life when a baby was born. They prayed for prosperous families when someone married. They wailed and prayed when one of our kin died.

They instilled in me the habit of karakia. All my life I have prayed as they did. Even today, although the world has changed radically from that of my ancestors, I still pray every morning and every night. I do it for the same reasons the old people did — to keep the sky in its place and to keep the earth in its place. To maintain my contract with the physical world and the spiritual world by weaving a skein of karakia between both. And to negotiate the passage of those whom I love as they traverse the bright strand between.

Chapter Two

In the Shadow of Hikurangi

I BEGIN WITH my mother.

At the time she and I must have been visiting Hinu-o-koko, the family land where my maternal grandparents lived, just outside Tolaga Bay on the highway between Gisborne and Ruatōria. The chanting came from Puketawaī marae, carried crystal clear on the wind.

Blood, dawn, incantations, a profile limned with crimson — from the very beginning, Mum was emblematic. No wonder, therefore, she has forever been such a potent and hieratic force in my life.

THE NAME PEOPLE knew her by was Julia Keelan. If, however, my mother was introducing herself on the marae, she would have begun by locating herself within that Māori reality I have spoken of, identifying herself tribally rather than individually, reeling off genealogical connections that go back to the beginning of time: 'Ko Hikurangi te maunga, ko Waiapu te awa, ko Porourangi te tangata. Hikurangi is the mountain, Waiapu is the river, and Porourangi is the ancestor from whom my tribe takes its mana, its prestige.'

Pākehā find this process elliptical and tortuous, not to say lengthy. To be frank, so do some Māori. When a welcome prefaces an important event, they will arrive later rather than face the prospect of sitting for two or three hours listening to speakers establish their credentials by way of genealogical litany. Not until later in the ritual would my mother have said: 'My name is Julia.'

The pōwhiri, however, has a specific function. It is an opportunity to force time to stand still, to go backwards before you go forwards. During that time you pay attention to and elaborate on your whakapapa with its complicated stories of how bloodlines connect you to the listening iwi. In Māoridom this is the movement from ahau (me) to koe (you) to koutou (us) to mātou (I am part of the us) to rātou (I include all those kin who are ancestors) to tātou (we are all one, living and dead). Actually tātou includes non-people like the meeting house, which is addressed as the male or female ancestor he or she takes their name from. Or a river, tree or rocks.

And so, if you want to know about me, first you have to meet my ancestors. They belong to a time Māori call 'i ngā wā o mua', the days that have gone before us. The phrase alludes to a particular way of looking at the past as something that doesn't lie behind us but is in front of us; that goes for the ancestors, too, not comfortably dealt with and consigned to the past tense but watching over us and still waiting to be accounted to.

Another way of viewing this phenomenon is to say that Māori walk backwards into the future. All those ancestors sitting in the room behind our eyes walk along with us, too.

A bit disconcerting to think about, isn't it?

MY MOTHER WAS very proud of her tribal ancestry and history. Her originating ancestor was a man named Paikea, who arrived in Aotearoa from a place called Hawaiki on the back of a whale. He was the whale rider and he had a grandson named Porourangi, after whom my mother's tribe, Ngāti Porou, takes its name.

As a little boy I was always proud of Paikea, but had many playground scrapes with other ratty boys who would encircle me, jeering: 'Thinks his ancestor rode a whale. How dumb is that?'

'Just because your people can't ride on whales,' I would answer, 'doesn't mean mine couldn't.'

'How did he stay on then?'

'By holding on tight, of course.'

'And how did he breathe when the whale went under the water?'

I was already learning to be creative. 'He breathed the air from the whale's blowhole. How else do you think?'

'What about when the whale went really deep, like for half an hour or even two hours?'

'Paikea took a deep breath before the whale dived and held it.'

'And how did he talk to the whale and tell it where to go?'

Oh, some questions were too difficult, and I would push my tormentors away until they scattered like black-backed gulls.

'Your ancestor didn't ride on the whale. He was inside it like Jonah and was shat out when it arrived at the beach.'

My mother's people also referred to a particular waka called *Horouta* as our first ship. Captained by Kiwa and Paoa, when it first made landfall the men and women on board trekked inland from Ōhiwa to populate other tribal areas, and later the canoe sailed onward to land at Tūranganui-a-Kiwa, the current location of Gisborne.

They also talked of a sixteenth-century warrior named Tū-whakairi-ora, and some believed the tribe could equally have taken our name from him. In a lifetime spanning 100 years, Tū-whakairi-ora set about conquering neighbouring iwi. He also happened to marry a certain woman named Ruataupare, who was so irritated when people considered her husband more famous than she that she left him to found her own dynasty.

My mother loved that story.

She also spoke somewhat enigmatically about having ancestors among what she called the Uepōhatu, or Ngā Iwi o te Ao Kōhatu, The People of the Stone World. They were descendants of the great demi-god Māui, who fished up New Zealand, and they lived on the mountain before the coming of Paikea and *Horouta*.

Mum was always proud and immensely respectful of having such ancient ancestry; it gave her mana. There was nothing worse than not having a tribe to belong to or lacking mana. Without a tribe or mana you were an orphan in the world, travelling without protection. Her ancestry was fundamental to who she was.

You also needed to have — apart from river, tree or rocks — a mountain.

4.

MOUNT HIKURANGI TAKES its place in my whakapapa as the epic manifestation of my mother's mana, strength or prestige. Of course it was not only her mountain, it is the mountain that all Ngāti Porou regard as theirs. She always kept a close eye on Hikurangi whenever we were travelling through the East Coast. This part of Aotearoa ranged from Whāngārā in the south to just beyond Ruatōria in the north. It was bounded by the sea on the east and, to the west, the tribal territories of Te Whānau-a-Apanui, Tūhoe, Te Aitanga-a-Māhaki, Te Whānau-a-Kai, Tai Manuhiri, Rongowhakaata, Ngāti Kahungunu and others. As we traversed the massive flanks of the mountain, she would acknowledge it with bowed head. Throughout her life she steadfastly took her bearings from Hikurangi and never showed her back to it.

Mum's awe of Hikurangi was not without foundation, no matter that the mountain was not particularly pretty, being somewhat lumpy and formless. At 1920 metres it was the highest point on the Raukūmara Ranges, but because of her reverence of it, from the very beginning the mountain played an enormous part in my own psychic life, looming over it and through it. Hikurangi's potency came not only from its brooding physical presence but also from the stories attached to it.

For instance, when Māui went out fishing with his brothers and he dragged Aotearoa up from the sea, it was because his fishhook had caught in one of the crevices of the mountain. When this enormous fish of Māui had finally ceased its struggles and rose through the water, Mount Hikurangi was the first part of the land to broach the surface. The force of the streaming water began to bear the canoe, *Nukutaimemeha*, carrying Māui and his brothers, dizzyingly down the slope. The brothers cried out in terror, clinging to the sides of the waka as it tumbled downward — until, luckily, it was caught in a high cleft of the mountain.

I would watch from the window of the car and hope to catch a glimpse of the sails and broken bailer of the waka because, so I was told, sometimes the mountain revealed these antediluvian artefacts to those who believed. Did I believe? Did I *what*.

The word Hikurangi means Summit of the Sky, and the mountain is often regarded by Ngāti Porou as a lodestone for the universe. If there were ever a map of the stars and planets, the cosmological significance of Hikurangi would be acknowledged by its cardinal appearance. Why? It was the first point on the earth's surface to be touched by the new day. And so I have always liked to think that, if ever you were lost in space, all you would need to do was wait until the sun came up. What would you be waiting for? Why, the flash of sunlight on the sacred mountain! Once you saw that sword of light, then you could calibrate your position. You would say, as my mother always did: 'Ah, ko Hikurangi, there and *mark*.'

There was another story about the mountain, and it had to do with the Waiapu River. I still gasp at the immensity and psychic power of the imagery, for some people say that the river was the birth cord connecting the sky to the earth. Perhaps that was why Ūawa became the location for Te Rāwheoro, the most famous whare wānanga, spiritual as well as temporal, in the land.

Most of what we know about this Māori university — the great library of Alexandria is its equivalent — comes from the important texts of the priest Mohi Ruatapu, who wrote down its history and practices in the 1870s. His manuscripts are considered to be the prime source of our knowledge of nineteenth-century Māori intellectual attainment. Ruatapu described Te Rāwheoro as a place of tohunga whose task it was to conserve and practise the spiritual arts, and to anoint younger acolytes into the priesthood.

It is no wonder that as a young boy born within that region, where the river fed the placenta of my world, I always had the sense of the birth cord and of blood inheritance. If I were to trace the spiritual source of my work, there's no doubt in my mind that one of the tributaries would take me back to Te Rāwheoro.

Even further back to those Stone World people, descendants of Māui who lived on Hikurangi mountain.

Chapter Three

A Colonised World

1.

INTO THIS WORLD, Turi-teretimana Keelan was born on 18 April 1922.

Of course the world was not just a Māori one now, because some 153 years earlier, in 1769, a second ship had arrived to anchor off Mount Hikurangi. The ship was called the *Endeavour*, and to local Māori it looked like a huge island with wide bluff bows, a raised poop and a square stern. The large sails made the island appear to be carrying its own clouds above it. On board was James Cook, the most important Pākehā claimant of Aotearoa.

Can we read something psychic into the arrival of Cook at the same place as Māui's waka? As a boy I liked to think so. After all, here was the pito, the umbilical cord of the world. It was the birthing place renowned among Māori as a site where the profound and the magnificent could occur. Showers of stars were a constant over Hikurangi mountain. Oral Māori stories in 1910 still refer to the appearance of Tūnui-a-te-ika, Halley's Comet, in the sky overhead.

Halley's Comet, ugh. What a lack of imagination. The Māori name is more colourful, referring to the male organ in tumescence, spilling its seed through the night sky.

From the sublime to the real, it appeared that the *Endeavour* wasn't the only vessel to arrive within the shadow of Mount Hikurangi. There were also stories of Chinese junks and Spanish caravels coming to grief on those shores or having been blown off course. Way off course.

As far as Cook was concerned, I imagined his arrival as some dark blood clot sloughed through the uterus of earth and sky, bringing a new destiny into collision with the old. And what a collision it was! Although the meeting was initially marked by diplomatic negotiations on the part of Ngāti Porou, Cook's compulsion was conquest. Instead of acknowledging Māori courtesy and cordiality he, like all explorers before him, did the usual thing of claiming — without the knowledge of the current indigenous occupier — the country for his sovereign. Then, in the absence of any consent or acquiescence, he named or, rather, renamed places he came across, immediately superimposing an English consciousness.

Of course Māori didn't know what Cook was up to. How could we? More to the point, would we have objected if we had known that Cook was claiming, mapping and naming our country? You bet your sweet life.

The grandfather of my warrior ancestor, Tū-whakairi-ora, for instance, had been murdered in a dispute regarding crayfish pots.

Worse were Cook's attempts to incorporate Māori geography into the naming. Like as not, he got it wrong. When he asked about a good anchoring place, it sounded to Māori that he was asking what direction the wind was blowing, which was north-west. He was told, 'Te raki.' He heard Tologa — Tolaga.

And then Cook's scientist, Joseph Banks, uplifted plant species to take back to England. His was the first act of biotheft committed in New Zealand.

2.

THAT WAS THE beginning of the end for traditional Māori society.

On the East Coast and throughout Gisborne and Hawke's Bay, expansion was spearheaded by a group of whalers and traders. Their *modus operandi* was to set up their entrepreneurial efforts under the protection of chieftains of tribal clans and then further the infiltration by marrying high-ranking Māori women.

These swashbuckling men were known as *Messieurs the Whites* — I don't know why they had a French name — and quite a few of them appear in the genealogies of Māori families, including mine. They came mainly from England and Scotland, but also numbered the occasional American (including black American), Spaniard and Frenchman. According to 'An Old Colonist' in 1868, 'Most of the whites had each a domestic establishment, with an aboriginal lady at the head of it, and the good old plan of having a pet chief who took you in charge and, whilst plundering you himself, preserved you from others was still in vogue. "Messieurs the Whites" led a pretty considerable, careless, reckless, Godless kind of life, drinking and gambling, having, in these halcyon days, full liberty of action.'

My *Messieur* — or, rather, *Monsieur* — was the Scot, George Babbington, known among Māori as Hōri Paputene. We think he was from Glasgow; he arrived on the East Coast around the 1830s, and he did pretty well by running the whaling station at Māwhai, near Tokomaru Bay. In 1847 he had three boats and twenty men working for him; he also kept a store. The high-ranking woman he married was Mere Karaka Tiritapu, and among their children was John Babbington, my mother's maternal grandfather.

I was always very proud of my connection to the patriarch George Babbington but it sometimes got me into difficult encounters with others who might not have wanted me as a relative. For instance, when Jane Cleghorn and I were married and went on our honeymoon to Britain, in 1970, we travelled on the MV *Akaroa*. I noticed on the first-class passenger list that a Mrs Babbington was travelling on the same ship.

'I should say kia ora,' I said to Jane.

'I wouldn't if I were you,' she answered.

However, I had the bit between my teeth and at an on-board dance nothing could prevent me, during a waltz, from steering Jane in the direction of Mrs Babbington and her partner. She was looking haughty and regal, and Jane and I weren't looking too bad ourselves in our best finery. Finally, accidentally on purpose, I bumped Jane into Mrs Babbington.

In a rush of excitement I smiled my best smile and said, 'We must be related.'

Mrs Babbington took one look at me and fled in the opposite direction.

When we arrived in the UK, Jane and I embarked on a tour of the country by buying a minivan and sleeping in it to save costs. For some reason I had got it into my head that I was related to Anthony Babington who, so I thought at the time, had married Mary Queen of Scots. That his surname was spelt with one 'b' in the middle was a minor matter — if James Cook could misspell, so could anybody else — and so whenever we fetched up in a city Jane would go off to visit one of the castles associated with Queen Elizabeth I while I went in search of Mary.

'Happy dreams,' she would say.

Jane knew I often had those kind of 'if only' dreams about Mary successfully taking the English throne and installing my ancestor alongside her. Recently, however, somebody who shall remain nameless rained on *that* parade. It turns out that Anthony Babington had been a young Catholic nobleman who was the chief conspirator in a 1586 plot to put Mary on the English throne, but he never married her.

Of course, when the British — or rather the English, as I have problems implicating my Scots and Irish ancestors in what Westminster did — brought the rule of law and order to New Zealand, they were really paving the way for governing the country. Those same *Messieurs* were among the whites who objected. They were setting up their own kingdoms, in George Babbington's case maybe some Antipodean *Brigadoon*. They lost, England won.

British officials signed a treaty at Waitangi on 6 February 1840 between Queen Victoria and some Māori tribes. The Māori understanding was that we would maintain our mana and be above Queen Vicky. Even when we allowed that the Crown could be equal to us, much to our consternation when the new government of tauiwi legitimised itself we found ourselves below. Very soon British culture displaced Māori culture altogether as settlers arrived. We called them by the generic name Pākehā.

By 1858 we were already outnumbered. Let's be fair, what with the

Dutch, French and Germans pitching flags in the Pacific as if it were a pin cushion, English colonisation was arguably more advantageous than any other.

Colonisation by Christian conversion, mainly Anglican, soon followed. Māori were fascinated by the Bible, which appeared to be tribal stories told in a similar vein to our own and, in 1841, only a year after the Reverend William Williams set up the Poverty Bay mission station, we were attending services in our thousands: 3200 in Waiapu and Tokomaru Bay, 2500 at Ūawa and Tūranga. Three years later, it was estimated that 4300 of the 6000 Māori inhabitants of East Cape and Waiapu, 2300 out of the 4000 at Ūawa, and 6000 out of the 10,000 at Tūranga and Māhia were Christian. The consequences for Māori spirituality, Te Rāwheoro in particular, were catastrophic.

With their superior technology, the settlers began to establish another Britain in New Zealand. In the rohe of Ngāti Porou, small colonial settlements like Tolaga Bay, Tokomaru Bay, Tikitiki and Ruatōria began to ring the coast. Old tribal tracks were taken over as carriage and wagon ways and, later, they were amalgamated to become the future State Highway 35. Like the earlier whalers and traders, settlers found amenable hosts in the local iwi, who embraced change and challenges, presuming that they would absorb these new people and the culture they brought. Yes, Ngāti Porou were outnumbered, outflanked by Christianity, and then — we were outgunned.

First by other tribes, particularly Ngāpuhi, who accessed guns, pū Pākehā, before other tribes and began a series of ferocious intertribal Musket Wars in the 1820s. Then by Pākehā, who waged wars against Māori from the 1860s to the 1880s. Around mid-1864, there were over 20,000 men fighting 'rebel' Māori and, I kid you not, more British troops in New Zealand than in any other country in the world.

Don't even get me started on the disease and disillusionment that led many commentators to consider that Māori would die out by the end of the nineteenth century.

Ngāti Porou's situation was complex. When the Pākehā Wars began in the Waikato in the 1860s and the people there proposed to have a Māori King, Ngāti Porou was divided in supporting that notion or the Pākehā Queen. And when emissaries from the Pai Mārire — a religious movement established by the prophet Te Ua Haumēne — came from the north-west to seek our support against Pākehā, we had two choices: either join the rebels or become kūpapa, loyalists to the Crown. But Ngāti Porou was already seriously compromised by an infusion of Pākehā blood, let alone our newfound Anglicanism. In the wars that followed, we chose mainly to be loyalists, although family on one side often fought against family on the other.

All lost out in the end because the government's punishment — land confiscations — did not distinguish between who was loyal and who was not. Generations of settlers benefited from the reparations, amassed holdings and controlled the country.

By the time my mother was born, the tribal territory of her girlhood had changed entirely. It was now called the East Coast, part of Poverty Bay, and her people were referred to colloquially and reductively as 'Natis'. Employed initially in the flax trade, they soon found themselves working in freezing works, the dairy and butter industries, and as stockmen on cattle and sheep runs. There was talk of building a wharf at Tolaga Bay that would be the longest in the Southern Hemisphere, to increase export opportunities. New Zealand became a sheep farm for Great Britain, and the East Coast one of its most important pastoral landholdings.

The Pākehā had become part of the whakapapa.

Chapter Four

Country of the Past

1.

I MUST APOLOGISE for the digression. Let's face it, when you're dealing with whakapapa you sometimes have to double back.

Let me return to my mother.

She was born when New Zealand was just recovering from the losses of Pākehā and Māori men to the First World War and the flu pandemic of 1918. The date of her birth, however, is a fiction. When she was fifty-nine and due for a pension, my sister Tāwhi took her to the Gisborne courthouse, the Tolaga and Tokomaru bay post offices, Tolaga Bay School and Mangatuna Native School, in an attempt to obtain a copy of her birth certificate. Tāwhi also wrote to government offices in Palmerston North and Wellington, but to no avail. Even the usually reliable family Bible was no help, as my grandmother Putiputi had forgotten to enter my mother's name. The nearest we got was finding a baby with a similar name, but the father's name was different — and the young girl had died at birth.

My mother was very upset about this, and Tāwhi and I made matters worse by treating it as a joke. 'Guess what?' Tāwhi said. 'Mum doesn't exist! If she does, her name isn't Julia and her father isn't her father and she's supposed to be dead.'

Dad tried to placate Mum. 'Don't worry about it, dear,' he said. 'The authorities in those days were always getting Māori names, dates and places wrong. Count yourself lucky you were registered at all.'

'Maybe my uncle went to register me,' Mum agreed, 'and those stupid people thought he was my father so put his name down. Perhaps he had gone to inform them of his daughter's death as well as to register my birth. Yes, that must explain how things got mixed up.'

Tāwhi and I sometimes never knew when to drop something. We did not help by laughing at the predicament. Unaware that Mum was truly grieving, my sister went waltzing around the kitchen waving a towel, wiggling her hips, rolling her eyes and singing a calypso song: 'Woe is me, shame and scandal in the family!'

'I didn't even want a pension,' Mum muttered. 'I don't like taking a handout from the government, I'd rather keep working for my living.'

When the climax of the song came, I altered the words: 'Her father's not her father but his daughter don't know!'

My mother lifted her face to the light. This spelt danger. It indicated that she was spiralling.

Immediately, our father intervened. 'You two should know better,' he said. 'You know your mother's deep respect for whakapapa. What's the matter with you both?'

 2.

DAD WAS REFERRING to the huge sheets of genealogy Mum had written in her own hand, copying painstakingly from family ledger books. They lined the hallway of our house at 11 Haig Street. Who would think that such an ordinary three-bedroom house in a Gisborne suburb would contain centuries-old histories?

From the road, you wouldn't know. There was a wire fence, a gate to keep in our pit-bull cross Tanner — well, actually, to keep people out, so my sister Gay says — and a piece of Grecian statuary that would not have looked out of place in *Downton Abbey*, which the family called 'The Lady at the Gate'. The house itself was white, the roof was in need of a new coat of red rustproof paint. You could tell that a home handyman had been at work adding two bedrooms and other extensions, including a huge carport, that the council hadn't found out about yet. Open the front door, however, and you were in the presence of the whakapapa. There it was, with the names of the ancestors, ever branching along the hallway.

Getting the names right and ensuring your father was your father really mattered. Māori called this focus tika. The word refers to the absolute requirement of ensuring that your information is correct, though some people translate it morally, as telling the truth. Indeed, tika is one of the prime requirements of any research into mātauranga Māori, Māori knowledge, and my mother upheld it with unfailing precision. The consequences, in terms of correct descent lines, were unthinkable and too disastrous even to contemplate. They could lead to spiritual disruptions in both time and space. Old lives could be extinguished and new ones cause a rewriting of the present and future.

Today, the consequences are equally momentous. The entire Waitangi Tribunal process, which decides on land claims, is predicated on correct genealogical information. In the case of my father and his tribe, Te Whānau-a-Kai, some pretty grievous errors have meant that other iwi have claimed our ancestors as theirs and gained ownership of lands and rights that are ours.

And they know it.

Yes, while my mother's grievance appeared to be on a smaller scale — though for Māori there is no such measure between a large thing and a small — she had something to spiral about. Whakapapa was the prime way to maintain her identity, for her to affirm who she was and the people she came from.

3.

AND SO THE birth certificate that Mum found was inscribed with details belonging to a dead child. As well as that, she was also named after an uncle called Turi, the same one who registered her in this way and had decided it didn't matter if she was given a Christian name of the wrong gender. These two incongruities bestowed on my mother an interesting complexity. I remember one day at school being given a smoky piece of glass to watch an eclipse of the sun, and I looked at Mum through it. There she was, sometimes seen brightly and then darkly.

My mother made the matter all the more interesting when she decided to invent herself. By deed poll, she became Turi-teretimana Keelan and she assigned to herself the birthdate of 18 April 1922. She also gave herself that name of Julia.

I like to think that her choice was appropriate, patrician, as there was always something Roman in her bearing. Indeed, looking at her I always sensed why early explorers in their comparisons thought of Māori in an Arcadian way: lean, tall, well shaped, an attractive way of speaking, aquiline nose, dark-coloured eyes and motivating intelligence.

Her mother was Hoana (Putiputi) Babbington, the daughter of Mate Tautau and Reneta (Len) Tūpara Babbington. Len was a grandson of the aforementioned *Monsieur* George Babbington, whose entrepreneurial abilities had set up their father, John Babbington, as a leading townsman in Tokomaru Bay. Indeed, the Babbington strain has made my kin large-framed, handsome and very fair people. The strain of blond or red hair that survives in our family comes from this Pākehā ancestry. It surfaced in my daughter Jessica, and through her to my grandson James, so, no, it wasn't the postman.

Although her name was Putiputi, our maternal grandmother was commonly known as Flowers. Raised in Tokomaru Bay, she had two brothers, Morgan and Hātea, who were wonderful singers, but she did not grow up with them. When she was still a baby, her Grand-uncle Moana, on the Tautau side, asked her father Len if he and his wife, Wharerautawa, could adopt her — they were childless. She was adored by her grand-uncle and in every respect was a favoured foster child.

I can never think of Flowers without associating her with a popular Māori love song that goes something like this:

E putiputi koe katohia, you are a flower from an old bouquet,
I've waited patiently for you each day!

But I need to undercut that sentimental song by applying tika in the telling of her childhood story. It is a disturbing one. My grandmother was raped by a relative when she was twelve. She may have been a lovely flower, but her childhood was blighted by this brutal experience. Over time, the enduring kin relationships between families reasserted themselves, so some of my cousins may be asking, 'Why bring this up now?' Well, it's because for years Mum had to defend Moana Tautau, who reputedly put a mākutu on the family of the boy who committed the act and, certainly, their family was plagued by death: Mum's best friend at twenty-one, a sister at nineteen and three brothers, who died young. When Mum met one of the brothers, his feet were festering, and she asked in all innocence, 'What is wrong with your feet?'

Mum never liked the implication that the misfortunes of that family had to do with a mākutu placed by Moana Tautau. 'He could never have done it himself as he did not have the requisite powers or skills to secure the intent,' she told me, 'and nor would he have gone to a tohunga and asked that it be done on his behalf.' Mum would have felt vindicated by subsequent genetic research which confirmed that the premature deaths in that family were caused by an inherited defect passed from generation to generation. 'Moana was a loving man,' Mum always said.

4.

FLOWERS MARRIED THE tall, handsome and laconic Kereama Hātarei (Graham) Keelan who was born on 6 June 1862; Kereama's father was Wī Koka Keelan. It is through Papa Graham that I have a direct connection to Waikato through the Irish policeman William Thomas Keelan.

Yes, an Irishman in the whakapapa. He was born in County Cork, went mining in Australia and came to New Zealand as a soldier fighting against the Māori during the Land Wars in the 1860s. He ended up changing sides and marrying one, Hana Konewa.

Now here is an interesting link in the genealogy, because my mother has penned in the names of Hana Konewa's father, Rāwiri Tangaroa, and Hana's mother, Tarati Te Angiangi, a member of the kāhui ariki, the Waikato royalty. Oh, Rāwiri and Tarati's love story was so fascinating! Remember those Musket Wars I earlier referred to? Well, the story goes that Rāwiri Tangaroa was captured by Ngāpuhi during one of those battles. The name most associated with these conflicts is that of the great Ngāpuhi chief Hongi Hika, who became a Christian early on and in 1820 visited England, where he met George IV. Hoping to be given muskets and other weapons, he was instead presented with cash and a suit of armour. Undeterred, on the voyage back he stopped off in Sydney. There he bought the muskets with which, after returning to the Bay of Islands in July 1821, he sallied forth on epic waka voyages of conquest and revenge against tribes to the north. Hongi Hika must have appeared like some avenging god: his suit of armour flashed in the sun and he fired continuously from four or five muskets, loaded quickly by attendants.

As far as Ngāti Porou was concerned, Hongi Hika wished to avenge the death of his wife at our hands and therefore, during 1821 to 1823, his ferocious focus was the East Coast. On one particular campaign five waka arrived at the rivermouth of Whareponga. From there, the Ngāpuhi warriors travelled inland to assault a fortress known as Kōkai. Now I don't know whether or not Rāwiri Tangaroa was taken on this particular raid on the pā and surrounding territory of the Te Aowera people; it may have been a different assault. But if it was this one, let's imagine that he was one of the children acting as sentries who had spotted the invaders. At the time he was twelve years old.

'The warriors are carrying sticks on their shoulders,' Rāwiri reported.

'What kind of sticks?'

'They look like mamaku,' Rāwiri answered. He and the children had never seen muskets before, but they were silver like mamaku tree ferns.

Ngāpuhi chose a good time to attack Kōkai. The able-bodied men were out gathering food and only old people, women and children were in the pā. Alerted to the approach of the Ngāpuhi warrior party, Rāwiri and the defenders were able to slash the vines restraining large boulders so that they rolled downhill and into the path of the approaching enemy. However, boulders versus muskets? It was not long before the defenders were decimated.

Rāwiri Tangaroa was still throwing rocks at the invaders as they entered Kōkai.

'Give up or else you will be killed,' they said to him.

Instead, he laughed. This enraged the warriors, but Rāwiri Tangaroa must have been very pleasing to look at: I'll use an old-fashioned word, 'comely', to describe his appearance. Just as he was about to be shot, one of the warriors exclaimed, 'Do not touch him! Look at his face!'

In those days Ngāpuhi reaped slaves for many purposes, and because of his beauty Rāwiri Tangaroa was taken back to the north where, according to family history, it was planned to put him to breeding duties, as if he were a stallion, to sire strong and beautiful children from the mares of Ngāpuhi. How long Rāwiri Tangaroa lived among the Ngāpuhi people I don't know, but enter the aforementioned Tarati Te Angiangi, a princess of the Waikato, who was on a royal trading mission. She was reputed to be much older than he was but, in the quaint parlance of the time, on first glimpsing his form and face she felt a great desire for him. During her trading negotiations, she raised an imperious hand and said, 'Add the slave to my livestock, feather cloaks and greenstone. I shall take him back to Waikato as part of the payment, tribute and exchange of trade between us.' Her wish was their command and, for the rest of his life, my forebear, Rāwiri Tangaroa, lived in the Waikato.

We go back to Wī Koka Keelan, who was the grandson of the union between Rāwiri Tangaroa and Tarati Te Angiangi. When the scourge of the Pākehā continued to whip the Māori of the Waikato, his mother Hana Konewa decided to send Wī Koka to the East Coast; he could take refuge among the people of Te Aowera and assume the mantle of his grandfather, Rāwiri, who had been captured and taken those two generations earlier by Ngāpuhi. Wī Koka managed to get past the cordon of Pākehā soldiers ringing Waikato and walked through the Waioeka Gorge, travelling at night to get away. The symbol of Te Aowera is the morning star, and I like to imagine that Venus was shining when he arrived. He was greeted with great joy by them — it was as if Rāwiri Tangaroa had himself returned.

Safely living among the Ngāti Porou, Wī Koka met and married Turuhira Mahemahe and they settled at Te Aowera, Rāwiri Tangaroa's ancestral marae. By the way, Turuhira was a twin, with an identical sister, Katarina. My grandfather Kereama was never sure which one was his mother. Whenever he wanted to suckle, he would run to whoever was around.

The Keelan clan is famed for having twins. Local boys were often cautioned about going out with Keelan girls because, watch out, you may have a good time but will end up with two dropkicks instead of one. My wife Jane escaped the birth of twins, but whenever I took home my daughters, Jessica and Olivia, my aunties would jest, 'Where are their sisters?'

 5.

SO FAR, SO good. Now, in those days, Māori families were pretty large and they stayed that way right up until the mid-twentieth century. For instance, Kereama was one of eleven siblings, and the sheer numbers don't make easy the telling of the story of a Māori family. I've included a photograph of Papa Graham with John, Sarah, Rūtene and Claude, but there were also Dick, Kopa, Mere, Lena, Joe and Tom — and even listing them like that doesn't do them or their families justice, not to mention extended kin through their marriages.

It's my own fault, and I am kicking myself that I did not go this year, while I was writing this memoir, to see my mother's cousin Sue Nīkora, also known as the Queen of the Keelans. The trouble is, as you will discover, I have been tipi-haere here and tipi-haere there all over the world. Sorry, ancestors. And although I have been vain enough to think that I had competent kōrero to be able to give a fair picture of the Keelans — and Babbingtons, too — I don't. Not, anyway, for the generations three, four or five times removed from mine.

In the case of the magnificent Keelans, Sue or one of my cousins Josie,

Trudy, Molly, Tunis or another of the cuzzies are better placed than I am to tell the story of the family's aristocratic origins, dynastic succession and the ways in which we connect with other whānau groups of the East Coast. They grew up within the architecture of the wider families, and I didn't.

Not only that, but, what with all the travelling, I haven't kept up with the regular Keelan dialogues so don't know whether the new stories that are being told have made the old stories that I know wrong. There's a well-known expression that one must swallow a toad every morning so that when you go out you won't find anything more disgusting. I don't think I should make my proud Keelan relatives swallow a few toads, so I won't offend them by serving anything worse. Meantime, I shall limit myself to telling you about Papa Kereama, who acknowledged the mana of his new bride Flowers and lived with her at Hinu-o-koko rather than her with him at Tokomaru Bay. Close to the Ūawa River, it was our family marae.

'This is how my darling fell in love with me,' Kereama used to tell his grandchildren as we crowded around him while he slurped from a jug of homebrew. 'As you know, I broke horses in, eh. You can see how tall I am, well, the horse didn't have a chance because I could keep my feet on the ground while it bucked and snorted and tried to unseat me from my saddle.'

Yes, he was *that* tall, just like his stories.

'Anyway, I noticed your grandmother. She was one of the girls who was always looking at me. After all, aren't I handsome like our ancestor Rāwiri Tangaroa? I wore spurs that used to ring and jingle, jangle. But although she liked looking at me, my darling played hard to get. I had to let my horse woo her for me. It would dance and prance until she fell in love with me. The horse made me look really good.'

Oh, I was putty in Kereama's storytelling hands! I could just imagine him, a smiling man with a twinkle in his eyes, making his stallion perform a high-stepping, butt-swaying saucy rumba or tango for a shining-eyed girl called Flowers. Among the horses he owned were two named Cinderella and Starlight, after the movie steeds that heroes like Hopalong Cassidy and Gene Autry rode in the Western musical films that Māori loved in the 1940s. Indeed, Kereama was well known for his equestrian skills; today he would be called a horse whisperer. He would tap on Starlight's front feet and the horse would go down on its knees so that he could get on more easily.

Well . . . maybe he exaggerated a little about how tall he was.

Although Kereama was afflicted by gout and ill health throughout his working life, he nevertheless was able to make a good livelihood breaking in horses, and he took fencing work wherever he could get it. You can still see his fences standing, and he was regarded highly by the farmers of the district.

6.

MY GRANDPARENTS KEREAMA and Flowers kept up the Māori habit of large families by having thirteen children. The number makes me feel rather faint: how did they manage to raise them all? Be patient, bear with me. There is no way of cutting corners in telling of the aunties and uncles. Two of them I didn't know, the titular eldest, Rangiora, and Te Rōpiha, who died as a baby. Rangiora, however, lives on in the stories Mum told of him.

'He was my favourite brother,' she would begin, her eyes lighting up. 'Whenever there were dances at Tolaga Bay I would watch him dancing with his girlfriends and wait patiently right to the end, because he always saved the last waltz for me. He would look around the dancehall asking, "Where's Turi?" and pretend not to see me. I would rush up to him, "Here I am, here I am!" and I would go right up on my toes and he would reach down and put his arms around my waist and off we would go: "When I grow too old to dream, I'll have you to remember . . ."'

As for the other aunties and uncles, let me introduce them to you as if they had all gathered for one of the regular family reunions at Hinemaurea ki Mangatuna marae. The marae was the gathering place of our local kin, Ngāti Ira and Ngāti Kahukurangi, and as a boy I sometimes liked to sneak up on my relatives unawares and listen in as they sat talking in the sunlight. 'Gee, boy,' they would say, pretending to be surprised, 'where did you come from?'

Kararaina (Aunty Molly) was the girl after Rangiora. She was a huge woman with bad teeth — no, *no* front teeth — and a large laugh. Like the rest of the Keelan clan, she had a wicked sense of humour.

Hiro (Aunty Hero) was next; thin, wary, always watching, it seemed, for whatever was coming down life's highway. On the lookout for me, too, no doubt, with my spying ways. She had me sussed, yup.

Then there was Tū Maurirere (Uncle Nacy, popularly called Nasser). Here he comes from his truck bringing crayfish to the feast. They are big and red, claws going snap, snap, *snap*: 'Don't try to sneak up on us, Witi, or otherwise you will geddit.' In those days the crayfish were enormous, half my height from flapping tail to tips of waving front feelers.

Mum came next, and she was probably in the cookhouse helping get the kai in the big pots on the boil. Tāwhi Pare (Aunty Polly) would probably be with her, a colourful bandanna around her hair and wearing a flower-patterned dress. When Aunty Polly walked, she had a slow, swaying gait, and those flowers looked as if they were bending to let her through. Wally Kaa was lucky to marry her, and he connected us to one of the most famous families of the East Coast — I thought of them as a samurai clan of imperial Japan.

Āpirana Hiki Toa (Uncle Api) was the brother after Tāwhi Pare. 'We were like two peas in a pod,' Mum would say of him, 'and, on cold days on the way to school, he would say to me, "Hop onto my back", because I never wore shoes and sometimes there was frost on the roads.' Apparently my nature was most like Uncle Api's, so I often missed knowing him as well as I should have. He had a mobile face, sometimes serious, but at a hui you could identify his sudden burst of laughter anywhere: 'That's Uncle Api.' He was patient with me, the curious little boy who would just arrive and depart, and was always asking questions he tried his best to answer. My cousin Tunisia (Tunis for short) always does a double-take when she hears and sees me, because I sound and look like her dad. If I had asked him, I'm sure he would have given me a ride on his back, too.

Tainakore (Aunty Dinah) was the next child, a very beautiful woman with high cheekbones. She was a nurse, and I was always in awe of her. She would have dispatched me from listening in quick and smart. 'Go away and play with the other kids!'

Then came Violet, a softer version of my mother, Te Ohomauri (Uncle BoyBoy) and Mohi Tūrei (Uncle Brownie). Uncle BoyBoy liked to tease me, he *sparked*, and together with his older brother Api he was a boss of the council gangs working between Tolaga Bay and Tokomaru Bay. As they already had the equipment, they began to look after all the Māori cemeteries along their council routes: 'Seeing as we're passing, may as well clean up the old people, otherwise they'll get cross at us.'

Looking at them all across the marae I see that I have inherited the main physical traits of the clan: a large forehead, Roman nose and wide lips plus the low, clipped Keelan way of talking. Pity I didn't score the cheekbones and Kereama's imposing height, but I suppose you have to miss out on *something*.

Friends from Auckland, artists Gretchen Albrecht and James Ross, on a trip around the East Coast, once stopped at Hinemaurea and upon looking at all the photographs in the meeting house exclaimed, 'My God, Witi is everywhere in this house!' Their comment reminded me that when I was growing up I was fully aware that one of my worst fears was being fulfilled, and that I was looking more and more like my mother.

Of course the longer I looked, the more I saw my aunties and uncles, and the older I get the more their genetic inheritance has settled in. They found a way of reminding me in no uncertain terms of my obligations to them, their history and their mountain, by having me wear it on my face. Now *they* sneak up and eavesdrop on *me*. I suppose I asked for it.

Still, they could have allowed me to look a little more like Rāwiri Tangaroa. And they could have turned down the volume a bit when they gave me the Keelan teasing humour.

My friends do not call me Wicked Ihimaera for nothing.

Chapter Five

Keeper of the Fire

1.

MĀORI FAMILIES WERE hard-working. Mum's most enduring memory of her mother was of Flowers, and the other women, constantly washing clothes in boiling hot coppers. Another memory was of young mothers with babies on their hips staring from doorways while old, out-of-work men drank on the steps of their houses.

Yes, this is the tika. Although I have described them in their days of emotional largesse, having large families trapped people, left them strapped for cash. The impoverishment of Māori communities was also the result of their entrapment in a larger cycle caused by the land confiscations.

Only the early ohu system of communal farming and gardening kept families fed on a sharing basis. This system had reached its zenith on the East Coast in the mid-eighteenth century under the great Ngāti Porou ancestress, Hinematioro. She was so much a cynosure of her times that tribes outside the East Coast often referred to the region as Hinematioro's land. As a young girl her beauty was considered remarkable, as was her generosity. According to contemporary description, although her main iwi was Te Aitanga-a-Hauiti, she owned many gardens, though that term seems to me inadequate for her huge estates, which stretched from Whāngārā around the coast to Te Kaha. I can imagine early Pākehā scholars scratching their heads and sniffily asking each other, 'What is the equivalent to our British culture?'

I reckon her properties were the equal of any of their manorial estates or dukedoms.

Sydney Parkinson, a botanical artist on the *Endeavour* with Cook, could have given them a clue: 'The country about the bay is agreeable beyond description and, with proper cultivation, might be rendered a kind of second Paradise. The hills are covered with beautiful flowering shrubs, intermingled with a great number of tall and stately palms, which fill the air with a most grateful fragrant perfume ... and between the hills we discovered some fruitful valleys that are adapted either to cultivation or pasturage. The country abounds with different kinds of herbage fit for food; and, among such a variety of trees as are upon this land, there are, doubtless, many that produce eatable fruit.'

Indeed, Cook was aware of Hinematioro when he first landed at Ūawa in 1769. She was one of a number of arikinui of Pacific Island countries, and she would have reminded him of Purea, the greatest wahine ariki then living in Tahiti, from which he had come after observing the transit of Venus. Hinematioro was so sacred that she was carried everywhere on a litter. Her pathway was strewn with appropriate karakia, so potent that for her to even touch the ground was to place her retinue in danger from the gods. The Reverend Richard Taylor remarked in 1815 that she was Queen of a large district, and Samuel Marsden also gave her royal status. She lived to become a beloved matriarch, able to protect her people until 1823, when the Ngāpuhi raids reached her island fortress on Te Pourewa. In attempting an escape, her canoe capsized and she drowned.

Subsequent Ngāti Porou leaders built on Hinematioro's example, including the politician all idolised, Āpirana Ngata. In the 1920s, when Kereama and Flowers were raising their large brood, Ngata had convinced the government to institute an ambitious scheme to help them and other families: he secured funding so that multiple owners could better develop Māori blocks.

Even so, life was not easy. Although Flowers and Kereama could survive within a society where the land and sea provided and food was shared, for the most part it was a hand-to-mouth existence. Life was made bearable only when my grandfather obtained money-paying jobs when he could and where he could. When there was no work to be had, he either worked communally or sat with the other men, either on the doorstep of his own home at Hinu-o-koko or on Hinemaurea marae, drinking his white-frothing homebrew out of those ubiquitous jars.

He gave me a swig of the stuff once. Ugh.

I DELIBERATELY DARKEN the palette now.

Within the family my mother was the fourth daughter. Her eldest sister, Mate, was brought up by Mum's grandparents, and there were already two sisters, Molly and Hiro, and two brothers, Rangiora and Nacy, who could help in the family home at Hinu-o-koko and with cropping the land. While my mother never lost the aristocratic bearing that came from her Keelan and Babbington ancestry, she was by force of economic circumstance the sibling who was informally adopted out under what was known as the whāngai system. This mainly provided for a grandparent to raise grandchildren, but it could also mean children being taken to look after elderly relatives, or to live with another family or to be adopted by a childless couple.

The primary metaphor of Mum's early childhood was the kāuta, the kitchen. It was usually a small whare separate from the rest of the house, having a dirt floor, a fireplace with hooks above it on which could be hung blackened pots, a large, draughty chimney made of corrugated iron and a small brick hearth. Every morning, she blew on the embers from the night before to make the fire come alight; she never had to use a match. If there was no fire, there was no cooked breakfast.

She was called keeper of the fire.

This may sound lovely and sentimental, like a fairy tale about a young girl sitting among cinders, but I don't think anything will prepare you for the reality of the situation. It's illustrated in the narrative that my mother told to me of how, in 1928, when she was six, a man driving a horse and buggy appeared at Hinu-o-koko and took her with him.

This is the story. Imagine it happening in sepia.

The man in the buggy was my mother's uncle, Dick Tūpara Tikitiki. He was the one who had registered her birth and came to see Flowers with a special request. Two old women, wonderful weavers renowned for the beauty of their sacred work, needed a young girl to prepare the food and other common household tasks. Could Turi go to look after them? Flowers agreed; after all, Mum was named after her uncle. On that very day, while Mum was playing with her brothers and sisters, Flowers told her to get on the buggy with her uncle and go. Just like that. In the clothes she was wearing. No shoes. No sentimental goodbyes. No saying 'E noho rā' to the rest of the family. Just instructions from Flowers to go with Uncle, look after the old women and keep their fire alight. And because Mum was obedient and loved Flowers, she did as she was told.

Uncle Dick took Mum to the place where the two kuia lived, in a valley full of rainbows. The road didn't even go to the land where they lived. He stopped at the side of the road, pointed to a curl of smoke, 'Haere ki te whare', and then left.

The two weavers were Hauwaho and Kaingākau, and they lived with a brother, who was somewhat simple, in a small whare that was not as nice as the one at Hinu-o-koko. Way over the other side of the paddock was the kāuta, separated from the sacred work of the weaving. Mum was in awe of the two kuia, who welcomed her kindly. They dyed and wove mats of all colours: reds, yellows, purples, greens, blues — you name it.

As soon as Mum arrived she was treated as an adult. No excuses for being six. She was put straight to work because the weavers were busy with making mats for a very important meeting house that was under construction. And because Flowers had told her to be obedient, Mum did the work without complaint. She was shown the place where she was to sleep, on the floor at the foot of the bed of Hauwaho, and that is where she slept for three years.

Every morning my mother woke at the same time as Hauwaho, Kaingākau and their brother to say karakia. Straight afterwards, Mum would run over to the kāuta, barefoot in all weather, to blow on the embers. The kāuta was in bad condition, with rain coming in through the roof, and when she first arrived Mum had a lot of trouble keeping rain out. But she solved the problem: she patched the roof and holes with pieces of wood cemented with clay. In the first few months, though, she got a lot of stern rebuke from the two kuia, who wanted her to learn faster.

Once the fire was alight, Mum took the bucket to the spring to get water. The bucket was as big as she was. But she figured that problem out, too, and made a sled from two planks of wood to carry the bucket. She then fashioned a harness for herself. After a while, though, she made friends with the weavers' pet dog — it was as old as they were — and taught it to take the harness in its teeth and pull the sled. That dog was Mum's best friend and they loved one another very much. Together they would take the water back to the kāuta, where Mum would fill the pots and bring the water to the boil. All this, before dawn.

Now Hauwaho's and Kaingākau's and the old man's main diet was eels, tuna, and dried shark meat. Hauwaho showed Mum how to catch tuna, only once, and from then on she had to do it by herself. No excuses, no 'Can you show me again?' Mum would gather worms — under cowpats was the best place to find them — and thread them onto a whītau, a flax thread. Then she would get her dog to drag an old tin basin down to the river. There she would sit, dangling the whītau into the water, waiting for the eels to bite. Once this happened, *flick*, Mum would pull the tuna out and into the basin. *Flick*, and she would pull another eel out. *Flick*, another. *Flick*, and another. In all that time the dog would sit silent because he knew that his life, and those of the old people, depended on Mum's fishing skills. She was also the one responsible for curing and drying the shark meat. The job was hard and made her hands raw.

People regularly dropped by to either pick up the woven mats Hauwaho and Kaingākau made or else to leave orders with them. They brought a bag of flour or tinned food in exchange for the beautiful work. Hauwaho would give the flour to Mum and say, 'E Turi, make us a flat bread.' They never had butter with their bread. As a special treat they would sometimes get some dripping for Mum, for they soon grew to love her. She was obedient and did her work well.

Whenever the two kuia were working, Mum would feed them with a long fork, mārau, putting bits of eel or shark or potato on the end, because they were not allowed to touch food. 'Homai te kai,' they would urge her, 'homai.' Sometimes they teased her, moving their faces this way and that, to make it difficult for her to put the food into their mouths. After all, she was just a child, and they knew that a child likes to play games.

Very soon Mum had all the household tasks well under control. Her one dress was falling apart and she decided she had better learn how to weave so she could make a new one. She asked Hauwaho to show her, but the old woman said, 'No, e Turi, your job is to keep the fire alight.' Mum felt very sorry for herself and was embarrassed because her body was showing through her dress. She always had great modesty; although she loved when visitors came, she began to hide because she was so ashamed of her clothes. One night Hauwaho surprised her. She said, 'This is for you, e Turi.' The two kuia had woven her a beautiful cloak of plain flax, so soft on her shoulders that it made her feel like a princess.

Mum never spoke ill of those three old people. They were as kind to her as they could possibly be, often giving her hugs whenever she felt lonely, so she was not without love or affection. But she was always wondering when Flowers was coming to get her. She would go out to the road with the dog and sit there, waiting. One day she saw two older children, a boy and a girl, coming along the road, but she was so shy that she hid in the grass. When they drew abreast she saw that they were two of her siblings. She sprang out and ran to them, saying, 'Have you come to get me? Have you come to take me home?' They didn't recognise her, because she had grown so much, and, frightened, they ran away.

Mum never realised how hard she was working. She just had no comparisons to make. When she did find out, I think it took her a long time to understand it all.

Well, the old people did their best. Sometimes they got sick; Mum was sent out to gather herbs to make them better. She and her pet dog began to do more and more heavy work. Mum loved that old dog. She depended on him. He was obedient to her. Then one day, when Mum and the dog were returning with the water from the spring, the dog began to pant in a strange way. It lay down. When Mum saw that her dog was going to die she got so angry that she picked up a stick and started to beat the animal, trying to make it stand up. 'Get up, kurī!' she yelled. 'We have to get the water back to the kāuta.' The dog just couldn't do it. Quietly it began to whimper, and then it died. Just like that. One minute there, next minute gone.

I never knew my mother to cry. She always took tears as a sign of weakness. But when the dog died she didn't want to go on herself: blowing on the fire every morning, covering the fire every night, cooking and sleeping on the dirt floor.

Mum was nine when she left. She has never spoken about why. She insists she never ran away. She has always said, 'I just left.' I don't know where she went to, but I think it was to stay with her eldest sister, Mate, in Gisborne.

Flowers went to the town to get her. 'You have to go back,' she said.

She never did.

3.

NOW THE TIKA to my mother's story.

First, she was sixty-five when she told it to me in 1987, and one of my daughters was misbehaving and not being obedient at the kitchen table so there was a point in telling it. In the process Mum may have turned the story into a morality tale about a previous generation's hardships, more improving than real. She may also have been hinting at the fact that no matter a family's proud status, in any society, there is always the possibility of hard times and personal sacrifice.

Second, I was so affected by the story that I wrote it down straight away. In my narrative she was six, but, about ten years later, Mum wrote her own account of the story in which she begins: 'When I was about nine, one of my Tūpunas Dick Tūpara Tikitiki came over home talked to Mum and Dad then took me away from my parents.'

Clearly there's a three-year difference in her age, and my mother's version should be honoured. She gives details: the house was called Te Mahanga, and it was situated below Te Arawaere cemetery. Mum refers to a young girl of four years old, Teddy Milner, who was also living at the whare, but she does not mention the brother of the two weavers, or the pet dog. When she first arrived she was lonely, frightened and homesick. She writes: 'Hauwaho was a tiny old lady with a Moko with shoulder length curly hair and everyone called her Shirley Temple. The Tūpunas belonged to the Ringatū faith and prayed and chanted from three o'clock in the morning until dawn.'

More details: Mum made a broom of mānuka brush with which she swept the floor. The woven mats, kits and hats covered the whole floor, and some were strewn over the rafters. A man named Peta Kōmaru saw a mat that Mum had made, liked it and took it with him. Mum writes of a tenth birthday in which Hauwaho baked her a cake in a camp oven: 'Hauwaho forgot the sugar! I will never forget that cake as long as I live.'

Third, Te Mahanga was flooded many times so it was decided to move it to Mangatuna, where it stood on the left side of Hinemaurea meeting house. During Cyclone Bola, however, Te Mahanga was swept away — Mum calls the meeting house 'she' — to join the two tīpuna, Hauwaho and Kaingākau, who always lived within her heart.

The valley, of course, remains. Today, if you get into your car at Tolaga Bay and drive to the valley it will only take, say, fifteen to twenty minutes. But one has to remember that the world my mother lived in, in those days, was one without cars, where people either walked or rode horses, and therefore what takes us fifteen minutes might have taken them half a day to a day. Apart from which my mother was remembering how life was in childhood, when everything was larger, wider, longer.

The point is that time and distance don't really matter. My mother, her mountain, her people and the way they lived, and her stories became a taonga, a treasure, handed down from her generation to mine in all their variation, mystery, wonder and fascination.

The whakapapa at 11 Haig Street is not just a genealogy. Although it comprises only names, all I have to do is to hongi, press noses with them, and the stories spill out. As for that three-year difference between being six and nine, there may have been a reason for it, which I will come to later.

4.

MEANTIME, LET'S TAKE up my mother's story from the time she was ten. Mum was adopted out again to keep the fire for her father's brother, Rūtene, and his second wife, Kararaina. They lived at Anaura Bay and needed help with the children.

I don't know how long Mum was with Rūtene and Kararaina but she was approaching her teens when she returned to Tolaga Bay. There is a photograph of her in the family album, the earliest we have of her, which shows a shearing gang; they are within the inverted V of one another's legs, in a line going up a hill slope, smiling, and Mum is full-faced, with wild bushy hair. According to those who knew her, she was built like a man, with wide shoulders, but those hips gave her away; she was lightly muscled.

At fourteen, Mum left the coast to return to Gisborne and her sister Mate, who was married by then to Pita Kaua. Mate had turned herself into a teacher, how is a mystery to me, but this aunty was always a woman of iron determination and able to negotiate the upper rungs of Māori Anglican and Roman Catholic societies without being compliant. Mum got a job as a cook and housemaid — perhaps Aunty Mate found it for her — for the Ogilvy family who lived in Cobden Street. Mr Ogilvy was the postmaster in Gisborne at the time, and he and his wife had two sons, John and Jim. Mrs Ogilvy was very fitness-conscious and, every morning, would swim in the sea, a pretty extraordinary occurrence in the 1930s.

I suspect that it was under Aunty Mate's influence that Mum grew up into a well-groomed young woman and certainly into her inheritance as coming from two patrician families of the East Coast. It's a remarkable transformation and you can see the beginnings in photographs. The first I have chosen for this memoir reveals her as buxom and bushy-haired and wearing rural trousers; in the next, with my father at a Gisborne dance, she is slimmer and beautifully dressed, but that hair still needs to be tamed; by the time you come to the photograph after my birth, she is positively stylish in hat and dark suit, striding confidently along a busy street.

I like to think my own capacity for reinvention and shape-shifting through my life comes from her. Blood, as they say, will out.

My mother must have been around sixteen when her grandfather, Len Babbington, sought her out to come up to Tokomaru Bay to be the keeper of his fire and look after him and his wife, Mate. At the time Len's father, John Babbington, patriarch of the Babbington clan, was still living; he was ninety-seven when he died in 1939. Mum recalls how Meimei Aiopa used to drive John Babbington into Tokomaru Bay in his Pontiac to see his son Len. Mum herself learned how to drive, and took over the chauffeuring duties. She was a familiar sight taking both men on drives in his Essex with a dickie seat. But she must have been hankering after some independence from family duties because on the recommendation of the Ogilvys she managed to get part-time housekeeping jobs with the Fraser and Loiselle families.

Mum was seventeen when her favourite brother, Rangiora, told her he had answered the call of Āpirana Ngata and enlisted in 28th (Māori) Battalion to fight in the Second World War; of the 3551 men in the 28th, a third came from the coast. Mum had a premonition, a very bad tohu, about Rangiora's enlistment. When she farewelled him on the military train which left Gisborne for camp at Palmerston North, she was extremely distressed.

The last waltz my mother had with Rangiora was at the railway station before he boarded; the battalion's story is eloquently told by Patricia Grace in her novel *Tū*. I imagine Mum in a white dress, going up on her toes, and dancing with her brother. His mates whistle and cheer as they glide and dip in each other's arms.

'And when I grow too old to dream, your love will live in my heart.'

Mum stayed with Grandpa Len until he decided to go and live at Hinu-o-koko with Flowers and Kereama. Eventually she returned to Gisborne and, on the recommendation of the Loiselle family, got a job with the Nathan family in Gisborne at Tukura Road. She was on the way to making her life mean something.

My mother was never too proud. Even into her seventies, when she should have been retired, she was working in a kitchen, this time as a cook at the Sandown Hotel on Childers Road. The Chinese owner relied on Mum to get there every morning to make room service breakfast for businessmen and families who were checking out before the dining room opened.

One of the enduring memories I have of my mother is hearing her rise before dawn from beside my father at 11 Haig Street and going down the hallway, past the whakapapa, to the bathroom to wash, shower and change into her kitchen clothes. Daily, she emerged from a passage in time, appearing through the names of the ancestors. Came the moment when I heard the sliding door to my bedroom open. 'Are you awake, son?'

I was always awake for my mother. I loved the ritual nature of our farewells when she would bend to kiss me on the forehead.

Next moment the darkness would streak with crimson.

Chapter Six

A Literary Whakapapa

1.

THERE'S A MĀORI saying that goes: 'Te tōrino haere whakamua, whakamuri. At the same time as the spiral is going forward, it is returning.'

I like to think of the spiral as being an appropriate symbol for the way that Māori tell stories. We progress our narratives by way of their circularities and, where one spiral touches another, it has the power to take us back as well as propel us forward.

This is what has happened to the main spiral of my story. Another spiral has touched it and propelled me forward to the late 1960s and early 1970s, when I began my literary career. With it came an encounter with whakapapa: by genealogy can one be granted land, language and culture, yes. What is granted, however, comes with responsibilities and restrictions. There are also implicit custodial obligations.

2.

I WAS TWENTY-EIGHT when my first book, *Pounamu Pounamu*, came out in 1972. I had worked hard to become a published writer, and I will be covering this career in a later book. Suffice to say, at this point, that within a very short three-year period I had made myself known, within literary circles at least, as a new kid on the block, and a Māori kid at that.

Of course there were other writers around, like my cousin Arapera Blank, J.C. Sturm, Rowley Habib (Rore Hapipi), and an old guard of Pei Te Hurinui Jones, Harry Dansey and others. But I came out of nowhere when nobody was looking. I rode a big wave of publicity, which got bigger when the *Auckland Star* published one story from *Pounamu Pounamu* in their Saturday edition for six weeks. I was on tour for the book from Auckland to Wellington, and I had every reason to be proud of myself.

Then I hit Gisborne. My minder, Ted Bland, went to stay in a hotel and I turned up at Haig Street. I will admit to overconfidence and arrogance: I truly expected Mum and Dad to be pleased that I had become a writer. No sooner had I put my suitcase down, however, than I sensed the mood. Mum was dressed in a blue dress for the launch of the book at Muir's Bookshop, and Dad came from the bathroom and stood in front of her while she tied a knot in his tie.

As she did so, she asked Dad, 'Have you told our son about the visitors we had last week?'

'No,' Dad answered. In explanation he turned to look at me and said, 'Hēnare Ngata, Toko Te Kani and your mother's chief from up the coast, Api Crawford, came to see us.'

My mother had huge respect for Api Crawford. I saw her flinch at the mention of his name.

'Oh?' I asked. ' Did they get their invitations for tonight?'

'They came around to ask us if we knew you,' Dad said.

Knew me? In my vanity and puzzlement I thought, 'Didn't they read the newspapers? It wasn't as if I've been hiding.' I realised that, of course, although I had appeared in the Maori Affairs magazine, *Te Ao Hou*, I had mainly been published in Pākehā magazines like *Landfall* and the *New Zealand Listener*.

'It's your own fault for using that old surname of ours, Ihimaera,' Dad continued. 'You should have used your own.'

The whole conversation went to a level I had not expected.

Mum turned to me. 'You should have asked their permission before you published your book.'

I couldn't believe my ears. 'Why?'

'They are your chiefs, son, you know that,' she said. 'And you should have told the people at Waituhi you were writing about them, and all the other people in your book.'

'The book's fiction, Mum. It's made up.'

'Made up?' she asked. 'How can that be if you use the name Waituhi in it? Anybody who reads your book will know that Miro in the stories is your kuia, Mini.'

I had told Nani Mini that I was calling her by another name and, actually, she had been cross. 'Are you ashamed of me? And are you ashamed of Waituhi?' It had been a difficult dilemma. I would never have won whether I called the village by its own name or not, so I conceded on the name of the village but I did not call Nani Mini by hers. The reason was personal. Nani Mini was mine and I was not about to share her with a reading public.

My mother's criticism continued. 'Everyone will know that Mr Hōhepa, who puts a mākutu on the postmistress, is Te Kani Te Ua. Not to mention the chief who chops down the door of the storehouse — we know it's Moni Taumaunu.'

'So you've read the book, then?' I asked.

Mum was persistent. 'They are rangatira, son, they have their own mana. You should have respected that. You come from a line of chiefs, too, but you have not proven yourself.'

She finished Dad's tie and he patted her on the shoulders: 'There, there, dear.'

Meanwhile I was trying to catch my breath: what was happening?

'So what did you say to our chiefs?' I asked Dad.

'I told them who you were,' he answered. 'Hēnare and Toko both know you, and Hēnare said, "Oh, you mean Witi?" And I said, "Yes." And Toko didn't seem to mind. He went, "Hear, hear, Witi!"'

Dad was looking at Mum, hoping she would calm down, but she was still really, really upset. 'Api, however, didn't take what Dad was saying, and he turned to me directly and he asked, "So, Julia, where does your son come from? By what right can Witi claim to do what he is doing, writing about our people?" He knew who my mother Flowers was. Not to mention the mana of the Keelan line. How dare he!'

'I had to get between Api and your mother,' Dad continued. 'They were having a ding-dong battle over your whakapapa, and Mum was taking him back through the Babbington and Keelan genealogy, but Api would not budge — no writers in them. In the end I said to him, "Look, don't ask Julia that question. Ask me." I referred him to the book your Uncle Win edited, the Māori language book by Hēnare's father. And Api had to back down, and he said, "Oh, so the right is through Win? That's okay, then." And then they left.'

I turned to my mother. 'And what would you have said anyway, Mum?'

She was not unkind. 'Son, I tried to establish your right through our family waiata composers and haka composers, but what you are doing is not the same, it is different.' And then she added, 'Kia tūpato, be careful. Your own people are watching. They are the ones who matter. You must make sure your work has mana. It must have reo. It must have mauri.' And then she asked me, 'Have you had the book blessed yet?'

'No,' I answered.

She gave me a dark look. 'Don't you know anything?' Then she turned to Dad. 'We cannot go to the launch with an unblessed book. We'd better have a karakia before we get in the car.'

As Dad started to say a prayer over *Pounamu Pounamu*, I opened a small crack in my eyes and whispered an apology. 'Oh, book, I am so sorry. You and I didn't expect any of this, did we? My mistake was that because I wrote you in English and as fiction I forgot that you were still Māori. Forgive me and go well in the world. We just have to make the best of it.'

After the karakia, Mum still had questions. 'I need to know exactly why you have done this, son, why you are writing about us.'

'You're the people I know.'

'Why don't you write about the people that Pākehā write about! Kings and queens or princes and princesses or rich people?'

'I'm not a Pākehā, Mum, and I want to be a Māori writer. Who else can I write about if I want to be that? And I don't know any kings or queens or princes or princesses! You and Dad are the queen and king of my life, and all the people out at Waituhi, they are my life's princes and princesses. I am their own true subject.'

She wasn't about to be swayed by the flowery way I said it. She took my chin in her hands and looked into my eyes. I tried to turn from her penetrating gaze, but she would not let me do that. Then she nodded, satisfied. 'In the future, be careful, son, lest your good intentions come back to punish you.'

It was clear that Mum didn't like this new career of mine, and that I should have made a stronger separation between Māori and *Māori*, but I had already set my course and the distinction would be forever blurred.

Today, *Pounamu Pounamu* seems such an inoffensive, nonconfrontational little book with its unabashed lyricism. Māori, however, with their deep analytical ways, really had to adjust their thinking about it. I suspect one of the questions was to do with the fact that while they spoke to each other in Māori through action song and waiata, they saw *Pounamu Pounamu* as showing themselves to the Pākehā 'other'.

3.

NOW THE TIKA. A whakapapa is a cosmos, a map of a universe. Māori sometimes say of their ancestors, 'Kua whetūrangatia rātou — they are the myriad stars', and at a tangi someone who has recently died is often farewelled with the words 'Haere ki Paerau — go to the threshold of the heavens.'

Perhaps instead of ancestors the room behind my eyes is a beautiful dark sky filled with sparkling stars.

For Māori writers of my times, however, as few as we were, there was no such universe, no such whakapapa. Of course some people will say that is nonsense because, after all, there was a vast number of oral practitioners to be inspired by, and an oral inventory of Māori traditional stories to draw from. Yes, that is true, but we were writing ourselves into existence in English and moving from the known into the unknown, an altogether different darkness, in an altogether different language. Where were we planning to take the literature, the inheritance of our ancestors?

This chapter is titled 'a literary whakapapa' because I realised, that evening, while my mother was tying a knot in my father's tie, that they were not the only ones in the Māori community wondering where to fit this new art Māori writers were practising. What was its genealogy? What was its tribe? Who were its chiefs? It wasn't even in the reo; it was some unblessed *thing*, a wilful child operating outside the accustomed norms.

I realised that not only would I write it into existence but I would also have to be its custodian. Not only to talk the talk but walk it. Ever since, I have asserted its rights not only as a writer but as one of its elders. Others were doing the same in contemporary art, music, dance, theatre, television and education.

Together, we established a period that some critics define as a cultural renaissance. Eventually our practice revealed what had always been there, the connection of our work to the oral traditions of our ancestors.

And our acceptance came to pass.

Chapter Seven

The Joining of Paternal Genealogies

1.

THE GREAT CREATION myth of the Māori involves the arrival of something out of nothing. The nothing is known as Te Kore, The Void, and the tendency is to think of it as an emptiness. I prefer the way in which classicist Agathe Thornton looks at it as the Greek equivalent of Chaos.

Te Kore evolved over a timeless time into Te Pō, otherwise known as The Night. The Māori text is splendid, offering a dizzying number of transformations of blackness: Te Pō Nui, Te Pō Roa, The Big Night, The Long Night, The Night Without End, and so on.

Then from out of Te Pō came Te Ao, The World, comprising Papatūānuku, the earth mother, and Ranginui, the sky father. They had generative capacities, and their copulation resulted in the making of a male pantheon of gods and separate kingdoms — forest, sea and wind, and so on — for them to rule in and, incidentally, to fight over. Definitely the first patriarchy. No women allowed.

Don't think, either, in the Māori Genesis, that there were only a few brothers. They numbered in the hundreds, each with their own territories and tasks. No wonder Māori were always saying karakia; all those gods, let alone god territories, that had to be negotiated, say, as you were taking a walk down to the sea or going out to do some fishing.

The gods lived in the crowded spaces between the eternal embrace of Papatūānuku and Ranginui. They discovered their predicament only when Uepoto was washed beyond the parents' clasp in the mimi, or urine, of his mother and discovered that there was a beautifully scented and light-filled world outside.

Naturally the gods debated how they might find release from their confinement.

Tū, god of war, said, 'Let us kill our parents.'

Tāwhirimātea, god of the winds, was horrified at the proposal: 'No.'

It was Tānemahuta, god of the forested earth, who suggested a compromise, 'Let our parents live, but one high above and the other far below.'

There was much disagreement among all the gods, but, in the end, Tānemahuta broke ranks and over a timeless time tried to wrest the parents apart, so that all their children could fully stand. However, Ranginui always foiled the attempts by holding fast to his wife; some of the brothers also tried to stop Tānemahuta. In the end, Tānemahuta triumphed by placing his hands on his mother and, with a savage kick, he sent Ranginui spinning away.

Early folklorists, mindful of children as readers, rendered the separation myth in pretty picture-book form. They preferred not to add illustrations of the god brothers chopping off Ranginui's limbs to prevent him from re-embracing Papatūānuku, or drawings of the raising of poles between earth and sky to keep them apart. Then there was the sacrifice made by Pāia, who willingly knelt between the parents; he became the Māori version of Atlas, forever holding his father up on his back.

As a boy, I was constantly awed at Pāia's great strength. 'How heavy Ranginui must be,' I thought with amazement.

Once the separation was achieved, The Light, Te Ao Mārama, came flooding in between.

Indeed Te Ao Mārama also came with many layers of metaphor and meaning, among which was one about parental sacrifice and from that followed independence, knowledge and awareness. Because of The Light, all humankind, and all with whom we shared this world, were able to live. It was only to be expected therefore that in their karakia the old people honoured the sacrifice of the sky above and the earth below and their generosity in providing the bright strand between.

As I turn from my mother to my father, I make my mihi to the primal parents with full awareness of the brutality of their separation. I foreground my parents' generosity and ability to forgive.

There was a lot they had to forgive me for.

AND SO I trace the spiral of my father's whakapapa.

I begin with his father, Pera Punahāmoa Ihimaera, and Grandad's many mountains, and with the answer to a question that may have been puzzling you: Where did the 'Smiler' come from?

'The early missionaries had difficulties saying our Māori name,' Grandad told me when I asked him. 'They kept on mispronouncing it and then said, "Well, it sounds like Smiler, so why don't we call you that?"'

We've been saddled with the name ever since. Such a prosaic lack of imagination. And I've had jokes made about being 'Witty' Smiler, and no doubt my sister Gay has had similar jokes about hers. Poor us, eh Gay.

Pera was born on 2 October in either 1888 or 1889 (in Pera's own whakapapa book the year alternates) and was one of the last full-blooded Māori in Poverty Bay. As I write those words *one of the last*, I start to shiver, and I can sense Grandad's formidable ancestors crowding forward to stare out of the room behind my eyes — 'It's our turn now.'

According to family history, Grandad's mother was from lands that bordered the district, and this gave our family an expansion to those other mountains and other affiliations I have referred to. Her full name was Hine Te Ariki Pera, although in Grandad's book there is reference to another name 'or Taniwha Parewhai'. She was born circa 1867, the daughter of Pera Punahāmoa and Te Rina Parewhai (sometimes spelt Terina or Rina), and was from Whakatōhea, Te Whānau-a-Apanui and Raukawa (Heretaunga); as well, she had ancestral lands in Te Whānau-a-Kai.

The first-mentioned, Whakatōhea, occupied the eastern part of a bay that Cook named Plenty compared with our Poverty; it was a large arrowhead of coastline from Ōhiwa Harbour eastward to Ōpapa, and thrust inland through the Waioeka Gorge to Matawai. The tribe was descended from two great ancestors: Tūtāmure, whose people had come to Aotearoa on the *Nukutere* canoe, and Hineikauia, whose ancestors arrived on the *Mātaatua* nine generations later. Like my mother's Uepōhatu, Whakatōhea also had a Stone World people. They were known as Te Tini-a-Toi, the multitudes of Toi, and the tribe intermarried with them too.

By all accounts, Hine Te Ariki was a formidable chieftain of the Ngāti Ruatakena, one of the subtribes of Whakatōhea. She claimed Tūtāmure meeting house as her marae; the dining hall, Hineikauia, was built on land she donated with her sisters. She also asserted rights in the subtribal lands of Ngāti Ngahere and Ngāti Irapuaia. Assuredly Hine Te Ariki's alternative identity as Taniwha Parewhai symbolises with some accuracy — 'taniwha' being the word for a being with ferocious qualities — her inherited prestige. According to my father, 'Whenever Hine Te Ariki stood to speak, other people sat down.' He added with a twinkle in his eye, 'Being over six feet and broad-shouldered probably helped.'

Comparatively speaking, the Whakatōhea tribal lands were not large, but they controlled a valuable coastline and therefore north–south sea lanes, and were richly endowed with traditional kai from land and sea. During pre-Pākehā times, the tribe needed all the six-footers they could get, both men and women, to hold off other iwi wishing to wrest their strategic position from them as well as their highly desirable food resources. Auē, during the nineteenth century the tribe suffered a greater threat, this time from Pākehā settlers looking for prime coastal real estate with a flat hinterland. Despite their welcoming settlers, including both Roman Catholic and Anglican priests, they were invaded by government troops in 1865. The Crown used the excuse of the killing and beheading of missionary Carl Sylvius Völkner as pretext, and went so far as to hang six Māori (some say seven), including the chief, Mokomoko. And then they confiscated the land.

On 17 May 1866, just before he was hanged, Mokomoko turned to the hangman and said: 'Tangohia te taura i taku kakī, kia waiata au i taku waiata. Take the rope from my throat that I may sing my song.'

It was a stirring utterance. Those words and their cadence have haunted me all my life.

Shockingly, Whakatōhea today has only recently reached its settlement claim and apology, not only for the land confiscations but also for Mokomoko's hanging. It's been a messy, long drawn-out business, one that Pera was involved in as a member of the Whakatohea Trust Board. I only wish that I had seen Grandad in his role as a leader and negotiator.

3.

IMMEDIATELY YOU CAN sense a different, darker, family history.

It's a history of people pushed to resist and then to rebel and to stand their ground. And this unflinching position can be seen not only in the tribal whakapapa of Grandad's mother, but also that of his father Ihimaera (Te Teira) Te Hānene Ringarore, the Honey Gatherer, born circa 1863.

For many years I always thought of this ancestor as being from Te Urewera, but his father Te Teira Te Hānene was from Nūhaka and it was through his mother Turuhira Tāmaku that the primary connection is made to Te Urewera — specifically the Ngāti Whare iwi. They are one of many peoples who once were clustered under the general rubric of Ngāi Tūhoe, the mountainous heartland of the North Island of New Zealand; they're on the western side, clustered around Te Whāiti and Minginui.

All my life, I have felt a ridiculous amount of pride at being of direct descent from the Urewera iwi. At first it was a romantic, idealised pride, founded on pretty folk tales published for English children about an enchanted land where a mountain (Te Maunga) married a Mist Maiden (Hine-pūkohu-rangi) and, lo and behold, the Children of the Mist were born. At least the folk tales got one thing right: the presence of yet another Stone World within the folds and peaks of the mountains. When Ngāi Tūhoe arrived on the *Mātaatua* and *Rangimatoru* waka, they absorbed these 'faery folk' into their iwi.

Proximity to Waituhi added a frisson to my pride. Te Urewera backed onto Te Whānau-a-Kai lands, and I can remember a stirring moment at Waituhi in the early 1950s when a delegation from Te Urewera arrived for a hui at our family marae of Rongopai. Through a curtain of swirling dust they appeared, the darkest and most majestic apparition I had ever seen.

'Sit up straight,' Grandad said.

My spine was already vertical and my hair standing on end.

Some of their warriors were riding horses. They must have come over Rua's Track from Maungapōhatu along the Hangaroa Valley by way of Waimana and down the Wharekōpae River. The women were garbed in black and their heads were wreathed in greenery. And they were chanting karakia and their warriors were throwing dust in the air.

I tell you, by the time they arrived at the marae, even our mountain was bowing in homage to theirs.

There's nothing romantic, however, about Te Urewera history. Unlike other tribes, they remained powerfully isolated from Pākehā settlement behind the palisades and ramparts of their natural mountain defences. Then, in 1863, they were accused of sheltering one of the leaders implicated in Völkner's murder. They were cruelly punished with land confiscations, including their only access to kai moana. A few years later, they were again implicated in providing sanctuary for the rebel leader, Te Kooti Arikirangi Te Tūruki.

4.

I DISCOVER I must, by way of background, make a detour here, to Te Kooti.

Those who know the 1826 novel, *The Last of the Mohicans* by James Fenimore Cooper, will recall that, apart from the white trapper and hero, Natty Bumppo, or Hawkeye, there are two main indigenous protagonists, Chingachgook and Magua. The story takes place during the Seven Years War, 1757 to 1764, when the French and British fought over who would control the scattering of colonies that had been established mainly along the upper east coast of North America. Chingachgook, who has a son called Uncas, is the good Indian because he sides with the American settlers; Magua is the bad Indian because he fights with the French against the settlers. The French soldiers think Magua is on their side, but he is a fascinating and ambivalent character who identifies with neither; he is all the more intriguing because he has been 'civilised' — can speak French and English, and has had experience of high culture. Known as Le Renard Subtil, the cunning fox, Magua is condemned as a savage, unredemptive killer; he earns a double condemnation when he turns on the very settlers who were civilising him, and then embarks on a killing spree.

In Aotearoa, there are arguably three such Magua figures, but they leap out with even greater intensity because they are real and not fictional. There are some suggestions that Cooper gained inspiration for the motif of savagery in his novel not only from events in North America but also from the killing by Māori of over seventy white sailors and passengers on the *Boyd* in 1809, when it landed in Whangaroa Harbour to collect kauri spars. Widely reported and sensationalised, the incident teaches us to take heed of context, which has to do with the concept of utu: the reciprocal retaliation for the spreading of a disease by a previous ship which had come a year earlier. Undoubtedly, the *Boyd* incident, reported as a massacre, set the seal on Māori as barbarous savages during the turmoil and confusion that filled the years before the signing of the Treaty of Waitangi.

The three Magua figures are: Te Rauparaha, sometimes known as the Napoleon of the Southern Hemisphere and often depicted as a wolf; Tītokowaru, the great Taranaki warlord of Achillean epic proportions; and, on the east coast of Aotearoa, we had Te Kooti.

All have been represented as barbaric savages, inhabiting the darkest corners of the New Zealand Nightmare, but they and many others had good cause to fight against the government troops who invaded their lands, from 1845 to 1872. These wars have been known as the New Zealand Wars, the Land Wars or the Māori Wars, and, by Māori, as the Pākehā Wars. In the majority of cases, Māori were responding to prior acts against them by soldiers or settlers. They were not the aggressors; they were compelled to take utu. *Lex talionis*, an eye for an eye, was not unknown among Māori.

Te Kooti's four-year guerilla-type action occurred during the final four years of the wars between Māori and Pākehā, and this late campaign is often referred to as the Te Kooti Wars: some military historians consider it the most savage of the lot.

I will be returning to the Te Kooti Wars later but, for now, let me quickly go over the prophet's early life, and I ask you to note the context: born circa 1832 of neighbouring kin, Ngāti Maru, Te Kooti was a Christian and involved in coastal trading with Pākehā settlements in Poverty Bay. When the Pākehā Wars began, he actually joined the government forces that fought Pai Mārire supporters — their earlier emissaries had managed to attract rebel sympathisers — at Waerenga-a-Hika, not far from Waituhi, in November 1865. However, instead of being praised, Te Kooti was arrested for being a spy and sent, together with 300 other men, women and children, to imprisonment on the Chatham Islands.

When the lives of Te Kooti, Te Rauparaha and Tītokowaru are compared, it is clear that Te Kooti's had the greatest religious dimension. While he was on the Chathams the Angel Gabriel visited him and told him to found a church based on the Old Testament and customary Māori beliefs. Thus did Te Kooti transform other prisoners into his followers. He believed his mission was to lead them out of slavery as Moses did in Exodus — and his disciples were known as Ngā Iharaira, the Israelites.

My friend, historian Judith Binney, who died in 2011, was of the opinion that the escape from the Chathams was the result of unfair and possibly illegal duress. The prisoners had been sent to the islands only for a specific time and, when that time expired, who could blame them for taking the matter of release into their own hands? In July 1868, Te Kooti seized a resupply boat and, together with the Iharaira, sailed to the mainland with the express purpose of fulfilling the Angel Gabriel's instruction to establish a spiritual settlement.

Instead, although he was adamant that he did not want to fight Pākehā, Te Kooti was met by militia under the control of Major Reginald Biggs, who asked him to lay down his arms and submit to arrest and reimprisonment. When Te Kooti refused to do this, a force under Biggs's control relentlessly pursued him. Again, Judith Binney queried whether Biggs had the authority to take this action.

Astonishingly, Te Kooti and the Iharaira were triumphant in their rearguard defensive exodus through the dense bush of the East Coast and Poverty Bay. Not only that, but the prophet's charisma inspired local Māori to join his church, which he called the Ringatū, 'Ringa' meaning hand and 'Tū' meaning upraised. The upraised hand is always the gesture made during concluding cadences of Ringatū prayers: 'Korōria ki Tō Ingoa tapu, Āmine. Glory to Your holy name, Amen.'

Because he continued to be pursued by troops, Te Kooti made a formal declaration of war. Acting on this declaration, he attacked the military garrison at Matawhero in November 1868, and executed not only Pākehā but also Māori prisoners, including women and children — around sixty were killed, roughly equal numbers of Māori and Pākehā.

The detail is messy: you could use the word massacre, but don't forget that declaration of war, and that in war both civilians and military are casualties. Whatever the case, to this day some Māori families in Poverty Bay hold an abiding enmity towards Te Kooti or any attempts to redeem him.

From this point on the war escalated, with savagery being exhibited on both sides. Te Whānau-a-Kai's anecdotal evidence of the Battle of Ngātapa in January 1869, where the Iharaira were brought to account for the Matawhero killings, records that the militia executed 120 defending the pā to enable Te Kooti to escape, for £5 a head. Judith Binney, however, refers to 130 male prisoners — rounded up, incidentally, by Ngāti Porou kūpapa — being shot, and she does not mention any price per dead rebel.

Now let me join this aside to my narrative about Te Urewera.

Te Kooti escaped into the region's high mountains and forests. He was followed relentlessly by government forces who, finding him difficult to capture, applied a scorched earth strategy: smoke Te Kooti out by punishing those tribes who supported him. They waged this strategy between 1869 and 1871, killing or imprisoning suspected sympathisers, destroying villages and their crops and stock. Te Kooti managed to escape to the King Country. Decimated and starving, Ngāi Tūhoe submitted to the Crown. Between 1896 and 1901, 23 per cent of the population of the area died, succumbing to disease and deprivation. Throughout the twentieth century, confiscation and its consequences threatened to bring Ngāi Tūhoe to their knees. From time to time their leaders have continued to be imprisoned.

As writer Kennedy Warne has said, 'Te Urewera history can break your heart.'

Chapter Eight
The Māori Israelites

1.

WE SHOULD RETURN to Ihimaera Te Hānene Ringarore, the Honey
Gatherer. His first name has always held a fascination for me and,
indeed, translates as Ishmael; it comes from the Old Testament, Genesis,
chapters 16 to 25.

Let my ancestor explain himself. The night sky is above, the campfire
of the faithful awaits. And the Honey Gatherer throws a cloak of many
colours over you.

'Korōria ki Tō Ingoa tapu.

'I raise my hand and give glory to God.

'The patriarch, Āperahama, was in his eighties and his wife, Hara,
some ten years younger than him, was barren, i whai tamariki māna.
Yet Īhowa, God, had made a promise to Āperahama that his seed would
be as numberless as the stars. See them? Are they not like many eyes of
heaven?

'But the years passed and with every year Hara's heart became heavy.
She was already long past child-bearing. She had a handmaid called
Hakara — from Egypt she had come, the land of the Pharaohs. Hara
entreated Āperahama to sleep with the Egyptian and, from that union
was born a son, ko Ihimaera was his name; Āperahama was eighty-six
when he was born.

'Oh, it was thirteen years before Īhowa honoured his covenant that
ngā Kīngi and nations would come from Āperahama and Hara's seed.
Can you imagine how long that felt to Hara? Āperahama was ninety-nine
years old when, miracle of miracles, Hara found herself pregnant. And at
ninety years of age, she delivered a legitimate heir, ko Īhaka.

'The Paipera Tapu says that Hakara had flaunted Ihimaera in Hara's
face and that when Īhaka was weaned Ihimaera mocked his half-brother.
Angered, Hara told Āperahama to cast them out. Āperahama grieved
over this but Īhowa told him, "In all that Hara has said to you, hearken
to her voice, for in Īhaka is my covenant." But Īhowa did not forget
Ihimaera and also said, "From the son of the bondswoman will I make
a nation." Therefore Āperahama rose up early in the morning and took
bread and a bottle of water to Hakara and sent her and Ihimaera away.
They wandered i te koraha o Pērehepa, in the wilderness of Beersheba,
dying almost from thirst. Īhowa, however, did not abandon them; He
sent an angel to Hakara.

'The angel showed Hakara a well, and she and her son were saved.

'And his seed, too, was as numberless as the stars.

'Glory to Your holy name.

'Korōria ki Tō Ingoa tapu, Āmine.'

Īhaka's son Hākopa, Jacob, fathered twelve sons, who became the twelve tribes of Israel. Ihimaera also fathered twelve sons, who became the nomadic Arab nation.

When I was in New York in 1988, the Jewish ex-congresswoman Bella Abzug and I were talking at a cocktail party and she took a shine to me, until she asked me what my surname Ihimaera meant. When I told her she was taken aback and said, 'I like you, Witi, but if only you weren't named after the progenitor of the Arab people.' Later in my life I was to ponder those difficult questions of legitimacy and illegitimacy between brothers.

THE OTHER PART of my ancestor's name, Te Hānene, was also intriguing to me, firing my imagination. Was Ihimaera literally a man who gathered wild mānuka honey to feed the rebels while they were on the run, or did the name, with its biblical resonances, have some more figurative association?

Nor do I know at what point he became a Te Kooti follower and Ringatū adherent, but he may have joined the Israelites during the prophet's pell-mell flight through Te Urewera. According to Dad, he became an important lieutenant for Te Kooti. As I write this memoir, I can feel the Honey Gatherer shaking me hard: 'Witi! Stand up straight! Remember!'

Let me give him imaginative voice, and let him tell you of his experiences of civil war in Aotearoa. In the particular is the universal, so let what he tells us stand for the experiences of all those iwi fighting during that turbulent time against the government-led troops.

Therefore let us return to the campfire. There, oh ancestor, throw dust in the air, take the rope from your throat and sing your song:

'Ko te tangata he toa, ko te wahine he toa,' he begins. 'The man is a warrior, so too is the woman a warrior. When we go into battle, all of us go. Not just the men by ourselves, the women and children, too. If you are ever against us, don't spare the women or the brats we have because in war gender and age make no difference. The fight is not over until we are *all* dead.'

Hine Te Ariki stands beside him. 'When the wars began the Pākehā called them the Māori Wars. What did we call them? The Pākehā Wars! Te matauranga a te Pākehā he mea mō wai rā mō Hātana! Mō Hātana, I tell you!'

'The wars were fought in the Waikato, the Taranaki, the King Country, the North,' Te Hānene continues. 'Then they came to the East Coast twenty years after they had begun. I heard that the prophet Te Kooti had escaped from his island imprisonment on the Chathams, seized a boat and was on his way back to the mainland. I said to Hine Te Ariki, 'We must go to meet him and the 297 who escaped with him.'

Hine Te Ariki begins to intone a karakia. 'Let our people go, Pharaoh, let us be freed from the slavery of Egypt. Let us proceed without pursuit to our promised land of Canaan.'

Around the campfire the Ringatū faithful raise their hands. 'Korōria ki Tō Ingoa tapu, Āmine.' The sparks rise up like fireflies.

'The prophet landed at Whareongaonga,' Te Hānene says, 'but to that place to meet him came the cohorts of Pharaoh. They comprised Major Biggs and eighty militia, and Biggs said to the prophet, referring to his European name, "You, Coates, throw down your arms and surrender." When we would not, Biggs fell upon us with his devil's horde. Repeatedly he tried to stop our pilgrimage here, to the Urewera. He attacked us with 140 soldiers at Pāparatū. He fell upon us again at Te Kōneke. As we traversed the Ruakituri, Biggs tried to stop us there also — this time with 236 men.'

Hine Te Ariki takes up the story. 'The Lord was with us and He turned the weather against Biggs. Even so, many of our followers were killed. So it was that the prophet said unto Biggs, "Three times you have attacked me and three times I have asked you to leave us alone. You still pursue us in our pilgrimage, but if it is a fight you want a fight you will have. Therefore I shall take my people up unto Puketapu Mountain and from there in November I will come down from the mountain and fight you. Take heed of my declaration of war."'

In the firelight the faithful show the sign of the upraised hand and chant and sing. 'E te Atua, show us the way to escape the net of death so that we may live to glorify Your holy name, Āmine.'

Te Hānene continues, 'Te Kooti asked me to be one of his lieutenants in the attack on Biggs's military garrison at Matawhero. He said to me, "You, Honey Gatherer, will you be my left hand of God with which to smite the Egyptians?" Oh, my heart rose up with pride that I had been chosen! I kissed my beloved wife. Of course she wanted to come with me, but not this time. On Monday 9 November at 6.30 p.m. I led my squad of men on the run toward Matawhero. We went by way of the Ngātapa Valley, past Repongaere Lake. There we waited. Under cover. One minute to midnight—'

In the grip of memories, Hine Te Ariki cries, 'Attack!'

And the faithful, speaking in tongues, begin to relive the assault on the military garrison. 'Au! Au! Kia kutia! Whiti whiti e! Close your ranks! Cross over! Whano, whano! Go! Fight!' They are peering into the fire, watching the slaughter, the men, women and children of the garrison falling like angels to the attack. And then, there is Biggs, Te Kooti's nemesis, also falling to the ground.

Hine Te Ariki turns to Te Hānene. 'The Pākehā say you massacred sixty-three people.'

'Did we? It was a military attack. War is war.'

'They say that some of the victims were in a church praying when you killed them.'

'Were they? I can't remember a church or people praying. I returned to you and our people on Puketapu Mountain. I said, "We must flee for surely the cohorts of Pharaoh will want to take utu on us." They pursued us, oh, how they pursued us, and in the pursuit many fell. I remember a young boy, ko Rōpata tana ingoa, he was reloading my musket. He said to me, "Here you are, e tā," when a bullet smashed through his brain. No time to say goodbye. There was a sweet girl, too. What was her name?'

'Hīria,' Hine Te Ariki remembers. 'She was seven. She fell far behind as we ran, so I pushed her into the flax and told her we would be back for her. When we returned we found her body floating in a stream, slit from throat to stomach. Friendly Māori fighting on the government side were being paid for each rebel they killed and, after all, although she was a child she was also a warrior.'

The fire burns, the fire burns, the flames tongue the night. The faithful offer prayers for the souls of the dead, 'E te Atua, homai te aroha ki a mātou mate. O Lord, give Your love to those who come to You. Korōria ki Tō Ingoa tapu, Āmine.'

Te Hānene raises his hand. 'Christmas 1868, do you all remember?'

A moan rises and the air is filled with thrown ash and dust. 'We had taken refuge in our clifftop fortress at Ngātapa. That's where Pharaoh, with 700 troops, caught up with us, and there did he lay down his siege. He built a series of forts coming closer and closer. We were running out of ammunition, water and food.'

'Then on the ninth day,' Te Hānene continues, 'death rained down upon us from the cannon that had been brought by Pharaoh. They say between eighty-six and 126 of us went to God that day. I myself was wounded, a bullet in my neck and another in my left thigh, I could hardly hold my rifle or stand. I pleaded with the prophet, "You must escape, you must leave us. If we all stay here, you will die with us. You must go. Let me continue to be your left hand of God. Let me stay with the weak and wounded to cover your escape. And you, Hine Te Ariki, you go too."'

'I said goodbye to Te Hānene,' Hine Te Ariki says. 'The back of the pā was a steep cliff leading down into forest below. On the evening of 4 January 1869 we made flax ladders for the prophet and all the able-bodied men and women to climb down.

'By a splintered moon I watched them leave,' Te Hānene continues. 'The next day the soldiers took our fortress. They found only the wounded, fourteen men, sixty-six men, the rest children. We did not expect mercy, and mercy we did not get. Instead the soldiers herded us to the cliff edge over which our prophet had escaped. They laughed and said, "Follow them." And they raised their rifles to execute us.'

The faithful around the campfire raise their voices again to God. 'Oh Lord, they tasted the bitter taste of death. They ascended to You by the whirlwind path of Enoch. Korōria ki Tō Ingoa tapu, Āmine.'

'The wind howled with the voices of spirits,' Te Hānene remembers. 'The sky was red and bloodied with the dawn of a day that none of us would live to see. We would be cut down, the children, too. One of the old women, Whaiora, yelled out to a soldier, "Hey, one last puff of your pipe, eh? And give the children quick deaths so they won't feel the pain." And suddenly the soldiers were raising their rifles. Quickly I said to everyone, "Hold each other in companionship so that we all go together to the throne of God. And come nearer to the cliff so that when we are shot we shall fall over it. Let us not give Pharaoh the pleasure of more of our scalps, eh?" Oh, the air was so cold, so wonderful to breathe! And as the soldiers took aim, I began a haka of defiance.'

The faithful leap to their feet. Feet rise and fall, spittle sprays, eyes bulge, the world trembles. 'Ka mate, ka mate, ka ora, ka ora! It is death, it is death, it is life, it is life! The hairy man comes from out of the west. The sun rises! The sun rises!'

'The shots rang out,' Te Hānene says. 'I felt a bullet hitting me in the chest. And then I was falling, and all around me the others were falling too, crowding the air. I remember the impact of hitting the trees and tumbling through them to the ground. Others were falling beside me. I saw Whaiora, she was still breathing. She crawled over to me and pressed some leaves to my chest to stem the bleeding.

'Suddenly there was the sound of government Māori coming for our scalps. Whaiora pulled some dead flax over me and said, "Live! *Live!*" Then she rolled away, drawing attention to herself. I watched as a soldier took her by the hair, forced her to sit up and slit her throat.'

Te Hānene is silent a moment. 'I lived on. Two others survived. Somebody has to bury the dead. Despite our wounds we were able to follow after our people. I was reunited with my dear wife. After the war was over we went back home to Te Whaiti.'

He upraises his hand.

'My name is Te Hānene, but people call me The Honey Gatherer. I am the Ishmael who wandered the desert.'

'Korōria ki Tō Ingoa tapu,' the faithful intone. 'Āmine.'

3.

THE POINT IS THIS.

I am my history's witness. There are moments when my work becomes a wero, a challenge. It is ruthless, giving no quarter and taking no prisoners. Pitiless, it can go for the jugular without caring for the consequences, to itself, me or anybody else.

Where does the wero come from?

Just as I like to think that one of the tributaries for the wairua in my work will take you back to the teachings from Rāwheoro, there's no doubt in my mind that the main source of the wero is through Pera's whakapapa, particularly to the chronicles of the Iharaira. When the Ringatū give the sign of the upraised hand, the gesture is similar to that required by a court of someone giving evidence. You swear to tell the truth, the whole truth and nothing but the truth; the *whole* truth.

Most times literature forgives and forgets. In my case there is an explicit obligation to forcibly remind.

Te Kooti was pardoned in 1883 and thereafter lived peaceably at Ōhiwa, going about his great work of reconstruction: establishing meeting houses in the form of whare karakia, churches. He created its liturgies out of the Old Testament, his priests proselytising among the Iharaira. One of those liturgical morning prayers had woken me to consciousness as a child, and whenever I am within a Roman Catholic church I get that same sense of holiness from their Mass.

Hine Te Ariki and the Honey Gatherer must still have been in Te Whāiti when, in June 1884, Te Kooti returned to open one such meeting house, Hinenuitepō, at Murumurunga marae. The people say his horse shied and, at that moment, Te Kooti saw that there was a carving of a lizard, face down on the central pole of the front porch; it looked as though it was preparing to eat up the land beneath. Te Kooti predicted that the meeting house would be completely consumed and only the threshold of the house would remain as the meeting place for the survivors.

Two children were born of Hine Te Ariki and the Honey Gatherer's marriage, Te Raukura and my grandfather; sadly, Te Raukura died in childhood. Grandad, however, has left his own personal account of his birth and early childhood, part of it in his own handwriting. He gave it to my sister Kararaina after she had asked him a question and shown interest in whakapapa. She endeared herself to him a few months later when she and her husband, Gan, took him Māori kai: kina on one visit and kōura mara just before he died. Most of the details about his family in this memoir are taken from the book:

'I am known today as Tame Ihimaera was born of goodly parents October 2nd 1889 by law Real date 1888 and was given the name of my noble Grandfather Pera Punahāmoa a name of ancestral significance and according to custom and tradition one born of chief leneage was adopted by my Grandparents that I May be raised under the influence deserving of that rank incidentally my parents of adoptian were all versed in Maori Lore Arts and Crafts being particularly outstanding in building and carvings which adorned many meeting houses in various parts of North Eastern Hawks Bay.

'Well I don't know exactly where I was born but I know this much when I was old enough when maori woman soon they going to bear a child the husband prepare a whare kohanga or whare tapu. Only a priest or tohunga attend to her till she get her baby. soon she get her baby she be kept in this house for 8 days only her mother or tohunga allowed to visits her till that time was up then she came out of this house, before the people could see her, and that how most of our children was broad into this world, probly I was born in one of this house.'

By then Hine Te Ariki and the Honey Gatherer had moved to Waikaremoana where, in the uneasy peace and shattering aftermath of the savage government incursions, Te Hānene made his living felling bush. One day, in the year 1912 according to Grandad, the Honey Gatherer was out bushfelling. A tree fell and a branch broke off and hit him on the head, killing him.

We now follow the spiral of Hine Te Ariki's life.

Widowed and with a son in tow, she could well have returned to Whakatōhea or even travelled to Waikato as, through her mother, Te Rina Parewhai, she was related to Te Puea of the Waikato. Instead, after a period of mourning, she took up with a fine man named Manu Tāwhiorangi (Ereātara), who was also a Ringatū follower and came from Ngāti Porou. I don't know how or where she met him but Ringatū were great travellers, holding services at one marae after another — and, well, he was a six-footer like she was and maybe, some enchanted evening, they looked each other in the eye across a crowded marae. During the early part of the relationship, Hine Te Ariki sent Grandad to Nūhaka to be brought up by the Honey Gatherer's sister, Mihi. He writes of these early days:

'When I was 6 or 7 Knowing a bit of this life, dayley life. we make tops. String art wrestling boxing art of bow and arrow and many other sports conected the art of self defence. When I was about ten I start to attend the Nuhaka school about 5 miles away we used to walk every days to school sometime one of us have a horse and we used get on this horse about 5 of us. When I was about 12 years my uncle start to put me on unbroken horse or wild horses many times my life in danger of falling off or been kick by a horse.

'My grandparents very Religious make us prayer night and morning and so Religious they were they wont let us play on sunday even we have to piel potatoes on saturday night and cut our meat get ready for Sunday meal.'

4.

NOW AT THIS point I have to divert a little to tell you about Mihi's husband, Te Teira Meihana, who had been another of Te Kooti's very close followers.

As a boy, my father knew Te Teira Meihana, who gave him three taonga, which our family treasures to this day. Dad stayed with the old man and would go into the bush with him. They camped out in a tent where Te Teira would tell my father about Te Kooti and the flight of the Ringatū through the land. During one of these headlong escapes, some time in the late 1860s, Te Kooti received a message from another rebel chief, Rewi Maniapoto, of the Ngāti Maniapoto tribe.

You know the story of Rewi, don't you?

During the Waikato Wars he led a defensive movement at the Battle of Ōrākau in 1864, immortalised as Rewi's Last Stand. During the three days between 31 March and 2 April, 300 defenders of a hastily erected redoubt fought 1400 colonial troops. They repulsed attack after attack but the writing was on the wall. Even so, Rewi vowed: 'Ka whawhai tonu mātou, ake, ake, ake! We will fight on forever!' A third of the defenders were women who, when offered safe passage from the redoubt, responded: 'He kakī anō tikanga, me te tangata, me te wahine, me mate katoa. There is one rule for the men and the women, all will die together.'

However, on the third day, when the soldiers finally breached Ōrākau's defences, the survivors managed to battle their way through the military lines and, splitting up into small groups, made it to the safety of the bush. Nevertheless, 160 defenders were killed either in the redoubt or while on the run. One of those small groups was led by Rewi, who sent a message to Te Kooti: 'Can you come to my aid?'

Te Kooti's reply, sent from one warrior to another, was conveyed by way of a song. The prophet had one of his men memorise the words and then he composed the melody, the rangi, for it. He sent the song to Rewi by way of the warrior. It goes like this: 'Ki kona kea e Rewi, I greet you, Rewi, and hope that you prevail against the soldiers. Auē, it is not a good thing to see our land being broken up like a biscuit. Alas, I cannot come to you at Te Kūiti. Like you, I am being chased hither and thither like a bird in the forest. But fight on, dear friend, fight on.'

The second taonga is a simple story about Te Teira. He taught Dad how to shoot, giving him six bullets: 'Six bullets, six pigeons,' the old man said.

When Dad came back with his six pigeons the old man was astonished but pleased. And then Dad handed him three bullets back.

'How could you shoot six pigeons with three bullets?' Te Teira asked.

'I waited until they were ready to kiss,' was my father's simple, boyish explanation.

The third taonga is contained in one of Dad's ledger books; occasionally he liked to write down memories. One early morning, when he was in the bush with Te Teira, Dad went to wake up the old man. Old habits die hard and Te Teira still slept with a loaded rifle by his side, just in case of a constabulary attack. He brought the rifle to Dad's forehead.

'Don't ever do that again,' he said.

And then he told Dad what happened to Te Kooti's body after the prophet died on 17 April 1893. There are varying accounts of how, after lying in state, Te Kooti was spirited away and reburied where he would not be found. Some people had feared that the prophet's head would be chopped off by the soldiers and put on public display. A number of Ringatū families are guardians of the stories relating to the secret burial location.

Mine is one of them.

WITH HER NEW husband, Hine Te Ariki began a fresh life in Waituhi, in the lands of Te Whānau-a-Kai, where their marae was Tākitimu. She herself had more than an ancestral property connection. She also had a spiritual one as her name was that of an uri taniwha, a merwoman, who lived with an underwater tribe within the deep pools and caverns of the Waipaoa River. When the first human, Tūmokonui, settled in the valley, the merwoman took him as her husband, thereby combining both human and fantastical histories in our blood. She was like an Arthurian Lady of the Lake, except that her domain was a river.

Hine Te Ariki summoned her son Pera Punahāmoa to join her. For most of their lives, Hine Te Ariki and Manu Tāwhiorangi lived near a creek that feeds into the Waipaoa River. They built a three-bedroom house, painted white, on high terraced land known as Waituhi 2E. She had three children to Manu, two of whom were boys, named Iriopeta (Sid) and Weretā (Doey). Both died before they reached the age of eighteen; Sid at Te Aute College when, during a rugby game, he caught a chill and succumbed to pneumonia. A third child, my Grand-aunt Mini, was of hardier stock. You only had to take one look at her to know that she was a survivor.

Hine Te Ariki transcended tribal identity and location. Her chieftainess ways established themselves in the lands of Poverty Bay and, according to my father, her charisma elevated her to the highest paepae, perches, of leadership — although many of the male leaders of the tribes never liked it. You think she could be stopped from standing to speak on the marae, not only in Waituhi but on all the marae as far as the Māhia Peninsula, up the East Coast and over to the Bay of Plenty? Try, and like as not she would turn her back to you, bend and point to the place where you came from.

She started taking Dad with her to the many hui. On one occasion things became so vehement that, as a four-year-old, he ran out onto the marae and stood in front of her skirts to defend her. 'Auē, te hōhā o te tamaiti nei,' she scolded him, trying to push him behind her with her walking stick. Nevertheless, she was very proud of him for his action.

Dad's relationship with Hine Te Ariki's and the Honey Gatherer's kin remained close all his life. Indeed, sometime in the 1980s or 1990s the elder Toko Te Kani went with other rangatira to Te Whāiti-nui-a-Toi to ask the gatekeepers of the Whirinaki Forest, Ngāti Whare, whether they could have a tōtara for a waka they were building.

The people said, 'No, but if you come back with Tom Smiler we have to give it.'

To undercut any assumptions you may have — after all, we always associate leadership with having the accoutrements of personal glamour — I have to caution you that from the one photograph I have of Hine Te Ariki she is a solid-looking woman of plain and ordinary looks, dark of face and having an impassive expression. She wears a hat, plaid shirt and a full-length bell skirt. Her face is almost half hidden by the brim of the hat. The shadow gives us respite from the history of scorched earth in her eyes. You can sense those eyes staring out of the photo, out of the past.

In the family's pantheon Hine Te Ariki has blended with our uri taniwha ancestress to become our kaitiaki. Forest families look to a particular bird as their spiritual guide and protector; sea families look to a shark, octopus or stingray.

'If ever you are in trouble and need help,' my father would say, 'always call for Hine Te Ariki.'

And so there are many times when I have asked for her assistance, and Hine Te Ariki always comes to me as a swirling in the air or perhaps two eyes looking up at me from under the surface brim of the water.

Or maybe when I look into the river what I see is her eyes looking out of mine: 'So, Ihimaera, tēnā koe, e te mokopuna.'

Chapter Nine

Migrant Chieftains

1.

THE NEW ZEALAND WARS over, let me turn to the years of Māori recovery and to the genealogy of my paternal grandmother, Teria (sometimes the name is spelt Te Ria) Pere Halbert.

It is through Teria, or Daisy as she was commonly known, that Te Whānau-a-Kai has the primacy in my whakapapa. Her ancestry granted me what are known as take tupuna, ancestral rights, in the Tūranga or Gisborne district, as our tribe was the first to occupy, clear and continuously cultivate and live on the land.

Some of the following narrative is simplification, which is making me a bit nervous because you can't really simplify whakapapa as you can make too many errors. This is why the work of the Waitangi Tribunal in sorting out treaty settlements is such a tortuous and lengthy business. However, here goes.

No other tribe in Gisborne has a longer history than Te Whānau-a-Kai. We whakapapa back to the Ngā Ariki of our own Stone World, to Paraki and Tūī, and then to the great chief Ruapani, whose pā was at Popoia, Waituhi; around 1525 he was considered the paramount ariki of all the Gisborne tribes.

The problem is (for those who see it as a problem) that, although the patriarchy of the gods led to that hierarchy which, in human history, saw male leadership privileged over female leadership, our claim to be an iwi comes from Ruapani's *female* line. They were women chieftains with their own hereditary title, distinction and, most important, those take tupuna of which I have spoken.

However, unlike Ngāti Porou tribes, which have women's tribal rights enshrined in their names, Te Whānau-a-Kai's name is that of a male ancestor. And because that male ancestor just happens to be the third in ancestry from the warrior chieftain Kahungunu, the overriding male mana of that line from Kahungunu to his son Māhaki to his son Kai (or Kaikoreaunei) has meant that for many years an assumption was made that Te Whānau-a-Kai was a subtribe of Te Aitanga-a-Māhaki.

Wrong.

2.

I CANNOT BELIEVE I have just written those words, 'just happens'. Somebody like Kahungunu doesn't *just happen*. Born in Kaitāia, he was already tall and handsome as a boy, and to top it off had a sexual entitlement that made women faint and men very, very envious. His lineage was royal, coming directly from Tamatea-ariki-nui, captain of the *Tākitimu* canoe through Rongokako to Tamatea-ure-haea, who was Kahungunu's father. As a young man he became renowned for his industry and skills as an architect: he planned and supervised the construction of many pā. No wonder he was welcomed throughout the land.

He also became famous for his high-ranking marriages, nine in all. His first wife was Hinetapu, whom he left when he set off on his southern wanderings. When he arrived at Whakatāne he married Waiarai. In Ōpōtiki he married Te Hautāruke. He travelled further around the East Coast to Whāngārā, where he took up with Ruarauhanga. Then he journeyed inland to Poverty Bay, where he married Ruareretai, who was the daughter of the aforementioned Ruapani.

There may not have been a method in his marriages, but the pattern is clear: with each marriage, and the children of the marriages, he was establishing a dynasty like no other.

I'll let my sister Kararaina tell you the rest of the story. She was always good at dramatising it with the rise of an eyebrow, a coy look and a droll manner.

'After Ruareretai came Hinepuariri and her sister Kahukura-waiaraia at Whareongaonga. It was Hinepuariri who let the cat out of the bag, the boastful girl, about the size of Kahungunu's penis. But she made it sound like she was complaining when she said that most of it remained, er, outside. Well! This little bit of gossip travelled far and wide and piqued the interest of the beautiful Rongomaiwahine of Nukutaurua. She was lounging with her handmaidens and when the story reached her she sighed, "Oh the fault is not Kahungunu's. What a pity that Hinepuariri's pool is clearly too shallow."

'Well! That sounded like a challenge to Kahungunu, didn't it! So he decided to journey to Nukutaurua on the Māhia Peninsula to look at the proud woman who, perhaps, was the owner of a pool that wasn't, er, shallow and in which he could comfortably bathe. Of course he fell in love with her but the trouble was that she already had a husband.

'Anyway, he was welcomed to Nukutaurua and invited to sleep in the same whare as the proud princess and her consort. So near and yet so far — sigh. How could he get her husband away from her side long enough for him to sneak beside Rongomaiwahine and ... well ... you can join the dots yourself. I am a lady, thank you very much.

'That's it! He would eat a lot of kina, sea urchins, and that would fill him with obnoxious-smelling gas. And then . . .

'Well! All night he farted and farted and made people gag and run for fresh air. But there was still no respite for the beautiful Rongomaiwahine, whose nostrils twitched and wrinkled until she could bear no more.

'And she turned to her husband and blamed *him*! "Tama taku tai, get out of my perfumed bed and go sleep somewhere else." And when he did that, guess who was waiting to claim the empty bed space?

'Well! It wasn't Elvis Presley.'

In his old age, Kahungunu married one last time, a woman named Pouwharekura. By the time he died, apart from the sons I have already mentioned, he had sired many other children. Today the Ngāti Kahungunu dynasty stretches along the eastern seaboard from Māhia to Masterton and has the third largest iwi population in New Zealand.

His domination, however, meant the decline of Ruapani. Fortunes wax and wane, don't they? Leaving Popoia Pā, Waituhi, Ruapani moved inland to Lake Waikaremoana. There, his descendants, Ngāti Ruapani ki Waikaremoana, set up a perilous existence between Kahungunu on one side and Ngāi Tūhoe on the other. That common refrain, land confiscations, applies to them as well and, like us, they suffer from the attempts of the larger iwi to claim the land and the lake as theirs. It is a shocking indictment to see them struggling today to establish themselves in their own right.

YOU SEE THE problem for Te Whānau-a-Kai, don't you?

It was in the layers of male titles that superimposed the mana of Ngāti Kahungunu and his descendants over ours. Yes, the superimposition may also have bequeathed us another waka and more mountains, but, as my cousin Josephine said to me once, 'Although we are proud to have *Tākitimu* as our waka, our tribe didn't marry into Kahungunu's. He and his descendants married into ours.'

Actually, that sounds a similar sentiment to the one expressed by Rongomaiwahine's and Ruataupare's descendants, too.

The grandson of Kahungunu may have given his name to our tribe, but his two wives, Te Hāki and Whareana, were the ones who counted. When Kai married the women they in no way gave up their rights of hereditary title to their husband.

Chapter Ten

She Comes, Teria

TERIA, MY GRANDMOTHER.

She was sitting with me on the highest terrace of Pukepoto, the ancient hill fort that was the northern gateway to the village of Waituhi. The day was cold and I was wearing a warm coat. Teria had put on a heavy coat also, and a wide-brimmed hat with a dark veil.

Earlier Teria had caught me looking up at Pukepoto. I was entranced by the gigantic crescent staircase of terraces, like the poutama pattern, the wondrous Stairway to Heaven.

'What's up there?' I asked.

'Let's go and see,' she smiled.

My grandmother had taken *ages* to climb up the hill. I ran up the ridge before her, yelling, 'Hurry up, Nani!' Down below was the village itself and, beyond Waituhi, river flats widespread and country towns afar.

Finally, breathing hard, she made it. As she sat beside me, the wind caught the veil of her hat, covering and then uncovering her face. 'I haven't been up here for years,' she said.

And then the hill breathed *in*.

'Ah, mokopuna,' Teria began, her voice low and thrilling, 'we have ruled here for over a thousand years. This was our land, this was our life. It is your life and land now. It has been yours even before you took your first breath. It comes to you from the time of the gods.

'We have eternity in us.'

MY GRANDMOTHER TERIA was born on 22 July 1893. Beauty has a charisma of its own and, as you can see from the early photograph that accompanies this memoir, taken when she was about sixteen or seventeen, she was a striking young woman. Even at this age she appears self-aware and there is no doubting her intellect. The brow is narrow, the nose finely sculptured and aquiline, and the eyes are proud. Her hair is pulled back, making her appear somewhat severe; unbound, it is lustrous, thick, flecked with auburn. I like to think that Teria is looking beyond the photographer as if he is of no account.

I wish you could have heard my grandmother's voice. It had a singular beauty and was mostly modulated in a ravishing, intimate way. When she wished to be forceful, however, as she often had to be, it could rise to the pitch of its passion.

Telling Teria's story poses a logistical problem, mainly because of that Halbert connection. For all of us who descend from Wī Pere, the turn-of-the-century MP for Eastern Māori and minister of the Crown, the House of Halbert is our implacable default position. But the history of this Māori House of Windsor is long and complex and would comprise too big a digression when I want to keep the focus on my grandmother, so I'll deal with it later. Let me, however, quickly sketch in that Teria's father was one of Wī Pere's two surviving sons, Te Moanaroa, who married Rīria Kaihote Wātene from Wairoa. Teria was in the third generation from Wī Pere himself, the fifth of fourteen children, and she appears to have been treated with special affection by her grandfather and her father.

As a boy I was told so many stories about Teria that I could never differentiate between what was real about her and what was unreal, and so, as with my mother, I was always looking at her through a prism. Not knowing what was true and untrue gave her an interesting complexity.

There is no doubting, however, that the 'real' Teria was the Māori woman who, along with her elder sister, Mana, took to the marae as to the manner born. You can see her lack of fear in the forward stance she has taken in the photograph. She also took this fearlessness into the realm of Pākehā physicality. She rode in the Gisborne hunts, appears to have been a tomboyish roller skating champion in the days when this was an indoor sport on wooden floors and, according to my dad, was adept in the art of fencing.

I have always credited Teria as being the one who turned my life from fact into fiction. I often imagined her, a beauteous young woman in flowing gown at a ball after a hunt.

Can you blame me, therefore, for always associating her with the goddess Artemis?

 3.

MY FATHER NEVER told me how Teria met Pera Punahāmoa. As a boy I could not understand the attraction. For one thing Grandad was nine years older; for another, he had an unprepossessing appearance and I remember him as being the same height as her or possibly even shorter — what happened to his mother Hine Te Ariki's six-foot genes?

The stories told about Grandad, however, gave him qualities that emphasised his physical prowess, and I like to think that Teria would have been more impressed by his personal history. From the age of twelve he was already working with gangs felling timber, and our family's strong association with shearing as a livelihood began with a muscular Pera turning, during his teenage years, from bushfelling to shearing.

I don't know whether Pera was accepted as an equal by the somewhat autocratic Halbert family, but I can imagine Hine Te Ariki giving them what-for if they ever considered Teria was marrying beneath her. Why do we fall in love with a particular person anyway? And how could a young boy like me make a judgement about what attracts one person to another? Perhaps Teria was drawn by his leadership and determination. In the small community of Waituhi, Grandad would have stood out, having assembled a six-stand gang and successfully secured shearing contracts around Waerenga-o-Kurī. When motor-driven machines first came in, replacing blades, the handpieces became so hot that they were often difficult to hold. Every shearer had a bucket of water near his stand, into which he would plunge the handpiece to cool it down. But not Pera — he would carry on shearing regardless.

And where it counted, in sport, Pera had all the credentials of a gladiatorial hero. The YMP (Young Māori Party) Club was the backbone of his rugby career. He was regarded as quite a player in his day, and is believed to have been selected for a representative team. When news of his selection came out, however, he missed the opportunity because he was working in the bush and could not be found. Charlie Pere, my father's uncle, told Dad that, in a game involving well-known boxer Tom Heeney, although Heeney upended Pera he was able to recover and run eighty yards to score a clinching try. He may have had short legs, but have you seen short men run? Off like a rocket and when they're tackled, whoa, they can't be knocked down.

As it happens, the union comes with an intriguing subtext, as Grandad may have appealed to Teria because he was her salvation. The details were told to me by my cousin Elizabeth, in the late 1950s, when we were teenagers. If ever there was a lookalike for Teria, it would have to be my cousin, whom I adored when I was young. She and I had streaks of rebelliousness, especially where our elders were concerned, and, because the Smiler clan was so moral, we loved to undercut them.

We were playing a game of marbles and Elizabeth was cleaning up. 'As if our grandparents can talk,' she said, smacking one of my marbles right out of the circle. 'Nani Teria was married to somebody else when Pera stole her from her husband.'

Stole her? Now that appealed to my romantic nature. 'That can't be true,' I answered, hoping it was, as I managed a comeback with my favourite black toa. How satisfying to hear the crack as it connected with one of Elizabeth's defenders.

She sniffed with disdain, pushed a wing of hair back from her face and thumbed one of her marbles over an impossible distance to claim the circle again; she always had an unerring eye. 'Not only that,' Elizabeth continued, 'but Teria's husband is still alive and living in Te Karaka.'

Grandad's stocks soared with me but, no matter that I pestered my father, aunties and uncles to verify the story, nobody would admit to it. I went even further, asking if Pera and Teria had, in fact, married. The aunties didn't like that question one bit. Even today, on one of the genealogy websites you can access, there are four question marks querying my grandparents' marital status. Eventually, I found a mention in one of my father's ledger books. The phrases crossed out are his own deletions:

'My Dad Tame or Pera married my mother Teria Pere in 1914. My mother had ~~already married~~/a liaison with a man called I think ~~name crossed out~~. They had a child but she died as a baby, my mother left him because I heard he was playing around with other women so Mum Teria left this man ~~name crossed out~~ & went to live with Pera in 1914. ~~They had a great life together over 42 years till she died 1956.~~'

Only one paragraph, but so resonant. I don't know whether Dad crossed the name of my grandmother's husband out because he did not have evidence to substantiate it or because he wanted to be tactful. If the latter, he hasn't done a good job of the obliteration and you can still see the name, as if Dad wanted any reader to follow it up if he or she wished to. I should mention, however, that although Dad mentions the word 'married' there is a typed reference in Grandad's whakapapa book to the marriage as being 'by MAORI TRADITION'.

For many years I imagined my grandfather coming to my grandmother's rescue out of the west, like Sir Walter Scott's hero, Lochinvar, in his 1808 poem. And there my grandmother was, in wedding dress and veil, her hair threaded with pearls, waiting for him to carry her off on a white steed:

> One touch to her hand, and one word in her ear,
> When they reach'd the hall-door, and the charger stood near;
> So light to the croupe the fair lady he swung,
> So light to the saddle before her he sprung!
> 'She is won! We are gone, over bank, bush and scaur;
> They'll have fleet steeds that follow,' quoth young Lochinvar.

Whether Teria's husband or kinsmen ever caught up, I don't know. I presume that some agreement was reached to enable her to marry her second husband.

I loved my grandmother deeply and she me, but my relationship with Grandad became deeply conflicted. Physically strong and a hard worker, he expected everybody, including his horses and dogs, to work as hard as he did. Whenever he and I got together, I constantly brushed him up the wrong way with my own strength, which was not physical but mental, something that he couldn't see.

When Elizabeth told me the story of how my grandparents got together, however, I could see him as a hero. After all, he had saved my grandmother.

And I was still, then, obedient to him.

Chapter Eleven

Czar of All the Russias

1.

TERIA SOON FELL pregnant with my father. One might have expected her to be delivered in a hospital — she would certainly have had the choice — but instead she followed Māori tradition. Her female relatives put up a canvas shelter and she was in confinement for a few days. She gave birth to a son, born Te Haa-o-Rūhia Ihimaera Smiler, on 26 June 1915, and named to commemorate a sovereign on the other side of the world, the Romanov Emperor Nicholas II, known as the Czar and Autocrat of All the Russias.

The naming of children by Māori reflected the changing nature of their world. Certainly children were still given names of tribal heroes and heroines to acknowledge whakapapa links, but a double aspiration began to occur during those years: the conferring of Pākehā names to smooth one's passage in the outer Pākehā world while still maintaining Māori names to ensure the same passage through the inner, tribal, world. If you look at some of the other family names of my father's clan, they are all of a piece: Caesar, Mafeking, Tunisia, Tripoli and Egypt, as well as Victoria, Albert and George after English royalty.

For most of his life, however, Dad was known as Te Haa for short, and he was most often addressed as Tom, which was also his father's European name. To differentiate them, Dad was called Tom Junior, even into his nineties, which kind of kept him young all his life.

I'm not sure how long Teria suckled her newborn son, but it wasn't long. Dad writes in his ledger book: 'And then Hine Te Ariki came and took me away.'

When I read those words I still gasp at their simplicity and affecting beauty. My father was Teria and Pera's first child and a son. How could they give him up at birth? Not only that, but this was Teria's first living child; it must have been so difficult for her.

Give up my father she did. After all, it was the custom for the first born to be raised by the father's parents, and so Dad was taken by Hine Te Ariki and Manu; they had the responsibility of inculcating custom into the child. There was a practical function to the arrangement, too, as it enabled Teria and Pera Punahāmoa to maintain their economic livelihood as a husband and wife bushfelling team at Tauwharepārae.

Hine Te Ariki's daughter Mini, who must have been about ten, became both a young mother and sister to the infant. Throughout their lives, my father and Mini were possessed of love and loyalty for each other, and, when I was born, Mini transferred all those feelings to me.

MY FATHER WAS the eldest of fifteen children — yes, another large family in the whakapapa.

As he once told me, 'I think one of the reasons why Hine Te Ariki took me was because, when I was born, I had an abscess in my head, somewhere near the fontanelle. The scar is still there. I was skinny, emaciated, my eyes sunken into their sockets, and the abscess, constantly weeping, still hadn't healed after a year. In the end, I was bedridden and people were waiting for me to die. I was told by my Uncle Charlie Pere that Hine Te Ariki came into the room with a plate of kūmara. Looking at me, she started to eat some. I saw her eating, pointed to the kūmara and started to beg like a dog, "Mmmn, mmmn." She put some more kūmara in her mouth, mashing it because it was too hot, and then put it from her mouth into mine.'

My father survived, but infant mortality was obviously high; Māori of all ages died young in those days. My father was three during the 1918 flu but he has memories of tents above the meeting house, either Tākitimu or Rongopai, to take advantage of the cool breezes coming off the hills and siphoning into the valley where the sick were taken. Whenever anybody died, the tents looked like waka, their white-winged flaps transporting the dead to God. Similarly, around the 1930s my mother remembers tuberculosis tents circling Tolaga Bay, where her friends would go to either convalesce or, like as not, succumb.

Even if you lived, life expectancy during the first fifty years of the twentieth century was not high, and I can still remember the shock when I realised how young Teria had been when she died in 1955. She was 62 years old.

Education was a hit-and-miss matter, too. My father began his education when Grandad enrolled his brother, five-year-old Win (Winiata), at Patutahi Primary School, and decided to enrol Dad, who was seven, at the same time. Dad had a natural intelligence and, by Primer Four, he had already caught up with the younger children. He was put straight into Standard Two and then, a year later, into Standard Four, and a year after that, Standard Six.

All this time my father was still staying with Hine Te Ariki and Manu Tāwhiorangi. Sometimes he would see Teria and she would entreat him to stay the night. He always answered, 'No, I have to go home to my Nani. She'll miss me.'

3.

MY FATHER CALLED his grandfather Manu, Pā.

'Pā had the best horses in Poverty Bay,' Dad told me in an interview in 1997. 'They were chaff-fed, grain-fed. Manu was a farmer on forty acres of his own land, cropping maize and oats, and he also had some lease-land. He also used to grow grass to sell as hay and seed.

'In the 1920s the Okitu dairy factories started up at Mākaraka, one near the railway station. Hine Te Ariki and Manu ran a herd of cows, and the revenue they got from the cream was exchanged for flour, butter and other goods. I recall that no money was exchanged, only goods. Hine Te Ariki was a good milker. She would climb a hill, see where her cows were, sometimes a mile and a half away, put two fingers in her mouth and whistle her dogs to bring the cows in.

'In those days everybody lived close-knit. We stayed in our own homes but we shared everything with each other. My grandmother used to save milk and take some to my Uncle Tip (Tīpene) and others after each milking. If anybody killed a beast they would go around sharing the meat. Any meat left over was preserved in a big drum filled with fat from the pork. The fat preserved the meat and it lasted for months. If somebody didn't have kūmara, resources would be shared so that everybody could get through from one season to the next. It was not unusual for families to feed up to twenty people at dinner, including those who were passing by or staying temporarily.

'Our day normally started at five in the morning. Pā used to start the Ringatū hīmene but sometimes he would call out to me, "E Haa, māhau rā te hīmene, you start the waiata." When I was very young I used to get frightened of the droning sound and would hide my head under the blankets.

'We had prayers for up to an hour, and then we were out of bed by six. Breakfast was cooked in the kāuta on an open fire and normally comprised a cup of tea and oven bread. We always blessed the food before eating. In fact, there was a prayer for just about everything. Then Pā and Hine Te Ariki would go off to work: "Right-o, haere tātou ki te mahi."

'One of the main occupations was tending the kūmara plantation. I remember how Pā would say a karakia before digging the kūmara out of the ground. In those days people were always so careful handling kūmara and other garden crops. I remember helping the old man put the kūmara one by one into a flax basket, so carefully, that they wouldn't get bruised. If they got bruised they could go rotten in the kūmara pit. Then I would help him carry the kit to the pākoro, all the time he'd be saying in Māori, "Careful, careful, e Haa!" The pākoro was a small raupō house in the pit, so low you couldn't stand up in it, where the kūmara were stored. It was constructed so that when it rained the rain would fall away on the outside of the pit and not come inside. Pā would crawl inside and I would start handing him the kūmara, one by one. Always he would be cautioning me, because I was always in a hurry, "A! A! Don't tip the kūmara! Be careful! Kei marū! You might bruise the kūmara!"

'I loved watching the way he put the kūmara into the pākoro: the first row on the solid ground, then the next row on top of it, giving a slight careful twist so that each kūmara fitted in nicely. The big kūmara were always placed at the back of the house and the small kūmara to the front. Always so much care! The reason? Because Māori lived from season to season and those kūmara had to last a year, between one harvest time and the next, so that there was sufficient food to keep everyone alive.

'I remember once I tried to go into the pākoro to help him, but he wouldn't let me, just in case I passed wind, because even that could make the kūmara go off.

'Kūmara was the main diet, supplemented with pūhā, pumpkin, ironbark pumpkin, and Māori bread baked from flour, water and sometimes yeast. Not many potatoes were grown at the time.

'Our main drink was water. Whenever it rained we had to catch water by any means and put it into three twenty-gallon wooden casks. We didn't have a tank. Sometimes, however, we had to get our water supplies from the Waipaoa River.

'I remember one day, Pā said to me, "Haere, tama, ki te tiki wai." We took two of our casks on the sledge down to the river. It was in flood and the water was dirty, and I wondered why we were getting this dirty water. We started to bucket the water into our casks.

'"This water is too dirty, Pā," I said. "How can we drink it?"

'"Don't ask too many questions," Pā answered. "Turituri."

'After we had taken the water home, he proceeded to bucket the water into the third cask, which was empty on the kitchen bench. When it was filled he said to me, "Go and get a mug." He turned on the tap at the bottom of the cask and the water came out clear! I was so astonished, until he told me his secret. At the bottom of the third cask was six inches of shingle, which filtered the impurities out of the water. Much later in life, I used this same principle when digging a well. I shovelled some shingle into the well because the water was so yellow. After a while, it came out clear.

'These are some of the ways by which the people showed their simple, natural wisdom. And at the end of every day's work, there was a prayer of thanksgiving before going home.

'I have to say that I have never wanted tribal leadership. When Win was alive, I told him to do it. He used to say, "You're the eldest." Today I have realised that I have had to grow into this role of a kaumātua. I have tried to do my best according to Hine Te Ariki's and Pā's teachings.

'It was they who taught me to care, to look after people, to be unselfish, to give more than you take, to look after the kūmara, the royal children who will take the Māori into the future, and to try to stop them from being bruised.

'And always to have aroha.'

I don't know why my father's two simple tellings of storing the kūmara and of purifying the river water with his Pā affected me so much. In the first instance, I think I tried to apply them to my own work, because was writing so different to storing kūmara? I began to think of my work as kūmara, which I could offer to people to enjoy; Māori say that the kūmara does not tell you how sweet it is until you taste it, and I wanted it to be sweet. Second, sometimes I think of the rewriting process as a purifying process, adding a layer of shingle at the bottom to filter out the impurities. Man oh man, my father's Pā would probably reprimand me for the heaps of shingle I have had to sometimes use to ensure that the words come out clear as the water of the Waipaoa River.

Finally, Dad is right: the children are royalty. Every child is a prince or princess, an ariki. They are our future, and I am writing this memoir so that they know.

I didn't realise, however, how much my father's story had affected my own world view until 2009 when I was offered, and accepted, the University of Hawaii's Citizen's Chair. I followed the Father of Pacific Literature, Albert Wendt.

I found myself living in Honolulu. There, I rented the beautiful apartment of friends of mine, who left me their car to use, along with 'Anything you find in the refrigerator'. Superb wine awaited me, as well as fine cheeses and other delicacies.

A few months later, at the back of the refrigerator, I found the potato.

Now I don't want my friends to get upset about this story. Who knows? I probably bought some potatoes when I first arrived and one dropped out of sight where the moist conditions encouraged it to develop a blackish-greenish tinge and stimulated it to sprout knobbly growths, kind of like a miniature triffid. I showed the potato to my friend Glenn Yamashita, who told me I should put it down the waste chute, but I couldn't do that.

'Why not?' he asked, astonished.

I began my explanation. 'In legendary times, a potato could mean all the difference between living or dying. A potato, for instance, figures in our family history because Hine Te Ariki fed my father with one, chewing it in her own mouth and putting it into his so that he would not die of starvation, but its importance is more profound than that.'

Warming to my subject, I related the story of how the kūmara, sweet potato, had been brought from Hawaiki to Aotearoa on that very same canoe, *Horouta,* which had been the first ship of my mother's ancestors. Seedling cargo on the waka was spoiled when *Horouta* foundered at the mouth of the Ōhiwa River.

A young voyager by the name of Pourangahua offered to return by canoe to Hawaiki to obtain a fresh supply. He came to shore at Parinuiterā where his uncle, Ruakapanga, had a potato plantation and was only too pleased to offer his nephew a replacement cargo. However, Pourangahua had a problem. When he had left Aotearoa the kōwhai trees were already beginning to bud and the planting season was near. If he didn't make it, and the seeds were not sown in the ground, there would be no crop to feed the people in the spring. They would surely die of starvation.

As it happened, Ruakapanga had the fastest transport going at that time: two pet giant albatross called Horangārangi and Te Ungārangi.

'The birds would carry Pourangahua back to Aotearoa,' I told Glenn, 'but they came with a set of strict instructions. Pourangahua was not to fly them anywhere near Mount Hikurangi because an ogre lived there and would engage them in battle, he was not to touch or pull out their feathers, and he was to feed them and give them water before he sent them on back to Hawaiki. Pourangahua agreed and, astride the two birds, off he went! Of course, no sooner had he gained altitude than he disobeyed his uncle's instructions. Maybe he was in a hurry to get back to see his girlfriend.'

'Is that in the story?' Glenn asked, noting the contemporary tone and knowing my penchant for embellishment.

'No,' I answered. 'It's a possibility, though, don't you think? Anyway, Pourangahua flew right over Hikurangi where the ogre attacked him, and the two albatrosses had to fight back and were grievously wounded. Then, when Pourangahua was approaching Aotearoa, the birds began to circle and circle because they were looking for a place to land. Impatient, Pourangahua plucked a feather from each bird to begin their descent.'

Naturally the people rejoiced to see Pourangahua and the new kūmara seeds. But there was no rejoicing for the two giant albatross. Auē, Pourangahua even forgot to feed them and give them water. Knowing that they would not make the return home, they began to weep for each other. The tears formed a particular pattern on the sand that Māori call the roimata toroa, the tears of the albatross.

To get back to the story, Glenn and other Hawaiian friends kept on advising me to get rid of the triffid potato. They even spirited it out of the apartment while I wasn't looking, dropping it into the waste chute, but I had nightmares about what they had done, so went down and retrieved it. After all, the whole of Ireland had suffered many deaths when the great potato famine began in 1845 (some people say 1846.) The statistics are tricky: nearly a million died, and the numbers who emigrated depend on what years you include, two million perhaps, mostly to America.

In the end, after two weeks of eyeballing it, I ate the potato. I made a ritual feast. I roasted the potato, slathered its crevasses with butter, placed it in the middle of a nice lettuce and tomato salad and put every little dried black piece of it in my mouth.

You owe me, Dad.

I have never been able to leave any food on my plate or on anyone else's plate. At high-class restaurants I suffer dreadfully if friends don't eat everything. Rather than have me embarrass them in public, they ask for a doggy bag — and even that makes them shudder — so I can take the kai home.

I have a carved panel in my house in Herne Bay, carved for me by my cousin, Greg Whakataka-Brightwell. When he asked me what story I wanted to have carved on it I immediately thought of Pourangahua on the back of those two pet albatross.

I wonder why Pourangahua wasn't punished? In most mythologies punishment is usually the punchline: 'You fly too close to the sun you get burnt.'

In Māori myth, however, clearly a Māori Icarus doesn't fall into the sea. Gods and humans with supernatural powers can get away with anything.

It wasn't Pourangahua, however, I wanted to honour. The carving was to remind me of the two birds whose sacrifice saved a nation and enabled it to develop in the new world.

I NEED TO get a move on.

Sometime in the early 1920s Hine Te Ariki and Manu Tāwhiorangi moved from their home to Tākitimu marae, where they supervised the building of the meeting house; it never used to be on the hill but on the flat where it was too wet. While living there, the two old people drew their water from the horse trough.

During the summer break of his final year at primary school, 1927, when my father was twelve and on a visit to his parents, Grandad took him shearing.

'Do you want to hop on a stand?' Pera asked.

So began my father's origin story of how the family's shearing tradition was passed on.

The next year Dad began to attend Gisborne Boys' High School. In his day, the only way to get to Gisborne was by horse, pushbike or foot. The quickest route was by way of the ford across the Waipaoa River at the Dodds's place, which cut three miles off the journey. One day Dad and Win were doubling on a horse when they came across a harvester, a haymaking machine, the first they'd ever seen.

The horse shied, throwing Dad and Winiata off, and bolted.

That same year Uncle Charlie Pere formed a hockey squad and marked out practice fields across the road from Tākitimu marae. George Tūpara was an exciting, fast hockey player who was also a great striker; he could get the ball into the goal. Dad, now thirteen, was not interested in hockey because Mini, who was playing for YMP in the city, would always return home from a hockey match with bruises all over her legs; she may have been goalie and, in those days, they never wore pads.

One day, Charlie Pere yelled out to Dad to join in. Mānuka sticks were the hockey sticks of the day and, from that moment, Dad was hooked. He was so good at the game that he was soon playing men's senior hockey.

However, rugby was the preferred sport at high school, and there Dad excelled. His great competitors on the field were Murray Sharp, Bobby Green and Bruce Jenkins. In his ledger book Dad writes about how he managed to balance out both sports, hockey and rugby: 'I had to play hockey at 1pm at the hockey reserve. Finished at 2pm to go to the Oval to play against the Auckland team at 3pm that same day. I did that all season. Play hockey at 1pm, then go & play rugby at 3pm for our senior Club side Marist. Our hockey team Waituhi & Marist football team won the competitions that year.'

My father also took up boxing, but his brothers, Win and Mike, were better, and Win became a schoolboy champion. Dad also had excellent grades in maths and French. I can still remember how dumbfounded I was when I introduced Dad to a French friend, Véronique, who had come to stay with us, and he began to talk in his schoolboy French.

'Your father's accent is so antique,' Veronique exclaimed. 'It is so ancien!'

That grand old woman, Hine Te Ariki, died in 1932; she had contracted the flu. Dad, aged sixteen, was out getting firewood on the sledge. He had cut some mānuka and was on his way back along the hill ridge behind Rongopai. Then, from far off, he heard wailing coming from the direction of Tākitimu. He had a terrible feeling of emptiness. After Hine Te Ariki's tangi, Pera came to pick him up and take him home. At the time Manu was mourning, and Mini could not bear the idea of Dad, in particular, leaving them both. My father writes: 'We had lived together all our lives and we loved each other. Mini said to me, "Please don't leave me, stay with me." So I said, "Okay." I told Dad, "I'm sorry, Dad, I have to stay with my aunty."'

According to Dad, he kept up his schooling and was top of 5A: he had a phenomenal memory and learned the facts in his history, science and other textbooks off by heart. However, tragedy struck when his

Pā, Manu, died; my sisters tell me this was in 1933. My father became the breadwinner for himself and Mini, and began shearing on a more regular basis. He missed school for three weeks because Pera needed his help in his crutching gang. 'I was all set to sit my matriculation, but the headmaster would not allow me [because of my absence] so I told him where his school could go.'

When Dad told me this I could not help but feel a sense of pain for him. He was always such a natural and intuitive learner and could have become a fine scholar. I have a feeling that the unconscious denial of schooling always coloured his view that education was an intrinsic right.

The bus service from Waituhi to Gisborne, which began in 1933, proved to be a great boon for Waituhi people. Only a few people had cars or trucks, but now everyone could go to town.

Having left school, Dad went out to work with Pera Punahāmoa: 'My early teens I began laboring for my dad scrubcutting, fencing, thistle cutting & any laboring work on farms. I & my brothers & other extended members of the family and friends [were] fortunate to get this work due to the good relationship my father had with the farmers & the sheep stations in the district we were never out of work for long. Thank you father & Mum for your loving care. Moe mai, e hika mā.'

As well, Dad was already shearing 300 sheep a day, a tally that he maintained all his life.

Mini began to walk out with George Tūpara, a man younger than she was; I called her Nani and him Uncle. Once he winked at me and said, 'Your Nani found me irresistible. Can't you see how handsome I am?' And indeed he was.

As for Nani Mini, she was a small, dark woman with an ageless, wry look and deep, wise eyes. I always referred to her as my old Incan princess. She did not object, having the same flat face, hooked nose and petite, and sturdy, stature — I think she only heard the word 'princess'. However, sometimes she would demur by telling me, 'You mean your *young* Incan princess, don't you?'

'Two's company, three's a crowd' was Dad's explanation about the reason why, finally, he left her and returned to Teria and Pera.

I AM TELLING you all this about my father not just because I am proud of him, but also because, as a small boy, hearing all the stories about his sporting prowess made me want to emulate him so much that it hurt.

When young, Dad continued to gain local attention within Gisborne sporting circles. From local rugby he graduated to Māori rugby. 'There was no division between junior and senior rugby in Māori games,' Dad told me. 'You were thirteen or fourteen and you were playing rugby with mature men. That's how you learned to play. You also learned to tackle low because players would put their elbows and knees up.'

I can still hear Dad's call across the paddock to the referee: 'That tackle was too high, ref, too high!' Like so many old-timers, he thought the contemporary game was not as good as it was in his own day. 'Players get away with too much, and the refereeing is bad.'

Like his father before him, Dad's abilities in Māori rugby got him noticed when one day YMP and Celtic were playing a senior match. Pita Kaua gave Dad a YMP jersey and said, 'We're one player short. You're our fifteenth player. You want to let your Māori brothers down?'

Dad thought he'd play flanker, but Pita said he was to play wing. His job was to mark Alec McInerney, top sprinter in Poverty Bay and very tall at six feet four inches. 'Don't let him through,' Pita warned him, but to no avail. McInerney kept on scoring and it was doubtful if anybody, let alone Dad, could have stopped him.

The YMP players, Tom Dennis included, were pissed off and said to Pita, 'Tom's a useless beggar. It's better for us to play short.' The Celtic crew were up by five points. Pita said to Dad, 'You'd better shake your ideas up.'

Dad began to tackle McInerney, ball or no ball. Five minutes were remaining in the game when Pita called the play, 'Taha ka pō, blind side.'

When the ball came out of the scrum, Pita passed it out to Dad's side and he went wide past McInerney and took off, past the halfway mark, past the three-quarter mark. He could hear Celtic players trying to catch him, but he was too frightened to be caught. His YMP mates were yelling, 'Go, go, go, you little beggar, go, go, go!'

He was fifteen years old and he crossed the line and wanted to put the ball down beneath the goalposts. Pita Kaua yelled out, 'No! If you don't fall on the ball, we'll kill you.' My father scored an eighty-yard try. It was enough to get him a jersey representing Poverty Bay.

Later, Dad took on golf when he went to stay with his Uncle Rongo Halbert for a year. He managed to get down to a three-handicap within a year and won the Poverty Bay Māori Tournament. He could hit the ball past 300 yards.

My father also played lawn tennis at annual Māori tennis tournaments. People tend to forget that Māori were playing tennis in the 1890s, and by the early 1900s most marae had lawn tennis courts; Māori played with improvised racquets. By 1926 the popularity of tennis as an iwi sport was so great that Sir Āpirana Ngata created the New Zealand Māori Lawn Tennis Association to coordinate the intertribal matches that had arisen. That first association had some powerful men involved, among them Tai Mitchell, Pei Te Hurinui Jones and Tukere Te Anga. Tribes sent their best players to the tournaments.

In 1932, when Dad was seventeen, he won the junior lawn tennis title by accident. Jack Baker put Dad's name down for the championships without his knowledge. He had no racquet, no shorts and no shirt, but he couldn't back out and, protesting, let Jack dress him: his shorts were halfway down to his knees and had to be tied around his thin waist. His brother Win had been given a new racquet so Dad played with the old one, which had broken strings.

Dad reckons he won the championships because whenever he hit the ball with that old racquet, the ball would do strange things. Instead of going in the direction it was hit, the broken part of the strings would deflect the ball another way. Not only that, when the ball landed on the ground, the spin of the broken racquet would make it bounce backwards or sideways. He knows the racquet won him the championship because after the match it was restrung and he began to lose.

In 1933 Dad won the doubles championship with Fred Keys from the King Country. Keys was the top player in the tournament, good at the overhead smash, but his brother had to pull out as his partner. Jack Baker organised for Dad to replace him.

Not long after that, Dad and Winiata went to Ngāruawāhia; it may have been the year that Uncle Win won the junior title. At the time Ngāruawāhia was a major centre of Māori lawn tennis, and the young generation of tennis players was regarded by their elders as setting an example of modernity to their generation. The two brothers must have cut manly figures in their white shirts and trousers. While Dad was playing, one of the officials came up to him and asked, 'Are you Hine Te Ariki's grandson? There's somebody wants to see you.'

That somebody was the patroness, Princess Te Puea, who, because of her relationship to Dad through Hine Te Ariki's mother, asked him to represent her at the closing ceremonies of the hui. Later, she asked him to come and stay with her permanently.

The connection between Dad and Waikato remains to this day. When the Māori Queen, Te Atairangikaahu, came to Gisborne in 1996, she asked Dad to sit with her during the ceremonies. The relationship continued with me, and we always had a special greeting for each other. When she died in 2006, I grieved deeply for her and wondered what life would have been like for Dad had he accepted Te Puea's offer and stayed in the Waikato.

I began to play lawn tennis myself when I was at high school, and I realised why Dad was such a good player. While others were busy slamming the ball, he was busy pointing it and placing it. He was extremely clever, dropping the ball just over the net, lobbing it high over his opponent's head, placing it in a leisurely fashion and with extraordinary finesse.

One of my proudest moments was to play in the father-and-son regional Māori Poverty Bay championships at the Gisborne Tennis Club sometime in the 1960s; we may have won it. What really happened was that Dad kept playing at the net and would put out his racquet here and there, and when occasionally the ball went past him, I would tear after it wherever it was heading.

'Go, go, go, you little beggar, go, go, go!'

My father extends his racquet and pretends he has missed the ball. I race from one side of the baseline to the other, listening to his voice lilting with love and joy. His expectations give my feet wings and I achieve the impossible. I reach the ball. It is almost at the double bounce when I scoop it up and slam it back over the net.

I would have done anything for my father.

Chapter Twelve

The Spiral Always Turning

1.

THE SPIRAL ALWAYS turning, and the forward spiral of my kōrero has rubbed against another, which is running parallel with it. We will have to cross over for a moment, but we will come back again.

So what does this new spiral want?

Ah, to ensure you do not lose sight of the fact that, as I've previously mentioned, early to mid-twentieth-century Māori families were pretty large. And I haven't introduced my father's siblings to you yet. Forgive me, therefore, as I take you back for a moment.

Having been brought up by his paternal grandparents, Manu and Hine Te Ariki, Dad never really got to know his brothers and sisters until he returned to them. He was nevertheless the one whom Teria appointed as trustee, along with Winiata (Win), to look after the papakāinga land.

Uncle Win, the second eldest, was brought up by his maternal grandparents, Moanaroa and Rīria. Unlike Dad, who finished school early, Win was sent to the Mormon-run Māori Agricultural College, the first such built outside the United States. He became a first-class student and rugby player — Dad always put his skills down to the application of American gridiron techniques to the New Zealand game. Win later went to Wellington, where he graduated from Victoria University, then a college of the University of New Zealand, with a BA in 1948. One of his contemporaries, Hēnare Ngata — the same elder who had come to see Mum and Dad to ask if they knew this new writer, Ihimaera — gained his law degree at the graduation ceremony, and his father, Sir Āpirana Ngata, was given an honorary doctorate.

Uncle Win's photograph was on my mother's wall with the family whakapapa. He was resplendent in his academic gown, and his wife, the beautiful Aunty Margaret née Black, wore a beautiful floor-length dress and lacy half-gloves. I think Mum hoped that the photograph might give me a model to aspire to. When I wasn't doing as well as that, I would duck my head as I passed along the hallway: 'Sorry Uncle.'

Uncle Michael (Mike) came next. All the Smiler boys were handsome, but chiselled Uncle Mike was the looker among them. Because Teria sent him to Manu and Hine Te Ariki to be raised with Dad, they shared a strong bond. When Mike grew into manhood he became as much a sporting star as Dad and Win. Another of my mother's whakapapa photographs was of the three Smiler brothers, sitting in singlets and shorts, arms crossed over their chests, after winning a local boxing championship. And there I was, skinny and studious, with not a bicep in sight, ducking my head again: 'Uncles, sorry.'

Next was Uncle Puku Uenuku (Puku), another to make me feel wanting; and then a daughter, Aunty Meritaiakupe (Mary), interrupted the flow of boys. Her brothers and sisters all acknowledged her as the Big Sister. Actually, we *all* bowed down to Aunty Mary, she was that kind of imposing woman, big in body, voice and argumentative spirit. After her came Aunty Joey Teo Merengi (Joey), the beauty of the family, Uncle Hiri (Sid), Uncle Hani (sometimes called Tote), Uncle Ihimaera (Danny), Uncle Mafeking (Mafe) and Aunty Alice. Papa, Te Teira and Cissie had died as infants and Weretā as a young boy.

I realise with awe that sometime or other in my boyhood I stayed with *all* my uncles and aunts, something that I doubt many of my cousins would be able to say. They all tried to invest in me some gift: Aunty Mary, generosity; Uncle Mafeking, well, he became a New Zealand snooker champion but I never had his unerring eye; Aunty Joey, hospitality; Uncle Danny, he was fantastic at playing the Spanish guitar but no matter how much I tried, I never mastered the art; Uncle Hani, like Win, obtained a university degree, and to him I attribute my doggedness; Uncle Sid gave me laughter; and Aunty Alice sweetness.

Yes, even the Wit*sh* — the pet name Teria gave me — sometimes required sweetness.

The tika. As a child I loved growing up into two huge families, the Keelans and the Smilers. There came a time, however, when I understood that I was not only growing up into them but also into every Māori family on the East Coast and the Gisborne district. When I say that I was related, therefore, to every Māori in Poverty Bay, that was the truth. Eventually, there came a time when I wanted to hide from them and then to escape.

2.

BACK TO THE main spiral now.

When the Second World War began my father wanted to go, but Teria refused to let him. I don't know the reason why she said no and I find it puzzling, given that her grandfather, Wī Pere, had supported the First World War. Times had changed since then, however, and perhaps, like the Waikato princess, Te Puea, she had grown cynical of Pākehā.

Many other Māori in the district signed up, particularly from Ngāti Porou where Tā Āpirana was the great recruitment officer. His face would be the Māori version of the moustachioed Lord Kitchener in the iconic poster, 'YOUR COUNTRY NEEDS *YOU*'. Instead, Te Haa remained in Gisborne.

'In 1942 I met this girl, Julia Keelan.' These are the words with which my father begins his reminiscences in his battered ledger book. 'She was cooking for the Nadens in Iranui Rd. I courted her & then she left to go to work at Hedley Reeves Tolaga Bay.'

My mother remembered the detail of their first meeting. 'I was living with my sister Mate and one night decided to go to a dance,' she told me.

She put on a dark blue satin dress trimmed with sequins, pretty spectacular against her dark colouring. In those days the dances were held either at the Selwyn Hall or at Poho-o-Rāwiri meeting house, Kaitī. Mum's close friends, Mandy and Nan Bartlett, were also living in Gisborne, and the three girls would go together, sometimes being chaperoned by dating couples like Haddo and Polly Ngaira.

'It was either Mandy or Nan who hooked up with two men,' Mum continued, 'one of whom was this older fellow. I ended up with the younger one but halfway through a dance Mandy (or Nan) said to me, "Let's swap, I want to see what your fellow is like", and I found myself dancing with your father.'

Dad has a different story. He saw Mum in her lovely satin dress and his interest was piqued by her attitude of independence. When the swap happened, and he was dancing with her, he knew he wanted to get to know her better.

By the way, my mother was in earshot in the kitchen in Haig Street when Dad was telling me this story. She came to the doorway and said, 'Your father was fast, but I wasn't one to go with any sweet-talking man, even if he was Tom Smiler.'

That first evening Dad asked if he could take Mum home, but she already had somebody who was doing that, or so she said, and she answered, 'No.'

As bold as brass Dad said, 'Well, how about tomorrow?'

At the time, Dad was living with Win and another brother, Puku, in a small whare at 165 Crawford Road, which Teria had bought for Win. My father had a good job at the nearby freezing works. Although shearing was his trade, whenever the season was over he had an open invitation to work in the fellmongery department, where he was a foreman curing sheepskins.

He told me that as soon as he met Mum he lost interest in all other women — and there were a *lot* of women in his life. As for Mum, she was twenty and Dad was twenty-seven; seven years' difference, hmnn! During the following week he must have made enquiries about where she worked because one afternoon he was waiting on the street outside the Nadens' house and he asked her to go out with him. She told him she would meet him at the movies, but when she got there — 'He had another girl with him!' she called from the kitchen, overhearing his story among banging pots and pans.

'I tried to explain to your mother,' Dad continued, 'that the other girl was just a friend and that she needed help — she wanted me to drive her somewhere. I asked your mother to wait while I drove this other girl where she wanted to go. She said okay.'

'No, I didn't.'

'I drove like blazes there and back. Your mother was gone. She hadn't even waited.'

'I wasn't going to wait around for him,' my mother said as she appeared at the kitchen doorway again, a look of mirth on her face, 'even if he was your father.'

My mother was referring to Te Haa's profile in Gisborne. Of course Māori knew who Tom Smiler was; his descent lines and sporting accomplishments were reflected in his physical grace and sense of self. He wore his confidence lightly, however, almost as if he was unconscious of his looks, his abilities and attractiveness. He was considered quite a catch.

3.

AFTER SIX MONTHS of Te Haa's relentless pursuit, my mother thought things were getting too serious. Anyway, she knew her parents would have been dead against her getting married before she was twenty-one — that age her generation chose to define 'adulthood' and, in the case of women, when she could marry without parental consent. Indeed, it was a boundary that Mum in her turn imposed on all her children, much to our personal cost. 'You are not getting married until you are twenty-one,' was the constant refrain to my sisters. And so my mother left Gisborne to escape my father — 'I wasn't going to be another one of his conquests' — and to work for the Reeves family at Tauwharepārae Station at the back of Tolaga Bay.

It was while Mum was back on the coast that she learned her favourite brother, Rangiora, Serial No. 62591, one of 128 men of Ngāti Porou C Company of 28th (Māori) Battalion, had been killed on 26 March 1943. He was twenty-nine.

> So kiss me, my sweet, and so let us part
> And when I grow too old to dream
> Your love will live in my heart.

Led by the charismatic Captain Arapeta Awatere, Rangiora was one of the ninety-seven men who died at Point 209, Tebaga Gap, in north-west Tunisia. The mission had been to take and hold two positions. One was Point 209 and the other a similarly high position that the battalion had named Hikurangi. The most famous of the fallen was Second Lieutenant Moana-nui-a-Kiwa Ngārimu, who was posthumously awarded the Victoria Cross. I like to think that the Hikurangi in Tunisia became the point from which the dead soldiers made their spirit journeys back to Mount Hikurangi in their homeland, there and *mark*, as my mother would have said.

When we were children I was fascinated that every year Mum put an advertisement in the bereavement column of the *Gisborne Herald* to honour Rangiora. Dad always said to me, 'I was not your mother's first love, her brother was.'

Whether Rangiora's death had anything to do with Mum's feelings about Dad, or his persistence, I don't know, but Dad visited Mum at Tauwharepārae. She decided to return to Gisborne, where her heart was starting to turn towards him. They continued to see each other, go to dances at Poho-o-Rāwiri and on other dates.

One never imagines one's mother as an object of desire; it's embarrassing for any son to contemplate. The first time I was ever confronted with the notion was the time, as a small child, I was walking down Gladstone Road with her on a Friday night. All of a sudden, a red-faced man burst violently out of the crowd, picked me up and stared at me.

'Is this yours, Turi?' he asked her.

'You're drunk,' she said. 'Put him down.'

The red-faced man had his face close to mine. I can remember the smell of beer coming from him. 'Your mother did this to me,' he said. 'You should have been mine.'

Compelled to think of my parents as sexual beings, I have often pictured myself at the carved portal of Poho-o-Rāwiri, looking in. The meeting house is crowded with young men, both Pākehā and Māori. They are looking across the huge divide of the dance floor at the pretty girls. Alas, to reach the object of their desire they must get past the stern old women, chaperones sitting around the perimeter or on guard to stop the girls sneaking out with a dangerous boy. There is an orchestra playing on the flower-decked stage, some Glenn Miller tune — let's make it 'Moonlight Serenade'. A group of young men are smoking near the band and a few daring girls join them, and the haze of the smoke gives the scene a lambent golden glow.

Suddenly there's a break in the crowd and, on the dance floor, two couples are dancing. As they waltz past each other, one of the girls whispers to the other girl — and they swap partners.

I look at my mother and she smiles, her eyes twinkling: 'So you've come to spy on me and your father, have you?'

She is slim and attractive in a shimmering sequinned dress. Whenever she moves the sequins flash like tiny mirrors. Her high heels make her stand straight; she wears a necklace of greenstone shards. Her hair is thick, full and a bit untamed because the sparkling butterfly comb she usually wears has a broken clasp. She has made herself up very lightly, a dash of lipstick and that is all.

As for my father he looks dangerous, with somewhat slanted eyes and shining black hair. He wears a shirt, tie and a double-breasted suit with the hint that there's a handkerchief in the top pocket. No doubt about it, this boy's dressed to kill. He holds my mother easily.

She looks at him thoughtfully. And I do, too, because I got to *know* this man, and as much as I loved him I could have warned my mother about him. Indeed I once asked him a question that staggered us both with its terrifying assumptions about the love and loyalty between a father and a son. He was astounded and just stared at me. 'Why ask me that question, son, why?'

I suspect I knew the answer but I was much too afraid to admit it.

Dad must have been counting the days to Mum's twenty-first birthday because, as the time approached, he suggested she accompany him to a Mormon hui tau, which was being held in Hastings during the Easter weekend of 1943.

They got on the train together and, on the way to Hastings, Dad proposed. My mother's first thought was that now she was twenty-one she could make up her own mind about what she wanted. All her life she had been the keeper of the fire, always looking after other people and having responsibility for them. She saw Dad as a way out.

'Better to be an old man's darling than a young man's slave,' she thought to herself.

I always assumed that this was an original adage of Mum's until I discovered that its first usage dates from playwright John Heywood's *Dialogue of Proverbs*, published in 1546. Dad never seemed to mind that she voiced this to us all her life; it became something to smile about between us.

He was determined, and he'd thought ahead because he had the licence in his pocket.

She said yes.

THE MORMON HUI tau that Mum and Dad went to needs some explaining. It's very simple, yet complicated. Although my grandfather Pera had been brought up as Ringatū, he converted to the Church of Jesus Christ of Latter-day Saints, or Mormons.

The Mormons had begun proselytising among Māori, whom they regarded as 'The Chosen People', soon after the church was established in America by Joseph Smith in 1830. The missionaries who arrived from the east in 1854, with their upraised hands, had been foretold by Māori seers like Pāora Pōtangaroa. It was not until 1881, however, that Māori became a specific group for conversion.

For their part, Māori were attracted to the notion that they were a Lost Tribe of Israel. Nor was it unexpected that Māori would turn to Mormon teachings, especially since some practices paralleled those of Māori culture: particularly the focus on family and whakapapa, and going to another place after death — a Mormon rather than a Māori Hawaiki. And those upraised hands, for Ringatū, only confused matters.

By 1897 there were 4000 Mormon adherents in New Zealand, most of them Māori, and by the 1930s it was a common sight in rural Māoridom to see pairs of fresh-faced young American men, dressed in dark suits, tramping the dusty roads and handing out the *Book of Mormon*.

There are two family versions of how Pera became a Mormon.

The first, prosaic version, which the family tells, has it that in the early 1920s Pera played host to a man who, after an argument with him about religion, left the *Book of Mormon* on the shelf. One day, when it was raining, Pera picked up the book and started to read it and was immediately converted by its stories. They told of an Old Testament people who had fled the biblical Middle East and established a race of fair and delightsome people in the Americas; Christ visited them immediately following his crucifixion.

The second version is the one that I find more captivating and which, along with the story of my grandfather stealing Teria from her husband, worked its way into my imagination. Pera is ploughing papakāinga land during a late and golden afternoon when, suddenly, he looks up and sees an angel coming to rest on earth.

'Huh? He aha tērā?'

Printed on his retina was an after-image. The clouds had rolled back, revealing a blue kingdom. Something golden was fluttering down from the sky.

Pera Punahāmoa shook his head again. He took a cloth from his trouser pocket and wiped the sweat away. 'E hika,' he exclaimed.

The angel was standing on the roadside. He was blond and had blue eyes and looked like Jesus in a cotton suit. 'Kia-a orai-a, ee hor-a,' the angel said in an American accent. He had a hideous Midwestern crewcut and looked like he'd just flown in over the rainbow from Kansas or Salt Lake City.

'Kia ora,' Pera replied.

The angel came closer, leaned on the fence and blew away a feather that had fallen on his shoulder. He plucked a straw and began to chew on it. Still blinded, Pera saw golden rays emanating from the angel.

'Ko ko-ay a Pera Punahāmoa?' the angel asked. His Māori accent was atrocious.

'Āe,' my grandfather nodded.

The angel smiled, a sweet smile, which showed perfect white and even teeth. 'Ah,' the angel continued, 'ten-ay ko-ay.' The golden rays began to shimmer, spilling their radiance across my grandfather's face. 'The Lord has great work for you to do. He has blessed you with great strength and prowess. Such men or women are valuable to the Lord, and because of this suffer temptations beyond those of ordinary mortals. That is why He, the Lord thy God, has sent me.'

'He aha?' Pera asked.

'The Lord wants you to cleave unto His ways now and to be a living witness and testament unto all your people that He lives. And He has sent me, one of His angels, to tell you this.'

'How do I know you are an angel?'

'I have wings,' the angel said.

'So do birds,' Pera answered, 'and devils.' He paused, suspicious. The angel was smiling with those clear cornflower-blue eyes, amused. Pera knew he had to test the angel. 'And what do I get if I help God?' he asked.

'Why, the Lord will help you to prosper and, as He did with Israel, bless the fruit of your loins. You are descended from a Lost Tribe of Israel, and your seed shall be as countless as the sands on the beach or the stars in the heavens, and He will be with you all your days.'

The slick-sounding promises left Pera unconvinced. 'I will wrestle with you,' he said, 'and if you are truly an angel, God will take my strength away so that you can defeat me.'

The angel roared with laughter. 'I accept your challenge,' he said.

'The best of three falls?' grandfather asked.

'Yup,' the angel answered, spitting on his hands.

Well, how would you react if an angel appeared to you out of a glowing, falling sun with the potent message that Māori were descendants of a Lost Tribe of Israel?

Of course, in my version, the wrestling with an angel is a metaphor for my grandfather's study of Mormonism and his eventual conversion. He was soon baptised; I imagine that Hine Te Ariki would not have been happy with him. Not only that but Pera was persuasive, and after some years Teria and his children soon followed him into the church.

Dad remembers his adult baptism this way. 'We were dressed in garments as white as snow and waited in a line on the banks of the Waipaoa River. People were singing while they were waiting, praising God for bringing them salvation:

Come, come ye saints, no toil nor labour fear,
But with joy, wend your way.
Though hard to you this journey may appear,
Grace shall be as your day.

'As I was waiting my turn, I saw the people being totally immersed. They were like white moths fluttering in the river. When it came to my turn I crossed my hands over my chest, the elder held them with one of his and cradled me with the other, and then firmly pressed me down.'

1.

NOWADAYS, YOU DON'T see the great religious meetings that Māori attended in those days. They were the equivalent of the revivalist tent meetings that dominated American religious history during the 1930s and 1940s. Perhaps the modern-day version would be the smaller but nonetheless just as potent Destiny Church rallies, which attract 2000 or more.

The Mormon hui tau were huge and rambunctious; the Catholic version was the hui aranga, and the Anglicans had their hui tōpū. When Mum and Dad arrived in Hastings they were married by Te Tuati (Stuart) Meha, a prominent Māori patriarch of the Mormon Church, on 27 April 1943, nine days after my mother's birthday. One of Meha's granddaughters is now married to my cousin, Winiata.

Meha is a reminder of amazing times when Māori like him were visiting Salt Lake City or the new temple at Laie, Hawaii, and establishing a greater bridgehead among Māori. Indeed, he once strongly proposed that the Mormon Church ally itself with the Rātana Church to create a Māori-based religion that would have had wider affiliation in Aotearoa. This somewhat visionary proposal was regrettably turned down by Church authorities.

My parents returned by train to Gisborne, and my sisters have told me their version of events: 'Mum said goodbye to Dad at the railway station because she felt the need to tell her parents she was married now. Dad agreed she should go, and she caught the bus back to Tolaga Bay, arriving there around nine in the evening. Kereama and Flowers were in the sitting room and when Mum admitted her news they said, "We know."'

How did they know? My sisters were at a loss to explain, suggesting that the details were as fluid as memory.

Around ten days later Mum was still up in Tolaga Bay, so Dad decided it was time for him to go and collect his wife. According to his narrative, Mum wanted them to work as a married couple on a station, so they both obtained jobs at Tauwharepārae Station, where she cooked and he was a fencer and general hand. They were paid '£5 a week all found', which meant that the jobs came with free food, bed and lodging.

'I learned a lot about sheep farming,' Dad writes. 'In October we were shearing. So our life [began], involved in shearing maize picking freezing works etc & [then we were] blessed with children.'

2.

AS YOUNG CHILDREN, my sisters and I always loved the story that Mum would tell us of how she met our father, married him and came back on the train from Hastings. We would ask for it often, and she told us time and time again, and we never tired of it.

The 'First Telling', as I have called it, was in 1950 and I have previously written the account as fiction. My sisters and I were in bed, sleeping, when lightning flashed.

A huge thunderstorm came up from the south. Our father was working somewhere up country, and my mother was sleeping with the baby Viki in the cot beside her. My sisters Kararaina and Tāwhi and I were frightened by the thunder. We saw the candlelight shining under the doorway of our mother's bedroom and, when the lightning flashed, nothing could stop us from opening it and running to get into bed with her.

Our mother was never conventionally attractive but she had a way of angling her face to the light that made her look almost beautiful. When you looked at her straight on, you simply saw her Ngāti Porou ancestry at its most ordinary, the fullness of the flesh and the softness of the contours that shaped her cheekbones.

'You children should be asleep,' she said.

'It was Kararaina's idea,' I answered. Talk about ganging up on the younger sibling.

The bed was warm, and we felt safe to be close to our mother. Surely the thunder and lightning couldn't hurt us now. After a while, Kararaina asked, 'When will Daddy be coming home?'

'Oh, when he's finished his work. Next week perhaps. But if he's not back by then we'll go picking blackberries and maybe I can get a cleaning job. Don't you worry, children.'

There was a pause, and then Kararaina asked, 'How did you and Daddy meet each other? Did you fall in love with him straight away? Was he as handsome as a prince? Did you live happily ever after?'

My mother's laughter trilled through the bedroom. She was a good storyteller. 'Yes, your father was as handsome as a prince. I thought he was the most handsome boy I had seen. The trouble was that he knew he was good-looking and he had girlfriends who were much prettier than me. But for some reason, we continued to go out, even if his attitude was rather arrogant. For instance, he asked me to go to a dance and I said yes. There I was, waiting at the front door for him when he came along, and he had another girl with him! I don't know why I let him get away with it, but I did. I guess I was in love with him.'

'You were married in Hastings, eh?' I said.

Our mother smiled and nodded. 'We were booked on a train to return to Gisborne on 28 April 1943. In fact the weather that night was really awful, as bad as it is tonight. There were a lot of slips on the track and whenever we went over a railway bridge we could see that the rivers below were really high and swollen. At one point, as the train was going along a cliff, the water came rushing down the hills, and we thought it would sweep us away. The journey was really frightening. But I was with your father and he protected me. I wanted nobody but him. Anyway, although the train was supposed to arrive in Gisborne in the early evening, the weather caused delays and we didn't get there until ten or eleven. I know it was very late. And guess what?'

'What, Mummy?'

'Your grandmother Teria was there to meet us.'

Kararaina and I looked quickly at each other. Our mother had begun to rock back and forth with Viki, the baby, humming a lullaby. Her face tilted upward, the planes flattening out, bringing her eyes, nose, lips and chin into sharp relief. The pupils had widened and her eyes were dark and staring.

Our mother was spiralling out of the lovely story, and if she went any deeper it would be difficult to pull her up. Whenever she spiralled, Mum's whole body went rigid. Her toes paddled as if she was swimming.

Quickly I brought my mother back to her story. 'So Teria came to the railway station to meet you and Daddy?'

'Yes, she had come to meet your father. As for me, I went up to Tolaga Bay to tell my parents that I had married him.' The rain dashed against the window.

Kararaina plucked at Mum's nightdress. 'Where's the happy ever after? There has to be a happy ever after.'

Our mother smiled in a distracted manner. 'Why, of course there was a happy ever after.'

She pierced me with her glance.

'You were born.'

NOW THE TIKA. Let's face it, there are always questions you can ask about my mother's narrative. Some aspects of the First Telling puzzled me, especially when compared to later versions. There appeared to be a wilful attempt to obscure and confound some of its truths. As I was to discover, the interpretation of them depended on what position they were viewed from, or who was telling them.

For instance I was always puzzled about how Dad and Mum managed to keep their plans to marry a secret from Teria and Pera. They were adults, so why bother to keep it a secret anyway? Then there's the difference between the ten days that my sisters said my mother was at Tolaga Bay and the three months she told me, and here I have to take my mother's version as definitive. I always grew up with the story that I was a premature birth — my sisters confirm this — and this makes better sense only if Mum didn't return to Gisborne with Dad until late July or early August.

One thing is for certain: my mother had been disarmed by love. Although it had rendered her defenceless, she had promised to honour and obey. And then I came along.

My mother had made her bed. She would lie in it.

Witi Ihimaera, six months old, 1944:
A miniature amber votive Buddha
sitting on a blanket.

The Babbington kaumātua surrounded by whānau. In the middle, Mōkena Romio Paputene. Back standing (from left): Morgan Babbington Jnr, Tūtawa Pēwhairangi, Bill Wirihana, Rēnata Tūpara (Len) Babbington, Tate Kōpua, Hōri Ryland, Ihaia Hutana, WĪ Karaka, Rev Mohi Erewini, Eparaima Hau Whakataka, May Hale, Heke Terure, Erekana Pēwhairangi, Mikata Kōpua. Hidden: Mrs Cockery and infant. Second row seated: Te Raiwa Hale, Miria Wirihana, Hake Paputene, Te Ārai Wini Paputene, Mōkena Romio Paputene, Tū Wirihana Pōtae, Tau Ānaru. Front row: Pinerete Rārere Tupene, Whainoa, Ani Erewini.

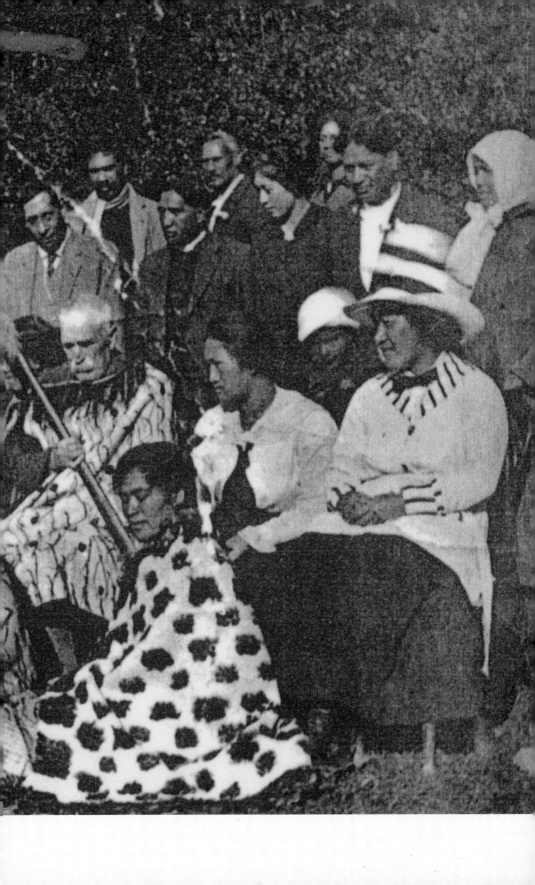

ABOVE My mother's
grandfather, WI Koka
Keelan, son of William
Thomas Keelan, with
his wife Turuhira
Mahemahe. Date unknown,
but likely to be
taken in the 1920s,
though Turuhira may
have been painted in
posthumously.

LEFT Kereama Hātarei
(Graham) Keelan,
circa 1940s. The older
I get the more the
Keelan and Babbington
genetic inheritance has
settled in, and I now
wear them on my face.

LEFT Hoana Putiputi Babbington, known as 'Flowers', with Moana Tautau, her beloved uncle, circa 1900. 'You are a flower from an old bouquet, I've waited patiently for you each day.'

BELOW Nani Flowers, circa 1950s. The Babbington strain has made my kin large-framed, handsome and very fair people.

PAIKEA'S JOURNEY MAY HAVE BEEN AN ENDING FOR HIM, BUT IT WAS JUST A BEGINNING FOR US. THE MĀORI JOURNEY WILL NOT BE OVER UNTIL WE REACH THE STARS.

ABOVE Mount Hikurangi, first place in the world to greet the morning sun. There is nothing worse than not having a tribe to belong to. Without a tribe you are an orphan in the world. You also need a mountain.
Tairāwhiti Museum, Te Whare Taonga O Te Tairāwhiti

RIGHT Paikea on the whale, gable of Whitireia, Whāngārā: 'Moni, Moni! If Paikea was able to tell his whale where to come, whales must speak Māori!'
Tairāwhiti Museum, Te Whare Taonga O Te Tairāwhiti

ABOVE A Keelan reunion at
Hiruhārama marae, circa
1950s. Graham Keelan is
second from left with his
siblings John, Sarah,
Rūtene and Claude Keelan.

BELOW LEFT Flowers with Rangiora
Keelan, my mother's favourite
brother, prior to his departure to
the Second World War, circa 1939.
BELOW RIGHT Mum (on the right) with
her friend Tuini Ngāwai, 1930s.

Julia Keelan and Te Haa-o-Rūhia (Thomas) Smiler
Jnr, early 1940s: Turi-teretimana Keelan's
transformation from Tokomaru Bay girl (previous
page) to a young woman around town in Gisborne,
early 1940s (this page), to wife and mother in
the 1950s (opposite page, top and middle).

'IN 1942 I MET THIS GIRL, JULIA
KEELAN.' THESE ARE THE WORDS WITH WHICH
MY FATHER BEGINS HIS REMINISCENCES IN
HIS BATTERED LEDGER BOOK.

BELOW Julia Keelan with
her sister Mrs Mate Kaua,
Gisborne, circa 1950s.
I like to think my own
capacity for reinvention
comes from my mother.

Gladstone Road, the main street of Gisborne, 1930s:
Gisborne in 1952 had a rural respectability,
rather like a well-groomed sheepdog.
Tairāwhiti Museum, Te Whare Taonga O Te Tairāwhiti

OPPOSITE TOP Witi Ihimaera and his sister Kararaina,
circa 1948.

OPPOSITE CENTRE Witi Ihimaera at Mrs Cole's piano recital,
Christmas 1954.

OPPOSITE BOTTOM Witi's first front-page newspaper appearance
with, from left: Kohi Rangiuia, Bill Kaua, Mum, Pani Whatuira
and Dr Skinner at the Mataatua meeting house, Otago Museum,
Dunedin, 1955: 'This will be ideal,' the photographer said.
Evening Star, Dunedin

Madge Cole, music teacher, Gisborne, 1950s: 'Mr Cole? Mr Cole! Would you kindly escort these people off the premises immediately.'

OPPOSITE TOP Mum with her Kaitī neighbour, Mrs Walker.

OPPOSITE BOTTOM Gordon and Jeanne Waugh and extended family, next-door neighbours, Haig Street: Gordon and Jeanne became Mummy and Daddy Waugh.

Hine Te Ariki Pera with her grandson, my father, Te Haa-o-Rūhia, and Hine's pet ram, circa 1918: 'So, Ihimaera, tēnā koe, e te mokopuna.'

Pera Punahāmoa, my paternal grandfather,
late 1950s: One of the last full-bloodied
Māori in Poverty Bay.

Witi Ihimaera, second from left,
front row, Gisborne Intermediate
Hockey Eleven, 1955.

PART TWO

A LITERARY WHAKAPAPA
A NEW ZEALAND CHILDHOOD

Chapter Fourteen

7 February 1944

1.

THE OLD PEOPLE say that Teria was attending a huge Māori tribal gathering when she heard that my mother, Turi, had come to term two months early and that I was being born. Although the gathering was an important one, involving chiefs from throughout Poverty Bay and the East Coast, Teria made her apologies to attend the delivery. When she arrived at the hospital she was alarmed at the difficulties of the birth; the doctors told her that they could save my mother or me, but not both. Because my father was not there, they turned to Teria as the relative present: the choice was hers.

The old people say that, in the moment of decision, Teria experienced a sense of foresight. She saw me in my mother's womb and that I was struggling to free myself of the birth cord, which was wrapped around my neck. She could well have stood by and let me die, except that when I revolved she saw that my left eye was swimming in blood. As soon as she saw that eye she remembered that at her own birth, so she had been told, her eye was also bloodshot and that she too had been strangling in her birth cord.

Realising that our births were similar, Teria decided to try to intercede with an appropriate karakia. She began to chant, and I was encouraged by its rhythms, because I began to twist and turn myself free and unwrap from my umbilical cord. In the chant a child cried to be fed the royal food, the sweet potato, brought by Pourangahua:

> Pō! Pō!
> E tangi ana tama ki te kai māna!
> Waiho, me tiki ake ki te Pou-a-hao-kai,
> Hei a mai te pakake ki uta rā,
> Hei waiū mō tama;
> Kia homai e tō tupuna, e Uenuku.
> Whakarongo! Ko te kūmara ko Parinuitera.
> Ka hikimata te tapuae o Tangaroa,
> Ka whaimata te tapuae o Tangaroa,
> Tangaroa! Ka haruru!
>
> Ka noho Uru, ka noho i a Ngangana;
> Puta mai ki waho rā ko Te Aotu,

Ko Te Aohore, ko Hinetuahoanga
Ko Tangaroa! Ko te Whatu-o-Poutini, e!

At the end of the chant I slithered into the world.

'Haramai tama i te maru aroa o wai matua,' Teria said. 'Welcome child, to the world made by Tāne, the domain of humankind.' With that she placed her mouth over the soft fontanelle of my head and blew: 'Haaaaaaaaa.'

So was my first breath given unto me.

The old people say that I cried at Teria, demanding that she acknowledge me as her grandson. Laughing, she held me in her arms. 'All right then,' she said, 'it is you who I will accept and it is you who I will give my blessing.'

This is what the old people say.

 2.

AND SO I come to the day I was born.

It has taken a while, but I wanted to honour the Māori process of the pōwhiri and to introduce myself to you as I would on the marae. In so doing, I have tried to give you a glimpse of the compulsions that have led to my living within a tribal mind and to pay due acknowledgement to my tīpuna and iwi and the people who have shaped me. They comprise a long line of ancestors, stretching before me and going back to the very beginning of time, to whom I am accountable and with whom I have an implicit contract: it's my turn now to be kaitiaki, guardian of all our worlds.

But autobiography, biography and memoir are inadequate genres within which to write a tribal life story. They have a habit of reducing the life, and the characters within it, to a selection of that life's inhabitants. Not only that, the tribal Māori mind does not proceed in a linear fashion but, rather, by way of those circularities I have already introduced to you.

Never mind, I shall try to do my best though I have a sneaking suspicion it must be easier to be a European. You don't have to acknowledge, to be inclusive rather than exclusive in defining the complexity of all those relationships that have compelled your life forward, by way of whakapapa, in such a huge way and on so many circular fronts. Māori have no option but to keep track of our relationships as they have happened through the large families, generation after generation, as well as in adjunct ways through the process of whāngai, the raising of children by grandparents or close relatives. Sometimes I am staggered at the capacious memories that Māori speakers have as they recite genealogy, even their ability to recall ancestors who may have been taken to other tribal areas — such as Rāwiri Tangaroa was during the Musket Wars.

Why this emphasis on kaitiakitanga, on guardianship? There's a saying that encapsulates this obligation: 'E kore au e ngaro, he kākano i ruiruia mai i Rangiātea. I am from a seed that was planted at Rangiātea, the homeland island from which we migrated, and I will never be lost.'

No wonder that when I began travelling the world my father would say to me, 'Never forget, son, if anything happens to you while you are overseas, don't worry. If you are born a Māori, you die a Māori. The last obligation your people have to you in life is that, no matter where you die, they will come to bring you home.'

3.

I WAS BORN on 7 February, although for many years I liked to tell people my birthday was 6 February, Waitangi Day. I often wondered why my mother had not been able to arrange matters in, well, a more politically appropriate and congruent manner. Not until much later, when I was around thirteen, did I discover that 7 February was also the birthday of Charles Dickens, the great English novelist. Not that this helped me any.

I was not born in a ponga hut and I was not raised on a marae. My world had long been compromised. Instead my place of birth was a maternity ward, and that was the beginning of many disconnections I would experience as I grew up and away from the traditional umbilical cord of the old Māori world. Like all people born in Aotearoa New Zealand, my life has been negotiated primarily through one frame of reference or the other, Māori or Pākehā. The outcome of these constant negotiations fashioned a particular New Zealand childhood, which some might recognise, others not.

Whatever the case, it *was* a New Zealand childhood.

My name came from Dad's best friend, Witi Taotū Teka, who joined Dad and his brothers at Crawford Road. Actually there are three of us named after Teka, so he must have been a very popular man; his nickname was Ping. He had a sister, Rērere, or Lil, who had no children and perhaps this is why she had a special affection for me; she was another of my grandmothers. Whenever I went past Nūhaka I always had to call in.

Sadly, over the years I lost touch with Lil, but in 1984 I remembered her and asked her to join the special train bringing all my relatives down from Gisborne to the opera *Waituhi: The Life of the Village*; she got on at Wairoa. I was so busy at rehearsals that I couldn't join the train until Masterton. I walked through the carriages greeting everyone and then I came across Lil, in coat and scarf with that lovely face of hers.

'Just because I am coming to the opera doesn't mean I forgive you for not coming to see me more often,' she said.

Boy, did she make me eat crow.

According to my mother, I was born around 9.50 a.m. I'm sorry to say there's no tribal preamble to my birth as there had been for the great warrior Tū-whakairi-ora. Have I forgotten to tell you the story?

As you may recall, he was one of my mother's ancestors. Pre-European history was filled with internecine warfare — an eye for an eye, a tooth for a tooth, that sort of thing — and Tū-whakairi-ora was the main character in one of the greatest revenge cycles of Māori history. The series began when his grandfather, Poroumata, was murdered by a number of rival clans. Poroumata's daughter, Te Ataakura, bore two children, and the second was Tū-whakairi-ora. Much to Te Ataakura's delight he wriggled, kicked and shifted so much in her womb that she knew her prayers had been answered: 'Ah, yes, move violently within me, son. It is for you to requite the death of my father.'

Such divinations clearly place destiny's mark, for those who seek it later, when trying to understand the origins of greatness.

Spurred on by his mother's words, Tū-whakairi-ora spent most of his young years proving to his clan that he was indeed the avenger they were waiting for. He was soon rewarded with chiefly feathers and the taiaha to achieve the task. The gods also honoured him with supernatural trappings: a clap of thunder announced his coming.

Finally, when the auguries were auspicious, Tū-whakairi-ora led his clan against those who had been complicit in the killing of his grandfather. The old texts name six pā which faced his warriors. Together with reinforcements, the defenders committed a huge force to the battlefield. What was Tū-whakairi-ora's attitude? 'Though the enemy may come in his many thousands, he is but food for my weapon.'

Alas, unlike Tū-whakairi-ora, I did not move violently in my mother's womb, but that did not stop me, when I grew older, from asking. Even when I was wailing in her arms, still no tohu appeared, no portent in the sky, no glorious chorus of birdsong or sighting of something strange and wondrous, like a taniwha off Young Nick's Head.

'Not even a rainbow?' I teased her.

Let's face it, Mum was much too busy concentrating on herself, no wonder she missed any signs. Legs in stirrups, already in the middle of a breech birth, growing unconscious as the chloroform took effect. Her first child coming out of her like a back in the rugby match, left arm ready to fend off the world and head tucked under his right shoulder. No, all I got from her was not a comet streaking through the sky but, rather, the messy stuff about blood, mucus, and how mine had been a difficult birth.

Nor had my father, Tom, the courtesy even to be there, though probably that was because I hadn't given him due warning. How was he to know I was coming early? He was on the job at the freezing works, where he had managed to get some temporary work, and sauntered over to the Cook Hospital Maternity Ward at lunchtime; was he ever surprised. I shouldn't be too hard on him as, even if he had been there, men were usually kept at arm's length by a medical establishment that believed it was better for the mother to be left alone to get on with it.

There was a reason, though, why Teria was attending my birth. She anticipated that my mother would give me up to her, just as she had given up Dad to Hine Te Ariki, and so she asked: 'Homai taku mokopuna ki ahau, e Turi.'

'Confronted with this dilemma, your mother said no,' my father told me some years later.

And so, unlike my grandfather or my father, or my grandmother or my mother, I was not brought up by any grandparent. When I asked Mum herself why not, all she did was to lift her face to the light. It was a particular stance she took, almost as if she was ready to attack: eyes wide, looking down high cheekbones, nose narrowed, face almost in rictus.

'I held you in my arms,' she said.

My mother must have had a very strong will not just to stand up to Teria but also to the customary norm of whāngai. As I was to discover, the practice was widespread and far more common than people today realise. As an expanded adoption process, although no formal papers were signed, the custom was a powerful way of maintaining cohesion and unity, and of extending relationships through whakapapa. And this may have been the case for the first son and first daughter, I have no quarrel with that. With younger children, there might also have been some reciprocal obligation, which, in my mother's case, she was to fulfil on behalf of the family; she would have done this gladly. Nor should any fault be attached to Flowers; she was not to know that Mum would be unhappy, perhaps it was the luck of the draw.

In not giving me up, however, was my mother saying that she was not prepared to take the risk with me, even if it was Teria? Apart from her own experiences, she would have seen some of her peers, especially in the 1920s and Great Depression of the 1930s, placed in situations that led to mental and physical punishment and sexual abuse. Being male in a society that privileged male over female children does not make me any happier that, in my own generation, I saw female cousins who were little more than work slaves for the families who adopted them. Actually, being male did not save you from that same situation either.

In my case, my mother said, 'No.' She was a modern Māori woman living an urban life now, and perhaps she thought — or hoped — Teria would see that times had changed and that notice should be given on some of the old customs. Mum was the one who taught me the power of that word 'no' and that it was always easier to say 'yes'. When the river is flowing it is always easier to go with the flow. She wasn't talking about herself when she explained, 'The people of courage are always the ones who stand up when one by one everyone else goes with the consensus.' Her view has always shamed me because, like my father, for most of my life I have preferred to say yes. I have always believed that it is better to open a gate than to close it. When I was elected to the Queen Elizabeth II Arts Council, for instance, I said in my introductory remarks: 'I must warn you that if ever there is any doubt about a decision and it comes to a split vote, I will always vote in the affirmative.'

At least people have always known where I stand.

There was, actually, was very little that was equivocal about my mother. This is difficult to explain, but the moral code she had been brought up in meant that she thought in absolutes. It was either black or white, right or wrong, left or right. You either did it or you didn't. As well, it was either yes or it was no; not yes, *but* or no, *maybe*. When my mother said no to Teria, she meant no.

The problem was that my grandmother was not accustomed to being denied. In this case she had Māori custom on her side, and Mum was caught in a bind, as she always acknowledged tikanga and kawa. In this case, the kawa, the right that Teria wished and expected to exercise, was the same right Hine Te Ariki had invoked — the eldest grandchild to be brought up with the paternal grandparents. Teria's demand was a crucial moment in my mother's life and it defined her relationship with me, and with my grandmother. And because Teria was so persistent, other relationships had to adjust, including that of Teria's to Grandad.

The agreement was not easily won. First of all, Teria tried to persuade Dad to return with his family to Waituhi, but Mum did not want to live there; she was staying put in town. I suspect that having won her independence from her own Keelan family, she was not about to surrender it to Dad's. Teria then began to appear at the house in Crawford Road. At the gateway she would wait and, like Māori women of old, call for me, karanga after karanga in her beautiful voice. And I, so I have been told, would recognise that voice and kick and wriggle and want to be held by her.

'What could your mother do?' my father asked me. 'She couldn't let Teria just stand there in the road, with cars going past and neighbours watching on, doing karanga after karanga to you! So although your mother was breastfeeding you, she would allow Teria to take you for a few hours. As the weeks went by, however, Teria insisted, "More time, Julia, more time I say!" And your mother would allow you to go with her overnight. At least that was halfway to fulfilling her obligation. She would put you in a blanket, prepare milk in a bottle and take you out to the front gate. Sometimes Pera was with Teria, and he was always irritated at her behaviour. But your grandmother took little notice of him or any of us, really. Only you, and you were such an ugly little thing. Scrawny. No flesh. You know what she would say to your mother? "Give my grandson to me, Turi, homai taku mokopuna ki ahau." Just those words, nothing else. Then without looking at me or your mother, she would turn and take you away.'

Teria was demanding and forceful. After a few months, she was taking me to Waituhi for the weekends. The irony is that, while I love my mother deeply for defending me and not giving me up, part of me would dearly have wished to have gone with Teria and been brought up with her.

For one thing, I would have learnt how to speak the reo, the chiefly language. From the very beginning of time, the reo has always been sacred whereas English is profane. The reo was the language communicated with the gods through sung karakia, chanted whakapapa, recited and declaimed whaikōrero and incantatory waiata. And it has lost very little of the ihi (energy), wehi (dread) and mana (force). English once had this power when its reo was runic and talismanic; no longer. The words have lost all their spiritual and psychic qualities, and the English language is now of such common and base matter that it has been robbed of its mysteries.

I have some proficiency in the reo but Teria would have ensured my excellence in it: I know, but I don't *know*.

Teria would also have embedded the chiefly arts of the marae strongly within my make-up. I wonder if she was attempting a rescue mission to give me sufficient Māori upbringing to see me through my life?

To this day, therefore, I always envy my peers who have had a traditional Māori education. When I see them performing whaikōrero, haka and waiata before a Māori audience, I am overwhelmed with excitement. While I am confident and second to none in the Pākehā world, they are my superiors in the Māori world. Their expert ritual recitations of reo are beyond my capabilities, and their understanding of tikanga, the Māori way of doing things, is something that evinces my complete admiration.

When, as a young boy at primary school, I tried to involve myself in the Māori cultural class it was too late. I was always the Māori kid with the big eyes who was put in the back row of the kapa haka group not only because I was bone skinny but so that I wouldn't get in the way.

My mother, when she said 'No', placed my feet on a pathway that led away from the Waituhi Valley. I have learnt to live with my inabilities but, oh, sometimes I catch my breath when I see that other *me*, the one who could have been the young man, in the front row, leading a fiery haka. Or when I am on the marae, I delight in the high school boy in uniform confidently and proudly paying tribute to the meeting house, his language passionate and soaring, his choreography immaculate and so pleasing.

My marae was to be found in another world.

I was destined to do another kind of haka.

Chapter Fifteen

The Medicine Woman

1.

FROM THE START, I was surrounded by loving whānau and had people crying over me from one village to the next. Indeed, a month after my birth, Mum and Dad were in Ūawa and met the Mormon patriarch Te Tuati Meha, who was there on Church business. He was so overjoyed they had a child that he blessed me and kept on blessing me every time he saw me. No wonder I have had such a fortunate life.

Despite Meha's blessings, I was a sickly child. I was over two months' premature, which was no help for life expectancy; Māori mortality rates remained high. To top it off, as I grew older I had chronic breathing problems, and the Pākehā obstetrician who delivered me didn't think I would live beyond my first year.

Perhaps this was why my mother took to sprinkling me with water, which was one of the ways Māori, particularly Ringatū, had of providing protection. She learned to do this when she was staying with the two old weavers in that valley full of rainbows.

The Māori word for water is wai, and it has great resonance in our lives. When a person has concluded a speech, for instance, you will hear people call out, 'He wai!', which is an exhortation to sing a waiata, a song that blesses the words you have spoken. One particular proverb has the line: 'Homai te waiora ki ahau, give to me the healing waters of life.'

Whenever my mother was anxious about me, or any of her children for that matter, she would sprinkle water over our heads, even though we did not want her to. We ran laughing away from her as she pursued us. When I became a teenager Mum still didn't stop. I'd be listening to the radio and all of a sudden I would feel drops of water and turn around to catch Mum in the act. As an adult, I worked for Foreign Affairs and travelled a lot overseas, and Mum still kept sprinkling me because she was apprehensive for my safety. 'You're leaving on the plane tomorrow,' she would say. 'I'll do this now, rather than in public, just in case, you never know.'

Because of my sickliness, Mum and Dad became anxious parents of a child who appeared to be battling for every breath. Dr Bowker, kindly, with bright blue eyes, curly grey-brown hair and a stoop, would welcome Mum to his rooms with a cheery, 'So how's the little boy doing?' He would pick me up and shake me to see if I still rattled, and gloomily give her the prognosis. Then there were the Plunket nurses who arrived in their little cars, uniforms and caps, regularly every week. They would tick off my weight, height and disposition in their books and write comments in it, presumably 'Still Alive'.

In her position as my kuia, Teria rallied around my parents and encouraged them to try to carry on with their lives as normal. My visits to Waituhi turned into extended weekends when she 'forgot' to return me to Mum and Dad on Sundays and kept me on Mondays or Tuesdays. Conveniently I hadn't, so my cousins loved to tell me, 'taken to the breast'; they knew that kind of information made me gag.

'You were a bottle baby, not like us,' they said.

My mother soon realised that Teria was a law unto herself, but that did not stop her from reprimanding my grandmother for her baby-snatching. 'Witi's mine, Teria, not yours.'

Teria's answer? 'He is better out here at Waituhi where he can be looked after by his whānau rather than in the town where there's only you.'

And so, no matter that I coughed and my breathing was constantly raspy, Teria wrapped me up warmly in blankets ('In cotton wool more like it,' my cousins liked to suggest) and shared me around the village. Whenever she got sick of me ('Which was like never,' my cousins said) she gave me over to be strapped to the backs of the women whenever they went out to plant potatoes or harvest maize; for some reason their constant bending and chatter was soothing. No doubt I was also put with the other babies beneath the trees, guarded by protective older children, when the whānau were picking fruit. And somebody please tell me that I was scolded when I was wracked with coughing or wouldn't sleep or ... ate dirt?

'Oh, you loved eating dirt,' my cousins said. 'It was your favourite kai. We loved feeding you with it.'

Ah well, if they did, at least it was Waituhi dirt.

Nani Mini soon included herself in the act, grabbing me from Teria whenever she could. My Aunty Tilly, Mini's eldest daughter, liked to tell me the kinds of stories about wet and shitty nappies that make a grown man shudder. 'I took you to dances with me,' she told me, 'and you really made a mess of my love life because everyone thought you were my baby.'

'And you were a real crybaby,' my cousins said. 'Talk about tangiweto, a wa a wa a waa!'

Against all odds I managed to survive my first year, and then my mother became pregnant with my sister Kararaina, who was born in 1945. Dad decided not to stay at the freezing works, which was the destination, along with the Wattie's canning factory, for most newly urban Māori. He followed Grandad by making his career in the shearing business. Mum, Kararaina and I followed after him, Mum working at the table as a fleeco with her sisters-in-law Mary, Waina, Betty and others. All the babies were put in a row to one side in a bale of wool; I was the coughing one. The experience had a side-effect, which is that whenever I smell the beautiful aroma of newly shorn fleece, I always want to roll in it and go to sleep. There was one farmer and contractor, old man Gemmell, who took a shine to me because, like him, I had no hair. His favourite nickname for me was Baldy. He should see me now.

There were also golfers who told me that Dad, blissfully ignorant of my sickliness, would sometimes leave me at the clubhouse to be looked after by all the doting women while he played with his chums; sounds like Dad. I met one later in my life, a jolly buxom woman with permed blonde hair out of a bottle and bright red lipstick. She pinched my cheek and said, 'Who's a big boy now, then?'

I thought, 'Oh no, this Pākehā lady has seen me without clothes on.'

Soon pregnant again, Mum gave birth to a baby brother, Thomas, who died in 1946 at five months with a congenital condition called a hole in the heart. Mum says I was much too young to remember my brother's death, and perhaps she is right because I would have been only three years old. But I have memories of an incident that matches some of the details of his tangi.

My mother is sitting with other women on the porch of Poho-o-Rāwiri marae, at the base of Kaitī Hill in Gisborne. She is sitting beside a white casket. Inside the casket is a small baby. My mother tells me, 'Go and play and make your brother happy.' I scamper to the front of the meeting house where there is a slope, and I start to roll down it, over and over.

The death of Thomas spurred Mum to try to find a cure for my own coughing and gasping for breath. She finally turned to her own Māori community of faith healers for a cure.

MY MOTHER HEARD that Hōri Gage, the great Māori healer and leader of the Ringatū, was visiting Poverty Bay. She bundled me up in blankets and took me in the car to see him.

She always liked to be formally dressed whenever she went to see important people in the community, so she put on a dark blue suit, stockings, gloves and a hat and drove me to Mangatū; driving was still an uncommon accomplishment for a Māori woman. As for the formal way she dressed, she modelled herself after her half-sister, Aunty Mate, who was fashion conscious, always wore beautiful clothes and was powdered to perfection. Look at photographs of Māori in the 1950s, especially Ngāti Porou men and women, and you'll see what I mean; the women are stylish, the men are rakish.

Indeed, there were, on the coast, a number of young Māori women of fashionable appearance and formidable intellect, among them Peggy Falwasser and Lorna Ngata. In my own Keelan clan, a later generation could look to Sue Nīkora, who was a tutor to the children of the King and Queen of Tonga, and, today, my cousins Josie, the family activist, Molly Para, young-adult health professional, and her sister, Ngawini, who works for Foreign Affairs. They are the exceptions to the rule in Gisborne these days, where Māori — and Pākehā, for that matter — look as though they have chosen their all-weather fashion-statement shorts, trainers and caps at that huge red barn known as Te Warewhare.

But to get back to my story, when my mother arrived at Mangatū she suffered a setback: Hōri Gage had already left to return to his own ancestral lands near Whakatāne. She sank to her knees, cradling me in her arms. Gage had been her final hope, and no amount of sprinkling water was going to permanently ward off the possibility of her first son's death.

I know all this because survival narratives are always central to any family, and my mother told them to me to try to instil in me the value of life. I may be the eldest but compared with my brothers and sisters, I have always been the sickly runt; and, of course, my mother had already lost Thomas and didn't want to lose another son. Stories of my survival were therefore dispensed along with all the cod liver oil, malt and other less mentionable concoctions and therapies with which my mother plagued me as a boy. My siblings did not think of this as special treatment. I made them look good.

Much later, it was intimated to me by yet another one of those seers who seemed to hover over my life that I would not live beyond the age of thirty. That only served to affirm the doom and gloom with which my early years were surrounded. Of course I am over double that age now, so every year since I have considered a bonus.

My father's approach to my sickliness was much more practical, if wrong. He was always robust, and he refused to believe in mollycoddling, favouring fresh air, open windows, cold baths and the like. When I grew older and still had various ailments he liked to threaten me with a health camp; there was one on Gladstone Road, Gisborne, close to Te Hāpara Primary School. As we drove past he would point out the children exercising, not a brown one in the bunch, and say, 'You'd better get better, son, or else!' I was therefore putty in his hands when he applied his own remedies to get me well, including one that was popular among Māori in those days — dabbing benzine on a cloth and getting me to inhale it. It's a wonder I didn't turn into a petrolhead.

So there she was, my mother, on her knees in the mud at Mangatū when she felt a gentle tap on her shoulders. 'You should take your son to the medicine woman,' a voice told her.

'The medicine woman was called Paraiti,' my mother told me, 'or

Blightface, because she had a red birthmark over the left half of her cheek, running all the way from the hairline to the neck. Like Hōri Gage, she was a Ringatū follower of the prophet Te Kooti's spiritual ways.'

My mother stood up straight away, and drove me from Mangatū to Whātātutu, where Paraiti was going about her work. Among the stories of childhood, this was the one that I could imagine fully. Stars wheeling above, an anxious white-faced mother speeding down dusty roads looking for a scarred witchdoctor, a child coughing his life away — you know the sort of thing.

Where was my father? He never figured in the narrative. Whether or not he gave Mum permission to take the family car, which was a four-door Austin, I don't know, but she took it anyway.

The work of women (and men) like Paraiti was illegal and frowned upon, and they were forced to practise in a clandestine fashion because in 1907 James Carroll had introduced the Tohunga Suppression Act. Ostensibly, the legislation was an attempt to restrict the rise of a famous prophet, Rua Kēnana, but its wording extended to anyone considered to be a witchdoctor or faith healer. Maybe there were a few who deserved the malevolent bone-rattling image, and muttered spells and threw bones on the fire, but most were revered prophets or natural healers. Paraiti was one of the latter, a medicine woman.

When my mother finally found Paraiti and delivered me to her for inspection, was she welcoming? No, first she tried to intimidate my mother with her scar and then scolded her by saying, 'You should have come straight to me instead of going to Pākehā doctors. Why do you think I will be successful when they haven't been?'

My mother was not a woman to be deterred easily. I can imagine her holding her own.

Paraiti must have been in her late seventies by then. A girl during the Land Wars, she had lived through the 1918 flu and no doubt witnessed many changes as New Zealand became colonised. Grumpy though she was, Paraiti looked at me, sighed, shook her head but said she would treat me. From what Mum told me, for the next week I was kept in a makeshift tent filled with herb-infused steam; sometimes Mum would join me in the tent, cradling me as I tried to sleep during the night. Every now and then Paraiti trickled mānuka honey down my throat. Some days later she began to karakia, to pray, and, as she did so, she hooked a finger into my throat and pulled out threads of phlegm.

Paraiti saved my life, but maybe my mother's constant wai also had something to do with it. For instance, many years later I was on my way to the United States, this time for four years to work as a diplomat in New York, and made a visit to Gisborne to say goodbye to Mum and Dad. At the airport, it was usually my father who came by himself because my mother always hated my going overseas, as if she would never see me again. Sometimes, with bitterness, she would say, 'You can't wait to get away from me, can you?', which was often true.

But *four years*. The most time I had ever been away was three. So, this time, Mum came to the airport with Dad. When the boarding call was made she looked at me and said, 'You were the only thing that was ever, truly, mine.'

I was walking out to the plane when she realised she had forgotten something. I heard her call out to me, 'Son, wait.'

She dashed into the terminal, where she must have asked the man at the counter of the food bar for a paper cup of water. I knew she wanted to sprinkle the contents over me but I was already out of reach.

'Come back,' she cried.

My heart was aching so much, and I just wanted to get on the plane before I crumpled into an emotional heap.

In exasperation she threw the paper cup in my direction. Well, I was wearing a very nice suit, so I ducked. What would you have done? The cup hit the shoulder of a fellow passenger on the flight and some water splashed on him. I said to him crossly, 'You've just received my mother's blessing.'

A few years ago, when I was looking after my grandson James, for some reason I remembered my mother sprinkling water. He was at that stage in life where he was constantly catching a bad cold from other children at the crèche, so I thought I would bless him. However, James was so difficult to keep in one place for long that I had to chase after him. He giggled and laughed, thinking this was a great game.

By the time I had done the job satisfactorily, he was, well, somewhat bedraggled. My daughter Jessica doesn't miss anything. When she came in and saw him, she got that 'Hmmmnnn' look in her eyes. 'Why is Jamie so wet, Dad?' she asked.

And so my story begins.

 3.

IT STARTS LIKE THIS:

I am a five-year-old Māori boy standing at the side of Lavenham Road with Teria outside her and Grandad's rambling homestead. We are waiting for the school bus. There are other, older, cousins at the bus stop, too, and Teria is giving them instructions to look after me. I am going to school at nearby Patutahi and this is my first day.

I am excited. I am not afraid, I truly want to go to school. As for Teria, she must have had conflicting emotions. 'Well, this moko will be living among Pākehā soon, but I hope he has been filled up with as much of his culture as I can give him. As for the future, he is in God's hands.'

The bus arrives and I get on it. When I arrive at Patutahi Primary my cousins take me to the school office to be registered. I can't remember what happens at school, but I must have enjoyed it because, when I return to Waituhi on the bus and Teria is there to greet me, I am brimming with excitement.

She asks me a question. She says, 'E Witsh, so what great wisdom did the Pākehā teach you today?'

'I learned a nursery rhyme, Nani,' I answer. 'It was about a boy called Jack and a girl named Jill.' As I skip along the path to the homestead I start to recite it. 'Jack and Jill went up the hill to fetch a pail of water. Jack fell down and broke his crown and Jill came tumbling after.'

Anybody in the English-speaking Commonwealth will immediately recognise the nursery rhyme. In my own generation we were all taught it and, when enticed, will always recite it in that same sing-song manner we learned as children.

Teria looks at me, puzzled. Then she asks, 'Who are Jack and Jill? Why aren't they called Tama and Meri? And why is Jack wearing a crown? It's his own fault if he falls down and breaks it! And what are Jack and Jill doing, going up a hill to fetch water? What a stupid place to put a well.'

Comes my second day at Patutahi Primary School and Teria sees me off again. It must have been another exciting day and, at the end of it, there she is waiting when I return to Waituhi.

'So, e Witsh, what was the great wisdom you learned from the Pākehā today?' Her intonation conveys suspicion and I am not too keen to tell her.

'I learned another nursery rhyme, Nani, about a little girl called Miss Muffet.' I look at her cautiously as I recite the rhyme. 'Little Miss Muffet sat on her tuffet, eating her curds and whey. Along came a spider and sat down beside her, and frightened Miss Muffet away.'

Surely this is inoffensive enough for Teria? But she starts to critique this nursery rhyme, too. 'Who is Little Miss Muffet? Why isn't she Little Miss Mahapihi? What's a tuffet? What are curds and whey? And what a silly girl to be frightened of a spider and run away! Why didn't she say kia ora to it?'

It wasn't until I was much, much older that I realised how truly wise Teria was. With her questions she was conveying to me that I was moving into a world that was not a Māori one, where Pākehā names and attitudes would provide the prevailing context of my future. And their world was an upside-down nonsensical place where people built wells at the tops of hills. It was a place unlike the Waituhi Valley, where people did not talk to spiders but ran away from them. Its values were anathema to ours.

I know that some people will say, 'But Jack and Jill and Little Miss

Muffet are just nursery rhymes!' and part of me would agree with you. However, they also come from a Western European narrative and they map out that culture's values system. Many of us learned the rhymes by rote without questioning them. For instance, what's a tuffet? What are curds and whey? Some of you will know, but I suspect the majority won't.

Teria, from the very beginning, taught me always to question. Not to take for granted. She also taught me that it all depends on the story that you hear.

My sister Kararaina and I decided, when we were teenagers, to regender the Jack and Jill story because, when you look at it, the nursery rhyme emphasises male power. We went around the house at Haig Street singing at the top of our lungs: 'Jill and Jack went up the track to fetch a pail of water, Jill fell down and broke her crown and it was Jack who tumbled after.'

We did the same with the Miss Muffet nursery rhyme: 'Little Master Muffet sat on his tuffet eating his curds and whey. Along came a spider and sat down beside him and—'

What do you think Little Master Muffet would do?

'Squashed it!' Kararaina and I sang.

All my life I have been writing the story of the spider. I was at a Commonwealth Literary Conference in Canada in the 1980s, giving an address, such an inoffensive occasion, when Teria's voice resounded in my ears: 'E Wit*sh*, so what great wisdom is the Pākehā teaching you today?'

Instantly a door opened on my memory and I was that little boy walking home with a beloved grandmother, and she was teaching me possibly the greatest lessons of my life. I couldn't continue my talk. For reasons which I will explain later, I had become the boy — and then the man — who never cried, and there are very few occasions when I will weep; I simply won't allow it. But on that day my eyes flooded, then poured, with tears.

There's a character in Shakespeare's *The Tempest* who most represents me as I was at that time. His name is Caliban and his island has been conquered by the white wizard, Prospero. Caliban has a powerful speech that goes like this:

This island's mine, by Sycorax my mother,
Which thou tak'st from me. When thou cam'st first,
Thou strok'st me, and made much of me, would'st give me
Water with berries in't; and teach me how
To name the bigger light and the less,
That burn by day and night. And then I lov'd thee,
And show'd thee all the qualities o' th' isle,
The fresh springs, brine-pits, barren places and fertile:

Curs'd be I that did so! All the charms
Of Sycorax, toads, beetles, bats, light on you!
For I am all the subjects that you have,
Which first was mine own king; and here you sty me
In this hard rock, whiles't you do keep from me
The rest o' th' island.

Teria, my grandmother, held my island. She was mine own ariki, my beloved ruler.

She has always been my Sycorax.

Chapter Sixteen

Crossing the Paepae

1.

SO MUCH FOR my being small, sickly and premature. There I am, in one of the few early photographs that survive of me, naked, chubby, somewhat roly-poly, sitting on a blanket. The photograph is yellowed with age, making me look like one of those miniature amber votive Buddha that people like to display on family altars.

The only possibility is that the photograph might not be of me at all, but of my sister Kararaina. However, when I was in my teens and asked my mother, 'Are you sure it's not Kararaina?', she was very cross at the question. The next time I looked at the photograph it had the name 'Witi' inscribed at the bottom of it in no uncertain terms.

There's another photograph, taken when I had just begun to walk. It also shows a pudgy boy, and my grandmother Teria has me by the hand. Isn't she handsome? The willowy young woman has acquired the stronger frame, the typical Pere build now; she still possesses sculptured features and indeed her hair is wavy and strong. I remember her profile as being somewhat Italianate; the closest to it is that of the dramatic soprano, Renata Tebaldi, whose heyday as a Verdian soprano came in the 1940s and 1950s. I never saw that profile of Teria's in anything other than a proud angle of repose, with the touch of a smile on her lips.

Most of all, I recall her voice. It was low, it caressed, and when she said my name, 'E Wit*sh*', the first syllable was higher than the second, the voice falling into sibilant tenderness. Well, most of the time anyway, because, according to my father, once I started to walk I liked to play running-away-from-grandmother games with her. Then her voice would rise, becoming inflected with exasperation: 'Auē, he hōhā te mokopuna.'

After all, I was a boy.

If I had known she had a weak heart, I would not have been so unkind to her.

My sister Tāwhi was born, and then Viki, and this compelled my parents to make a decision. Now that they had a family of one son and three daughters and, seeing that I was going to school, they decided that we should give up travelling with Dad. Instead, Mum would return to 185 Crawford Road, Kaitī, with us. My father, however, would continue to travel the district and beyond, shearing, scrubcutting or shepherding, coming home when he could.

I INVOKE THE concept of the paepae, the door sill of a meeting house with its protective powers, when I say that my mother and sisters and I crossed over the threshold, into the Pākehā world. Without the protection of our father we moved from a sacred world into one that was without sacredness. This must have occurred in 1949, and the change could not have been more momentous. From living in Te Ao Māori we moved to living in Te Ao Pākehā.

If I use the word 'Oz', that is because, to my childish mind, I had been transported to a similarly fantastic world as the film of *The Wizard of Oz*, where I would have to show heart, bravery and ingenuity if I was to succeed. Some sense of destiny was at work, propelling me from the glowing pounamu landscapes of Māori country to the sparkling emerald possibilities of the Pākehā utopia; I doubt if Māori of that time ever thought of it in its alter-ego, dystopic sense. Nor, like my mother, was I prepared to disdain my fate. There was no doubt that I would succeed. Much later, of course, I saw that that the Oz imagery was wrong. A bold refocusing of the lens enabled me to adjust my thinking.

What I had done, in fact, was move from Te Ao Māori into a more magnificent Te Ao Māori, one in which Pākehā also lived. Ah, but at the time, was it like that? No.

Let's look a little more closely at that Ao Pākehā of Gisborne.

The first observation is that Gisborne may once have been Māori but, except for Poho-o-Rāwiri meeting house, which had opened in 1930, there was no other physical architectural manifestation of the Māori world within the town limits. This is probably why it was easy for Pākehā to impose their history. In possession of the geography and the naming of places, they substituted Gisborne for Tūranga and Kaitī Hill for Tītīrangi. It was only a matter of time before most of the Māori names were erased, along with their histories. Like most New Zealand towns, Gisborne is filled with British names — Oxford Street, Cambridge Terrace, London Street, Belfast Crescent, York Street and Glasgow Crescent. One suspects that those streets with Māori names have been maintained because, well, they have uncomplicated spellings and, even then, some are misspelt anyway.

The second observation is that the Māori history as told in Te Ao Pakeha was either rewritten or relegated to the status of folk tale or myth. Witness what happened to the saga of Kupe, the first discoverer, who arrived in a catamaran circa AD 950. His canoe was filled with women, men and children and was well provisioned, but an 1898 painting by Louis J. Steele and Charles Goldie depicted the people in the waka as being in extremis. Steele and Goldie borrowed the imagery from Théodore Géricault's *The*

Raft of the Medusa, and their representation forever cast doubt on the survival skills of Polynesian sailors and the notion that they were sailing regularly across the Pacific and down to Aotearoa.

As for local Gisborne history, Captain Cook's arrival off the coast was celebrated and Tītīrangi's summit was claimed for a handsome granite memorial to him. And just in case that symbol of conquest didn't completely cow the natives, an old cast-iron cannon was mounted up there, too. The date of Cook's arrival may be wrong on the memorial, and the cannon may not even have come from the *Endeavour*. If so, that's a phantom ship and occasion we're celebrating.

The homicidal aspect of Cook's first encounter with local Māori in Gisborne was never part of the narrative I heard at school as a boy. Don't forget that Cook was the invader. According to my elder Toko Te Kani, 'The people wanted to see who these strange beings were. As they got closer, Cook and his men became hostile and six Māori were killed for showing fight against the interlopers. Cook named Poverty Bay unfairly because of the reception.'

Actually, nine Māori were murdered. The encounter took place at Te Toka-a-Taiau, which was a rock in the sea marking the boundary between Ngāti Porou and Rongowhakaata. The rock, by the way, was blown up to make way for the widening of Gisborne Harbour. Māori at least had the consolation that not only their history was being demolished but that of Pākehā, too.

Every Māori child in Te Ao Pākehā was forced to accept that Captain Cook discovered New Zealand, as if we didn't have prior rights or a history. He was portrayed as a good man who brought to us civilisation, as if we did not have one ourselves — and that we welcomed him with song and dancing (murder does not fit well with this phantom history). This version was uttered so frequently that you could hardly be blamed for believing it. The teachers kept repeating it forcefully, as if they needed convincing themselves and that their lives depended on it.

They found an unwilling believer in me. Many are the childhood scrapes I got into when I would insist otherwise. After all, to accept the Pākehā view would have been to erase myself. The point is that, though I may have been transported to a fantastic world, it was one which, to impose its power, mimi-ed on Māori. It created a new narrative that displaced the old.

When the leading statesmen of Te Ao Pākehā subsequently talked about their relationship with Māori, they preferred to couch it within the concept of 'He iwi kotahi tātou', we are all one people. These were the words uttered by Governor Hobson when the Treaty of Waitangi was signed between Māori chiefs and the Crown on 6 February 1840. However, the concept had a particular spin. It was not so much that we became one with the Pākehā but that the Pākehā authorised himself to bring us to the aforementioned civilisation and the light. He, for the Pākehā was invariably male — sorry, ladies, European women did not figure in the narrative either — claimed centre stage and his was the history that was told. Look at all the statues in our cities and towns, hardly a Māori or a woman in sight unless she was Queen Victoria.

So Captain J.W. Harris, on behalf of Sydney traders Montefiore & Company, arrived in 1831 to set up trading posts from Gisborne north and south along the coast. And Herbert Wardell has a place in the town's history as the first resident magistrate. At least he was under no pretence about his position among Māori, and admitted that he was there under sufferance, not as of right. Local Māori told him, 'We can be our own magistrates, let Pākehā magistrates attend to their own people.'

Nevertheless, within that uneasy period when the Crown was endeavouring to enforce its legitimacy, it became purchaser when it acquired its first block of Gisborne on 29 January 1857. The vendors were the main chiefs representing Gisborne tribes at the time. Among them was Kahutia, who gave or sold the land in the spirit of partnership.

The chiefs are reported in H. Hanson Turton's *Maori Deeds of Land Purchases in the North Island of New Zealand: Volume One*, published in 1877, as follows: 'Now we have fully considered wept over and bidden farewell to and entirely given up the land bequeathed to us by our ancestors with its streams lakes waters timber minerals pastures plains and forests with its fertile spots and barren places, and all above and all below the surface of the said land and everything thereunto pertaining we have entirely given up under the shining sun of this day as a lasting possession to Victoria the Queen of England and to the Kings or Queens who may succeed her for ever.'

The author of the report is credited as Donald (later Sir Donald) McLean, who was then Chief Land Purchase Commissioner, and he clearly knew his Shakespeare. His description echoes the sentiments of Caliban in *The Tempest*. To be fair, this same wording was pretty much standard in agreements between the Crown and Māori chiefs, and it is also not certain that McLean actually drafted this original resolution. Nevertheless, let me cast him as the white wizard Prospero who had full knowledge of the consequences for that native son of so generously giving over his inheritance.

And let me cast Kahutia as Caliban. The first thing that Māori do if a manuhiri, visitor, comes into our area is to honour our tikanga and after the pōwhiri extend the hand of friendship. Kahutia must have got sick of having his hand chopped off, because just three years later he said: 'I had the mana before the Pākehā came and have it still. We have done with the Queen from today.'

I love the absolute authority Kahutia was attempting to reclaim, don't you? I am sure other chiefs in Te Ao Pākehā were also trying to revoke original agreements, but it was too late to 'have done with the Queen'. In Gisborne, Pākehā persistence paid off when the government purchased the current site for the town in 1868. Kahutia and other early chiefs such as Te Kani-a-Takirau, Hirini Te Kani, Paratene Tūrangi and Ānaru Mātete are not to be blamed for eventually agreeing to the dodgy ad hoc land sales that secured the site. Colonisation had long reached the point of no return, and towns like Gisborne were springing up throughout the country. By the time of Gisborne's first European census a few years later, there were twenty weatherboard houses in the district, besides barns, stores, sheds and stables. And come hell or high water, more land was being acquired from the surrounding district.

Maybe the early Pākehā negotiators hoped for the best and assumed that, given time to accept the situation, Māori would get over it. They didn't.

ONE OF THE names in that first census is that of Thomas Halbert, who is described as a trader for W. Norris. Where the wife was a native, her name was not shown, so Halbert appears as the virgin father of two boys and three girls, who, because they were half-caste, are listed only with his surname.

I should not be so flippant. What's interesting was that Halbert was another of those *Messieurs the Whites* and, like my mother's ancestor, George Babbington, he was of Scottish descent, so I have one on each side of my family. Those Scots got around, making tribal alliances through well-placed marriages, but Halbert was in a class all his own. Let me take a little time to tell his story and subtitle it: The Kōtimana — the Scotsman — and his Six Wives.

At some point, his family had crossed the border into England, so he was born Thomas Lindsay Halbert in Newcastle-on-Tyne in 1802. In his late twenties, with his brother James, he set sail for the Southern Hemisphere. James liked the look of Australia and stayed there, but Thomas Halbert carried on to New Zealand. He landed at Māhia around 1831 aboard a three-masted whaler, and became the manager of one of Captain Harris's trading posts.

Some say that my ancestor was only the second Pākehā in the district. No wonder he commanded attention among Māori. He became known as Tame Puti, or Tommy Short, by the Māori, and rarity played to his favour. Despite his short stature and barrel chest, his appearance was no barrier to his marrying the first of his wives from the Rongomaiwahine iwi. Nobody seems to have recorded her name; I like to think of her as the lost wife.

Halbert left Māhia — and that first lost wife — in 1834 and set up on his own as a trader at Muriwai. If you believe that hoary story about Māori being attracted to gingas, then you can credit why Tame Puti soon contracted another marriage, with Pirihira Konekone, of the Te Aitanga-a-Māhaki iwi. By this time he was attracting attention for his business skill and acumen as a Pākehā Māori — someone working the borderlands of Māori and Pākehā for the benefit of both and, of course, for himself. However, on the personal side he quarrelled with Pirihira, who must have had considerable mana in her own right. Pregnant to Halbert, she went on to marry Raharuhi (Lazarus) Rukupō, one of the great chiefs of Tūranga, of whom more later. You have to tip your hat to Tame Puti, he was not single for long. I like to think of him as having risen to become a middle-level trader, but he was still looking to expand his interests. His third wife, Mereana Wero, was also from Te Aitanga-a-Māhaki, but she may not have come with good commercial assets. With his fourth wife, however, my forebear, Rīria Mauaranui, he got lucky.

Rīria was the daughter of the chieftain Ngārangi Piere, and therefore a direct descendant of many of Gisborne's chiefs, including Ruapani, Kahutia and Kahungunu; in her converged all the rangatira bloodlines of Te Whānau-a-Kai, Te Aitanga-a-Māhaki and Rongowhakaata. Born about 1815, she lived during that incredible time of internecine warfare, when tribes from Ngāti Porou, Kahungunu, Whakatōhea and Rongowhakaata, among others, battled each other for land. So highly respected was her whakapapa that when she became a captive of Tūhoe warriors at the battle of Hauturu in 1826, she was released to her people under Tūhoe escort as was her right and expectation. She was a child of eleven, and the likely reason is that her freedom came as part of one of those reciprocal exchanges that has always characterised intertribal dealings. I like to think it was for fear of retaliation had she not been released.

She must have met Halbert in the 1830s when she was in her early twenties. The question is, what on earth could Rīria or her father have seen in any union with him, three times married already and at least thirteen years older? They may have believed that Halbert's position as a trader would advantage them. And when Rīria gave birth to a son, William Piere (Wī Pere), on 7 March 1037, they saw Halbert claiming him and giving him his surname, Halbert. Indeed, on 18 December 1839 Rīria sold to Halbert the block of land known as Poupārae. As J.A. Mackay recorded in the chapter entitled 'The Old Land Claims' in his *Historic Poverty Bay and the East Coast, N.I., N.Z.*, 'His claim, which was dated 4 November, 1840, stated that the property contained 1,004 acres, and that the consideration in cash and goods represented £315, made up of:

Cash £80, four d.b. [double-barrelled] fowling pieces, 40 shirts, 36 axes, 32 plane irons, 60 blankets, 36 iron pots, 24 hoes, 400 lbs. of gunpowder, 10 pieces of print [dress fabric?], 500 lbs. of tobacco, 36 hatchets, 130 razors, 30 knives, 40 spades, and 22 pairs of scissors. The property, he said, was being used for rearing pigs for export. Witnesses to the sale were: J. M. Jury, John Campbell and Frederick Spooner.'

Auē, this was where Halbert revealed himself to be more interested in acquiring land than fatherhood. With Māori land disappearing from Māori hands, Rīria and Piere had believed that the best way to retain their properties was under the European title, which her husband conveniently provided. However, Halbert had already moved on to his fifth wife, Keita Kaikiri, and he sold Poupārae in 1841, disinheriting his part-Māori son. Fortunately, daughter and father were able to rise above Halbert's shenanigans and lay the foundations for Wī Pere's rise to tribal leadership. He was taught at Tokitoki in the sacred knowledge of the Māori House of Learning, and also in the profane Pākehā Anglican schooling system.

Halbert's sixth and final wife was Maora Pani from Rongowhakaata. Her story always fascinated me. Strong-willed, as a youngster she tried to join warriors travelling to a war in 1836, and was only discovered hiding in the waka when it was half a mile from shore. They threw her out but she was a fine swimmer and made it to land. She was very fond of the sea and is famous for a two-and-a-half-minute underwater battle with an octopus. Only her strength, skill and the fact that she was carrying a knife enabled her to defeat the wheke and, later, eat it.

With that number of marriages, no wonder that Halbert acquired the nickname of 'King Henry VIII'. He died at the age of sixty-three on 12 April 1865. Along with two brothers named Yates, he had been drinking on board a schooner lying in the Taruheru River near Mākaraka. On their way back to the landing place, their flat-bottomed boat overturned in a shallow and very muddy spot. The three men were all wearing heavy sea boots. One of the Yates brothers got ashore, but the other and my ancestor sank so deep in the silt they could not extricate themselves. I like to imagine them drunk as skunks and knowing that the tide was rising, toasting each other before they drowned.

Pass the whisky bottle, Tame Puti.

Chapter Seventeen

The Tide Incoming and Outgoing

1.

I SHOULD RETURN to my childhood in Kaitī.

My mother's morning routine was to give me and my sisters the usual doses of cod liver oil, castor oil and malt, followed by porridge, milk and bread. Then she would dress me in shirt, trousers and sandals. Much to my irritation, she forced me to be the best-dressed boy in the street, and, on my first day at my new school, Kaitī Primary, she pointed me in its direction. Off I skipped. I couldn't have been happier. I had already assumed the habit of independence and enrolled myself without any problem.

When Kararaina turned five, Mum again pointed me, with Kararaina clutching my hand, towards school with the instruction to enrol her, too. There we were, Kararaina with her curly hair and me nicely dressed, walking down the street. Tāwhi ran crying after us because she wanted to come to school as well.

'Go home, Tāwhi,' I shouted, throwing a stone at her.

Husky Preston was the headmaster, constantly smiling, and I had the good fortune to have a wonderful and sympathetic infant teacher, Miss (Mary Gillanders) Scott. I fell asleep often in class and she would forbid the other children from waking me up. What I most remember about her is her perfume and that whenever she moved she *crackled*, a sound associated with women who wore corsets. Classmate Beverly Bodle recalls me falling asleep in Miss Linton's class, too, while listening to Enid Blyton's *The Faraway Tree*.

I enjoyed school, especially the milk at morning break or hot cocoa in winter. After school I would race home, drop my school bag and then go out to play with my friends Spud Arthur, Graeme Hankey and others until it was dark. After that, it was back home for dinner.

My mother had very good culinary skills learned from being the keeper of the fire and from her housekeeping positions. She would feed us mostly lamb chops, pork bones or fishheads, boiled in the same large pot as the potatoes, pumpkin, kamokamo or watercress. She always gave us a pudding, mainly rice and peaches or a home-made cake with custard. In those days people had safes in their houses, not refrigerators, so she had her own garden where she grew vegetables and went to market for fresh meat.

Once, my daughter Olivia said to her, 'Grandma, your plates are always so colourful.' She was referring to the carrots, beetroot, cabbage, potatoes and meat that we were having for dinner.

Mum replied, 'I've always thought that if you have a little bit of green, a little bit of red, a little bit of orange and a little bit of brown then your diet will be balanced. It's only when you have one or two colours that it isn't.'

She could have taught those fast-food outlets a thing or two.

Teria would still collect me during the weekends. I can't imagine how my mother felt as I went running out the gate. 'Nani! Nani! At last you're here!'

IN OTHER RESPECTS, however, my mother was happy in Kaitī. One of the reasons was that the suburb, being the home of her southernmost kin, Ngāti Oneone, was still within the lands of Ngāti Porou. Originally known as Te Puhi-kai-iti, the suburb was dominated by Kaitī Hill, with Poho-o-Rāwiri at its base. In summer the hill was diamond sharp, cutting a clean edge into the sky. In winter it brooded with low-lying mist. Autumn brought flame to the poplar trees that lined the road circling up to the summit, and burnished reds to the fir and pine trees. In spring the grass was yellow and white with wild daffodils and daisies, and the trees were clothed in bright green leaves.

My friends and I played war games with toetoe spears on the grassy terraces. We rode cabbage-tree sleds down the bumpy slope and raced home-made carts down the road; ascending cars tried to avoid us. In the twilight the older boys liked to sneak up on parked cars in which young lovers were having sex. Once, a young man with his pants down around his ankles, butt-naked and red penis springing free, tried to catch us.

The special quality of Kaitī came, I think, from its separate identity from the rest of Gisborne, which was known as the 'Other' side of Kaitī Bridge. The gut of Gisborne port also created a division. At the mouth of the harbour was a huge reef where local Māori went at low tide — the shallow shelves with their many pools were rich in shellfish.

That same 'special' quality, if you want to call it that, came from the freezing works, the suburb's primary industry. Sometimes, herds of cattle or flocks of sheep would come along Crawford Road, destined for slaughter. My sisters and friends, sitting on a fence, would watch wide-eyed as the stock lowed and baa-ed, not wanting to think about what it meant. The sheep were led by a Judas goat that everybody called Mary.

'Don't follow her,' we yelled till we were hoarse, but they trotted placidly after her, without knowing that she was leading them to their deaths.

Once, Mary stopped to graze at our very fence. She snorted and blew snot at me, and pierced me with her horrible green eyes. *Watch out, little master, or you'll be next.* I almost fell off the fence in fright.

People from the 'Other' side often said that when the southerly wind was blowing they could smell Kaitī. They described the odour as a peculiar combination of dust, cattle and sheep dung, and blood. And us probably.

One of the enduring memories I have is of the clinking sound as the freezing workers walked along the street in the very early morning to go to work. The sound was their mugs and eating utensils banging together as they went through the dawn.

There was another characteristic of Kaitī: Pākehā and Māori lived cheek by jowl together — you couldn't get any closer — and the residents were mainly 'new' Pākehā. I grew up in ignorance of the enormous strains being experienced by our Kaitī kin. Much of their ancestral land had actually been taken to build the houses that made up Kaitī, with consequent loss of cultivations, sacred land and the cemetery at Rākauauē, which was once opposite the freezing works. Areas by the sea regarded as kāpata kai, or food storage, came under threat from sewerage systems, herbicides and general pollution.

Te Poho-o-Rāwiri was a classic case. Where it stands now is its third location. The town took the first site, which included the original village, under the Public Works Act when the harbour was excavated, and the second when it was extended. Toko Te Kani has said that our old people of the day didn't have a show of fighting it. Of course they were heartbroken. They had no other choice but to say goodbye to their kāinga, take the carvings off the wharenui and move to higher ground.

There was another, more insidious threat. Māori who lived in urban areas began to be called 'townies' by our country cousins, creating a kind of double discrimination, one Pākehā, the other Māori. We would always be less authentic.

Ironically, this double bind was the very bond that gave us commonality as neighbours with the Poms, Scots, Irish and Welsh who had come on a greater migration from the Home Country. Here in the dominion of New Zealand, they, too, became not the genuine article.

Then, again, maybe we all had to be less authentic before we could become authentically ourselves.

 3.

CRAWFORD ROAD RAN parallel to Gladstone Road, the main thoroughfare, although you couldn't see it. Our house, though calling it a house would be an overstatement, was on the higher eastern side. The homes opposite us — like those of my mates, Prince and Terry Williams — were on the lower western side. Behind them was Kaitī Creek, which ran sweet and slow in summer but could mount its banks quickly when there were storms.

We had important neighbours at No. 110. Lieutenant Colonel Arapeta Awatere, a relative of my mother, lived there with his wife, Elsie, and their daughters. His whakapapa also involved the times when Ngāpuhi raided the East Coast. Following the Musket Wars, Ngāpuhi sent young high-born men and women to intermarry with Ngāti Porou as a gesture of reconciliation, and one of those men became his grandfather.

Arapeta Awatere had an astonishing childhood, learning from tohunga, and his prowess in weaponry led to his winning, and being presented with, the taiaha named Tū-whakairi-ora. If anything was to mark him for war, this giving of a spear, named for one of Ngāti Porou's greatest warriors, was it. When the Second World War began, and the 28th (Māori) Battalion was formed, he became one of its foremost leaders. His understanding of both Māori and European military traditions — he had studied the battle tactics of everyone from Alexander the Great to Napoleon — combined to make him the leader par excellence of Māori men. He was also an estimable scholar, able to speak in many languages, and he had a great love of English, Latin and Greek poetry, which he could recite by heart.

Propelling Awatere's strategies was a certain inherited warrior fearlessness that made Sir Āpirana Ngata reticent about agreeing to his eventual appointment as commander of the Māori Battalion in November 1943. Whatever those concerns, Awatere led from the front and gave no quarter. And on his return from war in 1945, he spent two years on the road visiting hundreds of marae, wherever men had come to join the battalion, to walk among the families of those who had fallen.

One of those families was my mother's. She asked Awatere point blank how her brother Rangiora had been killed. 'He would not tell me,' Mum said. I think she was glad that he didn't. What had happened in war should stay in the domain of the war god, Tū.

Our house may have had electricity but I have no recollection of that. What I remember is, actually, a basic shack of the kind that the Railways used to house their workers when they were laying down tracks; or it could have served as quarters for the earlier builders of Gisborne Harbour. The front door was in the middle, and you entered immediately into the sitting room with the only bedroom off to your right; my sisters and I slept together in one bed in the sitting room. The back door was immediately opposite, leading to the lean-to kitchen having a wood and coal oven with hotplates, a bench with a tap, and a food safe over the bench. A pathway off the kitchen took you to the bathroom with its claw-foot bath and a basin as well as a tub for clothes. Further along was a tin-roofed dunny.

It doesn't sound like much, does it? But when you're a child you don't know anything different, you don't make comparisons. The circumstances of your lives are what they are.

There was a large empty paddock on our northern side, and on our southern side were our other neighbours, Mr and Mrs Walker. Like Mum, Mrs Walker was a grass widow; her husband was in the navy. She was always well dressed, a very thin woman with chalk-white skin and brown hair, and small eyes that seemed to be constantly squinting. The word febrile comes to mind when I think of her. She favoured fashionable coats with padded shoulders, and she was always puffing on Capstans. I liked the times when Mr Walker came home. He always enchanted me with magic tricks, like rubbing a penny and making it disappear and then finding *two* pennies behind my ears.

They had one son at the time, Graeme, and he became like a big brother. He had freckles and a wide, disarming grin. He and his friends thought nothing of including me in weekend jaunts to the McCrae Baths, where we would swim and, afterwards, share an iceblock with sherbert in it. I would give anything to taste an iceblock with just that piquant tang.

Whenever the women met on the street they called each other Mrs Williams or Mrs Smiler or Mrs Walker or Mrs Paterson or Mrs McKinley. Formal though those greetings were, the women looked out for each other. They were what I called 'The Watchers'. They kept an eye on us as we passed by on our way to and from Kaitī Primary School. They watched out as dusk was falling to make sure we would return from our war games on Kaitī Hill before it was too dark. They didn't have to worry: we were all so afraid of Poho-o-Rāwiri, with its fearsome red carvings, that we never liked being out late anyway.

Their strongest reprimands were reserved for when we played in the unsafe stream. They would yell at us like Mrs McFarlane, Ian's mother, 'Be off with ye, Little Graeme and Little Smiley. Get ye to yer muthers before the back of my hand speeds ye on yer way.'

I can't recall if any of the mothers had a telephone in the house, although I think Mrs Walker did so that she could talk to Mr Walker whenever he was at sea. Most times messages were shouted clearly through the air: 'Witi can stay with us for tea, Mrs Smiler. I'll get Mr Paterson to bring him home by seven.'

Within this realm of women we were safe, but life was always difficult. How hard it was for Mum I never knew until much later in our lives. Dad was paid by cheque, which could not be deposited until he could get to a nearby township. The cheques took three days to clear, and the delays meant that my mother was often out of money for a week or more. Mrs Walker was in the same predicament, and the two women soon pooled their resources. Whenever the money from either spouse came through they would dress in coat, hat and gloves and, with children in tow, go to the vegetable or the fish market at the port.

Sometimes there was a knock at the door as Ian McFarlane dropped by. 'Good evening, Mrs Smiler. Mum told me to bring around these chops that Dad brought home from the butcher's. They're extra and will go to waste.'

And of course, for Māori, there was always Māori kai. Still undiscovered as an acceptable food source by Pākehā, shellfood was a staple in our diet. One of the sweetest memories of my childhood is going shellfishing with relatives at Toka-a-Taiau, the reef that took its name from the rock landmark that had once been there.

One day, I made a discovery, a seahorse in one of the pools of the reef. I still 'see' it sometimes through the soft green water and drifting seaweed of my dreams. Look! Here it comes again, delicate and fragile, shimmering and luminous with light, just as it was in childhood.

IF IT WAS a sunny day, Toka-a-Taiau would already be crowded with other Māori from Kaitī searching for kai moana. There they were, the Williams family, the Terekias, regal Whaea Barbara Kerekere and her handsome children, the Te Kanis and others, dotting the water with their sugarbag sacks and flax kete. The women and children looked like they were kissing the surface of the water as they bent into the reef's pools and searched for pipi, pūpū and other food. They waved and shouted to us, and Mum would say, 'In we go, children.' We ran to join them, pulling off our shoes, grabbing our own sugarbags and racing each other down to the sea.

'You kids stay in the shallows,' Dad would yell. He would already be wading further out to the edge of the reef, where he joined the men in diving for kina, pāua and, who knows, maybe even crayfish. Breasting the waves, he had a sack clutched in one hand and a knife in the other. He used the knife to prise the pāua from the reef because if you weren't quick enough they used suction to hold onto the rocks really tight. Sometimes the men put on diving masks so they could see more easily underwater.

As for Mum, she liked nothing better than to be in the company of the women, especially those who lived around Poho-o-Rāwiri meeting house. Then she could kōrero with them while she was looking for seafood. All the long afternoon those women would bend to the task, their dresses ballooning above the water, and talk and talk and talk and *talk*!

For both Mum and Dad, much of the fun of going to the reef was because they could be with their friends and whānau. It was a good time for being family again and for enjoying our tribal ways. Dad especially, because he was so often away from home, had a chance to catch up with the local men. And for the other males, particularly those who worked at the freezing works, well, the sea and fresh air washed away the smell of the abattoir.

My sisters and I made straight for a special place on the reef that all the children liked to search in. It was our kōhanga, our ocean nursery, the place where all the kids could go, watched over by older siblings and cousins — except for babies like Viki, who were placed under the shade of a tree and looked after by a Nani who couldn't swim.

The pool was the place where the pūpū, or winkles as some call them, were in abundance; we all called it the pūpū pool. It was a semi-circular piece of broken reef, very long but not very deep. Just as well because Tāwhi, my sister, would have drowned, she was so short. But wherever Kararaina and I went, Tāwhi always followed, no matter that we scolded her and told her, 'Go back, Tāwhi! Go back!' As for me, the water only came waist-high.

The rocks surrounding the pool were fringed with long, waving seaweed. Small schools of transparent fish swam among the swaying leaves, and little crabs scurried across the dark floor. The many pūpū glided calmly along the side of the pool. Once, a starfish inched its way into a dark crack.

In that pool my sisters and I discovered the seahorse, magical and serene, shimmering among the red kelp and riding the swirls of the sea's current. Perhaps it had become separated from its colony.

We wanted to take it home. 'Can we, Dad? Can we?'

'If you take the seahorse from the sea it will die,' Dad told us. 'Leave it here in its own home, among its own iwi, for the sea gives it life and beauty.'

Dad told us that we must always treat the sea with love, with aroha. 'Kids, you must always offer the first catch of the sea back to Tangaroa, the god of the sea, for then, with that offering, he will continue to provide rich harvest. Whatever you catch after that is yours, but you must take from the sea only the kai you need and only the amount you need to please your bellies. If you take more, it is wasteful. There is no need to waste the food of the sea, best to leave it there for when you require it next time. The sea is good to us, it gives us kai moana to eat. It is our kāpata kai. As long as we respect it, it will continue to provision us. If, in your search for shellfish, you lift a stone from the reef's lap, return the stone to where it was so that the shellfish's kāinga remains the way they know it. Try not to break pieces of the reef, for in doing so you also destroy the home of the reef families that live there. And do not leave litter behind you when you leave the sea. It is an impoliteness to leave human waste in the domain of Tangaroa.'

Our father taught us to respect the sea and to have reverence for the life contained in its waters. As we collected shellfish we would remember his words. Whenever we saw the seahorse shimmering behind a curtain of kelp, we felt glad we'd left it in the pool to continue to delight us.

As soon as our sugarbags were full, all the children would return to the beach. We played together while waiting for our parents to return from the outer reef. One by one they would arrive, the women still talking, the men carrying their sacks over their shoulders. On the beach we would laugh and talk and share the kai moana between different families. We were happy with each other unless a stranger intervened with his camera or curious amusement. Then we would say goodbye to one another while the sea whispered and gently surged into the coming of darkness.

One weekend Mum and Dad took my sisters and me to the reef again. We were in a happy mood. The sun was shining and skipping its beams like bright stones across the water. But when we arrived at Toka-a-Taiau the sea was empty. No people dotted the reef with their sacks. No calls of welcome drifted across the rippling waves: 'Is that you, Tom? Julia? Haere mai!'

Dad frowned. He looked ahead to where the whānau were clustered in a large lost group on the sand. All of them were looking to the reef, their faces impassive in the sun.

'Something's wrong,' Dad said. He stopped the truck. We walked towards the others of our people. They were silent. 'Is the water too cold?' Dad tried to joke.

Nobody answered him. 'Is there a shark out there?' Dad asked again.

Again there was silence. Then Mr Williams pointed to a sign. 'It must have been put up last night,' he said.

Dad elbowed his way through the crowd to read it.

'Dad, what does it say?' I asked.

His fists were clenched and his eyes were angry. My father never swore, but the word that came out of him was a swear word, big, furious. Explosive and shattering the silence, it disturbed the gulls to scream and clatter about us.

'Tom,' Mum reproved him.

'First the land and now our food,' Dad said to her.

'What does it say?' I asked again.

His fists unclenched and his eyes became sad. 'It says that it is dangerous to take seafood from the reef, son.'

'Why, Dad?'

'The sea is polluted, son. There are pipes out there now, taking everyone's tūtae from the town and pouring it into the water. If we eat the seafood, we may get sick.'

My sisters and I were silent for a while. 'No more pūpū, Dad?'

'Not from Toka-a-Taiau, no.'

I clutched his arm frantically. 'What about the seahorse, Dad? Will it be all right?' In my mind, I always thought of the seahorse as the kaitiaki of the pūpū pool.

We walked back to the truck. Behind us, Whaea Barbara Kerekere began to wave a white scarf and cry out a tangi to the reef. It was a very sad waiata for such a beautiful day: 'Auē, auē.'

With the rest of the iwi, we bowed our heads. While she was singing the sea boiled yellow with effluent issuing from the sewer pipe on the seabed. The stain curled like fingers around the reef. When the waiata was finished, Dad called to the reef in a clear voice: 'E Toka-a-Taiau, we have been unkind to you. We have poisoned the land and now we feed our poison into your waters. We have lost our aroha for you and our respect for your life. Forgive us, friend. Forgive us, Tangaroa.'

He started the truck. We turned homeward to Kaitī and Crawford Road.

'There are other reefs,' Mum said to Dad.

In my mind I caught a sudden vision of many pūpū crawling among polluted rocks. I saw a starfish encrusted with ugliness. And flashing through dead waving seaweed was a beautiful seahorse, fragile and dreamlike, searching frantically for clean and crystal waters.

One of my sweetest memories?

Well, perhaps bittersweet. In urban areas like Kaitī, the tide was going out, just as it was at Toka-a-Taiau, leaving us isolated in the many pools and shallow shelves. Certainly my mother was right, there were other reefs, but one by one they went the way of Toka-a-Taiau.

How many reefs are left?

Chapter Eighteen

Sing, Memory

1.

IN 1950 DAD decided that he wanted to go to the fourth British Empire Games in Auckland, from 4 to 11 February, and our mother would go with him. The third games had been held in 1938 in Sydney, Australia, over twelve years before, so there was great excitement throughout the Commonwealth. The world was returning to normal after the Second World War.

What better place to have the games than in New Zealand?

Somewhere in the nation the Union Jack was being saluted daily. At school assemblies we always sang 'God Save the King' until he died and Elizabeth ascended to the throne. As a child, although I knew the problems of colonisation, there was something persuasive about the fact that New Zealand had been claimed by the English. If Pākehā life was inevitable, it may as well be the English version, and the existence of all those countries painted red on the globe clinched it; I felt they couldn't all be wrong, a 'common wealth' indeed. What might have happened, though, if the Dutch, who had actually 'discovered' us, in the person of Abel Tasman and named us Nieuw Zeeland, had claimed us? As for the French, or the Wiwi as Māori called them, they waited too long in claiming us for La Belle France and, while they were dithering, Captain Cook sailed past and decided to add us to Albion's property portfolio.

Counting travel to and from Auckland, Mum and Dad would be away for twelve days. But who would look after me and my sisters while our parents were away? Mum decided that Kararaina, Tāwhi and I would go to Anaura Bay to stay with my mother's Uncle Rūtene and his wife, Caroline, whom Kararaina was named after, and baby Viki would be looked after by Aunty Kaa. Rūtene and Caroline were the same people our mother had kept the fire for, following her sojourn with the weavers.

Of course Kararaina, Tāwhi and I didn't want to go. We had never been to Nani Rūtene's and Nani Caroline's place, but Mum said, 'You kids are growing up proper little Pākehā.'

This was true, though occasionally my coast cousins like Wallace would try to beat it out of me. While I may have charmed my uncles and aunties, as the townie child, whenever I visited the coast my cousins saw me as a moving target.

'You're all going,' Dad said, 'and that's that.' Just to sweeten the deal, he and Mum bribed us with toys they said they would bring back from

Auckland. I can't remember what they intended to do about our schooling: the beginning of the first term may have been delayed that year. Anyway we would only miss a few days and could go to the local primary.

Dad drove us from Gisborne, and the trip took the whole day. We knew we were leaving civilisation when the road turned to gravel and then ... no roads at all. No sooner had we arrived at Anaura Bay than Dad said quick goodbyes and was off.

My sisters and I must have looked as though we'd just flown in from another planet. I was in my school cap, shirt and tie, belted shorts, socks and shoes, and Kararaina and Tāwhi were cute in summer pinafores and hair curled with ribbons.

My cousins couldn't wait to get their hands on me.

On the first day Nani Caroline smothered us with kisses, said to her children, 'Look after your cousin', and then left me with them. What was she thinking? My cousins looked at me as if they hadn't had lunch. But she had warned them not to touch a hair of our heads and not to dirty our clothes, so I thought I would be safe.

However, my cousins had their own ways of getting around that prohibition. When Nani Caroline had exited the scene they rolled their eyes and asked me, 'Would you and your sisters like to go down to the beach and *play*?' There, after staring at the apparition I presented, they figured out how to handle me and leave me unmarked. One by one they kissed me on the cheek and said, 'We love you, cousin.' Then they lifted my cap, spat on my head and replaced it.

'Think you're better than us, eh?' Buddy asked. 'Just because you live in the town doesn't make a difference. We don't care that you speak all la-di-da and dress in fancy clothes.'

I felt the heat of humiliation on my face and I rushed at Buddy, arms up and ready, my fists bunched. I'd had a few boxing lessons from Dad and I was proud of my prowess.

'Hey,' Buddy said, pushing me away.

My blood was up and I got a few hits in. However, any betting man would have placed more money on Buddy, who was not only taller and heavier but more experienced. With a great sense of shock and pain I found myself floored with a bloody nose.

'You, you *rotter*,' I cried.

Buddy gave me a hiding. That might seem harsh to you, but it was my cousins' ritual, I suppose, and because I fought back I must have gained their admiration; I may have been a townie, but I wasn't a coward. We then played on the beach, rode some horses, and when we returned to the house I looked exactly as I had done before — except for that left black eye.

When Nani Rūtene asked the boys, 'Which one of you did this to your cousin?', I interrupted and told him that Blackie, one of the horses, had kicked me. It was really a survival strategy: I could see hidings every day stretching in front of me, and this was a way of preventing that.

My strategy worked. Of course that didn't stop me from being rolled around in cow shit now and then, or having my clothes taken off and constantly being thrown into the surf: 'Maybe he'll drown.'

Instead I survived.

More than that, I discovered a naturalness, an intimacy, that opened me up to different experiences: not just playing and swimming but also milking cows and going out on the boat to fish or collect Nani Rūtene's cray pots. Very soon my sisters and I asked Nani Caroline to keep our clothes safe in a drawer, and we borrowed clothes from our cousins for the rest of our stay. She mourned that my sisters and I did not know how to speak Māori and often called us her 'moko Pākehā'.

One day, Nani Rūtene and Nani Caroline told us that we were taking a trip to Ruatōria. They had business with Maori Affairs. That news excited everyone, and it also meant that we all had to take a bath. This was how they did it on the coast:

After evening kai, while the girls were doing the dishes, I went with the boys to the washhouse where we filled the copper and lit the fire beneath it. When the water was boiling we stood in a row and swung buckets down the line from the washhouse to the whare, where the bath was.

'Quick! Let's get in now,' Buddy hissed.

Nani Caroline saw him. 'Hey! You boys let Kuikui and the girls go first,' she yelled. 'You make the water too dirty with all the muck you pick up with your bare feet.'

'Yes,' Kuikui continued, 'all the cow shit from the milking, and we don't want Blondie's kutus floating in our water.'

We had to put on our clothes again and wait until the girls had finished.

There was something in the very idea of a bath that always brought out the lady in Kuikui. She emerged from her usual place in the kitchen in a long pink robe and towel turban, positively t-rrr-ipping on her toes to the bath. Following behind her came Matilda, Kathleen, Hope and Alamein like adoring acolytes, holding the scrubbing brush, shampoo and Sunlight soap, which Kuikui would apply to her hair, face and person.

This was no longer the Kuikui who tucked her dress into her pants when playing touch rugby with her brothers, nor the sister who yelled endearments like 'Hoi, kina-head!' or 'Gedoudahere, tūtae face!' This was some other more divine creation. Anybody looking on and listening in as she slipped into the bath would have thought this was Cleopatra swimming in ass's milk rather than in a rusty tub with a candle on the rim. Surrounded by the smaller girls, all in awe of her voluptuous curves, Kuikui would sigh, 'Make some more bubbles, dahlings' or 'Mmmm, more shampoo, sweetnesses' or 'Ooooh, just a little softer with the soap, babies.' And as they ministered to her, Kuikui let them in on the secrets of How To Be Seductive or What To Do If He Wants To Go All The Way. And if she ever heard the irritated yells of her brothers, 'Hurry up, Kuikui!', or the *thump* as a cowpat hit the roof, she simply ignored them: there was a big difference between brothers and *men*.

Was it all worth it? Oh yes, for to see Kuikui transfigured by soap and water, gilded by the moon, queening it across the paddock and around the cowpats back to the house, was to witness a vision. She was the Serpent of the Nile, Anaura Bay-style, preparing to go by barge to meet her hick-town Mark Antony.

Once the girls had finished their toilette I helped my boy cousins empty the bath and refill it. Have a bath in girls' water? No fear! We were just about to hop in for the second time when Nani Rūtene and Nani Caroline came out. 'You boys last,' Nani Caroline said.

Oh, my cousins were so angry because, had they known that their parents would pinch their water, they wouldn't have filled the bath to the brim. But finally it was our turn after all, and there I was, for the first time in my life, taking a bath with other people. Initially I was embarrassed about being in the middle with Buddy, Blondie, Jack and Dickie, especially since they were always dropping the soap.

'Whoops,' they would say as they hunted for it and ended up with a handful of you-know-what. They splashed each other, too. But very soon I forgot my inhibitions.

'Whoops,' I said as I searched for the soap.

We love you, cousin.

What did they mean, they loved *me*? It was *me* who loved *them*.

Nani Caroline was another of my grandmothers. My sisters and I grew strong and brown under her dictum, 'Work first, then you can play later.' I remember once that we were down at the beach and she glanced over to my sisters, and there they were building a sandcastle and looking for all the world as if they were on a beach at Brighton. And there I was, having come in from a swim, shaking myself like a little puppy.

'Are you having a good time?' she asked.

'Oh yes, thank you,' I answered.

'Would you like to sit with your Nani?'

'Uh huh,' I answered.

For a while we sat in silence, watching the waves come in and go out.

And then Nani Caroline said, 'All your bones are here.'

At the end of that holiday, when Mum and Dad appeared on the bluff I really didn't recognise them. Mum didn't recognise us either. 'Where are your own clothes?' she asked.

To be frank, I couldn't have cared less.

2.

FOUR MORE MEMORIES before I leave Kaitī.

I begin with something small, but it proved to be traumatic. One afternoon, on our return from school, Kararaina and I saw Tāwhi running down Crawford Road, screaming her head off.

'Mummy's bleeding,' she cried.

When we opened the door to the bedroom, the curtains were drawn and our mother was moaning in the bed she shared with our father. She had a white towel wrapped around her face and blood was seeping through it.

'What's wrong, Mum?' I was horrified.

She couldn't make words with her mouth, and Tāwhi began to wail, and that set Kararaina off. Eventually I deciphered what my mother wanted me to do. I was to make tea, feed baby Viki and put my sisters to bed.

It was all so simple really. Like many men and women of that era, my mother had had all her healthy teeth taken out. That was the accepted wisdom of the time; it was cheaper in the long run because you would never require a dentist.

For two or three days, my sisters and I ran the household. Although Mum wanted us to go to school, we didn't. Instead, we changed her bloodied towels and wiped the sweat off her face because she began to run a high fever. Her illness distressed us. Our mother was always so strong. This was the first time we had ever seen her vulnerable and defenceless.

Defenceless.

Not much later, an event happened that has imprinted itself forever in my memory.

Dad was still away from Crawford Road when, somehow, my mother's solo status came to the notice of a dark, stocky man who worked for Maori Affairs. He began to harass her; what was worse, he was a relative of Mum's so, when he first began to park his distinctive small black car on the road and came to visit, she welcomed him.

His first call occurred around my seventh birthday because I remember him being there that day. Mum and Dad had given me a trike, which my cousin Wallace pushed me off, and the man from Maori Affairs helped me back onto it. I was accustomed to rough and tumble, and that birthday was the best ever, ending with me and my friends floating some of my presents down the creek. Oh, the short interest span of the birthday boy.

My father resumed working out of Gisborne, and the man from Maori Affairs must have known that money was not coming regularly into our household. He turned up one afternoon and offered to help Mum; she said no. Kararaina was six at the time, Tāwhi was three and Viki was a year-old baby. On the man's next visit, his offer became sexual, and Mum rejected him. That only made his overtures more persistent, but, when she kept pushing him away, he became vicious. He threatened to make life difficult for her. He had friends in welfare, so he said, who could see to it that we would be taken from her.

One day Kararaina and I were walking home, and we saw the car of the man from Maori Affairs parked outside our house. When we went inside, we saw our mother struggling with him.

Don't ever think that young children can't recognise the presence of danger. My young grandson James constantly tries to stop me whenever he thinks his Papa is in a perilous situation. I drove him to exasperation at the beach once when I wanted to go for a swim, and all he could see were mountainous waves. 'Papa! Papa, no!' he cried as he waded out, breast-high. I had to come in, where he took my hand and firmly led me back to the sand and made me sit down, and then he joined me, gulping, and he gave me a look: 'Bad Papa.'

The strangest aspect of Mum's fight with the man from Maori Affairs was how silent it was, as if she did not want to frighten us. When she saw us she lifted her face to the light, looked at me and said, 'Take your sisters and the baby, and get out.'

I was too shocked and frightened, and stood stock still. But when the man backhanded her and she went spinning, and she said again, 'Get out, Witi, and take your sisters with you', I lost it.

In those days I had a bit of a lisp. A few years later, I actually went to speech therapy lessons to correct it. It's absurd, I know, but what I did was to cry out, 'Mithuth Walker! Mithuth Walker!' and I left my mother and sisters there and went tearing next door.

That brave woman came running, skinny and puffed from cigarettes though she was. 'What's going on here? Julia, are you all right? Who is this man? Whoever you are, get out! Get out!'

The man from Maori Affairs left, of course, and then Mrs Walker. I thought I had done the right thing, but my mother said to me, 'I don't want you to disobey me again, son. I could have handled that man by myself. Mrs Walker didn't need to be dragged into it. And you left your sisters in danger.'

I never liked letting my mother down. I felt deeply ashamed of myself.

Finally, 'Don't tell your father,' Mum said. I never did.

What happened next was surprising. As I have said earlier, I always thought of the women of Crawford Road as 'The Watchers'. News must have circulated quickly that Mrs Smiler was receiving unwelcome male attention. The women never mentioned it to Mum but, whenever they saw the man's car parked in the street, one of them would come striding over and say, 'Good afternoon, Mrs Smiler, I thought I would invite you

for a cup of tea' or 'Hello, Mrs Smiler, may I trouble you for some sugar?'
And if they didn't do that, they would stand at their front doorsteps
beating the carpet or smoking a cigarette so that the man from Maori
Affairs knew they were watching.

He soon gave up. I came across Mum and Mrs Walker talking in our
sitting room.

'He'll only go on to some other woman,' Mum said.

Could Mum have really handled him by herself? Probably. She was
always strong.

Why didn't she lay a complaint? Who would have believed her?

Next, I was invited to a birthday party by a young friend I shall call
Allan. I went into town with my mother and we chose a present for him.
However, the day before the party Allan's mother telephoned to say that
he was sick and that the party was cancelled.

'You should go and take your friend his present,' Mum said.

Mum walked me to Allan's address and, as soon as we arrived, we
knew something was wrong: schoolmates of mine were going through
the gate. Mum walked with me to the doorway and we knocked. Allan's
mother answered, and she went as red as a beetroot.

'Witi has brought Allan a birthday present,' Mum said.

Allan's father came to the door. He was uneasy and embarrassed but,
unlike his wife, not without courtesy. 'Now that he's here,' he offered,
'perhaps your son can join the other children.'

'No,' my mother answered.

I really would have loved to go to the party and, seeing as we were here,
why not?

My mother, however, was adamant. That day I learned that there was a
line she would not cross, and she expected me to be as unyielding about
it as she was.

When we returned home, however, and Mum was telling Dad what had
happened, he complicated the morality of the issue. 'Witi should have
stayed,' he said.

Finally, one evening almost a year later, there was a storm over
Tītīrangi. The gods were angry at something some mortal had done.
The thunder boomed and lightning flashed, and I was shaken awake by
Tāwhi, 'I want Mummy.'

The evening was similar to that of the First Telling.

Very soon Tāwhi and I were joined by Kararaina, so I said 'Okay', lit a
candle and we tiptoed to the door of our parents' bedroom and opened
it. 'Mum?'

She was asleep, and Baby Viki was in the cot next to the bed. Kararaina
reached out to wake Mum up.

'No, don't,' I said.

It was Kararaina who pointed out the movement of our mother's paddling feet, under the blankets, as if she was swimming. We uncovered her toes and they were rotating. When we did that our mother started to whimper.

'Where does she go to, brother?' Tāwhi asked. 'Our mother, when she dreams?'

It was such a simple question, but there was huge imaginative potency in it. Certainly there's a scientific name for my mother's disorder, something to do with the interruption of the circadian rhythms of the body during sleep.

I prefer the Māori explanation that there are some among us who are able to travel in their dreams. They travel when their aroha, their mokemoke, love and longing for others, needs to be expressed. Even in these great days of change, when nobody believes in such things, Māori still travel in this way to talk with whanaunga about old ancestral matters that must be resolved, breaches that should be healed, or to tell of taonga, family heirlooms, that need to be found. Most often the travel comes at moments of deep trauma, when something profound is imminent and will affect the whakapapa. Thus, they will travel to farewell someone who is dying and let them know how much they have been loved.

And then Kararaina said, 'If ever something happened to us, Mum will always come to save us, eh.' In her words was implicit faith in our mother, who never backed away from anything, who always confronted her attackers.

It wasn't a question. It was a statement of fact.

The walls of the house in Crawford Road fell away, leaving our mother and ourselves floating in some other dimension.

Chapter Nineteen

When the Shearer was King

1.

THE FOLLOWING YEAR, I enrolled Tāwhi at Kaitī School.

The secretary in the office gave me a form to fill in. I was accustomed to answering the questions, except that I couldn't work out what to write with my pencil in the spaces headed 'Father's Occupation' and 'Mother's Occupation'.

In those days, 'housewife' was not an occupation so that was easy. I wrote, 'She works at home', which the secretary in the office changed to 'unemployed'. For Dad I put down, 'He shears sheep.'

The secretary paused and then she asked, 'Is your father working right now?'

The shearing season had ended early that year so I answered, truthfully, 'No.'

She crossed out what I had written and substituted 'unemployed'.

Great. Now I knew. I had parents who were both out of work.

Let me just try to sort out that little mess and tell you where our family fitted in the New Zealand economic scheme of things. We weren't upper class, middle class or working class. We weren't Pākehā, we were Māori. We were that rural subsection of the New Zealand economy classed seasonal worker. And within that subsection we occupied a subcategory: indigenous seasonal worker.

New Zealand, on the whole, doesn't like that word indigenous. It smacks of the Mexican migrant worker, of being underprivileged, and surely we can do better than that, chaps? The fact was that in those days rural Māori were mainly seasonal workers, and most of us were shearers, fruitpickers and planters for the new forestry industry. Except for crayfishing, fishing was an industry yet to take off.

Shearing was the income-earner for the extended Smiler clan for the four months between November and the end of February; for the rest of the year the whānau lived mainly on the savings from the shearing. We supplemented our income by picking apples or other fruit in Hastings for contractors, travelling to Hawke's Bay to join other seasonal workers coming off the shearing season; we slept in workers' huts and caravans, and during one season my sisters and I joined cousins in Uncle Hape and Aunty Mary's VW Kombi. Sometimes Dad obtained contracts fencing or scrubcutting for local farmers and off he would go to live in a tent with other men while we remained in town.

The worst months for us as a clan were between September and October when money in the bank was low and no cheques were coming in from casual work. As far as food was concerned, however, the whānau had communal crops at Waituhi where, by careful management, we always put down potatoes, pumpkin, kūmara, maize and watermelon. At harvest time, the families would go out and pick what they wanted. Dad was able to get mutton through mates at the freezing works. He also grazed a small flock of sheep on Teria and Pera Punahāmoa's land.

We went to the beach to collect kai moana or into the bush to get pūhā and watercress. Sometimes we joined others on eeling expeditions or netting for flounder, Dad wading deep into the changing tide where the Tūranganui River reached the sea. We practised the usual Māori custom of storing kūmara and potatoes in a small home rua at the back of our house or salting fish, eels and meat and putting the food into a dry safe, away from rats.

One of the characteristics of this kind of living was that, after a visit to get potatoes or kūmara from the communal plot at Waituhi, or slaughtering one of his sheep, I would go with Dad to deliver sacks of food and meat to his uncles and aunties along the road.

'Tēnā koe, son,' they would say to Dad. 'Ka nui te pai mō tō aroha.'

Hello, son. Thank you for the tokens of your love.

2.

I TURN TO the role of shearing in the family.

Within the subcategory of indigenous seasonal worker, shearing clearly played the most important part as our major source of income. It was more than that: it was a family business, our way of life, the way that the huge Smiler whānau of uncles and aunties and rambunctious cousins kept ourselves together. Our family was so closely associated with sheep that Smiler was just another word for shearing.

We were Shearers R Us.

The history of the sheep industry is therefore an integral part of the whakapapa. From the time that James Cook brought the first sheep to New Zealand and settlers established the first sheep farms in the 1840s, the wool industry quickly asserted itself. From 1882, ships fitted out with refrigeration meant New Zealand could export lamb. Until Fonterra turned New Zealand into the dairy capital of the world, the main agricultural receipts came from sheep farming. The golden years began after the Second World War when pastoral farming, boosted by aerial topdressing, took off — and then came 1950, the boom year for wool. Up to then, the main destination of our wool was Britain, but the United States entered the picture; as a result of the Korean War, they decided that wool was of strategic importance and began to stockpile it. Wool prices tripled overnight.

Even as I write this I am smiling to myself and imagining the clatter of cloven feet, the sound of baa-ing sheep and shepherds yelling 'Hoosh! Hoosh!' as they herd a flock past the whakapapa and down the hallway of Haig Street. The entire economy of Poverty Bay, the East Coast and Hawke's Bay depended on the big sheep and cattle stations right at the back of beyond, along dusty roads which zigged and zagged down over culverts, through cattle stops, across fords, through gates that you opened and closed on your way in and out, around hairpin bends and over rickety one-way swing bridges at the very tops of the valleys. The huge two-storeyed homes, with names like Windsor, The Willows, Fairleigh or Tara, symbolised the industry's success. Some had been constructed of stone shipped from England, France or Italy. They had wide entrance halls, their floors shone with marble that had been hauled in by bullock teams. Their staircases were imposing and the hallways were panelled in English oak. The furniture, linen and sculptures had all been collected during regular visits by steamship to the Home Country. The master's study was filled with leatherbound books. There was always a deer's head over the fireplace.

Where were the Smilers? We were getting ready for the season. And that man moving easily between the masters shaking hands and greeting them? That's Dad.

Among the shearers, my father was a king. The closest equivalent I can think of when describing him in his milieu is an Italian word: padrone. He was the patron, the broker who negotiated the shearing contracts between the farm owners and the shearers. I'm staggered to realise that he was only thirty-six when he ascended to this status, and Mum was twenty-nine.

Let me update you on Te Haa-o-Rūhia and his wife, Julia. He is a husband and father of four children: a son he sometimes can't understand, and three pretty daughters. Marriage has matured him. He is still carelessly handsome, with a lock of shiny black hair flopping on his forehead, and he has filled out from Julia's home cooking, no longer lightly muscled but rather bulkier, stockier. Those somewhat dangerous eyes laugh a lot more now.

As for Julia, she has traded in her satin and sequinned dress for more appropriate clothes. These days her hair is kept in place by a wide ribbon. She likes to wear a shirt with pullover, and sometimes slacks rather than a skirt. Although she loves her son and three daughters, there are times when, caught unawares, she can be found mourning the 'blue baby' who, despite her lullabies, died so soon after he was born.

Although neither Te Haa nor Julia ever finished high school, they have done very well to raise themselves from housemaid and seasonal worker to housewife (employed) and shearing contractor. Te Haa has done so by virtue of his natural authority and his astute business sense. His school has been life, and his teachers, Manu Tāwhiorangi and Hine Te Ariki — as well as his parents, Teria and Pera Punahāmoa — have trained him to lead men and women. Like all shearing contractors, Te Haa has developed an infrastructural support system with the Bank of New Zealand, Dalgety's stock and station agents, the Shell petrol company and wholesale food suppliers.

Here's another of his talents: he keeps his own accounts. They're contained in school exercise books which are a bit battered now. When you open the brittle pages your hands start to shake at the way he has ruled the vertical columns, in red ink, and then the names of the members of the gangs in horizontal, in blue ink, and the amounts to be paid to them. The books contain listings of the small monetary koha for those who have lost a husband or have become ill during the season with the notations: 'He koha mo Aunty Maud' or 'He koha ki te whaamere a Cliff'. It doesn't matter that they don't work for the family any more, they are never forgotten.

Imagine him coming, approaching from behind, and looking over your shoulder. He has been out in the sunlight with his shearers, his head thrown back, a full-throated laugh surprised out of him by something one of the young shed hands has said. There are three cars in the drive and, one by one, the boys pile in and back out of Haig Street with a roar.

You hear the back door open and shut as he walks in. Along the hallway he comes, between the whakapapa that lines the walls, and the past is whistling and whispering: *Ask him now. When he comes in, ask him.*

You feel his presence behind you.

'Hello, son, so you are checking up on my accounting, eh?'

You wish you could turn to look at him. Oh, you could die for love of him. Instead, you say to Te Haa: 'I wonder, if ever we had been the same age, whether we would have been friends?'

 3.

THERE WERE A number of other shearing contractors operating in Gisborne, among them Red Fleming, Buddy Smith, Stan Pardoe, Roy Baker and Robbie Cooper. Dad and Cooper were very close, and Dad later worked for him when Uncle Puku took over the family shearing gang.

The contractors organised their own gangs, agreed on which farms would be theirs, picked workers of high quality and established the schedules by which the farmers were assured that their sheep would be shorn when the wool was at its best. When one contractor, say, Red

Fleming, had a night pen full of sheep all waiting and had problems when a shearer didn't turn up in the morning, he would ring up another like Stan Pardoe and ask for help. During shearing season, if ever the telephone rang between 5 a.m. and 6 a.m., my sisters and I always knew help was being asked for.

'All right, Robbie,' we would hear Dad say. 'I'll get a couple of my boys to go out to Huanui.'

If he couldn't find anybody, Dad went.

You can imagine, then, all the travelling the shearers did from November until the end of February. Many years later, when I was living in Menton, France, I saw a modern-day Romany encampment that had come up from Spain to camp outside Nice. My memory immediately went back to those shearing days when the shearers were Māori gypsies travelling from one farm to the next. I couldn't help writing about it.

My mother, sisters, brother and I loved the times when the summer holidays came, school was let out, and we could join our father for the shearing season. The trucks and cars gathered at Waituhi or Haig Street where the karakia would be given: 'E tō mātou Matua i te rangi, kia tapu tō ingoa, kua tae mai tōu rangatiratanga.'

Usually we travelled in convoy to ensure support for one of the other cars just in case its radiator boiled over, tyres were punctured, the battery ran flat or an axle snapped under the weight of our accumulated baggage.

One year Uncle Mafe's car broke down entirely. We were in the middle of nowhere so Dad hitched a tow line, which failed as we were going up a gradient. Uncle's car careened back in a wild ride to the bottom of the hill; the car's brakes weren't working. In the second attempt to get the car up the gradient, Dad lashed a spare tyre to the front bumper of our car and we pushed Uncle's car to the top of the hill. Uncle was supposed to wait for us at the top so we could get in front of him and prevent a dangerous no-brakes descent. He must have forgotten, because no sooner had he reached the top than over the other side he went, or maybe we had nudged him too far across the lip of the mountain.

The car rocketed out of control down to the bottom of the gradient. How Uncle managed to hold the road was a mystery. We agreed later that it must have been because the weight of all the people inside kept the car from flipping on the corners. On our own way down we had to stop every five minutes to pick up pots and pans, bedding, boxes of food and tin plates that had come loose on that pell-mell descent.

Then there were the fords where one car would get stuck in the middle of the river.

My aunties would laugh, 'We could do with a swim.' Out they'd get, their muscled arms pushing until the car was back on the road. One of my cousins, it may have been Elizabeth, discovered that she had natural flotation when she slipped and went tumbling along with the current.

'Help!' she cried. She couldn't swim. She bobbed along, kept afloat by her natural buoyancy, her red dress inflated by trapped air like a balloon. After that my uncles used to sing in jest, 'When the red red robin goes bob bob bobbin' along.'

More dangerous were the swingbridges when some of the boards gave way and the car's wheels went through. We'd all get out and carefully unload the car to make it lighter and then with an almighty *heave* my uncles would lift the car up from the holes in the bridge.

Often roads were washed out or blocked by slips or peppered with mud-filled potholes. Some places had no roads at all. When such hazards or challenges presented themselves, the gang looked to Dad to come up with a solution. While we kids went splashing in a nearby river, he would kōrero the problem with the adults and, by the time we got back, a new route had been worked out. Off we would go, backtracking or sidetracking or driving down to the riverbed and motoring along it until we could get back onto the road.

We drove, pushed, pulled and sometimes carried our cars piece by piece to get to the sheds.

4.

I NEVER NOTICED it at the time but, when other Māori families were fragmenting, the shearing kept the huge Smiler clan together. It replicated the dynamics of an iwi. My cousins and I were all raised in the woolshed and, there, we worked with our parents, uncles and aunties.

As babies, our nappies were changed by whichever cousin, aunty or uncle was nearest. Whoever was doing it would shout to the parent, 'E hika, he tūtae anō.' Another shitty nappy.

When I was seven I was a runner for whoever needed me: the shearers, the pressmen, the wool classers or the cook.

'Get me an orange cordial, boy.'

'Wipe my face for me, son, the sweat's in my eyes.'

'Tell the sheepo to bring more sheep into the pen.'

No doubt I made a thorough nuisance of myself, zipping here and there through the legs of the shearers, among the brooms of the sweepers, and around the hems of the wool classers. Nothing prepared you better for life than being able to negotiate the activity of the shed without tripping anybody up.

I graduated from helping the sheepo keep the pens tightly full to tamping the fadges for the pressmen or fleecos.

'Come and jump in the sacks, boy, and push the wool down.'

And then I worked as a skivvy for the pressmen.

The object was to get onto the payroll. There was no career path. The padrone was watching you and, one day, you found your name down on the list: 'General helper: Witi.'

To be frank it might have been better to remain unemployed. From the moment I was paid I was everyone's dogsbody.

The cook's assistant-to-the-assistant gave me my first lesson in life. I was the lowest of the low, and he had me chopping the wood, lighting the fire in the mornings, carrying water and peeling the spuds. The sheepo's assistant-to-the-assistant, mindful of his position and not wanting me to usurp it, said to me, 'You are a cockroach and cockroaches do not belong in sheds', and he kept me out in the farthest paddock where nobody could see that *I* was the one keeping the flocks bunched up and flowing into the pens. Sometimes, though, I skived off accidentally on purpose: it was worthwhile to get the occasional crack over the head by the sheepo, his assistant, and the assistant-to-the-assistant and to hear them being bellowed at because the shearers were waiting for sheep.

A boy had to do what a boy had to do.

A DAY OF shearing started at 5 o'clock in the morning and finished at 5 in the evening. We had breakfast at 6, half an hour for smoko at 9.45, an hour for lunch at noon, and another half-hour for smoko at 2.45. The three main meals were eaten at the cookhouse. Smoko was delivered to the shed: hot cocoa, tea for the non-Mormons, sausages, eggs, fried bread, and scones with lashings of butter and golden syrup. Sometimes, after afternoon smoko, the cook would stay at the shed to help the fleecos.

Our lives were driven by the phut- phut-*fart* of the engine, the whine of the driveshaft and the loud buzzing of the handpieces. Doors slammed as the shearers went into the pens, and the press clanked as a pair of cousins, Sam and Ivan perhaps, pressed the wool. People shouted all the time. In the background was the constant bleating of sheep and barking of dogs, and whistles as the shepherds moved sheep in the yards.

Sometimes the station owner or his manager would come into the shed. At those times, it was almost like the President of the United States had entered the building. Dad would stop shearing to exchange a few words with him, and Aunty Mary would assure him that the wool was being graded according to his expectations.

It was up to the shearer on the No. 1 stand to set the pace so that the gang could make the overall tally for the day. The other shearers liked it when Dad was top gun because he didn't set up a race with the others to see who could put the most sheep down the chute. Such a race resulted in exhaustion and hasty work, which often showed itself in bad cuts on the sheep's flesh.

If Aunty Mary heard too many shouts for 'Tar!' to go on the cuts, she would growl at the No. 1 shearer and tell him to slow down. The shearer who pushed the pace burned out his gang. Do that and you mightn't have anyone to work for you the next year. Not only that, but the top gun had to show some consideration for the new shearers on the board; the shearer who was a competitor was often not the best mentor. Although it was good to get the job done fast, it was better to get it done well. This was the reason my father was so highly thought of by younger men. He took the time to put down his handpiece and walk down the board to the No. 6 stand. He watched the rookie and gave advice on a better way of propping the sheep, how to count the number of strokes you were taking to remove the coat from the sheep, and whether you were using the correct comb.

My father had a fluid style and the ability to shear without cutting or marking a sheep; he also happened to be *fast*. Out he would come from the pen, dragging the sheep to his station. A pull on the cord to start the handpiece, and he was away. First, two strokes on the top of the head, then the shoulders and into the long blow up the back of the sheep.

One of my girl cousins, Cissie perhaps, would be waiting to sweep the wool away into its own separate pile on the board. Short strokes on the throat and insides of the legs, and longer strokes down and around the nipples or ure (be careful!) to the rump. Next, blows down the right side of the sheep. With deft movements, Cissie swept this grade wool away into another separate pile, flicking the dags out where low-grade wool could be salvaged. Best not to have long fingernails for that job.

Then came the part that I liked, the shearing of the fleece itself. I loved the way the fleece came off the sheep in one piece, like a golden coat. Dad would change the sheep's position in readiness so that it was lying with its left side facing up. He would begin the long curving boomerang blows along the right flank, stroke after stroke, driving the handpiece through the wool, the fleece peeling magically away. Then he propped the sheep on its bum and started the short horizontal strokes on the right side. At every stroke the fleece kept falling away. Both shearer and sheep would be encircled by the fabulous golden bounty.

Aunty Girlie would come along from the fleeco table to pick it up.

'Baaa!' With an outraged kick, the sheep would be sent down the chute into the outside pen.

Easy, eh? Now you try it.

Sometimes I would say to Dad, 'I'll get the next sheep for you.' In I would go and pull the sheep out. Occasionally I tripped and the sheep got away, causing havoc and hilarity as sheepos and fleecos dived for it.

6.

CHILDREN GET OLDER, they become wiser.

I have to say that although I was born into shearing there came a time when I began to dislike having to go to the sheds every summer. There was nothing romantic about it. People worked hard, rivulets of sweat were a constant, and it was a bone-wearying job. I created a lot of hilarity once when, after a school science lesson on the composition of oxygen, I told my uncles that they were working in foul air. Uncle Hape, referring to my father's nickname, Science, because he had such a wide range of knowledge, immediately proclaimed me Science Junior and hoped I would come up with a solution. From then on I was teased unmercifully by my uncles. They never understood that I was alarmed for them at having to work so long within a methane atmosphere.

I must have been somewhat arrogant, too. Although the cultural world of the shearing gang was whānau-driven, the financial world was not, and I objected to it. Indeed, my first inkling of the capitalist and class systems came from working in the shearing sheds, and I had a huge argument with my Uncle Puku, who was paying my girl cousins less per hour for their work than me and my boy cousins. In fact it was my cousin Josephine who alerted me to it.

We were shearing at Tangihanga Station, the farm owned by the Wī Pere Trust at Waituhi. Set up by an Act of Parliament in the early part of the twentieth century, the trust operated for the benefit of the descendants of Wī Pere and paid an annual dividend to family shareholders. And, of course, it provided employment for local families, including our shearing gang.

I was much too big for my boots when, during a smoko break, while all the shearers were relaxing, I decided to have Uncle Puku on about the pay discrepancy. 'Uncle, do you believe that people should be paid equally if they work the same amount of time?'

My uncle was always fair, and looked at me quizzically without answering. He didn't think I would pursue it.

I pressed on. 'At school we've been reading *Oliver Twist* and learning about the Industrial Revolution,' I told him.

Uncle Puku called to Dad, 'Tom? Take your boy out of school!'

The mood was warm and humorous: I already had a reputation among my uncles as a bookish boy and I was at it again. The whole shed started to listen in, the shearers, the fleecos, the pressmen and sheepos.

'So you think that shearers should get the same salary, even though I'm the boss and a better shearer than Cliff on the last stand?' Uncle asked.

'That would be good,' Cliff said.

'And you think that the women should get the same salary as the shearers, even though I'm the boss and shearers work harder than fleecos?'

I could see my aunties looking at each other. 'Hmmmn, do the men work harder than us?'

'And you kids, when you sweep the board or separate the dags, you should get the same?'

I had the temerity to answer, 'Yes.' Maybe I didn't like being pushed into a corner. Certainly, though, I didn't like the idea of reinforcing slave labour conditions through an inequitable payment system. I thought that the better principle was to pay by family group and not by individual, and that if a custom was oppressive it should not be upheld.

'Perhaps it's for you adults to sort out,' I answered, 'but what about my girl cousins? I don't think it's fair that they're being paid less.'

'Do you boys want your sisters to be paid the same as you?' Uncle Puku asked. 'If so, let me know and I'll divvy up your pay and you'll get less.'

Well, I could see from my boy cousins that if I pursued the matter and they lost, I would end up in the sheep dip. But as the engine started up, Aunty Girlie said to me, 'You ask such interesting questions, nephew.'

I hadn't known that as we were talking the station manager John Scammell had walked in and was listening in. He had a soft spot for me because I was a friend of Jay, his son. John must have calculated that the Wī Pere Trust would get a good profit from the wool that year, or maybe something in what I had said resonated with him. When we all received our pay cheques, my girl cousins got the same amount as the boys. The money may have come from the trust itself, but I think it probably came out of John's own pocket.

Uncle Puku was bemused. 'What the boss wants to do with his money is up to him, as long as it doesn't come out of the cheque I have to use to pay everybody.'

The arrangement was a one-off and lasted only as long as we were at Tangihanga Station, the trust giving their own working shareholders a bonus. The next year things went back to the way they had always been.

When Grandad discovered what John had done he was furious. 'You went over your Uncle Puku's head,' he said. He watched me become a (not very good) presser for the gang, and was in earshot when Uncle Puku asked me if I would like to learn how to shear.

Dad intervened. 'Shearing isn't your game, son,' he said to me. Dad was referring to some other ambition — he and Mum had a hope that I would become a teacher.

Grandad misread my father's comment as referring to what he felt was my lack of natural capability for the job. 'Useless,' he said.

My grandfather may have been right. There were two possible ways I could respond to his opinion. Either I could try to become what he wanted me to be or, recognising that I couldn't, hang my head and always allow him to keep his opinion and suffer his ignominy.

There was a third alternative, however, and it was the one I took. I would become what *I* wanted to be. Angered, from this time I truly became disobedient to him.

7.

THERE ARE MOMENTS of splendour that will never dim in the memory. One of these times occured when, after a day of shearing was over, the family would go down the river for a swim. At some point there would be a coy parting between the girls and boys, men and women.

'Why do the women swim separate from us?' I asked my cousin Sam when this phenomenon of the separation of the sexes first occurred.

'Because they're women and we're men, dopey.'

My boy cousins were not averse to giving their townie cuzzybro a hard time, but I gritted my teeth and persevered. 'And why do they go upstream and we go downstream?'

'Would you want to bathe in men's sweat, stupid? And they know you piss in the water.'

A code of modesty prevailed, which prevented the girls from bathing with the boys. Even husband and wives abided by it.

'Women to the right,' Uncle Puku would say, 'and men to the left.'

Every now and then we heard giggles and splashes from the women upstream. Sometimes the water brought down swirls of soap. Once there were squeals of horror, followed by silence. A bra came floating down. One of the shearers caught it in his fingers and lifted it up for all to see. It had hollows big enough to be used for teapots.

'Hmmmn,' he said, tongue in cheek. 'Must belong to . . .'

We waited on his every word, but he knew the price if he overstepped the mark.

The same code also meant that, although children could bathe in the nuddy, the adults had to cover themselves appropriately. Shorts for men, slips and bras and panties for women. I was ten or eleven when my mother said, 'Put some shorts on, son.' I had started to grow hair in my groin.

I wonder if the code had as much to do with Mormon practice as with Māori practice? And I shouldn't blame Mormonism really, as all Pākehā denominations had brought with them their Victorian attitudes to the naked body. Even so, I found it astonishing to watch as my uncles and Dad waded in for a swim in their long underwear.

'Gee boy,' they shivered to each other, 'this water is *wet*.'

Sometimes the shepherds came down and joined us. They were different from us, not cupping their genitals. They had milk-white skin and blond or red hair in their armpits and on their thighs, not to mention their you-know-whats, which were circumcised. Sometimes, when they lay down with us after the swim, they would talk about women.

'Well,' Dad would say, 'we'll leave you boys down here by the river.'

With a piercing whistle he would alert the women that it was time to go back up the track.

Now the tika. I don't know how other people grow into their sexual identity, but I do know that as a child I wrestled with it as much as I did with my cultural identity. These days, whether we like to admit it or not, the sexualisation of children is unavoidable; they cannot be hidden from visual and written sexual material, or, worse, aggressive or coercive behaviour by other children.

And then there's adult molestation of children. Although I like to think that I grew up in a more innocent time, of course that is not true. I have already described my best summer up the coast and bathing with my cousins. I wrote within the context of normal exploratory and spontaneous sexual play, and so it was. But if I was a parent with a child who was going on holiday now, I would prohibit him or her from being bathed in that communal manner or sleeping in the same bed.

I learned about sexuality and sexual difference not by being specifically educated in those two topics as children are today. I am a firm believer in sex education, not having been told the mechanics of sex by either parent and, like most of my peers, working it out for myself. Most of my friends had the same lack of parental explanation, and my sister Kararaina has told me of the trauma faced by young girls who suddenly started bleeding and didn't know what the cause was or what to do about it.

As far as how one should conduct oneself with girls, I learned that from watching the behaviour of my wider kin and, in particular, the visual cues as men and women responded to each other in intimate settings. You might have thought, for instance, that whenever we slept in a meeting house there would be displays of nudity. Far from it, both men and women were modest, draping their bodies with blankets or else changing into their pyjamas and nighties in the outside washhouse. Even when, at the shearing shed, we all went swimming in the river, the behaviour was decorous.

I've always felt it a pity that children learned about sex by talking about it behind the bicycle sheds or in the public bathrooms of the McCrae Baths or by observing graffiti in the public toilets in Peel Street.

As I grew older I recognised the potency of sex and, particularly, sexual desire. There were moments when I felt myself suffused, yes, even at the age of eleven, with sexual need. While childhood was indeed the time — I shall paraphrase William Wordsworth — when meadow, grove and stream, the earth, and every common sight, to me did seem apparelled in celestial light, it was also a time when, no matter that I was pre-pubescent, I would gasp for breath and feel my body's rushing carnal response to a school playmate, female or male.

Over the years I assumed the huge sexual *shake* was only an indication that I came to a sexual physicality earlier than most. But was the truth that, no matter the innocence of my experiences, I had become sexualised?

Even today I am much too afraid to admit the answer.

8.

ONE THING MORE.

My mother, always my mother, would say to me, 'Never leave your sisters alone with your uncles or your boy cousins.' I don't know whether Dad knew of her persistent instruction.

Why? Well, it has to do with that discrepancy when Mum told me she had been six at the time her Uncle Dick Tikitiki Tūpara took her to stay with the two weavers, Hauwaho and Kaingākau. You will recall that in her own account she wrote that she was nine.

I will honour my mother's narrative, but she may have been hiding something. She did intimate this to me that in those lost years when the Great Depression had struck without mercy and people were scrambling to support each other, she had been the keeper of the fire for another family. Mum told me only once, when we were alone one evening. She narrated it with eyes unblinking, in a monotone devoid of emotion. I may have caught her unawares, and then she looked at me, eyes wide, and retracted what she had said.

I used the basis of her account for the following story, with fictional names, and I present it with the proviso that it may or may not have happened. I am sorry that it's written in such a neutral third-person manner but I was so shaken by the story that this approach was the only way in which I could cope with the details.

They were Whiro, Old Sally, and fifteen-year-old Young Sally, their daughter, and the girl went to live with them because Old Sally was bedridden and needed nursing. The girl found the work difficult, especially when Whiro returned on Friday nights from the pub. In his drunkenness he began to lash out at her. Eventually, Old Sally managed to get her daughter away to a boarding school in Gisborne. She could do nothing for the girl.

Whiro's alcoholism meant that the girl and Old Sally lived in circumstances of increasing tension. The Depression only made matters worse, and the remote farm, two hours from a main road, fell on hard times. Old Sally tried her best to keep Whiro away from the girl, but when, in 1932, Sally fell ill, she knew it was only a matter of time before the girl would be violated.

Old Sally died less than a year later, when the girl was eleven. 'Run, girl,' she said on her deathbed. 'Get away while you can.' She had, in her own way, loved the girl but, even as she pleaded with her, she knew the girl would be faithful to her to the end and that she would stay.

At Old Sally's funeral, the girl was nowhere to be seen. When Young Sally turned up to mourn her mother, Whiro told her that the girl had left to go back to her own family. Young Sally wanted to believe her father. She wanted to believe him so badly that she refused to acknowledge the cries for help that came from the dog kennels. Even when she went down there and heard the dogs barking and a young girl calling to her, 'Sally, please Sally', and saw the young frightened eyes that peered at her from the kennels, she closed her ears and eyes to the girl's predicament. When Young Sally departed, never to return, she did so knowingly. She left the girl a prisoner.

Then Whiro took her from the kennels and led her into the house. He bathed her. He joined her by five dog chains reaching from his bed to the kitchen and bathroom.

That night he said, 'Come, girl.'

By the time he had finished with her, she was his. Whenever he said, 'Come', she came. When he said, 'Sit', she sat.

Now, here's the thing: I have wrestled with the question of whether to include this story or not, and there have been many sleepless nights between. I don't go out of my way deliberately to upset my relatives, least of all my sisters and brothers. There have in fact been many challenges in the writing of this memoir, and sometimes I've felt as if there are a whole lot of warriors out there, and no sooner does one perform his wero, his challenge, and puts his rākau or dart in the ground than another approaches.

The old people say that you have two choices: either you pick up the rākau or you don't and retreat. Actually, I have no choice.

I pick up the dart.

On behalf of my mother Turi-teretimana I raise the rākau in the air, proudly, so that all can see. She would want her life to be known to all of you, the mokopuna, and for me to tell you that you must never let sexual abuse of any kind — whether it is long-term molestation, rape, incest — define you or the life that comes after it. She would want to take you in her arms and cradle you and dry your tears and tell you that it was not your fault. Yes, it is trite to say that words are easy and actions are harder and, oh, Mum would know that sometimes recovery for the victim takes years and you run the gamut from self-disgust to feelings of suicide. But my mother would want you to fight hard, not to blame yourself, not to let what happened blight your relationships. Oh child, prevail, do not let it *win*.

Now, let us go forward.

My mother grew up; she grew stronger. All I know is that one day she was able to leave that farm, or perhaps Flowers or her brother Rangiora rescued her, and from there she went to stay with her Uncle Rūtene and his wife Caroline. If what I have briefly outlined to you above indeed occurred, it would explain my mother's caution to me about ensuring the safety of my sisters from men.

The irony is that in those days girls were the ones parents considered at risk. They never gave a thought to boys.

1.

AS YOU'LL HAVE realised, my memories of childhood are pretty clear. It's adulthood, where you can't make out the patterns and meanings, that causes me trouble.

My mother once said of me to my father, when he was telling me a family story and I corrected him, 'Look, Tom, if Witi remembers the incident that way, then that must be how it happened. He's like an elephant' — and she didn't mean it as a compliment.

Sometimes, when I go back into the past, it's as though I am sitting in that room behind my eyes with those ancestors and I am watching my life unspool, as if I am in a cinema of the mind. I can stop the memory, rewind it, stop it again for further examination, take a section of it for closer inspection, and then let the film proceed. Or *they* rewind it, growl at me for details I have got wrong and get me to fix it.

Take it from me, nobody ever wants a person who remembers what other people prefer to forget. In later years, when Dad in his old age was trying to sanitise some of the family's history, I caused him a lot of heartache. I would hold his chin in my hands, peer into his eyes and chastise him as if he was a child: 'Bad boy, Te Ariki. Don't. Do. That.'

Do you think *I* liked having a memory by which I could assess other people's penchant for fabrication? Life would have been much easier without it.

To undercut the capacious nature of my memory, however, I should add that it comprised not only my own faculties but also tribal and family memory. There were stories other people remembered and told about me rather than ones I remembered myself. And they told them again and again as if whakapapa needed to be constantly brought from the past into the present.

Most times I was not the hero of the stories at all but the butt of them. Such a one was the narrative Mrs Walker liked to tell to me as an adult, pantomiming my entrance to her house when Mum was being attacked by the man from Maori Affairs, yelling, 'Mithuth Walker! Mithuth Walker!' I didn't mind that she and Mum were howling with laughter, their eyes streaming with tears. What I was grateful for was that I had been remembered.

How awful it must be to be forgotten.

SEEING THAT I am in memory mode, perhaps I can deal at this juncture with that digression I put aside earlier: Wī Pere and the House of Halbert.

Why? I'm finding it difficult to juggle all the people in my life for you and, at this point, I've lost sight of Teria. There was clearly more to our relationship than the fact that I was the son of her eldest son, Te Haa. Something else accounted for the close emotional bond between us. In an attempt to explain it, I have offered up reasons like 'The manner of our births were similar' or 'My mother said no to her' (would that have not made Teria all the more eager to connect with me?) or 'I was a sickly child', for surely my sickliness would have appealed to Teria's tender heart.

Whatever the reasons, people persisted in telling me that I was a special grandchild. I don't like that description, though I have a sense that there is some truth in it. What I think is that Waituhi kin saw Teria bringing me out to Waituhi as a baby, and then they saw me with her as a boy. And I was serious, always well dressed, inclined to be silent and not like the boisterous cousins.

I was also the kind of boy who didn't mind when Teria wanted to take me by the hand. There's something endearing about a child who puts their hand up to you to hold. Even today, *I* still like holding my daughters by the hand as we are walking along a busy city street. Indeed, when my elder daughter, Jessica, and I were walking hand in hand when she was a teenager she looked at me askance and asked, 'Don't you think we're getting a bit too old for this, Dad?'

I thought 'Yes', and I should have sensed her reluctance, but I must have looked so disconsolate when I nodded okay. But afterwards, I had to have my say. 'Darling, it doesn't matter whether you're ten, twenty, thirty, forty or fifty or older, I'll always want to hold hands with you, so you may as well get used to it.'

I was somewhat shamefaced at my admission, though, so didn't carry through on my statement. Instead I dogged Jessica's steps with a hangdog expression until, some weeks later, as we were walking she took a deep sigh, thrust her hand out and said, 'All right! Take it then.'

In my defence, I like to think that Teria developed other relationships with her grandchildren just as warm and giving and generous as hers with me; they were probably based on other factors. Even though I don't like to admit it, I know that my relationship with each of my grandchildren is different. The elder grandson, James, likes to play with the iPad. His younger brother, Ben, is a lot more physical. And then there's granddaughter Aria, who has me under her pretty thumb.

In my case, Teria's relationship with me was protective; I have no idea, however, what she felt she was protecting. And yes, I acknowledge she did with me things that she didn't do with the others; I must admit I envied their more physical relationship with her.

When I was old enough to start remembering what we did together, it was always associated with driving to one hui or another: going to sleep in the car; waking up when we got to Waituhi or Te Karaka or wherever we went; sitting beside her in private at her home or in public on the marae; being obedient and not straying too far; and walking around Waituhi with her. Now that I think about it, maybe those walks were to build my stamina and help my breathing.

Whatever the reason, their importance became elevated in my work in this way:

Walk the proud land. Oh, how we walked the land, Teria and I, and how fearful I was that I might forget some small yet significant detail of what she told me. And as we walked she would point out the landmarks.

'Look: there, is the boundary between us and the Ngāti Porou to the east. There, we have the Whakatōhea and Whānau-a-Apanui to the north. There, to the south, are Ngāti Kahungunu. The Tūhoe, Children of the Mist, are to our west. Now, within Tūranganui, we have the Rongowhakaata confederation, Ngāi Tamanuhiri and Te Aitanga-a-Māhaki. The boundary of the Rongowhakaata confederation begins at the sea north of Muriwai and runs along the Oneroa Beach as far as Waikanae. There lies the boundary between Rongowhakaata and Te Aitanga-a-Māhaki, running to Mākaraka, south-west across the Waipaoa River to, and up, the Waikākāriki Stream, past Patutahi, then east to join the Ngāi Tamanuhiri tribal boundary. Watch even closer, mokopuna, for now I must point out to you your lands of Te Whānau-a-Kai. Commit what I tell you to memory.

'We are five miles from Patutahi. Ramaroa Pā is our ancient hill fort. Taumata-o-Tūmokonui is our highest peak. Our family marae is Rongopai, in the Waituhi Valley. Our closest kin in the valley are Ngā Pōtiki.

'E mokopuna, we have ruled here for over a thousand years. We had eternity in us. Then came the Pākehā.'

In later years, when I told my friends of those walks with my grandmother they would tell me of similar haerenga with their kuia. It is true indeed that the women are the keepers of the land.

There was also a tradition that my mother began, which Teria maintained. This was for me to take a nap as soon as my sisters and I returned home from school. Teria's version of it was to say to me, 'E Witsh, haere ki te moe.' My aunties and uncles told me that sometimes when they were talking too loudly she would admonish them saying, 'Quiet, e Witsh is asleep.' This clearly astonished them, 'E Witsh sleeps in the middle of the *day*?'

One afternoon I can remember waking up in a side bedroom and trying to find Teria in the homestead that everyone called the 'Blue House'. I stepped onto the verandah, intending to look for the bedroom she slept in with Pera. I took a diversion through the large kitchen at the back and walked through the living room: settee and armchairs, a ticking clock and a radio cabinet that always fascinated me. When switched on, the radio hummed and a large glass orb would glow like the Eye of Horus.

On reaching the bedroom, I came upon Pera fondling my grandmother. Her slip was half off her shoulder and her hair, unbound, shone in the afternoon light; a hint of a smile was on her lips. I didn't know what was happening between my grandparents but I saw enough to make me feel angry with Grandad. When Teria saw I was there she pushed him away, covered herself and came to me, shutting the door behind her.

Just before the door shut, I saw that Pera was angry too.

At some time when I was growing up, one of Teria's brothers, Koro Mafeking, stayed in a front room on the verandah. If Teria wasn't around I liked to visit him. He was bedridden, a large dark man who breathed in a very heavy way and had to be looked after. Retired from being a Māori Land Court clerk, he was surrounded with whakapapa and other books. Once my cousin Josephine came to empty his bedpan and help him take a wash from a basin of water. When I said I would help she said in her sweet voice, 'Not you, cousin.'

There were two special places at the homestead. The first was the large outside iron pump; you worked the handle to bring up the cool water from an underground spring to the tin barrel on the surface. Teria must have noticed my fascination with the pump because one birthday she bought me a toy, a deep-sea diver who descended into the barrel and could be made to ascend by pumping air down his tiny breathing hose.

The second place was a wall in the sitting room. On it were large framed hand-tinted photographs of my ancestors. One of them was a severe-looking man, Wī Pere, the parliamentarian.

I PRESS NOSES with my ancestor.

'Don't forget to mention my father's other children,' he says. 'I was not the only one in the first Halbert generation to work for the iwi Māori. From his second wife Pirihira Konekone came my elder half-brother, Ōtene Pītau; my brother and I were close all our lives. And he became as important a leader in the resurgence of mana Māori — and not only in the Gisborne area but throughout Māoridom. Let everyone know, mokopuna, that my brother hosted a legendary meeting of the Kotahitanga parliament. Just as I worked within parliament, he worked without.'

This is what happens when you hongi your history, other stories fall out. For instance, in acknowledging Ōtene Pītau I discover I must also make my mihi to the chief who adopted him, Raharuhi Rukupō of Rongowhakaata and Ngāi Tamanuhiri.

Born circa 1800 at Manutuke, Rukupō has often pounced on me and given me a *shake* to remind me of the mana in Māoridom. His early life was filled with travelling in Te Whakatōhea, Ngāti Porou, Ngāti Toa and Ngāti Wai. However, at the death of his elder brother, Rukupō returned to Tūranga, in the 1830s or 1840s, and was given the name of Lazarus, because he had been as one who was dead and now was alive again. He assumed the mantle of chieftainship and, although initially a friend of the early missionaries, soon came to believe in the proverb: 'E ngaki atu ana a mua, e tōtō mai ana a muri. The missionary comes to clear the path for the soldiers, who in turn come to clear a path for the land grabbers.'

When the Crown was going about the purchase of land to raise Gisborne as a town, Rukupō opposed the sales. He was at the Battle of Ōrākau in 1864 and, the following year, when the Pai Mārire envoys arrived in Poverty Bay, he supported them. Now Rukupō was not only a chief, he was a master carver, and throughout his early travels had participated in carving some important buildings such as Kaitangata on Mana Island and war canoes such as *Te Toki-a-Tāpiri*; he is regarded as one of the greatest tohunga whakairo Māoridom has ever known. In the 1970s, when I had achieved a modicum of fame, I wrote, for Foreign Affairs, a booklet called *Maori*, which was being distributed throughout the world. For publicity purposes I was scheduled to have my photograph taken by the Tourist and Publicity Department. I drove with the photographer to the Dominion Museum, Wellington, and without even noticing my surroundings found myself eye to eye with a magnificent carved whare rūnanga. I was just about to step over the lintel when:

'Wait a minute, hold on,' I said to the photographer. 'I have to take my bearings. Where am I?'

So, Ihimaera, tēnā koe, e te mokopuna. Eyes looking up from beneath the water / Teria asking me, E Witsh, so what great wisdom did the Pākehā teach you today?

And then I realised I was at the portal of the house known as Te Hau-ki-Tūranga. A memorial to his elder brother, Rukupō had constructed it during 1842 and 1843 soon after his return to Manutuke. I had never seen the meeting house before, but I remembered Dad telling me: 'The house was stolen from the people, son. Your ancestor Wī Pere, his brother Ōtene Pītau and sister Keita were among many people who tried to get it back.'

Well, the story was more complex than that and involved a visit by J.C. Richmond, the Minister of Native Affairs, to Gisborne in March 1867, twenty-four years after the wharenui had been built. Richmond, who was also during that visit acting director of the then Colonial Museum, saw Te Hau-ki-Tūranga. He clearly knew a work of art and this is an account, from Rongowhakaata sources, of the circumstances surrounding its removal:

'Richmond put forward differing versions of how he acquired Te Hau-ki-Tūranga for the Crown but the brief facts of the case, as related by other more reliable participants, are that, the day after his big hui with Tūranga iwi, he instructed Captain Fairchild, the master of the government steamer *Sturt* carrying the Crown party, to travel up the Waipaoa River, dismantle the whare and load it onboard. Despite being assured by Richmond that Māori had assented to the action, Fairchild encountered opposition from the few Māori then present at the scantily populated Ōrakaiapu kāinga. Together with Biggs he arranged the payment of £100 to unknown Māori to overcome this opposition, but later admitted that he doubted that the recipients of the money were the "right people" to deal with in this matter. After the payment was made, further Māori arrived and objected more strenuously to the assault on Te Hau-ki-Tūranga, but Biggs had departed and as Fairchild was not sufficiently adept with te reo Māori to debate the matter with them, he simply ignored their protests. Indeed, continued protests were forcefully overcome and Māori intimidated into permitting Fairchild to proceed.

'During the night, after Fairchild's crew had ceased their work for the day, Māori arrived with a team of bullocks and a sled, apparently intending to remove what remained of the whare to the safety of the bush. Again they were forcefully opposed by Fairchild's men, and in the morning his work was completed and Te Hau-ki-Tūranga was removed to Wellington, where it remains to this day.'

It can happen to you so quickly, being in one reality and then suddenly being given that vigorous shake to your soul. I had to take a moment to pay homage to the house and to the great achievement of my ancestor. Thus did I bow my head to Te Hau-ki-Tūranga, 'Forgive me for being so presumptuous as to saunter up to your doorstep, o sacred house, and not acknowledge your sorrow and that of your own, great rangatira.'

To continue with the Halbert offspring, from Thomas Halbert's fifth wife, Keita Kaikiri, came four of Wī Pere's half-sisters: Kate, Mere, Maata and Sarah, who were also as significant to politics as their brother. Remarkable women, they forged important alliances throughout the district with Kate becoming Keita (Kate) Wyllie (that's her place, the Wyllie Cottage next to the Gisborne Museum) and then Kate Gannon. She was a well-known public figure in Gisborne, maintaining a strong and vocal opposition particularly to Māori land alienation.

The blood from Thomas Halbert courses through the whakapapa lines of Māori whānau in Tūranga and also, by collateral alliances, creates a network of associations all aimed at one particular imperative, to retain Māori mana, and in particular land, at all costs.

Cut to 1971. While on honeymoon in England, Jane and I made a mad dash to the top of Scotland and en route stopped at Newcastle-on-Tyne. I wondered if Thomas Halbert had been sad to leave the city, freezing though the weather was.

But, ancestor, look at *you*, look at *them*, your children.

I think he would have been pleased.

Chapter Twenty-one

Wī Pere, Parliamentarian

LET US PAY attention now to Wī Pere himself.

The Halbert in his name tends to get detached as his political career takes over, an example of the way he shed his European identity like a lizard its skin, so from this point I shall simply refer to my ancestor as Wī Pere; after all, he himself quickly decided which of his two heritages he would favour.

In 1848 Wī Pere began his political career when, acting as proxy for his mother, he mediated in a war being fought between Rongowhakaata and Te Aitanga-a-Māhaki; he was only eleven. Four years later, he again intervened in an impending action involving the same two tribes, with success. As he himself wrote, 'I was frequently sent to settle minor disputes which were constantly arising, and never failed to avert bloodshed.'

My ancestor had an ambivalent relationship with Te Kooti Arikirangi. If we take 1832 as Te Kooti's birth year, Wī Pere was only five years younger and from 1853 you can chart the careers of both men as two comets in the sky. Although one was headed for ignominy and the other for acclamation, one was not *exactly* on one side and the second on the other.

For instance, at the time of Te Kooti's great escape from wrongful imprisonment on the Chatham Islands, Wī Pere was prevailed upon by Māori chiefs to persuade Te Kooti to surrender. 'I am in the hands of the Almighty God,' Te Kooti replied, 'and will not return until the Almighty so directs me.' Much earlier, however, Wī Pere had actually protested at the sending of Te Kooti to the Chathams without trial.

Again, although Wī Pere then joined the Native Contingent against Te Kooti and served under Major Charles Westrupp, he was known to be sympathetic to the rebel leader, a sense of respect that remained right up to Te Kooti's death.

IN 1857 Wī Pere married Arapera Tautahi O Te Rangi. They had a child, Te Pakaru, who died in infancy. Their son, Hetekia Te Kani, was born in 1858, their daughter, Mere Tahatū, in 1863 and a younger son, Te Moanaroa, in 1865.

My ancestor held the rank of captain in the forces under Major Rāpata Wahawaha, and saw further fighting under Major Pitt and Captain Thomas Porter. Before Te Kooti's infamous sacking of the military garrison at Matawhero in 1868, it was Wī Pere, aged thirty-one, who stationed sentries at Te Ārai, Ngātapa and Waikohu, nine men at each redoubt. But after a couple of months the commander at Matawhero, Major Biggs, called them in, substituting a smaller guard that rotated between the posts every three days.

Te Kooti took advantage of this and, in Wī Pere's words, 'Te Kooti swooped down through Ngātapa on to Matawhero, and Major Biggs and Captain [James] Wilson were taken by surprise and killed in their own houses, as also was my uncle and my brothers.' Not long afterwards Wī Pere himself was taken prisoner by Te Kooti. His companions were all put to death, but Te Kooti yielded to the influence of Wī Pere's iwi and spared him.

As I have mentioned, the relationship was full of ambiguity.

Now from this point I have to tread carefully because the regional history is a minefield. I will also have to beg your indulgence and patience as I try to explain why Wī Pere became the man many of his people considered could rehabilitate their political and social circumstances after the Te Kooti Wars.

Remember how I told you about the founding of Gisborne on land deals, some of them dodgy? Although that had continued with further suspect Crown purchasing, that was as nothing compared with its acquisition of land once Te Kooti was defeated. To cut to the chase, the Crown proposed to punish his followers by operating a new way of obtaining land.

Te Whānau-a-Kai, Te Aitanga-a-Māhaki, Rongowhakaata and other tribes were pressured to surrender the *whole* of their tribal lands to the Crown. (Even Ngāti Porou were on the list, and they were outraged for very good reason.) A Native Land Court was established so that Māori could come before it and, if they could prove they were not Te Kooti followers, they could claim their portions back. Yes, exactly.

On 18 December 1868 the Crown extinguished the Māori titles for all the following land: 'Commencing at Paritu on the sea coast, to the northward of the Mahia Peninsula; thence running straight to Te Reinga; thence along the Ruakituri River to its source in the watershed range dividing the East Coast from the Bay of Plenty; thence along the summit of the said range, that is to say by Maungapohatu and Maungahaumi to Tutamoe thence in the direction of the sea by Pukahikatoa, Arakihi, Wakaroa and Rakuraku to the sea at Turanganui; thence along the sea coast to the commencing point at Paritu.'

Wī Pere and many others considered the consequent work of the Native Land Court and its various commissions as iniquitous. Te Whānau-a-Kai, of course, could not prove that we were not Te Kooti followers, and we therefore suffered dearly. Fifty-six thousand acres were taken from Te Whānau-a-Kai, mainly the Patutahi–Kaimoe Block, and given to Pākehā soldiers and settlers seeking just reward for having fought for the Crown. Some Ngāti Porou, I have to say, also benefited.

Other reparations were paid. I have already referred to Te Hau-ki-Tūranga. Can you imagine what that must have been like, the lamentations of the people, on the day the ancestral house was severed from the earth? The reparations got even more personal when women were forcibly given to the soldiers as concubines.

The consequences? Well, just as had happened when Gisborne was purchased, the Crown thought that Māori would get over it. We didn't.

Instead, during the 1870s a repudiation movement emerged in Hawke's Bay. Wī Pere was one leader of the movement, Hēnare Matua was another, and many other chiefs joined them.

3.

WĪ PERE SAW that dealing with the iniquitous Land Court system meant long and fractious cases as Māori tried to claim back what was theirs — and they were often at loggerheads with each other. Looking beyond the court's work, he also divined the long and difficult rehabilitation, economic as well as political, that would follow. Inevitably Māori would sell what remained of their land, and the Crown was the only buyer in town.

He was attracted by an interesting alternative to partner with lawyer and politician William Lees Rees in creating a competitive commercial entity. And so another buyer came to town: the East Coast Native Land and Settlement Company, a 'land bank' wherein Māori could vest rather than sell their land.

I'm shorthanding again, always a bit of a risk, but the partnership venture ultimately attracted Māori landowners to commit to the company a quarter of a million of acres from Māhia Peninsula to the East Cape. The idea was then to settle some 2000 or 3000 families from Britain on the principal of cooperative colonisation. Wī Pere was attracted to Scottish crofters as a good fit with Māori landowners.

The Wī Pere–Rees initiative appealed so much to Māori that my ancestor was asked to go into national politics. In those days the Eastern Māori electorate comprised three main tribal groupings: Ngāti Kahungunu, Tākitimu and Mātaatua. In 1884, Wī Pere successfully contested the election. His support came from Tākitimu and Mātaatua, the latter containing the very important Ringatū vote; note the implications of the supporters of Te Kooti pitching in behind Wī Pere.

Another significant contemporary of Wī Pere in the repudiation movement was Riperata Kahutia. When her father, Kahutia, died in about 1860, she took over his attempts to redeem land that had originally been given away or sold, and to preserve Māori access to areas of traditional kai. In 1873 and 1875 she appeared at court hearings over a land block known as Awapuni, against other Māori claimants. Her kōrero at the 1875 hearing has gone down in Gisborne Māori history as one of the most eloquent and forceful of our ancestors. She spoke for over an hour, cross-examined others on their rights, and in the end won her way back in. One of her descendants, Pare Keiha, is just like her; he is the Māori pro-vice chancellor at Auckland University of Technology and his negotiation skills are formidable.

Wī Pere was forty-seven and on his way to parliament. What haunts me here is that he suffered two family deaths at this time: his beloved daughter, Mere Tahatū, died aged twenty in 1883, and his mother, Rīria Mauaranui, in 1884. Did she see her son leave for Wellington before she died? I hope so. Whatever the case, Rīria Mauaranui's place in Wī Pere's work and life is acknowledged in a most symbolic way. I remember the revelation of it like this:

'E Witsh, take my hand.'

My grandmother and I were standing in front of Rongopai, the painted meeting house that was also regarded as the marae of the Pere whānau. Although some of my cousins were afraid of it, I never was. I thought it beautiful with all its paintings of ancestors around the walls.

Not many people visited the meeting house. Apparently there was a tapu, a restriction on it, but Teria crossed the paepae and pushed open the front door. The movement caused dust to swirl like motes of gold which, as Teria used her hands to clear a pathway, only made the dust mount higher.

I couldn't see much to begin with. Then the sun shone through the doorway and the sparkling dust was like a golden pathway striking through to the middle of the meeting house. More than anything, I remember the odour of the floor. Compact hardened dirt, and the dry pungent tukutuku reed panels. Then came the sense of different pressure in my ears, of walking from the present into the past as we went inside.

'Let us pay tribute to our tīpuna,' Teria said. She led me slowly out of the sunlight, and I watched her as she criss-crossed the dirt floor, speaking to the various panels. They were painted with ancestors.

Deeper and deeper we went into the stomach of Rongopai. And there, at the back wall, Teria stopped. In front of us was a panel, and on it was painted a man with a tattoo wearing a funny hat and a military coat. He was in profile, and he was wearing boots with spurs.

'This is Wī Pere,' Teria said. 'And there is his mother with him.'

I couldn't see Rīria at first. Then I made out a figure sitting on Wī Pere's shoulders. She looked like a bird. Much later in life, I always thought of the figure as being like an owl, like Pallas Athena. At the time, however, I think I giggled. My childish laughter must have sounded shockingly loud within the house. Teria calmed me down; perhaps she asked the ancestors to forgive my intemperate humour.

'She offered guidance to Wī Pere,' Teria continued. 'She always whispered in his ear, just as I will always whisper into yours.'

If you ever go to Rongopai, at Waituhi, there is a wooden floor now, and a switch which, when flicked, turns on the horrible fluorescent tube lighting. Don't turn on the switch. Try to arrive when the sun is low enough so that when you enter the meeting house, you are ushered in by natural light.

Pay your own homage to Wī Pere and his mother.

1.

I NEED A flourish of pūtātara at this point, the equivalent to the trumpets that would have been used if the life of Wī Pere were performed like, say, *Henry V*, for it has all the drama of a Shakespearean play.

And with that flourish of trumpets, come with me for a walk down Peel Street, Gisborne, to the Peel Street Bridge and hang a right. See that obelisk on the riverbank? It's the Wī Pere memorial.

2.

SOMETIMES, WHEN THERE was not enough time to go out to Waituhi, Teria would take me to have fish and chips at the obelisk.

On the occasion that I am remembering, my sisters Kararaina, Tāwhi and Viki were with us. Teria purchased our meal from the Lyric Café, which was the best fish and chip shop in town, right on Gladstone Road opposite the Kings Theatre; I think it was owned by the Moleta family, who were part of the Italian community. Papa Moleta always had a beautiful clear-skinned Italian girl or handsome boy serving at the counter, and if he himself was around he liked to talk to his Pākehā and Māori customers.

Officially unveiled on 9 April 1919, the obelisk was over twenty feet tall. Made of handsome grey granite with red columns and ornamentation, it was situated on the town side of the Taruheru River; on the other side was where Wī Pere had one of his Kihipani (Gisborne) houses, the large and somewhat sumptuous Fitzherbert Street residence with a wrap-around verandah on three sides. The house is no longer there, its site now taken up by the offices of the Gisborne District Council.

There's a plaque on one side of the memorial, which reads: 'Erected by the Government of New Zealand and the Maori people in memory of Wi Pere, 1837–1915.'

I always associate those fish and chips outings with cold days. On this occasion my grandmother, sisters and I had our own separate newspaper packets, but usually Teria and I shared one. You ripped a small hole in the wrapping, and the smell and steam would waft out. Sometimes the chips were too hot and you had to blow on them to cool them down; your breath would turn to jets of mist. The meal was accompanied by raspberry or orange fizzy drink. My sisters and I poked out our tongues to show how bright red or yellow they were, and I chased Kararaina, Tāwhi and Viki around the obelisk or else played rolling down the slope towards the river.

No doubt Teria took the opportunity, when we had tired of playing games, to whisper in my ear more stories about Wī Pere and his days in parliament. My cousin Joseph Pere and others have written an excellent biography of our ancestor, and so too my Uncle Hani. He gave his manuscript to my mother for safekeeping and, if you would like to read it, it is under the bed of the room just off the dining area at 11 Haig Street. In both accounts it is clear that Wī Pere took to the debating chambers of the Pāremata (parliament) o te Pākehā as to the manner born. There is, though, one description of him that is a bit sneering: 'Wi Pere can be described as being of a very dark disposition and though only a half-breed is in disposition and taste "a Maori of the Maori". He is said to entertain an intense hatred of the Pakeha and his alleged connection with the Te Kooti troubles in 1868 has made him an unpopular man amongst the settlers.'

And here are extracts from another description of Wī Pere: 'His features are decidedly European … His manners are courteous and dignified … What a change in one man's life. The little wild-root eating savage metamorphosed into a grand courteously mannered member of the House of Representatives.'

With that dual heritage of his, while he could maintain his Māoriness, Wī Pere learned how to charm and lull sensibilities.

Once, when I was involved in the making of a television drama, the producer, Robin Scholes, needed an actor to play Wī Pere and, knowing I was a descendant, she exclaimed, 'Witi's got the charm, he could do it.' Alas, although the drama got made, Wī Pere wasn't written into the script so my cameo never came about.

What was Wī Pere's true purpose in parliament? I often heard it said admiringly by Māori relatives in the 1960s that he vowed to drive the Pākehā back into the sea whence they came. But that doesn't quite square with his intentions, as illustrated by the commercial operations. Nevertheless, I shall call him a Māori nationalist because in Hansard you can see him enunciating patriotic intentions. The words make dry and dusty reading but they are clear: let Māori control our own destiny.

However, at the same time as Wī Pere was ascending in national politics, his and Rees's company was having big problems. For one thing it required £500,000, which Māori did not have. For another, the government was resistant to the idea. For a third, clear titles could not be given on the major part of the land vested in the company, which pretty much negated on-selling to Pākehā settlers. For a fourth, Auckland investors were getting in on the act and changing the nature of the entire venture.

It was a bewildering time for Māori voters.

There was a celebrated hui at Pākirikiri, the home of Wī Pere's half-brother, Ōtene Pītau, in the run-up to the election of 1887. Four thousand Māori and settlers assembled to open a meeting house called Te Poho-o-Rukupō, which Ōtene Pītau had constructed to honour his foster father. Attendees also came to hear Wī Pere and James Carroll debate what was known as the Native Land Administration Act of 1886, which ended individual Māori land deals and private buying by Pākehā. It must have been enthralling to hear both speakers going hard against each other. Carroll brought up the settlement company; it wasn't looking good.

In that same year, Carroll defeated Wī Pere and took the Eastern Māori seat from him.

3.

FROM THIS POINT on, things started to unravel for my ancestor.

He was still fighting when he and William Rees went to London, in 1888, to raise capital. Rees appeared before the House of Commons. The Earl of Sheridan, head of the committee considering the matter, sought information from the New Zealand Premier, Harry Atkinson, who replied that the company did not have official backing.

As a consequence, Wī Pere and Rees sought to raise the capital by borrowing against the land, giving mortgage rights to the Bank of New Zealand. In 1892 the company was wound up, but it had been a sorry, two-decade-long saga of mounting debts and desperate attempts to pay them off, which still angers many Poverty Bay Māori.

In 1894 Wī Pere rallied and made a return to parliament as member for Eastern Māori. He was re-elected again in 1899; in that same year, with the land company debacle in mind, my ancestor managed to retrieve for his own descendants the entity that I mentioned earlier, which became known as the Wī Pere Trust. His state of mind about Māori politics and the difficulties of endeavouring to fight for Māori within the Pākehā political frameworks of the time can be gauged from the following story.

In 1903 Premier Richard Seddon offered the Māori King of the Waikato, Mahuta, a seat on the Legislative Council; this was following the submission of his sovereignty to the New Zealand government. A cartoon published at the time showed Sir James Carroll (Timi Kara) putting a hook in the mouth of King Mahuta. As a result the whole of the King Country was opened for Pākehā settlement. When King Mahuta came to Wellington to attend his first session of the council, Wī Pere looked at him intently and then smiled; there was an ironic lilt to his voice, one tinged with reflection and bitterness. He began his welcome, and the floor fell into silence.

'There was a certain owl,' he began, 'who lived in the darkness and fastnesses of the forest. While in his protected surroundings he was one day attracted by the joyful crying of the other birds outside the forest. Oh! thought the owl, what a lot of good things there must be there. He flew through the trees, but on reaching the forest edge his eyes were blinded by the light and he was obliged to perch on a tree. A man saw the owl and took a firebrand in one hand and a stick in the other. As he neared the owl it prepared to fly, but the man blinded the bird with the firebrand and stunned it with a stick. He then put it in a cage and made an ornament out of it.'

The Legislative Council began to laugh. They thought that Wī Pere was telling one of his usual nonsensical jokes. But he raised his hands to stop the laughter and put out his arms to King Mahuta: 'Welcome. The owl is you and we, the members of parliament are the other birds. The man is the prime minister, the firebrand is the bundle of notes for your salary, the stick is your oath, and the cage is the house of parliament.'

One gets the sense that Wī Pere realised that the Māori cause was at its lowest ebb. In that same year of 1903, Te Whānau-a-Kai made three major petitions about the Patutahi–Kaimoe Land Block, one put forward by Peka Kerekere and seventy-three others, to no avail.

What use, therefore, were the talking birds in the parliament of New Zealand? All of them had been blinded and stunned, and there they sat, the elected representatives of the Māori people, on the perches of the Pākehā. Wī Pere's words are a salutary warning to all those brave young Māori politicians who, today, still litigate on behalf of the people, in the cage that we know as Te Pāremata o te Pākehā.

My ancestor had a good innings. Although Āpirana Ngata won Eastern Māori from him in 1905, the Liberal government appointed him to the Legislative Council in 1907, a position he retained until 1912, when he was unseated on a technicality: despite his attempts to attend the meeting in Wellington, the council had completed its session. Still, he and Te Whānau-a-Kai, in 1914, kept petitioning for the return of confiscated land.

Wī Pere died on 9 December 1915 and his three-week-long funeral was held at Te Ārai, Manutuke. His embalmed body lay in what the newspapers described as 'an oaken casket'. Mourners from throughout the country came to pay their respects.

My father, Te Haa, was born in the same year that Wī Pere died, six months earlier. Dad liked to surmise that his great-grandfather would have held him as a child and blessed him, and it's not outside the bounds of possibility. Wī Pere's influence guided Dad throughout his life, and he constantly judged all his actions according to his ancestor's principles. The family and the land that supports us come first, everything else comes second.

Dad was the last living link to the times of Wī Pere. Touch him, and you touched our ancestor.

I have only been to the Waerenga-a-Hika vault twice and, of course, the first time was with Teria. Then I did not know where we were or what the place was. Only on the second occasion, when I was older and with Dad, did I realise I had been there before.

The first time, the car slowed down on the main road and then turned in. I don't know who was driving — it might have been Grandad.

'We won't be long,' Teria said. She put out her hand, and I took it.

As we walked along the driveway, I wasn't taking much notice of the surroundings — a few sparsely covered trees and, in the distance, maize fields — so I was surprised when I saw that I was in a cemetery.

Teria let my hand go and kept on walking. When I caught up to her, she was standing in front of the vault, in the place of the dead. My grandmother was uttering karakia, prayers of intercession, her lips moving, the words like whispers on the breath. The vault was dark, sombre and still. It was imposing, almost defiant, and the air around it was like a slow-moving river swirling into eternity.

And then she looked at me with a wry questioning smile on her lips.

'Do you want to say anything to your ancestor, e Witsh?'

'Hello,' I said. Just one word; she might have been expecting more. If so, on that day I may have broken her heart.

AGAIN, TIKA. NOTHING is simple. In his parliamentary years, Wī Pere had to spend quite a bit of time in Wellington, and there he met an Irish woman by the name of Annie O'Neill. When the affair became serious he confessed it to Arapera. She told him, 'That's all right. She will keep you warm at night.' Annie had two children by Wī Pere, called William and Albert. When Wī Pere died, Annie came to his tangihanga in Gisborne.

We cut to the early 1960s, when I was a student living in Auckland and failing my degree miserably. My father turned up one day on Wool Board business and asked me to accompany him. At the time he was also a trustee for the Wī Pere Trust; after many years of being run by Pākehā, the trust was now primarily run by family members.

Dad said he was trying to locate one of the sons of Wī Pere and Annie, I think it was William, so we went to Takapuna. I wasn't paying attention, but I remember the weatherboard house and the street, and walking up the front stairs and knocking on the door. I don't think that Dad had telephoned ahead, but he was greeted warmly. All her life Annie had received a pension from the trust, and Dad wanted to make sure William and Albert were receiving their cheques and that they were well. The trust continued to support the sons until their deaths.

5.

SOMETIMES, WHEN I think of Annie, the story of Hineahuone springs into my mind.

As you will recall, all the gods were male. According to Māori mythology, there came a time when Tāne, the greatest god of all, the one who had separated earth and sky, wanted to create a woman. Some say he was motivated by a greater desire than sex. He wanted to have children who would inherit the world he had created.

His mother, Papatūānuku, said to him, 'Use the red earth that you will find at my sexual cleft.'

From that red earth Tāne fashioned his woman, and she was known as Hineahuone, the woman made from clay. He then tried to mate with her. Some accounts of the story emphasise the hilarity of this moment, as other male gods, taking interest in this ritual, tried their penises in Hineahuone's mouth, ears, armpits, anus and other areas. This explains why there are secretions from those places. Finally Tāne found Hineahuone's vagina and entered her.

I was always fascinated by Hineahuone, mainly because not much is known about her — or, more to the point — asked of her story. I think this is the reason why the unknown Annie shares some resonance in my imagination with her.

Clearly, the way Hineahuone was made put her at a lower order than her creator — so has it ever been for the female race.

She was the first stone woman, and I imagine her lurching to life, uncoordinated, a pathetic, inarticulate female golem blinded by light and sinister shadows moving around her and hurting her. She has no other purpose in the mythic narrative than to produce a beautiful girl child halfway between godhood and humanhood and then she disappears.

Why doesn't the narrative allow her any maternal instinct and provide her with the opportunity to raise her child? She has performed what has been required of her as the receptacle for Tāne's sperm, and is done with.

PART THREE

TAMA O TŪRANGA
A GISBORNE BOY

Chapter Twenty-three

The Town Where Two Rivers Meet

1.

IN THE WINTER of 1952, Dad moved Mum, my sisters and me to the other side of town.

'This place is too small,' he told Mum of our Kaitī whare, 'and Teria has put a deposit on a house for us in Te Hāpara.'

My grandmother was full of surprises, in particular her business and financial acumen. She had secured Crawford Road for one son, Win, and now Haig Street for another.

'We can pay the house off and move in now,' Dad said.

The week before we left there was a lot of rain and the creek was running high. How thrilling it was to watch the brown, silty water flowing along it!

I was standing on the bank with Terry Williams, so it was probably a Saturday afternoon, and some of the older and braver boys leapt in with planks of wood and surfed along. Some of their mates had a rope slung from one side of the creek to the other. The boys would let go their makeshift surfboards and grab the rope before they were swept headlong further down to where the water disappeared into a culvert.

The next day turned out bright and shiny blue. I was playing again with my friends and we noticed a lot of people gathered around the culvert. The swollen tide of water in the creek had receded and there was a gap at the top.

A couple of men were in the creek, holding onto the sides and looking in. 'We'd better wait,' one of them said. 'The water level is still a bit high, but the lad is bound to be in there.'

I found out that one of the boys — or was it a girl? — had not been able to reach for the rope and had last been seen being swept further down and inside the culvert. I thought, 'But it is such a bright blue day.'

Recently I tried to find references to the event in the local newspaper archives, a death notice perhaps, without success. There were things in life that children could never be saved from, I guess, the capricious nature of circumstance.

However, perhaps the child made it out of the creek before arriving at the culvert. Or survived the terrors of being swept into the pipe and emerged, laughing, on the other side; I hope so. The incident became one of those unresolved matters that has stayed with me all my life. So many inconclusive endings and beginnings in all our lives.

My mother was upset to be leaving the women of Crawford Road. As our car backed out of the driveway, Mrs Walker kept puffing on her cigarette, pushing an unruly lock of hair back from her face. She was holding herself tightly in her fashionable coat as if she would break apart; even the padded shoulders could not disguise the frailty of her sadness.

As we left I shouted with excitement to Graeme: 'I'm to have my own bedroom.'

Some of the other ladies of the street had gathered to wave farewell. The formalities of address, 'Goodbye, Mrs Smiler', masked their sadness that one of their number was leaving.

2.

LET ME GIVE you a snapshot of Gisborne in 1952.

It was a harbour town positioned at a location where the Taruheru and Waimata rivers joined to create the Tūranganui River, the shortest in the Southern Hemisphere. Throughout my travels around the world I have never seen another town quite like it, except perhaps Launceston in Tasmania, or, at a pinch, Cork in Ireland. The main industry was centred on the port, which handled coastal shipping and was the hub of a thriving fishing fleet. The freezing works was there, together with a cluster of harbour businesses, as well as others scattered throughout the town like D.J. Barry's Ltd, long associated with liquor and fine spirits and branching out into cordials and fizzy drinks.

Today, Gisborne is a city of some 45,000 people, almost half of whom are Māori. In 1952, however, it was still three years away from claiming city status. The population was 17,300 and only about 1000 identified as Māori. Yes, only a thousand 'brownies', another of those reductive names, this time given to us by Pākehā city dwellers who cocked a puzzled eye that we had not stayed put down at 'the pā'. By this they were generically referring to the many marae clustered in the small settlements in the agricultural hinterland.

Were they ever in for a surprise. Over the next few years the rural to urban migration really took off, stimulated by the opening of new industries like Columbine Hosiery (by Dame Anne Salmond's lovely dad) and J. Wattie's Canneries (by the not so lovely Sir James, who had a habit of putting his foot in the proverbial).

Gisborne's city centre still looks much the same as it did more than sixty years ago, with the main shopping area strung four blocks along Gladstone Road from Kaitī Bridge to the fifty-five-foot Art Deco clock tower built in 1934. I was always ridiculously proud of the tower, which featured faux Doric embellishments painted beige (or, more politely, sand) and was floodlit at night. When it chimed the quarter, half, three-quarter and hour, you could hear the carillon all the way to the town limits. Right on 5 p.m. would begin the exodus of cars and cyclists from the city centre to the suburbs for dinner, which was usually served punctually at six.

In those days some buildings like Adair's, which was in the Spanish Mission style, were three storeys high; mostly, however, the profile of shops along Gisborne's main street was low, and the pavements had verandahs and ornate street lights. There were two pedestrian crossings, at Peel Street and Bright Street, and people parked their cars at angles; Fords, Vauxhalls, Prefects, Baby Austins (Gisborne was where they came to die) and the occasional raunchy Zephyr Zodiac parked outside the billiard saloon.

I actually think, despite the updated Gladstone Road and three sets of traffic lights, that Gisborne looked more prosperous in 1952 than it does now. It had a rural respectability then, rather like a well-groomed sheepdog. Today it looks a little, well, like a mongrel that has come to heel. Some locals still attribute this decline to the day when those same automated traffic lights arrived in the town. Until then there had always been a policeman standing in the middle of the road at peak hours; townsmen liked to judge him on his directing skills, pointing out to him when the traffic was banking up too far. On the day the lights began service, those same townsmen congregated to stare and cross and recross when the lights turned green and the mechanism buzzed — and then went back to their own ways and crossed the road when they wanted to, lights or no lights.

The main shops were department stores like the aforementioned Adair's, where the blue-rinse brigade took tea in the second-floor café, and on the third floor bought furniture and perambulators for their newly married and expectant daughters; daredevil children slid all the way down on the banisters between floors while Granny wasn't watching. McGruer's was also fascinating for kids, because it had a pneumatic tube system which sucked money upstairs and spat the change out downstairs. To my boyhood eyes all the stores along Gladstone Road were luxurious emporiums — others were Woolworths, McKenzies, Melbourne Cash and Thomas Adams' drapery. They were also magnets for my shoplifting cousins, who would use me to keep the permed and pearl-draped elderly shop assistants talking while they helped themselves to pretty paste jewellery. Although I was a good boy I tried once to nick stuff, and got caught. Any thoughts I might have had of a glorious criminal career were nipped in the bud.

Men got short back and sides at the Peel Street barbershop owned by Vic Davy Snr (later joined by Warwick Davy in 1967). Whenever there was a wedding or other special event, women went to get a set and perm at Daisy's Hairdressers or to Nita Teutenberg at Anita Fay's. The mother you thought you knew would come back looking strangely unreal and smelling of Rotorua, and at her appearance my sisters and I had been primed to say dutifully, 'You look pretty', even though she didn't.

Because Gisborne was a farming town, the main business hub was centred on either Williams and Kettle's or Dalgety's stock and station agents. Dalgety's had a large farming and machinery store a block from Gladstone Road, where Pākehā farmers and cow cockies came into town on 'Fry-dees' or for the cattle and sheep sales out at the Matawhero stockyards. The farmers dressed in tweed coats and hats, and, smoking pipes or cigarettes, debated the merits of the new range of Nuffield tractors and combine harvesters in the same rural nasal twang they used on their dogs — 'Gid in bee-hoind, Sam.' They were the overlords of regional agriculture, their air of affluence bespeaking a community that liked to purchase quality goods.

People smoked a lot in those days, so Gisborne Tobacconists was always busy selling the best baccy for pipes and the not-so-good for roll-your-owns.

The stock and station agencies were where the local mothers exhibited their daughters. It's always a bit of a shock to realise that those fine specimens of New Zealand womanhood didn't shave their armpits in those days and the main perfume was *Au de Naturel* — but that didn't turn the male species off, nah. Farming fathers and sons ran their eyes over the girls for breeding form, not for a whiff of scent. Big in the udders and wide hips for child-bearing were favoured.

And where would a likely lad in for the cattle sales take a daughter of Aunt Daisy when introduced to her? Definitely somewhere dark like the Ritz Cabaret or one of the local passion pits, as the three movie theatres were called. There, you could watch the red-faced farm lads forced to adopt that bent-over and hands-in-pockets walk that indicated they had a raging hard-on and no underpants to help restrain it.

The other alternative was to wait for the annual A&P shows where the cattle or sheep were not the only livestock on view. Mothers still looking for husbands for their daughters would parade them like prize heifers. If a boy was lucky, he could spirit her away (parents would discreetly look the other way to give him the opportunity, "Oh, has anyone seen our Sally?") and get her on the octopus or the ferris wheel. There, if he was lucky, a hand shoved into her groin would promise the possibility of sex on the next date at the Majestic.

I was still too young to think about *that*. I was more fascinated by a particular sideshow attraction: a shining globe at eye height, in which was a small mermaid, who waved and smiled at me. The barker proclaimed that anybody who could prove she was a fake could win

£10. I must have known that the mermaid was not real, but I think that was the day when I lost my heart to imagination.

People tend to forget the extraordinary role of movie theatres in Aotearoa — not just as passion pits but more seriously as purveyors of culture. In the 1950s New Zealanders loved going to the movies. Worldwide we had the fifth highest number of cinema-goers per capita in the world, and Gisborne had three of the best movie houses, each presiding over its own town block: the imperial Kerridge Odeon Regent, the Grecian Amalgamated Kings, and the Kerridge Odeon Majestic. Indeed New Zealand's great impresario, Robert Kerridge, actually began his career in Gisborne in 1926 by creating the Regent cinema out of an older movie house, the Palace. In 1946 he ensured that the sun would never set on empire, at least so far as film was concerned, by signing an agreement with J. Arthur Rank for the supply of British as well as Hollywood films. The Man with the Golden Gong entered our lives.

Sessions were normally at 2 p.m., 5 p.m. and 8 p.m., and additional children's sessions were held at 10.30 on Saturday mornings. If you were a child you paid 6d or 9d to go to a movie. Adults paid up to 2s 6d for the best seats, which were always the plush velvet ones in the back rows. You stood up at the beginning of movies when 'God Save the King' was played and a still of George VI appeared on the screen. If younger patrons showed disrespect for King and Country by remaining sitting, the frowns of outrage and spoken words of 'Show respect!' had you up pretty quickly.

Rae Wheeler was the beautiful manageress, and you were shown to your seats by a pretty usherette with a torch. There was always a first half, showing what were known as Shorts and Forthcoming Attractions. At halftime, the same pretty usherette would wander down the aisles offering ice creams and lollies for sale. Then the lights would dim and on would come the main film — *West of Zanzibar*, *Outcast of the Islands*, *King Solomon's Mines* or *Clive of India*. During the scary moments of a movie, some clown would start a train of Jaffas rolling down the aisle.

Whenever you walked through town on Fridays or went to the showgrounds, there was bound to be a street photographer to take your photo; just as well, else family histories would not have been so well documented. Every family went to Dunstan & Kinge Photographers, who specialised in weddings and portraiture, to have the required family photograph taken for the sitting room wall. The earliest family photograph shows Mum and Dad, me and my sisters. I was late getting home that day, I always hated having my photo taken anyway, and the reason I look so strange is that I was supposed to have had a haircut but didn't — my mother put a basin on my head and cut off all the hair showing beneath it. I swear to you, that photograph used to say to me

This is what happens if you don't listen to your mother whenever I walked past it.

You always dressed up if you went into town or the movies, regardless of whether you were a toff or the lesser kind. That's why the photographs of Mum and Dad are so wonderful to look at, with Dad in a fedora, open-necked shirt and well-pressed trousers and Mum in her hat, summer dress, handbag and gloves. You won't see me in anything less than a school cap, pullover and tie and with socks pulled up.

If you wanted to dine out during an evening or 'Take the missus out on a wedding anniversary', you also dressed up in your best bib and tucker and went to the Masonic Hotel, a stunning place that could have come out of Mayfair; it had a bar for the nobs. The hoi polloi were to be seen in less salubrious establishments like the Record Reign and the Gisborne Hotel; this was before the advent of the huge beer barns like the Sandown. At 6 o'clock the publican would call 'Time, gentlemen, please!' and the patrons would be turfed out. You could always drive out to Mākaraka or Ormond and score a crate or two from the backdoor bar.

Note the word 'gentlemen'. Ladies were never seen in a public bar.

Police patrolled the pavements — people still called them bobbies, and they wore distinctive cone-head helmets like those seen on TV's *Dixon of Dock Green* — to show that ours was a law-abiding community. The national air service was TEAL — Tasman Empire Airways Ltd — but only the wealthy ever flew. I kid you not, there is still a TEAL motel in Gisborne; some things get caught in a time warp. Most people coming into or out of the town travelled on the New Zealand Railways bus or the nifty railcars. They looked like red retro spaceships from *Flash Gordon Conquers the Universe* launching from the station near Waikanae Beach.

The main denominations were Anglican, Roman Catholic and Presbyterian. Sometimes I wondered whether the political differences between England, Scotland and Ireland were still played out in the colonies of Great Britain, through religion. I don't know where Presbyterian children went to school, but Anglicans sent their children to Gisborne Boys' High or Gisborne Girls' High, which, tantalisingly, was on the opposite side of the road. Senior girls and boys would congregate at the No. 8 wire fences edging the two schools. Younger go-betweens would be dispatched with messages of love to the swain or object of desire waiting on the opposite side: 'Meet me after school behind the bike shed.' Or 'I'll see you at Roebuck Road corner.'

Randier boys actually took Latin so they could go to the shared classes at Girls' High.

Catholic girls went to St Mary's, and Catholic boys went to Marist Brothers' High School, herded by brothers with hairy legs in long cassocks, shrilly giving orders via the whistles slung round their necks.

For non-Catholic boys there was always something about Catholic girls, who were unattainable — or so we thought — and seemed to float a few inches off the ground. Gisborne was not alone in revealing a healthy enmity between the two religions. Whenever a Catholic bishop visited the town, the girls were presented at a lavish ball, escorted by fathers or brothers. You could bet your life that an Anglican bishop was soon hot-footing it to town. Let the Battle of the Balls commence.

As for Mormonism, it wasn't considered a denomination. It was a sect and, what's more, it was *American*.

The sports grounds — rugby, hockey, netball and tennis — were all located at Roebuck Road, except for the McCrae Municipal Baths, which were on the banks of the Waimata River.

Men took their pay packet home to Mum, either their real mother or their wife, and she would take it, peel off a few notes and return them to Dad or sons and daughters; just enough to get them through to next payday. Mum would spend a little of the money on something for the daughter's glory box, so that once she got married, well, she would have sheets, towels, linen and other household items to begin life with. Did people put money in the bank in those days? I suppose they did.

And then, just a drive away from the town clock, was the esplanade at Waikanae Beach. Why, you could have been promenading at Brighton. There was a paddling pool for the tiny tots, a playground for the older children, and a changing shed for the adults before they leapt into the bright blue sea. At the soundshell there were summer beauty contests for local versions of blonde starlet Diana Dors, the British Marilyn Monroe. Mr Rank changed her surname from Fluck for obvious reasons.

Once, just as Māori had found Te Toka-a-Taiau good for shellfish, we had found Waikanae a good place to cast our nets for flounder. Not any more. We were in the perplexing situation of sharing the beach with Pākehā who went, e hika, to the beach for *fun*. They set up candy-striped umbrellas and picnic blankets and sat in the sun and got as brown as we were; how odd. (Skin cancer? What was that?)

'Look the other way, girls,' my mother would say to my sisters when blond lifeguards strutted past in skimpy costumes, their togs riding into the cracks of their butts.

As far as clothing was concerned, our mother was very puritanical, always fussing around my sisters' necklines and hems, pulling them up or down. When Speedos were in fashion and I had the body to wear them, I accidentally left my togs at Haig Street and asked Mum to mail them to me. They arrived in a small envelope accompanied by a long letter in which she patiently used words like 'unseemly', 'inappropriate', 'indecent' and so on.

Boy, she should see what people wear now.

Very soon, not only were we avoiding undressed lifeguards but also dodging young surfers riding the waves on huge wooden boards, the dinosaurs of the sport.

The pride of Gisborne, however, was the Eastwoodhill Arboretum. This was an astonishing colonial artefact — some might say *presumption*. Created in 1910 by William Douglas Cook, the arboretum was reputed to have the largest collection of trees usually seen only in temperate climate zones of the Northern Hemisphere; here they were, right in the middle of native land. Canadian author Margaret Atwood came to New Zealand in 2001, I think, only because the organisers promised a visit to the national arboretum.

If trees die out in Britain, no problem, Gisborne can supply the replacements.

3.

HAIG STREET WAS right at the town's western limits where there was a sign saying: 'Welcome to Gisborne, First to See the Sun.'

The suburb of Te Hāpara wasn't as established as Kaitī, but it was up and coming, with new wooden bungalows being built all around us. Mr Riki and his beautiful daughters, Mary and Rona, and sons, Hector and Mac, lived opposite; the Kururangis moved into a house on the corner. Pākehā in the street included the Whites, Lawrences, Gibsons, Candys, Malcolms and the Springay sisters. Next door No. 9 was empty, and at No. 7 was grumpy Mr Le Quesne, who had a BSA Bantam. Perhaps he wasn't grumpy at all but, rather, still suffering from being gassed during the First World War.

We got our groceries from 'The Blue Dairy' around the corner. Planes regularly flew across our house because the airport was at the end of Chalmers Road. The railway line from Gisborne to Hawke's Bay ran across the runway, so departure and arrivals had to be aligned with train schedules.

When we first arrived at the Haig Street house we unpacked with excitement. I can remember, though, coming across my mother standing stock still, as if taking a breath.

'What's wrong, Mum?'

If I had looked into her eyes I would have seen her trying to orient herself. After all, when we moved across Kaitī Bridge, we crossed the southern boundary of Ngāti Porou to what was known as the Tūranga side of town. In different tribal land, I imagine my mother was casting about desperately, taking a new compass bearing on where life was taking her.

Where was Mount Hikurangi? She bowed her head, submitting to the force of destiny.

Not that the relationship with our coast relatives was entirely broken. The Christmas following our move to Te Hāpara, my sister Kararaina and I went to Tokomaru Bay to stay with Aunty Dinah, who was a nurse. Despite the fact that she and Uncle Brian put stockings brimming with presents by the chimney, we were very unhappy. I found Kararaina weeping under her bed and slid in beside her.

'We just have to make the best of it,' I said.

Come to think of it, I was always being farmed out to other relatives, if not to be cared for, then to play with my boy cousins. One of my fabulous aunts, Huia Chrisp, would ring Mum up and say in her cultured voice, 'Julia? Is Witi available? I would like to pick him up so that he can play with Richard.'

Aunty Huia had been to the Sydney Conservatorium to study music, and on her return had married George Chrisp, a Second World War air force pilot. They were a handsome couple and bore handsome children in Richard, John and Christine. I can still remember watching and waiting for Aunty Huia to arrive with her white-rimmed movie-star glasses, fox stoles and clickety-click slingback shoes to bundle me into the car like a Māori Aunty Mame and take me to play with Richard.

In later years, after her husband died — he used to own Chrisp's Music Store — Richard wanted me to bring Aunty Huia up to Auckland. I wasn't aware that she was in her dotage and that she had an equally forgetful little dog called Bellamy. We had a crazy, wonderful, terrifying time as we all drove together to Whakatāne, where I picked up my cousin, Hineuru Blanche Robinson. She helped in the later part of the trip as Aunty Huia went from one episode to the next: 'Who are you? I'm being kidnapped! Help! You can't be Witi, you're so old. What do you want from me? Take my money, but please don't hurt my dog. Help!'

BACK TO MOVING DAY.

One of Dad's younger brothers, Uncle Hani, came to help and, in particular, clear rubbish off the section. This must have been shortly before he shipped off to join New Zealand's Kayforce in the Korean War. Whenever he was on leave in Tokyo, Uncle Hani would send my sisters exotic dolls garbed in kimonos. They peered at us with their beautiful lacquered eyes from behind a glass cabinet that Dad built specially to house our mother's precious treasures — crystal vases, porcelain tea-sets and so on.

Teria brought around a wind-up gramophone to give us a bit of music while we worked at the house. The number of shellac recordings were somewhat limited: Les Paul and Mary Ford singing 'Hold That Tiger' or

'Mocking Bird Hill' or 'The World Is Waiting for the Sun to Rise'. There were also two opera recordings, one of Enrico Caruso singing 'Vesti la giubba' and a soprano who I think was Amelita Galli-Curci carolling 'Caro nome' like a bird.

Kararaina and I thought the opera arias were hilarious and pretended to mime along with them. Much later, in adult life, I developed a love of opera, and Kararaina, recalling those years when we mugged to those scratchy recordings, said, 'Were you ever bitten on the bum.'

Haig Street had a half-verandah in the front, which Dad closed in to make a nursery for Viki. The house itself comprised three bedrooms. Mum and Dad slept in the front room, Kararaina and Tāwhi were in the one behind them and I was across the hallway. Yes, as the male heir, I had a bedroom to myself.

At the time, the hallway served as a gallery for family photographs. Over the years the gallery expanded, but it was still a long way from becoming Mum's corridor of whakapapa, a place that ultimately made a mockery of physical space. Where the walls collapsed around you and left you suspended in a continuum stretching back to Hikurangi and thence to the beginning of everything.

 5.

BECAUSE OF DAD'S role as padrone, Haig Street became a kind of halfway home for his shearing gangs. Not only that, but as most Māori had not yet made the step into suburbia, Mum and Dad's rural relatives would leave their children at Haig Street so that they could go to high school in Gisborne for a term or two. Kararaina, Tāwhi, Viki and I grew accustomed to the appearance and disappearance of all these young men and women — our cousins, too. They also included a gypsy boy from Romania; what he was doing in Aotearoa I'll never know. In later years I would go home and find a Swiss girl or German boy at home, awaiting their shearing experience.

The young shearers would begin to congregate at Haig Street in October, waiting for the season to begin. And they would assemble again after the season was finished, waiting around until a job came along. In the early days there were two young boys from Northland, Patrick Huhu and Fred Cassidy, who were like sons to my father. Then, later, among others, was a really lovely young Pākehā boy called Cliff Paine from Waipukurau.

While those young boys and girls were there, what did they do? Why, apart from going out to Waituhi with Dad to help him with the sheep he had there, they abetted him in putting up more of his illegal extensions — enlarging the kitchen and bringing the washhouse into the main body of the house.

Haig Street became a bit of a parking lot. Apart from Dad's big red truck, there were also the cars of those young men and women. Dad decided that he should concrete a driveway all the way to the back of the section. And then he decided to add his pièce de résistance: a huge two-truck garage. On the day that the cement on the concrete drive was hard enough, Cliff tried to teach me how to skate and promptly went arse over kite.

Did the garage ever house two trucks? Nah. Dad turned it into a motor-shop-cum-repair-shop-cum-lumber-and-roofing-yard-cum-scientific-laboratory. He filled the garage with planks, old farm machinery, stacks and stacks of timber of all sizes and lengths, some railway tracks and iron — *any old iron, any, any, any old iron*.

When he decided to build the carport and then roof it over so that it would become an outside dining room, why bother to go to a timber yard when he had his own supply? He pieced the carport together with bits of this and bits of that. No need for gauges or spirit levels, his expert eye could do the job just as well. The carport might have looked Frankenstein-ian, stitched together with odd-matching timber and battens and staples, but, as Dad would say, 'Nobody will know when the wood's painted.'

Haig Street was the 'House that Tom Built'.

More extensions were to come. The concrete was extended to include a path to the outhouse so that all the young women could have a nice clean walkway and, to relieve pressure on the sleeping accommodation, Dad built a small sleepout next to the garage for the boys. What else? Oh, he extended the living room and added a new room in the front.

That wasn't all. After a while Dad decided it was too much fuss going backwards and forwards to Waituhi to feed his dogs and look after his sheep. They began to be housed at Haig Street, too. Of course, sometimes they got out of their assorted kennels and pens, causing havoc in the neighbourhood.

The pathway to the outhouse needs explaining. It relates to the phenomenon of the night-cart man, who came every Wednesday night to change the piss and shit bucket in those days before inside flush toilets. All around the neighbourhood you would hear frenetic activity as households endeavoured to perform their bodily functions before he arrived. 'Hurry up with your business, Millie, otherwise the night-cart man will carry you off with the bucket.' Nobody, least of all the women, wanted to be caught in the outhouse.

A dread expectant silence would descend with the darkness. And then came the sound of the approaching truck, with its familiar odour of shit, piss and disinfectant like a miasma rising from a stinking bog. We all waited hushed in our houses, behind closed windows and curtains down.

Respect for the night-cart man made us discreet. But once, coming home late from my best friend Michael Wills' place — his mother had rung Mum to say that seeing as we were having fun playing with his new train set I should stay for tea — I saw the night-cart man's truck, laden with the reeking buckets.

I was hastening up the driveway when I bumped into him. He was coming down the driveway with our bucket on his shoulders. My eyes were dazzled by his lighted miner's hat. He struck terror in me when he said, 'Hello, Witi.'

How did he know who I was?

6.

I'LL BRING THIS snapshot of Gisborne in 1952 to a close by returning to the great impact of cinema on the Māori consciousness.

The big movie that year was actually not a British or American movie at all. It was called *Broken Barrier*, and it's worth stopping just for a moment to reflect on Māori within the history of the movies. Indeed, our appearances date back to 1913, when the Frenchman Gaston Méliès came to New Zealand and made four silent movies, with such titles as *How Chief Te Ponga Won His Bride*. Subsequently, New Zealand quickly took to the camera, and two pioneer film-makers, Rudall Hayward and his wife Ramai, made *The Te Kooti Trail* and the very exciting *Rewi's Last Stand*. Parallel to this development was the German film-maker, F.W. Murnau, who made the classic ethnographic film *Tabu, A Story of the South Seas*, in 1931.

Broken Barrier ended a very long drought in New Zealand movie history. Producers and directors John O'Shea and Roger Mirams made the film in black and white with a rickety dolly and two silent movie cameras; they added voice-over narration later. Folklore has it that one of the cameras was filched by some enterprising Kiwi soldier from 'a dead German in the Western desert' during the Second World War.

Filmed on location on the East Coast, *Broken Barrier* had Kay Ngārimu, one of my mother's relatives, in the starring role of Rami, the local girl who meets a Pākehā boy. No wonder Mum and Dad got Aunt Billie Hirini to babysit us while they went to the Gisborne opening.

Why was this film so important? It showed us to ourselves.

Broken Barrier is actually more sophisticated than New Zealand critics care to admit. When I was at the Turin International Book Fair 2010, I was taken to the magnificent museum of Italian film and realised how much *Broken Barrier* owed to Italian neorealism, films like Luchino Visconti's *La Terra Trema*, Alberto Lattuada's *Il Mulino del Po* and Giuseppe De Santis's *Riso Amaro*, starring Silvana Mangano. They were all in black and white, semi-documentary in style, filmed on rural locations among poor working-class people and often used local actors.

Riso Amaro ('Bitter Rice'), for instance, has strong resonances for Māori. Although set among the rice fields, it could well be the story of Māori itinerant shearers or orchard workers. In Silvana Mangano, my mother found a heroine with whom she could identify — and she bore a more than superficial resemblance to the Italian star. When she saw Mangano in Alberto Lattuada's *Anna*, she immediately bought a 45 of the movie's song, 'El Negro Zumbon'. She couldn't stop pirouetting around the house, rolling her eyes and trying to be provocative and sexy, but she was, really, just our mum. There she was, miming to the music and chasing after my sisters and me as we gleefully joined in the silly song about a tomato:

> *Tengo gana de bailar del nuevo compass*
> *Dicen todos cuando me ven pasar*
> *'Dicha, donde vas?'*
> *'Me voy a bailar, el baion!'*

No, I won't end there after all.

There was always random violence. Following the attack on Mum in Kaitī, she, my sisters and I were always wary. One evening, however, Mum and Dad decided to go to the movies and I was left in charge of my sisters.

All of a sudden a man arrived at the house and I managed to lock him out. He kept trying to get in, banging on the windows, so I rang the Regent movie theatre, and they flashed a notice on the screen: 'Would Mr and Mrs Tom Smiler come to the foyer, please.'

It was Mum's worst nightmare. She sped home with Dad to see what was happening.

The back door finally gave way, and when it opened the man lurched in. His name was Charlie and his wife was with him, and they were drunk. 'Is Tom here? I want my money,' Charlie said.

'You're not allowed here,' I answered. 'You should get out.'

The stench of beer was coming off him. 'No, I'll wait for Tom, and while I'm waiting you can make me and my missus a kai.'

'I told you to leave,' I said. Kararaina, Tāwhi and Viki were whimpering. What was happening?

Charlie backhanded me, and my sisters screamed. I fell on the floor, dazed, and watched as Charlie and his wife went through the cupboards, searching for a frying pan. They put some fat in it and placed the pan on the stove.

The fat caught fire. 'Shit,' Charlie said.

He went to the tap and got a pot of water to pour on the pan and, next moment, the flames flared and the cupboards above the stove began to burn. More dangerously, the fire rose above the cupboards and flowed like ribbons along the ceiling. When that happened, Charlie completely lost it, and he and his wife made for the door. Kararaina and I turned off the stove and I had learnt enough from Life Boys (the junior level of Boys' Brigade) to know that the best way to stop a fire was to smother it.

Kararaina and I were still trying to do this when Mum and Dad returned. Dad burnt his hand getting the fire under control and taking the blazing fat outside.

'Remember last time?' my mother asked. 'If something like this happens again, son, first get your sisters to safety.'

Today, realising the high mortality rates from fires in homes, I echo my mother's advice. When there's a fire, get out while you can.

Chapter Twenty-four

Becoming a Gisborne Boy

1.

DO YOU RECALL my telling you about Hineahuone, the stone woman?

After Tāne has made her and she has given birth to a daughter, Hineahuone disappears from all the texts. She's not important any longer, but I like to imagine a kinder scenario than disappearance for her. Although traumatised by what the gods have done to her, and the subsequent pregnancy and giving birth, she escapes eastwards. In her lurching steps she trails the afterbirth of her child. Ahead lies sanctuary in the biblical Land of Nod.

And so the story now turns to Hineahuone's daughter, but let me note again that the abandonment does not fit well with me — it's too convenient.

Her name is Hinetītama and translates as 'Girl of the Dawn'. It's a lovely name, speaking of the first woman and of a hopeful future. Bright and innocent, she is left alone in a carved meeting house with poupou, posts, that can talk. Under their care and tutelage she grows from childhood to womanhood, groomed, with all the connotations that word has, to perform her function in bringing humankind into the world. All the birds and animals of the forest are at her beck and call, caring for her.

Every now and then Hinetītama has a visitor. He comes striding through the forest and, when she reaches her sexual maturity, he begins to woo her. Presumably his courting of her is why Hineahuone is made conveniently absent in the texts, because I am sure that she would *never* have allowed it. Although Hinetītama repeatedly asks his name, he never gives it. Instead, he takes her virginity and mates with her. Although the narrative does not mention them, presumably she has children, both male and female, from the union.

However, Hinetītama's curiosity cannot be assuaged. She asks the posts of the house who her lover is. Eventually, succumbing to her constant questioning they answer: 'He is the man who constructed this house for you.'

And then: 'Tāne the husband is Tāne the father.'

This is the first incest.

According to the narrative, shame overwhelms Hinetītama. It's interesting that this must be a human trait rather than a godly one, because nowhere is there any mention of Tāne having such an emotion. She leaves Te Ao Mārama, The World of Light, and flees to a place known as Rarohenga, the Underworld. She reaches the guardhouse of Poutererangi and seeks entry from Te Kūwatawata, the guardian of the gateway.

'If you enter, you can never return to the light,' Kūwatawata warns her.

Taking one last look at the Overworld, she sees Tāne following swiftly after her. Some variations of the story, in an attempt to give him a quality we can sympathise with, tell us that he is in tears.

'Haere atu, Tāne,' Hinetītama farewells him. 'Hāpai ā tātou tamariki i te Ao. Goodbye, Tāne. Raise our children in the light. I will take them to me when they die.'

It's a noble leavetaking, isn't it? And with it, Hinetītama takes upon herself the sins of the father. Incarnated, she becomes the complete opposite of what she originally has been. From Girl of the Dawn she becomes Hinenuitepō, Great Woman of the Night.

The imagery all makes sense but, auē, because the narrative is written by men, Hinenuitepō undergoes a sinister change. She is crowned Goddess of Death and given all the imagery of malevolence. Teeth like a barracuda, eyes of obsidian and hair of writhing kelp. After all, death is to be feared, isn't it? Nowhere is there any sign of the mother who, with great love, takes her children to her when they go to her bosom after their sojourn in the light, to be cradled by her forever.

We cut to 2011. I was invited to give a DNA sample to the Genographic Project, a research partnership of National Geographic and IBM in association with the Waitt Family Foundation and helmed in New Zealand by the University of Otago.

When I decided to accept the invitation, I had Hinetītama in mind. After all, the project, not without controversy, is predicated on the existence of an original Eve, who lived in Tanzania several million years ago. Could not Hinetītama have been that woman?

She was a mitochondrial mother, and from her arose the children of men, generation after generation, to spread all over the world into Europe and across existing causeways into the Americas and other land masses. One of the greatest of those tribal migrations pushed eastward from the heart of Africa into Asia. The theoretical basis for the project is that mitochondrial DNA is passed from the mother to her children, both male and female and, therefore, you can trace the origins and movements of the populations as they moved across the earth.

In the case of Māori, the matrilineal evidence leads to a particular indigenous population who lived, some scientists consider, in the hills of Taiwan as the immediate source of our genetic origin. This occurred around five millennia ago, and there is sufficient linguistic, anthropological and cultural evidence to support this case. From this small culture, voyagers set out across the north Pacific, settling Samoa,

French Polynesia and other island groups. Eventually, from the island of Raiatea, reputed to be the mythical Hawaiki of the Māori, the original homeland, Polynesian migrants set sail some thousand years ago southward to a land of rumoured beauty.

Of all the world's migrations, ours is distinctive. The Māori are the pōtiki, the youngest of all the earth's peoples. The results of my DNA sample, when analysed, place me as belonging to the Mitrochondrial DNA Haplogroup B4a1a1a3.

I am proud to be numbered among the children of men. However, I know that there is a reason why Māori always begin their karakia when the sky becomes tinged with red.

2.

I JOYOUSLY BECAME a Gisborne boy. Every day I couldn't wait to go to my new school, Te Hāpara Primary. It was originally called Gisborne West; my Great-uncle Rongowhakaata Halbert is credited with the idiomatic Māori translation, 'Early Dawn'. How appropriate for all our eager young minds.

I'd jump out of bed, get dressed, have breakfast — usually porridge, bread and butter, and milk — grab my schoolbag, say 'Goodbye Mum' and go. With Kararaina and Tāwhi following behind, 'Wait for us, wait for us,' I'd run around the corner into Clarence Street and wait on Gladstone Road. Who was there? 'Gidday, John. Gidday, Kay. Oh look, here comes Sam!'

Right-o, off again with my friends down Gladstone Road, past the stately Art Deco house where the music teacher lived — dawdle a little because sometimes there'd be a pupil playing 'The Happy Wanderer' or 'Rustle of Spring' — to the Four Square shop at Lytton Road.

Who was waiting there? My best friend Michael Wills — 'Hello Witi, guess what I've got?' — to tell me what Mr Wills had bid for this week at the local auction house, a Meccano set, lucky thing. 'Come home with me after school and we can make something, eh?' His mother was welcoming and his ever fascinating family included a big sister named Delia.

Jabbering away, we would set off again along Gladstone Road past the Hēni Materoa Children's Home. If the day was sunny, the children were at their daily calisthenics, shirtless but hatted, like pale freckled fish flapping on the grass.

Across the pedestrian crossing I would go with more pupils — we were a veritable crowd of squealing children — and have a quick look in the tuck shop to see what kinds of pies they had today, before going through the school gates.

Try not to look at the 'Murder House', where the dental nurse used the horrible buzzing drill, and into the playground to play chasing games or hopscotch with Michael, Viv Gray, Sam Reihana, John Kīngi, bespectacled John Gribben, skinny Ray McFarlane, straight-haired Lorraine Cornish and pretty Polly Ngaira.

Was that the school bell *already*?

'Line up, children! Line up!'

Quickly I would get into my class group, stand to attention for the national anthem and wait while the headmaster, I think he was Mr Johnson, gave the morning instructions or news. With him were other members of staff like Mr Candy, 'Husky' Preston, who had moved from Kaitī, and Mr Gribben. Then on to inspection — no head inspection for lice today but I would thrust out my hands to show clean fingernails and that I had brought a clean hanky.

Quick march *left right left right* like a good toy soldier into the schoolroom. There, I would give the huge globe of the world a spin just to watch all those countries coloured red blur into one: New Zealand, Australia, Canada, India, South Africa . . . weren't we lucky to belong to the great British Commonwealth of nations?

Now hurry to help fill all the inkwells with dark blue ink and make sure each desk had a pen with nib. And then, first class, spelling.

'Hands up those who have done their spelling homework?'

Pick me, Miss! Pick me!

And then, second class, writing. 'Hands up who wants to come up to the board and write the word "friend"?'

Pick me, Miss! Pick me! (I was bad at spelling but would give anything a try and, in this case, was rescued by Lorraine Cornish, who hissed at me as I went up, 'End comes at the end of the word "friend"!')

And then third class, storytime! 'Hands up who wants a story?'

Pick me, Miss! Pick me! Can you read us *The Good Master*? Oh, has Jancsi managed to show his spoilt city cousin Kate yet that milk doesn't come out of bottles?

It's easy for me to smile at the young, eager and shining-eyed Māori boy that I was. I was at Te Hāpara Primary for three years. My favourite teacher, Barbara Hossack, was a major influence in my life; young, with black curly hair and flashing green eyes, she had me spellbound with her readings from Kate Seredy's books, *The Good Master* and *The Singing Tree*. I equated myself with the young Hungarian farm boy Jancsi and his father, Marton, who, in the second book, must go off to fight in the First World War.

Like other boys, I was devastated to watch Miss Hossack's budding romance with the handsome phys ed teacher, Colin Blows, and the morning the headmaster announced that they had become engaged left me down in the dumps and cross.

Another teacher was Sam Gribben, who also took the stamp club after school; all those beautiful stamps from exotic places like the Congo, Trinidad and Tobago, and Ethiopia filled my imagination with colour. It was through him that I became a member of the Boys' Brigade, and joined his son John doing 'good deeds' during the weekends.

I still bump into childhood friends from Te Hāpara. Vivian Gray is a professor of mathematics at Victoria University of Wellington, and Gillian Gibson and I often meet at the theatre or the opera. Gillian and her husband Sir Rod Deane have become great humanitarians and supporters of New Zealand arts and culture. I only wish I could meet Michael again; he disappeared from my life fairly soon after my years at Te Hāpara Primary.

As for Gillian, there has always been something of the 'Lady' in her and, whenever we are talking, just hearing her cultured voice is enough to make me flash back to a day at Te Hāpara School in 1953. Following an announcement at assembly that the Queen had been crowned and a New Zealander was coincidentally standing on top of Mount Everest, it was decided that we would put on a pageant celebrating both events. Gillian was chosen to play the Queen, a tall boy whose surname I can't remember, but I think his first name was Stan, was selected to play Edmund Hillary, and guess who Miss Hossack chose to play Sherpa Tenzing?

Yes, little kina-head himself.

The entire school, supported by the PTA, swept into action. Some of the fathers helped to construct a frame for Mount Everest which, to our children's eyes, looked as high as the sky. Other parents and students applied papier mâché to the mountain to give it bulk and stature, and added cotton wool snow. Behind, following the contours of the left side of the mountain, was a set of stepladders that Stan and I would ascend; we would always be visible to the audience.

The male parents also built a throne for the Queen, and some of the more artistic among them created Gillian's crown, golden sceptre and robe. Sure, they were only made of paste, cardboard, golden glitter and coloured glass, but, to us, they were as good as the real Crown Jewels and they probably sparkled brighter.

Let me colour the scene in a bit more. Other children were chosen to be an archbishop, royal holders of Gillian's long train, and sherpas. All classes had school projects on Westminster Abbey or the Tower of London or the Culture of Tibet. Rehearsals were held, appropriate music was found — probably Handel's 'Hallelujah Chorus' or 'Zadok the Priest' for the coronation ceremony — and we practised and rehearsed until we were word perfect.

Miss Hossack's instructions to me and Stan were very clear: 'Stan, you are to go up the ladder first, halt every so often and then look back at Witi and say, "Don't get too far behind, Sherpa Tenzing!" or "We're almost there, Sherpa Tenzing!" or "Come on, our destination draws nigh!" When you finally reach the summit, Stan, plant the flag and say to Witi, "We are standing on the highest mountain in the world!" Stay there and wave the Union Jack while the school choir sings.'

I don't think we knew in those days that Sir Ed actually said, 'We knocked the bastard off.'

And we could not have asked for a more perfect day. The sun shone brightly on the quadrangle. Our parents came in their Sunday best because, after all, the Queen was being crowned in Westminster Cathedral, wasn't she? Gillian arrived and everyone oohed and aahed at her royal robes and crown with its glittering Koh-i-noor diamond. She took her place and enunciated carefully, 'Oh, and a New Zealander is climbing the tallest mountain in the world at the same time as I am being crowned.'

That was our cue. Imperious, Gillian sat down on her cardboard throne and pointed to Stan, tall and white, and me, short, brown and grinning like a Māori Cheshire Cat.

'You're on,' Miss Hossack whispered.

It was a shambles from the start. Either Stan got stage fright or I was eager and impatient, probably the latter, but one thing is certain — I was the first on the ladder.

The script unravelled entirely. Instead of Stan delivering the words, it was me saying, 'Don't get too far behind, Hillary!' And although Stan tried to get past me, it was too dangerous, so I had to keep climbing, 'We're almost there, Hillary!' By the time my head poked out from one of the peaks of the mountain and I pointed to the summit, 'Our destination draws nigh!', gusts of hilarity were wafting up from the audience and threatening to blow us off the cardboard mountain.

My grandmother and my mother's responses to these primary school shenanigans were interesting. Teria smiled when she was told that Sherpa 'Witi' Tenzing had got to the top of Everest first. 'Ka pai koe, e Wit*sh*!' My mother, also, had no royalist affections. I can't recall that she was at the performance, though she tolerated my eagerness to play Tenzing — oh well, at least he's playing somebody like *us*.

You'd think that a botched performance like that would have nipped my dramatic career in the bud, but, for some reason, Miss Hossack trusted me with another. I was a Chinese marionette-maker who was asked by the Emperor of China to make a beautiful life-sized dancing doll. Why? The evil Genghis Khan with his Mongol horde had arrived at the Great Wall and threatened to break through and conquer all the land. My dancing doll, however, was the pretty Fiona Blair so no wonder the evil Khan was so smitten that he decided to turn away from the wall and all his plans of invasion and conquest. I had to wind Fiona up whenever her mechanism was slowing down. Up came her head, on came her smile, and there she was dancing so charmingly again.

In later years Fiona, who by then was known as Regency, danced into the life of young Tahitian lawyer, Charles Chauvel, newly arrived from Paris. They became the parents of young Charles, former Labour Party MP, and now working for the United Nations in Belgium.

My world was expanding, and of course at the end of the working week there was Teria come to pick me up from Haig Street.

One day I told her about the House of Beautiful Music on Gladstone Road that I passed on the way to and from school. The music teacher's name, so I had gleaned, was Mrs Madge Cole and I had taken to standing outside watching her pupils go in and out. I liked listening to the senior students playing 'Für Elise' or the 'Moonlight Sonata'. Mrs Cole must have noticed me, because one afternoon she came out and said, 'Would you like to come inside?'

She was beautiful and scented, always impeccably groomed, with lovely clothes, and she sat me down in her gracious drawing room while she continued her piano lesson. I was entranced. Her proud husband, John, adored her and they had two children, John Jnr and Patricia, who had golden ringlets.

I told Teria, 'I would like to learn how to play the piano.'

It was one of those things that young children say to their grandparents without really thinking. However, not long afterward, I came home to find my father unloading something from Chrisp's Music Store. My mother was furious with me. 'Why did you tell your grandmother you wanted to play the piano? Now she's gone and bought you one.'

The piano was new, an upright, the brand was Brasted, and Huia Chrisp arrived with some free music to give to me.

The purchase caused a lot of dissension between me and Grandad. He stormed over to the house and upbraided me in front of Mum and Dad. 'Your grandmother should never have bought it for you,' he said.

My mother was looking on, and after a while she stepped in. I thought she would continue growling at me but instead she turned to Pera and said, 'It's too late, it's done.'

Done? Didn't I have a say in the matter? I ignored Pera Punahāmoa and said to her, 'Tell Grandad I'll pay for the piano.'

He looked at me, incredulous. 'How do you think you can do that? You're just a boy.'

'I'll find a way.'

Chapter Twenty-five

Journey to Emerald City

1.

AROUND THIS TIME, Dad said he wanted to go to Wellington for a visit. His brother Win was an education officer and he, Aunty Margaret and the children had shifted into a brand-new state house in Rata Street, Naenae. Mum wasn't keen as she was pregnant with Derek and was as big as a house. But Dad persuaded her by saying, 'On the way we could stop at Waipukurau and see Cliff.'

Since coming to Gisborne and joining Dad's shearing gang, Cliff Paine had contracted poliomyelitis. This acute viral disease, which affected the spinal cord and nervous system, had been a somewhat regular visitor to New Zealand. However, the outbreak that began in 1955 and didn't taper off until June 1956 was particularly vicious, targeting those aged fifteen and over, and mainly people in rural areas; more than seventy people died. Schools went into lockdown, and I remember buckets of disinfectant appearing in our toilet block — the virus was considered to be transmitted by human waste. We had to wipe our hands with towels after using the toilet. It wasn't until the development of the Salk vaccine in the 1960s that the fight against polio was effectively mounted.

My mother was distraught when Cliff collapsed. After some time at Cook Hospital, where it was clear that his muscles had become paralysed by the virus, he was sent by ambulance back to his family.

'Yes,' my mother said, 'we should see Cliff.'

My sisters and I had never been on holiday as a family before, and the thought of driving all that way to Wellington was exciting. We couldn't wait. The only sad part of the trip was when we arrived at Waipukurau after a day's car travel. Cliff was lying in an iron lung, a compression chamber that helped to keep him breathing. We talked to his reflection in a mirror. His speech was punctuated by small gasps as he took air in and forced his lungs to work.

Mum just didn't want to leave Cliff's side. Although the plan was that we should go on to Wellington and arrive before nightfall, she asked Dad if we could stay the night and see Cliff again in the morning. Because her pregnancy was uncomfortable and tiring, he saw the sense in an overnight stop. He found a small hotel with a big bedroom and we bedded down together; it was part of the adventure.

My mother always sent money to Cliff's hospital so that they could give him better care. I don't know if he was aware of this.

2.

THE NEXT DAY we resumed our trip and arrived in Wellington in the early afternoon.

My sisters and I may have been townies to our Ngāti Porou cousins, but our Wellington cousins, Teria, Pera, Meri and Winiata Jnr, were on a different planet. Naenae was a state housing estate, freshly minted, with well laid out streets and weatherboard houses, each looking exactly the same as its neighbour. The symmetry was admirable and took your breath away.

The houses all had three bedrooms, one for Mum and Dad and two for children. The low-cost concept was a bold social welfare experiment, but nobody had told the architects that Māori, who were the main tenants, had five or more children. Perhaps the houses had been built on a smaller scale in the vain hope that we would get the idea.

The most amazing feature to us was that the toilet was *inside* the house and it flushed away your tūtae and mimi with water. My sisters and I flushed and flushed the toilet, apoplectic with mirth, until Aunty Margaret came and told us to stop it.

Later that afternoon, Uncle Win took us into town on the commuter train. I watched out the window as Wellington magically slid into view beside a perfect sea. We took the tram to the Wellington Zoo, where a big yellow parakeet, attracted by my yellow jersey, sat on my shoulder, said, 'Who's a pretty Māori boy then?', and promptly shat on me to show me that, although I might be yellow, I was a lesser bird.

I had my first encounter with Te Pāremata o te Pākehā, the New Zealand parliament. First impressions really matter, and I was awed by it. When I became a writer, my childhood impressions coalesced into an adult Ringatū perspective with attendant Old Testament imagery.

It was William Wakefield, brother of Edward Gibbon Wakefield, who in 1839 came on the *Tory* and then made what became known as the Port Nicholson purchase. He negotiated with Māori he thought represented the tribes of the lower North Island. They didn't.

The purchase was soon followed by the arrival of the *Aurora* in 1840 and four later vessels to the harbour first discovered by Kupe, a thousand years before, and founded by Tara. Although the Māori had named the harbour Te Whanganui-a-Tara, the Great Harbour of Tara, the Pākehā renamed it Port Nicholson, and later Wellington.

And so did Pharaoh begin his rule in Aotearoa. In 1865 he proclaimed Wellington as his capital of New Zealand, and shortly thereafter began to raise, in his Valley of the Kings, the edifices of his power and might. One of the first of his monuments was his temple to God, St Paul's, in 1866. Another was his Government Buildings, four storeys tall, completed in

1876 for his officials and overseers. His governmental papers had proper recognition of their status when Pharaoh caused to be built the General Assembly Library building, opened in 1899.

But the mightiest of the monuments was his new Parliament House, wherein his elected governors could meet to promulgate his laws and set his taxes. His architects began to build this imposing marble edifice in 1918 and, when it was finally completed in 1922, it was like unto a crouching sphinx.

To this place of might and dread, throughout the decades, Māori petitioners had come seeking justice. From the Far North, Hongi and Hone Heke. From the Waikato, Te Puea and others of the King Movement. From the decimated Taranaki, Te Whiti and Tohu. From the South Island, the rangatira of Kāi Tahu. Māori great and small, disempowered and displaced. Some, like my ancestor Wī Pere, had served within the Pāremata o te Pākehā in attempts to seek redress by representing the Māori within Pharaoh's Court.

'E hoa, give us back our land.'

Yes, there was no doubting the resonances, the *disturbances*, that were set up when I first saw that parliamentary precinct gleaming in the sun.

On that visit we were lucky enough to watch a debate in which Eruera Tirikātene was involved. He was a silver-haired, distinguished man, and afterwards, when he saw Uncle Win, he came over to say hello. As we were leaving, Uncle Win showed us, in one of the hallways, a large photo of a Māori delegation that had come to parliament only a few years earlier to present a petition on Māori land.

'Mum's in the photograph,' he told Dad. 'Can you see her?'

He and Dad pressed close to the photograph and although I asked, 'Let me see, too,' all I saw was a group of Māori with the prime minister in the middle.

Childhood is full of conversations overheard or eavesdropped upon. It's also made up of glimpses and fragments, which can be as potent as any full view. I made an assumption that Teria had been here on some business for Te Whānau-a-Kai.

We had early kai at Ngāti Poneke Māori Community Hall, and then Uncle Win left us to do some business. We walked up Lambton Quay to Willis Street and Cuba Street. I was fascinated by the lights and the sparking of the trams on their overhead lines. We saw a department store and went in. What happened next was the basis for this story.

Across the glistening sheen of the window shimmered our reflections. On the outside looking in.

'Can we go inside?' I asked.

'No harm in looking,' Dad answered.

'All right,' Mum said. 'But don't touch anything.'

We entered the gleaming swing doors, stepping into the perfumed and air-conditioned interior.

'Wow,' I said with awe. I led my mother along a carpeted walkway between glass counters. Together we stopped to look at rings and necklaces strewn inside display cases. We watched as people tried on high-heeled shoes and tall pigskin boots. Then we moved on, past the record counter through haberdashery into the women's wear section. A dress that might have suited Mum was on sale, and she fingered it curiously.

'Can I help you?' A shop assistant asked.

'Just looking,' Mum said. We walked away from the counter.

In the grocery department we joined a crowd watching a beautiful model carve a chicken with knife held delicately in red-tipped fingers. Then we wandered through the china department where crystal glasses, fragile ornaments and dinnerware bore runic names and twinkled on revolving stands.

For a short while we watched the programme playing on a black and white television set.

'Can we go upstairs now?' I asked. 'To the toy section?'

'All right,' Mum answered.

We followed electric arrows pointing the way. Suddenly, there was the escalator, the moving staircase between floors, a gleaming funnel bearing shoppers to the first floor. Before Mum could stop us, my sisters and I had jumped onto it. Screaming with delight, we waved to Mum and Dad.

'Come down from there,' she yelled. In her panic she put her hand on the rail. It moved beneath her touch and she recoiled.

'Do you mind?' A young girl glared.

'I'm sorry,' Mum answered. She stepped aside and let the shoppers file past her. As they moved on the escalator they looked back at her.

'What's wrong with you?' Dad asked.

'That thing. I'm not getting on it.'

'Why not?'

'You just get the kids to come down. And then we can go home to Win's place.' She saw us waving from the top of the escalator. She gestured back angrily. Then she noticed that a small group of bystanders was watching her. Some were grinning. Others were openly curious. Shoppers pushed past, stepping onto the escalator with the ease of accustomed habit, riding that short gap with an air of bored indifference.

Among the bystanders was a shop attendant. Mum caught his glance and quickly looked away. But she knew he would approach her.

'Is there anything wrong, madam?' he asked.

'Oh no,' Mum answered. 'I'm all right.'

'She's never been on one of these things before,' Dad explained. 'And, as you can see, she's pregnant and a bit afraid.'

At his words, Mum crimsoned. 'I'll take the lift,' she said.

The attendant smiled at her. 'But there's nothing to it, madam. Look, I'll show you.' He grasped the handrail and stepped lightly onto the escalator. He went up a few steps and then quickly turned back. 'See? Simple. Now you try it.'

'Let these other people go first,' Mum said.

'Oh, they won't mind,' the attendant said. He motioned her to take his place at the bottom of the escalator.

With an angry glance at Dad, Mum nodded okay. She looked up that frightening silver funnel. She looked down and saw the black divisions between each step appearing from beneath the silver footplate. She watched as they jackknifed into moving steps. She put out her hands to grasp the moving handrails and she raised a foot. 'No,' she said. She moved back. 'How dare you embarrass me in front of all these people,' she whispered to Dad.

Then she saw us running towards her. We had been chasing each other along the upstairs balcony and had come down the stairs. But instead of stopping with Mum and Dad we jumped onto the escalator again. Shouting and giggling, we chased each other up it, shoving and pushing past the amused passengers.

Mum ran to the escalator and yelled to us. 'Come back! Come back!'

I saw her face and froze. 'What's wrong, Mum?' And then I shouted across the space, 'What are you people doing to my mother?' My words carried through the store.

My mother tried to smile. This was the last thing she wanted, to be the centre of attention.

'Looks like you have to do it now,' Dad said.

The attendant came forward again. 'Once you get used to it,' he said, 'it's really quite simple, madam.' He demonstrated again how to step onto the escalator. People in the crowd offered encouraging comments.

'You can do it, dear. I was like you, love, afraid of the thing. Once you take that first step you'll be right.'

The escalator looked like a river running uphill. Mum put her hands on the handrails and then pulled them back again.

At that moment, someone in the crowd tried to give her a helpful push. Then a loud voice came from behind the crowd. 'What on earth is going on?'

'There's a Māori lady, she's pregnant and scared of the escalator.'

'What? Well, why doesn't she get out of the way then, instead of holding us up? She should use the stairs, they're made for people like her. Let me through, I'm in a hurry.'

Mum felt herself getting angry. She should get out of the way, should she? And stairs were for people like her, were they? Her anger rose above her fears.

She stepped onto the escalator.

The sudden movement beneath her feet threw her off balance. She felt one of her legs buckling as the escalator formed into steps. She grabbed with both hands first at the left handrail and then the right handrail. She sought her balance with her feet and hung on tightly as the escalator carried her upward. With dismay, she realised that the handrail was moving faster than the steps.

Then Dad was beside her. 'It's all right, Julia.'

The escalator carried them up to where we were waiting.

I never knew it at the time but my boyhood mind was constantly at work, trying to make sense of a new, changing, world. Although the Wellington experience was powerful, it was also disconcerting and freighted with signs and portents. Some I rejected, others I allowed to infiltrate my consciousness.

One question that resonated was this: Was Naenae to be our future? All spick and span and living like everyone else in the perfect harmony of a regulated estate?

In many respects, it was the same question as: Why build a well at the top of a hill?

Today, Aunty Margaret is a widow, but she still lives in Rata Street. For some years the bold state housing experiment of Naenae was maintained, and for many it did represent a version of the New Zealand dream — the three-bedroom house, not quite a quarter-acre pavlova paradise, for Pākehā and Māori wanting to live and work in Wellington. For a while the dream faltered, it wasn't a good fit, but today there are signs of revival. Someone even told me Naenae is thriving, affordable and mostly middle class. Cher, you guys. Go the Hutt.

I think the lesson was that there was nothing wrong with the dream.

It just wasn't ours until we made it *ours*.

MY BROTHER DEREK was born on our return from that visit to Wellington, and my sisters and I finally had the brother we wanted. Now we were five — me, Kararaina, Tāwhi, Viki and Derek.

Tāwhi, in particular, took to Derek very strongly. 'You and Kararaina have each other,' she said to me. 'I was supposed to have Tommy but he died.' As it happened, Tāwhi had to share this new brother with Viki.

Although Derek was a big baby, he suffered from what were known as convulsions, seizures that could come upon him day or night. During his infancy, therefore, he always slept in Mum and Dad's bedroom so that they could keep an eye on him. When Derek got older he was transferred to my bedroom where I was his watcher. Sometimes, when he cried, he would forget to breathe, almost as if his lungs had expanded so wide in his ribcage that they couldn't close. He had to be shocked into breathing again, and one of the tricks that Mum taught me was to run to the kitchen, fill a glass with water and splash it in his face. When he grew up and I told him what I used to do, Derek was not impressed.

But he survived, though my sisters and I still had to keep an eye on him. In particular, whenever we heard a plane coming in to land at the nearby airport, we would run out to protect him because the noise would bring on a fit. The worst times were when the plane was on the flight path right above our house. The plane must have appeared to Derek as some huge bird of prey swooping out of the sun — he would fall to the ground, kicking and convulsing. We ran outside and covered him with our bodies before the bird got him and took him away.

'There, there, brother, we've saved you.'

My sisters tell me that our brother Neil, who came ten years later, had the same affliction. I may have confused Derek and Neil, but I don't think so. My experience of my brother's seizures so worried me that when my own daughters were born Jane and I had them in our bedroom until I was satisfied that they did not show the same symptoms.

And so the lives of our family in Te Hāpara were eventful, but the events were all small and intimate. And *my* experiences at primary school, you wouldn't think of them as earth-shaking, but they all had their impact. Certainly I had graduated from nursery rhymes, and I was learning all the time about the world. What I was taking in, however, was not as important as what it meant.

There's another aspect to consider: the beginnings of a writer's life. In that womb of learning, what was making my creative subconscious move so violently, so eager to be requited? Was there something in the Kate Seredy stories that provided a template for my own creativity? And did I swap dancing doll for singing typewriter?

Can we see in the young music pupil's joy in piano music the beginning of his journey towards creating the singing word, literary waiata, in his work? And is the cheekiness of the boy who got to the top of Everest first so different from the adult who began to destabilise history?

In that trip to Wellington was there already an awareness of point of view, that a particular structure was being imposed? We could either belong or, if we didn't, forever exist as outsiders.

And in the story of Cliff's poliomyelitis and my brother Derek's convulsions was there something about our vulnerability that frightened me and made me want to create some certainty in our lives, even if it lay only in the hopes and dreams of my imagination?

All I know is that one day that creative subconscious put up its hand: 'Pick me, pick me.'

I was sitting in Miss Hossack's class and we were all playing up. We should have been outside letting off steam in the afternoon break but it was raining cats and dogs. So there we were, moody and vocal and kicking the furniture around, bored, bored, bored. No doubt Miss Hossack would have preferred that we were out of her pretty curly hair, but she was stuck with us, so she said, 'Get out your exercise books! We're all going to write a story.'

In those days you had a desk with an inkwell and a pen with a nib. Whenever you were fed up you wrote graffiti inside and outside the desk and sometimes admitted your feelings as in 'WS x AT' (which I did, and I'm not telling who 'AT' was). What I also remember is that for some strange reason the ink in the inkwell was purple; perhaps the Education Department had run out of blue or black.

I've told this story so many times before, to make myself the butt of a joke, so the actual words I wrote in my exercise book have probably been embellished for the sake of storytelling. However, it *is* intact, more or less, and it goes like this:

'Once upon a time there was a princess locked in a tall tower guarded by a fierce dragon. Every day she would see a handsome prince go past, and she would run to the window and cry, "Help me! Help me! Save me from this dragon!" But because she was so ugly, the princes on their white horses would take one look and keep on riding to rescue a more beautiful princess further down the road. Day after day this would happen until the princess got so sick and tired of waiting that she went out and married the dragon.'

As an instigating piece, it's not very good, is it? I wish I had written something of the quality of Janet Frame's first ever story about the bird and the hawk, but qué será será.

Sad to say, no rainbow appeared in the sky to bless my first words either and to offer the consolation that I might improve in the future. The rainbow god, Kahukura, hadn't appeared when I was born either, so what was new? Nor was Miss Hossack pleased with me; she thought I was playing the fool.

When I was much older — and a writer — and after I had read the piece to a laughing audience to show them that they could probably become better writers than I was if they wanted to, a man I didn't know came up to me. He told me I shouldn't be so embarrassed by the story.

'It shows that even as a boy you were subverting the main discourse,' he began. 'The princess is not pretty, as princesses are supposed to be, and the princes on their white horses are not chivalrous either. Nor does the princess wait around to be rescued by a man. No! What does she do? She leaves the land of safety and embraces danger by marrying the dragon.'

Was I flabbergasted by the analysis? Was I *what*. Clearly something was happening in that boyhood brain of mine, something springing up and motivated by that long ago day when Teria had critiqued those two nursery rhymes and told me I should always question what I was being taught.

Within the story is a young boy's first incipient and intuitive attempt to express, and answer, the imperatives of his Māori subconscious.

Now the tika. In the 1980s I was walking in Te Pāremata o te Pākehā on my way to the Maori Affairs Room when I suddenly remembered the photograph Uncle Win had pointed out to Dad on that first visit to Wellington. I thought I'd try to find it, so I went along one red-carpeted hallway after another — you could do that before security procedures became the norm. Of course, décor changes, photographs get taken down, paintings are moved. I don't know how long I searched before I gave up. In the end, I stood there. I realised that I was alone except, of course, that there are always ghosts.

In many ways that photograph, spectral and fragmented in my memory, became my 'Rosebud'. I began to add missing pieces to it. Uncle Win had alluded to the photograph's existence but, actually, all I needed for my imagination to be triggered was the *possibility* of it. When I had completed the reconstruction, the photograph had become a snapshot of an imagined moment — a moment in a narrative that *could* have been about a woman, similar to my beloved grandmother, who in 1949 visited Te Pāremata o te Pākehā to prosecute parliament for the return of her land.

Chapter Twenty-six

Wellington, 1949

1.

La luce langue, il faro spegnesi
Ch'eterno corre per gli ampi cieli!
Notte desiata, provvida veli
La man colpevole che ferirà.

Light weakens, and the beacon
That eternally courses the far-flung heavens is spent.
O desired night, you providentially veil
The guilty hand which is going to strike the blow.

The wind was in abeyance on the forecourt of Parliament Buildings, Wellington. The eastern wind was on one side, the southerly on the other. In between was the calm, like the eye of a cyclone.

Teria, however, was not calm. The child felt her fingers clasping his upper arms, almost hurting him. She was watching, intense, the consultation that was occurring between the prime minister and the chiefs of Māoridom, waiting on the red carpet.

'Kia tūpato,' she said. 'Now comes the time of the mihimihi, the speechmaking. We must listen carefully when the speeches are made to welcome us, because we must respond in kind. If we do not hear that is said then we cannot reply with all that must be said. So be alert because, after all, this is Pharaoh's territory, not ours.'

She directed the child's gaze across parliament grounds. 'See Te Pāremata o te Pākehā? It is a place of dread, mokopuna. From its halls the laws that control the lives of all Māori are promulgated.'

The pearls shimmered in her hair as she glanced at the prime minister and the chiefs of Māoridom. The prime minister's chief official, Tīmoti, was conversing with Whai, one of the elders. 'They are up to something,' Teria warned the child. 'But they had better be careful for they will get as good as they give,' she winked at the child, 'and receive more than they expect.'

There was a murmur of amusement from the ope. The Matua was in a fighting mood and those old fellas better watch out because she had eaten only a little breakfast that day and she was still starving. But behind the joking was a darkness, a fear, because in any encounter like this the forecourt was a marae, the courtyard of Tū, god of war. Any person, man or woman, who proposed to do battle here needed to be well aware of their weapons.

For a moment the child also felt fearful for his grandmother. He looked up and saw that the pearls in her hair, usually glowing, were darkening. The sky turning in her eyes, the eyes that took colour from the elements, on this day were deepening, dark green as the pounamu. He wanted to say something to her but, almost as suddenly as the wind had died, so too did the tumult and the ecstasy following their entry onto parliament grounds.

'Now it really begins,' Teria said. 'See? Whai is to be their first speaker.'

He stood on the red carpet, in his right hand a tokotoko, a walking stick, which he raised in a dramatic gesture. His voice boomed across the forecourt, his staff pulling the wrath of the heavens down, down to earth.

'Tihei mauriora,' Whai began, the words thrusting out, pushing out, into the world of light. 'I sneeze, it is life. Tihei uriuri, tihei nakonako, it is darkness, it is blackness. Lay, ha, set in its place, the sky above. Lay, ha, set in its place the earth below.' The words were rapid and recited in a rhythmic incantatory manner. 'Ka tau, ha, whakatau ko Te Matuku mai ki Rarotonga. Trace back to Te Matuku from Rarotonga, who dived to the spirit within, who dived to the spirit without.' Whai strode up and down the red carpet in time with the cadence of his chant, gesturing and brandishing his walking stick. His words were ancient and obscure. Right at the end, a giant tidal wave of voices joined with his.

'Hui e, haumi e, tāiki e. Yes, let it be done.'

Teria nodded with approval. 'Whai was always a great orator,' she told the child. 'One of these days, mokopuna, you must learn the reo, the ritual chants, the tauparapara and the pātere. Such chants dignify your speech. But hush, mokopuna, we must hear what else he has to say.'

Whai had paused, looking back at Tīmoti. Was that a nod that was exchanged between them? Imperceptibly, his stand altered and so did the quality of his kōrero. And then he deliberately turned his back on Teria and began to welcome, instead, the other tribes who had come to the hui.

('At this point,' the journalist said, 'I sensed that something was amiss. I can't put my finger on it, but it was as if the electricity in the air had turned from positive to negative. There was a strange unease, and some of the Māori people waiting on the red carpet were whispering to one another. The old Māori man I was standing next to explained it to me. "There's been a jack-up between Tīmoti and some of the chiefs of Māoridom. They must be in a hurry to get back to their meeting to treat the Matua like this. A chief is always welcomed in a chiefly manner with chiefly kōrero and speechmaking. They are welcoming all the other chiefs but not the Matua. To all intents and purposes they are treating her as an outcast. After all, she is a woman."

'And it was clear,' the journalist continued, 'that Teria recognised the slight and had taken offence. You know, sometimes distances seem deceptive. But when the sun came briefly through the clouds, it illuminated her extraordinary face, and brought her so close to me that I could almost touch her. The sunlight gleamed like fire on the pearls in her hair. I will never forget what she did. She looked up at the sun and her face was so deathly calm. And then—')

As Whai's voice spun itself out into the air, spinning, spinning, spinning, Teria lifted her head, as if to watch the words ascending. Higher and higher they went, and the sun shafted through them as they reached heaven.

She stared straight into the sun and did not blink. Instead she absorbed its power.

'Auē, e kui,' Aunty Mary said. There was confusion, anger, sorrow and embarrassment in the ranks of the ope. To stand here, like this, on the forecourt and be denied, for if they were not welcomed, they could not enter.

'Kia kaha,' Teria breathed. 'This is my fight, not yours. Nevertheless, close your ranks, all of you, stand close, closer still, for it is my great honour to feel your aroha for your Matua. Be one group and let us have the one heart and one purpose.' Her voice rose with authority. 'The red carpet of the Pākehā is before us and let nobody, Pākehā or Māori, stand in our way.'

Immediately, the ope began to acclaim her. 'Āe, āe, āe!'

The child watched as his grandmother imprisoned all eyes with hers. She lifted her hands to her head and began to pull her dark black veil back down and over her face.

'If a fight is what they want,' she said, 'a fight is what they will get.'

('The atmosphere was so tense,' the journalist said. 'The prime minister was watching bemused, as Bernard Scott hastily consulted with Tīmoti, but, clearly, the elders of Māoridom were adamant. "It is only the cock that crows," one of them said. Another interjected, "Better to put the kuia in her place now and not allow her the opportunity of appearing as an equal, with equal authority, among us."')

'So be it,' Riripeti said. She looked up at the sun again, full, glorious, a gigantic glowing orb of immense power. She lifted her right hand up to her veil and began to pull it across her face. 'Te Whānau-a-Kai hei panapana mārō, Te Whānau-a-Kai are a tribe who never retreat, whether we be men or women.'

('But I have yet to tell you of the most extraordinary incident,' the journalist said. 'I guess it will never, ever be explained. On reflection, I think it was entirely coincidental, but who knows? I have heard that some of your people have the power to make such things happen.')

The veil slowly descending. As it did so, the clouds began to join across what once had been a brief space of sunlit sky.

'So be it,' Riripeti said again.

With a ponderous rumbling, like iron gates closing, the sun began to go out.

PART FOUR

TŪRANGAWAEWAE
A PLACE TO
STAND

Chapter Twenty-seven

The Second Telling

1.

I'M TRYING TO keep the balance in my story. It's not easy, what with the huge cast of characters. At this point I know that I should summon my mother, Julia, to return.

Throughout my boyhood, my sisters and I always would ask her to tell us about the events of the story that had been so much part of the family folklore — the account of how my mother and father came back to Gisborne from their Hastings marriage in 1943, and its aftermath.

The account was one of those ritual invocations conducted when Dad was away. If it occurred in the evenings, we would begin by climbing on the bed while a storm cracked fierce overhead. Or if it was morning, we would sneak into Mum's bedroom while she was still asleep. Together, we would watch our mother's circling toes, moving under the coverlet. Inevitably the account would begin with one of my sisters asking a simple question: 'If ever we were lost in Te Pō, would Mum be able to find us?'

In my work I take traditional myth and concepts and fashion out of them new myths. Already, that simple event of watching our mother's circling toes was developing into an epic conceit. Eventually, in my reply, I began to incarnate the myth of the dream swimmer.

'Yes,' I would answer, 'even if we are lost in Te Pō, the great darkness at the other side of the universe, our mother will not be afraid. She will take her bearings from sacred Hikurangi mountain, and she will rise from Haig Street and begin her search. Through the hallway lined with whakapapa she will swim, ascending swiftly into the midnight air. Past the moon she will travel, her long white nightdress flowing behind her and she will shout to the planets, "Make way! Make way!" When she arrives at the rings of Saturn she will dive between them and move on fast beyond Pluto. And when she sees the stars showering into the black hole that marks the entrance to Te Pō, will she stop? No fear! Down she will plunge into the inky darkness.

'It might take our mother one year, a hundred years or a thousand years to find us, but we will be all right because we will be together and we will sing songs to each other in the darkness to keep ourselves from being afraid, eh, my sisters! And all the while, our mother will descend deeper and deeper into the maw of Te Pō where we wait at its intense and silent centre.

'But there will surely come a day when, all of a sudden, we will hear the darkness dividing and feel the touch of our mother's arms. And she will say to us, "Put your arms around my neck, children, because it's time to go home. We have to get back before morning because I need to make your father's breakfast."

'Clinging to her we will rise through Te Pō, watching as we finally reach the lip of The Great Night. Oh, the stars, my sisters!

'And our mother will wait for the sun to arise and to send a beam across the universe.

'"There it is, Mum."

'A twinkle in the distance flashes on Mount Hikurangi, there and mark. "Ah, ko Hikurangi tērā."

'Our mother has always loved us. Always.'

The story was a karakia, a childish mantra. After it was uttered, I would put my hands around our mother's circling toes. 'Wake up now, Mum.'

She would whimper, her head thrashing on the pillow. Her toes would try to keep on circling, but eventually they would cease their rotating movements and become still. I would watch her face as she rose through the surface of her dreams, like a swimmer arising from the sea.

A deep inward breath. 'Yes, son?'

'Now tell us what happened when you came back to Gisborne with Dad.'

IT WAS SUCH a simple story, really, of a young bride and her new husband returning from a secret wedding. Yet, whenever our mother told it to me and my sisters, I was always uneasy about the trancelike way she told it. Her eyes would become so still and dark, their irises diminishing. There was such a sense of innocence and hope in the story, but at the same time a sense of fragility. If innocence was a piece of glass and you dropped it, the glass would break into a thousand pieces.

Many years later, I decided to write the following version from the bits and pieces of information I had at my disposal. I sourced the dark resonances that I sensed lay beneath:

The train pulled into the railway station. The clock on the platform ticked 3.46 p.m.

Seated in the train, Turi took Te Haa's arm and hugged him. This man was hers. Who would have thought she would get married! 'I love you, Te Haa.'

He shrugged, grinned and winked at her. He only had to grin and he charmed the world. He bent to kiss her, and as he did so the window was splashed with sleet and rain; it streaked across Turi's image, scarring her. 'Almost there, Julia,' he said. 'I know my parents will love you as much as I do.'

Turi took consolation from his words. The trip had been a long one and she felt anxious at the prospect of meeting Te Haa's parents, let alone telling her own parents that she was married. All she wanted to do was to get it over with and settle down to life with her husband.

Then there was the matter of her virginity. What would her first night with Te Haa be like?

Her attention was diverted by a commercial traveller, sitting opposite, in conversation with a young passenger. 'That doesn't sound like progress, lad,' the commercial traveller said.

And here was the conductor saying, 'Five minutes to Gisborne, folks. Only five minutes more.'

The commercial traveller laughed and began to sing. 'Give me five minutes more, only five minutes more, let me stay, let me stay in your arms.' Others in the carriage began to join in.

Turi stood up and began to take the luggage down from the rack. Not much to start a life with. Everything she owned was in those suitcases. But she was strong, and a survivor. Once the war was over, why, there were better times ahead. She was startled to feel Te Haa's arms around her waist, pulling her down.

'Let me,' he said.

'I can do it,' she answered.

Te Haa smiled and said, 'I know you can, but let me. I know you've always done everything yourself in your life, but no longer.'

She looked at him and, after a moment's hesitation said, 'Okay.' But she had always looked after herself, and letting Te Haa take over was the closest she had ever come to surrender.

'Three minutes, folks.'

With a start, Turi saw that Gisborne had pounced out of the grey afternoon. Very soon, the houses began to stream past in the rain.

She put on her hat. She had a dark brown coat which she had bought because it was just like the one Joan Crawford had worn in *A Woman's Face*. Joan Crawford had acted the part of Anna Holm, hideously scarred on one side of her face. Embittered, she had lived a lonely life until she had plastic surgery. When Joan Crawford's face showed on the screen, healed, my mother had touched her own wonderingly.

She belted the coat and stood up. The coat, with its padded shoulders, made her look tall and shapely, and with the hat shadowing her brow and eyes, she was instantly intriguing. Yet, disarmed by love, she was for the first time in her life defenceless. She had given herself up to Te Haa and placed her future in his hands.

The time was 3.50 p.m. All of a sudden the railway station loomed ahead like a merry-go-round swaying in the rain. The train emitted a loud throaty whistle, and steam erupted with a hiss to billow across the windows. Turi laughed, put one hand up to her face and the other on the back edge of the seat to steady herself and ...

The train pulled into the railway station.

It was 3.51 p.m. The train driver applied the brakes and the wheels began to slow down and lock. For a moment they slid on the wet tracks, propelled onward by momentum. The couplings between each carriage began to jerk and clash as the train slowed to a halt. A final whistle, a blast of steam billowing across the platform, and the journey was ended.

'We're here,' Te Haa said. His voice betrayed that he was just as nervous as Turi was. He wondered why he had never told her his secret; it was too late now.

On the platform, heads began to crane and look into carriage windows. From the inside they looked like gasping fish, the mouths opening and closing in the joy of recognition. 'The waving hands are like white fins,' Turi thought. The passengers began to move out of the carriages and onto the platform.'

'Can you see your parents?' Turi asked.

'No,' Te Haa said.

She started to follow him along the corridor of the carriage to the exit. The commercial traveller was just in front of Te Haa, jumping down with great gusto. The train driver watched, amused, and gave a cheery wave of good luck.

It was then that Teria saw Te Haa. 'There he is,' she said to Pera Punahāmoa. Black-caped, she crossed the railway tracks to the platform; the stationmaster was talking to the engine driver. 'An hour and a half late, Bert,' he was saying. 'This train is getting later every week.'

The driver shrugged his shoulders. 'The sooner the viaduct is finished at Mōhaka the better. The real trouble's the rain. Just pouring off the hills, y'know.'

The platform was crowded with people. The rain was falling like bullets, and the people were hesitant to make a dash for it to their cars.

Teria stepped up and onto the platform. A pearl, which she had woven artfully into her hair, dislodged and fell into the mud and ...

The train pulled into the station.

The station clock, hanging overhead in an ornate metalwork bracket, announced the time in Roman numerals: 3.52 p.m.

From that overhead vantage point the entire length of the platform was visible. The platform was like a sea. In the crowd, a woman in black, accompanied by her husband, made her way from carriage to carriage. As she traversed the platform the crowd opened up, flowed and eddied around her.

'Here we go,' Te Haa said. He stepped from the train onto the platform. He put the two suitcases down. The commercial traveller, knowing that

Te Haa and Turi had just got married, said, 'Good luck, mate.' Te Haa shook his hand.

Teria saw him. 'There he is,' she said. She had not yet seen Turi, who was still standing on the topmost step of the carriage.

Turi looked down at Te Haa. She was almost beautiful. The light from the platform struck the planes of her face, and her eyes were glowing. Te Haa gave that handsome, sensuous smile. He put his hands firmly on my mother's hips to swing her to the ground and . . .

The train pulled into the railway station.

It was 3.50 p.m.

Suddenly Te Haa wasn't there and Turi felt herself falling. It happened so quickly, and it was so ridiculous to be falling that she felt like laughing at the silliness of it. She put her hands in front to protect herself as she fell and thought, 'Te Haa, I love you, don't do this to me,' and . . .

The train pulled into the railway station.

The train was late. 'There he is.' The huge front grille of the train pushed aside the rain. Turi, disarmed by love, was for the first time in her life defenceless. A pearl fell in the mud. 'Here we go then,' Te Haa said. He alighted from the train. He put the two suitcases on the platform. 'Good luck,' the commercial traveller said. Turi saw Te Haa below her and began to step down to him. It was 3.53 pm. Te Haa's hands were on Turi's hips and he was lifting her up in his strong arms to swing her to the ground and then she was falling. As she was falling she thought, 'No, I won't let this happen, I won't.' She saw that Te Haa was struggling in the arms of a strong man. Then she saw Teria and . . .

The train pulled into the railway station.

Turi fell. She fell twenty-one years in one second. She tried to find Hikurangi mountain but her mind was whirling so much that she couldn't focus.

'I was born into this life alone. I have always been alone. All my life I have had nothing. The world doesn't owe me anything. I will always be alone.'

She fell to the ground.

GISBORNE DOESN'T HAVE a railway station any longer. Passenger services were terminated in the 1980s, and although freight carried on for some years, that, too, has now ended.

The large ornate clock that once hung above the platform and fascinated me, that also has gone, but was it there in the first place? The sole photo I have been able to find of the platform shows no clock at all. All that's there now is a derelict building and associated sidings, and empty weed-filled pathways where the tracks used to be. There is always memory and, of course, railway stations even if abandoned and deserted are places where memories pool and swirl forever.

Even with memory, however, there is always a degree to which a person and their story is unknowable. For instance, in the above version, my grandparents were not in the train but were waiting for my father at the railway station. Was it there that Dad turned to my mother and told her, 'Yes, go to your mother and father, Turi, while I tell my parents'?

When she told me her version, my mother said, 'Your father went with Teria and Pera.'

I was puzzled. 'What do you mean?'

'He was supposed to marry somebody else.'

'Somebody *who!*'

'Somebody he was taumau'd to, an arranged marriage. They did things like that in those days.'

Oh, sometimes life is filled with unfinished explanations that reflect points of view that often don't fit with each other. I am tempted to ignore them, but if I do that am I not robbing life and its people of their richness — I wouldn't call this ambiguity, which suggests lies rather than truth but, rather, complexity? People are much larger than we think, and their motives in themselves may be construed in different ways when reflected through the prisms of interpretation. Mine is but one prism through which to see events, but it would be foolish and unfair of me not to acknowledge conflicting details and tellings. Along with that, I am more than happy to admit that, in arranging the bits and pieces I had, I got it wrong.

What really happened at the railway station? And which version possesses the emotional truth? None of us can assume to know. Certainly I don't assume that much.

As a young boy I figured that upon arriving in Gisborne Dad must have admitted to Mum that he hadn't told Teria and Pera Punahāmoa that he was getting married — he needed time to tell them the arranged marriage was off. It seemed entirely reasonable, therefore, that she should wait in Tolaga Bay until he had done this.

But this was not the reason at all. There was something else that Dad hadn't told her.

Chapter Twenty-eight

Haka!

1.

E HIKA, ANOTHER one of those backward-turning spirals has brushed against the main turning of the wheel, this gyre of my life, making me realise that although I have been writing this memoir in a linear fashion, my childhood, actually, wasn't like that.

It was organic. It was messy and, well, chaotic. You had to roll with it and the people in it or be rolled over by it — and them. It was difficult enough negotiating my way through the Pākehā world, let alone that other Māori world revolving alongside it and around it.

And the possessiveness of that Māori world! Sometimes I felt I belonged to everybody — my grandmother Teria, the great shearing and sporting family I was a part of, and my mother's equally possessive family up the coast. As children, my sisters, brother and I were constantly on the move with Mum and Dad out to Waituhi or up to the coast for whānau commitments, births, weddings, family anniversaries and death. There, 'up the coast' as we called it, the Babbington and Keelan families were like huge spreading trees with many embracing branches that intertwined with all the other families of the East Coast, and they embraced *us*. There was a strong female emphasis in the families — look at all the subtribes of Ngāti Porou named after women: Ruataupare, Hinerupe, Mate, Hinetāpora, Tāpuhi, Hinepare, Rākairoa, Hinemanuhiri and Iritekura. And let me bear witness to the many marae named after women.

Indeed, my mother had a special fondness for Hinemaurea marae. She was loyal to it all her life, and regularly sent a cheque towards its upkeep every year. She addressed her accompanying letter 'Dear Hinemaurea', and my sisters and I thought the marae was a real person. This was in the days before direct credit, so it really meant something for my mother to actually sign a cheque, put it in an envelope and take it to the post office.

Then there were the Māori church celebrations that constantly called to us, 'Haere mai, haere mai, haere mai'. I have already talked about the hui tōpū, hui aranga, hui Ringatū. On top of those were the national hui like those at Ngāruawāhia, where my grandparents regularly went to pay their respects to Princess Te Puea and then King Korokī; or the Golden Shears in Masterton, where Dad and my uncles went to compete for the title of best shearing team in the country.

Sometimes, when I am with Pākehā friends and ask them to join me at a hui, they will say they are too busy. Too busy? They should have seen my life or lives. They say, later, whenever I am hopping into the car, 'You know, you don't really have to go. It's a choice, you don't have to do it.'

Wrong. There is no choice. Māori must conduct themselves according to the principles of whanaungatanga, family obligation, and manaakitanga, supporting each other. Both principles involve reciprocity and honour of whakapapa.

As a child I found the reciprocal nature of family obligation sometimes difficult to sustain. I had no time to myself. I would tell Mum and Dad I had to do my homework and, although they understood, if a telephone call came from Tolaga Bay and we had to travel up there, they would say, 'You can do your homework later.' Off we would go in the car with a couple of mattresses in the back.

I soon learned how to do my homework anywhere, whenever and wherever. Today I can work in a car, on a train, on a plane. Because nobody knows when I write, people joke, 'Oh, Witi, he writes while you're looking.' People call me prolific but I am really only hard-working and hard-living. Getting on a plane in one month to go to Tahiti, the next month to Paris, the following month to London, the month after that to Oslo and then to Edinburgh and Banff — all of which were in my international programme for 2014 — is no different from travelling as a child and going one week to one kāinga and the next week to another.

The hui may be different, but a plane is only a bus, and I enjoy going on bus rides around the world.

AS IF LIFE wasn't busy enough, there were all the Māori sports and cultural activities. The Pākehā had their sports championships, Māori had theirs: rugby, hockey, golf and tennis. In Waituhi, for instance, Hine Te Ariki and Taraipene Tamatea founded the Waituhi Hockey Club in 1930, and Hine Te Ariki's daughter Mini and husband George Tūpara carried it on. This led to the founding of the Hine Te Ariki–Hana Konewa tournaments. They started first between Waituhi and Te Aowera and then went, well, as far as Māori are concerned, 'global', to other marae between Auckland and Wellington. In their heyday, forty to fifty teams, including an Indian one from Wellington, competed. My grandad, Pera, also played a big part in both Māori and Poverty Bay hockey as a referee, administrator and delegate for Māori teams in the Poverty Bay Hockey Association. He was the manager of the Waituhi hockey team that captured the Taranaki–Te Ua Shield in 1933 and throughout his life he played a part in organising annual Māori hockey tournaments.

At Haig Street you can see all the trophies that we hold for the hockey tournaments — the Hana Konewa and Hine Te Ariki shields and cups

— in an open compartment in the sitting room. And of all the games of hockey that were played, the ones that most people remember are those in the women's competition.

Here's how Māori women played hockey, Waituhi-style.

The day of the match was cold and wet, and the rain had made the ground mucky underneath. Four other games were on at the same time, but word soon got around, 'Hey! Waituhi are playing YMP!'

Nani Mini was huddled with the team. Aunty Joey was centre forward, Aunty Annie and Aunty Skin were inner right and inner left, and the wings were cousins Cissie and Wai. Playing at halfback positions were Aunties Bella and Rāwinia. The backs were the heavyweights, the dependable Aunty Girlie Wilson, aka 'Aunty Eyeballs', and Aunty Queenie. Goalie was Aunty Tilly, arms outstretched, splaying herself as much as possible from one side of the goal to the other.

'Okay, girls?' Nani Mini asked. 'Are you all ready? Just keep to your positions.'

'Hit the ball,' Aunty Bella interjected.

And if you couldn't hit the ball? 'Hit the player,' Aunty Queenie said.

The referee called the teams onto the field. He pushed his glasses onto the bridge of his nose. 'Let's have a nice clean game, ladies,' he requested, then blew his whistle.

'Come on the green,' came the chant from the left sideline. Green was the colour for Waituhi.

'Come on the black,' came the chant from the right sideline. Black was YMP's colour. And boy, was their team formidable, what with star players Dee at centre forward and Elizabeth at inner right.

Weight for weight, the teams were evenly balanced. The YMP women were all on deck: as well as Dee and Elizabeth they included Bobby, Cairo, Girl and Phyllis, who were all leaner, fitter and younger. However they had forgotten about older women who substituted tricks for speed, and they hadn't played sport with their brothers and men for quite a while.

Hockey one, hockey two, hockey three!

The sticks blurred and Aunty Joey finessed Dee by not quite touching on the third click. She scooped the ball back to Aunty Bella, who pushed it back to the hard hitter, Aunty Eyeballs.

'Ref! Where's your eyes?' Cairo roared.

Aunty Eyeballs wondered, 'Is Cairo referring to me?' She swivelled her eyes around, and one saw where Cissie was, but her other eye saw that Wai was better placed. *Whang*, and she hit the ball towards the right corner of the YMP half.

The Waituhi strategy had always been that once anybody got the ball they hit it out to the wing. The older women knew the younger girls didn't want bruises on their beautiful legs and would therefore fly down the line, keep out of trouble and then whack the ball into the circle of the opposing team. The theory was, of course, that the older women would be there to receive the ball — or at least one of them.

Good theory.

Wai positively streaked along the line after the ball. The YMP halfbacks chased after her, but not for nothing was Wai the last baton runner of the high-school track and field team. She picked up the ball, tapped it nicely, past the YMP backs. Only the goalie ahead. Now hit it into the centre where the aunties were.

Huh? Where *were* the aunties?

Oh, why did she always have to do this by herself? Wai dashed into the circle. She pretended to hit the ball to Cissie, and the YMP goalie turned to the left.

Gotcha.

Did I forget to tell you that Wai had a wicked eye? She had an inbuilt direction-finder. She needed no computer to calculate the distance divided by the width of the goal minus the mass of the goalie multiplied by the probability factor that the goalie might just stop the ball.

Up came her stick. *Wham*! I swear the ball caught fire, it was travelling so fast. It sizzled into the net before the goalie even knew it was there.

The Waituhi side of the field roared with acclamation. The YMP side screamed and squabbled with the ref.

'I told you girls,' Dee said, 'to watch these Waituhi women.'

Wai trotted back to the centre of the field, looking at her fingernails as if she'd broken one.

'Try that again,' Phyllis muttered.

Oh, they were magnificent, those Waituhi women. They had skill, strategy and, if not speed, the experience of modern-day Amazons. Directed by Nani Mini, they pulled every trick in the book to keep ahead. Nani Mini liked directing the referee, too. For instance, she liked to have one fullback way up to the halfway mark when the play was in YMP's half. That way she could often catch a YMP forward offside.

'That YMP girl, ref, look at her,' she would yell.

'Yes, I know, Mrs Tūpara.'

And if a YMP player was in the circle and about to aim at the goal, her favourite trick was to yell, 'Sticks!'

You never knew your luck. The referee might agree with you.

The half-time whistle blew. Waituhi were ahead three goals to YMP's (very lucky) one. Waituhi's tactic of hitting fast and regularly from the very start, getting as many goals as possible, had paid off.

However, the game was only just beginning. The real problem was that in the second half the aunties got slower and slower. Having too many babies and standing so long at the shearing sheds had given most of them varicose veins.

Dee knew it. Immediately after play resumed, YMP broke through the Waituhi lines. Despite a valiant stopping attempt by Aunty Tilly, Bobbie managed to get a lucky hit.

She started to trot back to her side. Aunty Rāwinia accidentally put her hockey stick out. 'Oh, sorry, darling,' she said as Bobbie tripped over and ended up with a face full of mud. Aunty Rāwinia went to help pull Bobbie up. By the hair. 'Only trying to help,' Aunty Rāwinia said.

To make matters worse, it began to rain. The ref looked doubtful about continuing the game. He consulted the two captains.

Call the game off? He had to be kidding!

As the aunties began to run out of steam, the play moved relentlessly into Waituhi's half. The greater fitness of YMP began to show as the women made lightning strikes into Waituhi territory.

The delectable Elizabeth scored a goal. 'Take that!' she yelled.

Waituhi three, YMP two.

None of this fazed Waituhi, for defensive play in the second half had mostly been the way their games had been going these days. Although one by one the aunties were coming to a standstill, their hitting power was as damaging and as accurate as ever. They gave battle cries as they hit the ball, orgasmic and thrilling to hear.

The objective became to stop the ball or get it off YMP and keep hitting it to the younger and fitter wingers, who could take the ball back up the field into the YMP half. It didn't matter what Cissie or Wai did with the damn thing once they were up there, so long as they kept YMP busy while the aunties had a bit of a breather. The primary task was to guard the circle at all costs.

However, the rain made the field muddy and the ball wasn't running as far as it would on a flat surface. To get the ball travelling, Waituhi had to resort to greater strength.

'Sticks!' Dee cried. Or, 'Raised ball!'

Each penalty against Waituhi meant that YMP could begin the game closer and closer into the Waituhi half. As YMP penetrated and pushed the Waituhi defence further back, slowly but surely the aunties were forced into a strategic retreat.

A cornered animal is always dangerous.

There was nothing more glorious to watch in hockey than Waituhi women on the defensive. They roared and screamed orders to each other:

'Watch the left! Watch the right! Watch the centre! Protect the flank! Keep an eye on that young YMP winger! Cover that gap! Keep together, girls! Only another quarter of an hour to go! Kia kaha!'

They shifted and dissolved fluidly from one defensive pattern into another. The defenders stopped the ball and hit it out to the wingers, but YMP had Cissie and Wai marked. Never mind, defend again and hit beyond the wingers to the far corner. Defend again, and hit.

Then YMP managed to get through the Waituhi defences and slam another goal home. The score drew at three all.

That did it. Defensive strategy descended into a free for all as both teams began pulling every trick in the book — and some moves that weren't in the book. It was the ref's problem if he didn't see what you were doing, but, if he did, never mind.

If a YMP player was dribbling the ball and got past you, don't worry. Stop the player either by tripping her up with your stick, tangling your stick with hers or, if necessary, pushing her off balance as she passes. The referee might blow his whistle, 'Obstruction!', but that would at least stop play for a while and allow the aunties to regroup.

If you were standing in the clear and with the ball, don't hit it straight away. Why waste a good shot? Wait until a YMP player was coming to attack you, then hit it.

If there were two attacking players, you could get them both. Easy! You pretended to miss the ball on your first stroke, because that way you could whack the first player, 'Whoops, sorry.' On your second stroke, that's when you hit the ball at the second player.

She shouldn't have been in the road anyway.

Oh yes, sticks was okay if there was a YMP player behind you who might cop your stick on your backswing. That way she could get carted off the field and, who knew, by the time you finished YMP might not have any reserves left. And if all else failed and you needed to protect the ball, pretend to slip and sit on it. Nobody was going to hit a poor defenceless old lady when she was down.

You never did any of the above in the circle, though, or the referee would call 'Penalty!' But if it was really necessary, a penalty was better than YMP getting a goal.

The Waituhi women trotted leisurely to their backline to prepare for a penalty goal attempt by YMP. Only four minutes to final whistle.

'Hey, ref!' Girl yelled. 'Tell Waituhi to move their big black bums, they're wasting time.'

Black maybe, but big? The aunties' feathers were ruffled that Girl could cast such aspersions on their beauty. They lined up to protect the goal.

The ball cracked out from the corner and across the circle. Elizabeth stopped it and Dee took the hit, *whang*. The ball sizzled and smoked, and even the line of aunties could not stop it from whamming into the goal.

'Good job, Dee,' the aunties accepted grudgingly. But as they trotted back to restart the game, it was clear that they had one thing in mind. They were down three goals to four.

Time to reclaim the game.

Hockey one, hockey two, hockey three! Aunty Joey won the ball and tapped it to Aunty Eyeballs, who had moved up to the forwards to give Aunty Annie a spell. Adrenaline pumping, the Waituhi forwards began to move like a juggernaut down the field. The backs moved in behind to support them, even Aunty Tilly left her goal, twirling her stick like a taiaha.

'Fall back!' Dee screamed to her women. 'Fall back!'

Waituhi kept up their momentum. They were going to war. Where was the ball? The rain was falling so heavily you could hardly see it. Ah, there it was!

'Watch out, girls!' Dee warned her players. Uttering a banshee cry, she ran at the wall of Waituhi women. Silently a gap opened, and Dee hurled herself in. It closed behind her. When the juggernaut moved on, there was Dee, dazed, going round and round in circles without her hockey stick and wondering what had happened to it.

'Elizabeth!' Dee managed to cry. 'Stop them!'

Elizabeth rushed at the Waituhi women. A flurry of sticks followed and there was Elizabeth, cartwheeling head over heels out of the pack.

Meanwhile, Aunty Skin somehow staggered against the referee, knocked off his glasses and trod on them. Good, he was out of the way.

'Back to the circle,' Dee ordered. All those huge solid Waituhi legs were like Birnam Wood come to Dunsinane.

Then Nani Mini yelled from the sideline, 'In you go, Joey!'

The game exploded. The Waituhi women formed a phalanx around Aunty Joey as she made for the circle. The referee still hadn't found his glasses.

Wham here, slam there, and two YMP women were down. Slash here, slash there, another two hit the mud. Boot here, boot there, and into a clear space sailed Aunty Eyeballs, her hair plastered on her face like a gorgon. Wielding her hockey stick with one hand, she gave a mighty swing. Oh yes, it was sticks, but, after all, if the referee didn't see it, that was his problem. The real fear was which eye was Aunty seeing the goal with?

Phew, the ball slammed in, rocking the goal backwards. All hell broke loose on the sideline, with YMP and Waituhi supporters embarking on a free-for-all. 'Ref, where are your eyes!'

The referee found his glasses. 'Oh, look at the time.' He blew the final whistle. In protest, a hail of objects and offensive substances rained about him.

YMP four, Waituhi four.

A draw, but boy, it was worth it.

LIFE WAS BIG, unruly and surprising. It was like another of those mainstays of Māori culture in those days, the kapa haka competitions.

Ah, an action song concert was like a Māori ode to joy! Today you can watch the teams on Māori Television, but nothing compares to the real thing. Therefore, oh memory, fly back to the 1950s and the annual Poverty Bay–East Coast Māori cultural competitions.

You think Christmas was the main event in the calendar? Forget it. Dial up April.

The venue was the Gisborne Opera House, now long demolished, a two-storeyed building with upstairs and downstairs decorated in fabulous gold and red. In its heyday, at the turn of the twentieth century, the theatre hosted overseas opera and theatre companies, which performed everything from Puccini and Verdi to Shakespeare and George Bernard Shaw. During the 1920s it became more versatile, even providing a boxing venue for the great Tom Heeney, a local boy, before he went to live in the United States.

By the 1950s, although Gisborne Opera House was still the place for first-class shows and the occasional visit of the New Zealand Players, valiantly dedicated to bringing culture to the provinces, it was more likely to feature local productions. Sometimes the Gisborne amateur dramatic company put on operettas and musicals like *White Horse Inn* or *Rose Marie*. Gilbert and Sullivan's *Pirates of Penzance*, *HMS Pinafore* and *The Mikado* were also regularly dusted off. In August the annual amateur dramatic competitions took place, and singers, tap and ballet dancers and elocutionists trod the boards.

Up to twenty haka teams entered each year. Waituhi always competed and, later, another team from the valley, which took the name of Tākitimu. The latter consisted mainly of the local Mormon families, which naturally included the Smilers; I never liked the way that the valley was being divided.

I was proud of my mother, aunts and other female cousins, all in the front and second rows. Behind them were my father, uncles and younger men, including Ivan and Sammy. And decked out in piupiu with a feather in his hair was little kina-head himself. Who could see me behind all those wide backs and huge thighs? 'Stay out of sight,' Uncle Puku ordered.

Here's how I observed the haka competition in 1954:

Although the haka competition was tough, Waituhi had succeeded in getting through the first round and were now among the twelve semi-finalists. We were on last, so were able to sit upstairs in the balcony watching the other teams. The Waituhi women were dressed in their headbands, bodices and piupiu. The men, too, were in piupiu, but wearing coats or jerseys over their chests. All of us were sweating, and our grease-applied moko were smeared.

We were quietly confident until Waihīrere kapa haka team took the floor.

The lights dimmed. The plush red velvet curtains swished back. Huh? The stage was empty. Normally haka teams were already onstage in their ranks. Then, from the side of the stage, a woman's voice called out authoritatively in the karanga:

'Tēnā koutou, rangatira mā, tēnā koutou, tēnā koutou, tēnā koutou.' To whistles and cheers, Waihīrere swept onto the stage, the men at an angle from one side, the women at a similar angle from the other. They were moving at double speed, making an X pattern. When they met in the middle, the scissoring effect was so dazzling that the hall raised a mighty cheer. No doubt about it, Bill Kerekere and the dynamic Bub and Nan Wehi had really brought style to the competition today. Waihīrere was always good, but this was *good*. Look at that!

And after their entrance, Waihīrere kept up their standard with impeccable performances of ancient waiata, action song and poi. Oh, their voices almost outdid the dawn chorus of the tūī! And their actions were crisp, impressive and as fluid as a rippling sea! The ingenuity and beauty of costuming made every performer on the stage look like a royal kōtuku in perfect flight! Not for them a front line that was, as with other teams, as crooked as a dog's hind leg. Nor for them one performer outshining the rest. They were a perfect team, and no wonder — they practised three to four nights a week, and three to four hours a night. And, later, they would introduce a fabulous paso doble and other rhythms cross-pollinating their songs and bringing the house down: 'Karanga mai ngā iwi korokī!'

Waihīrere rose to be one of the top groups in the history of kapa haka. Whenever I hear them today they make my heart soar. You know what? They were only across the river from us.

I HAVE TO admit that I had one shining kapa haka moment.

Quite by accident, Uncle Puku put me in the front row of the men. I was walking to my usual place in the back when he said, 'No, come beside me.'

Me? Was he talking about me? Hadn't he heard about my performance at the school pageant when I beat Hillary to the top of Everest? Apparently not.

The problem was that I was accustomed to being behind everybody else and copying what they were doing. I put my hands up in the air when they did. I stamped my feet when they stamped theirs. I might have been a split second behind, but when my uncles moved to the left I followed their massive thighs and moved to the left. When they flexed their huge popping muscles and their backs rippled, and they jumped, I jumped.

When you're in front you don't have anybody to follow.

What happened? I completely lost it. I went left when I was supposed to go right. I jumped when I should have squatted. I advanced when I should have retreated. And even when I got the action right, I was just that split second behind their beautiful timing.

I brought my uncles down on their *knees*.

Chapter Twenty-nine

Not Middle Earth, Māori Earth

1.

THERE IS AN extraordinary story to be told of high-ranking Māori houses, not only ours, maintaining their tribal mana during the late nineteenth and early twentieth centuries. In the process, they replicated all the qualities of the English upper-class gentry.

You need only think of the Ngata, Carroll, Tirikātene, Rātana and Pōmare families, and the amazing kings and queens of the Tainui people, to know that this is true. The families had remarkable style, a way of conducting themselves at the highest levels of Māori and Pākehā society, and it was reflected in their surroundings. They lived in palatial houses, had servants, and their good taste was reflected in their furniture and personal belongings.

Take the case of Hēni Materoa. Born in 1859, she was Riperata Kahutia's daughter and she married Sir James Carroll in 1881. In the Pākehā world Sir James had already proved himself the equal of any New Zealand gentry, but Hēni Materoa's mother considered he wasn't of sufficient mana — and he was also a Roman Catholic.

People called Hēni Materoa Te Reiri, The Lady. She and Sir James were childless, and perhaps this was why she always had aroha for the children of others. She gifted land for Awapuni School, and was remarkable in that she brought up thirty adopted children herself; someone should make a television drama about her. Her two-storeyed house on Kahutia Street was managed with grace and dignity, and she had a staff which included ladies' maids and servants. A chauffeur drove her around Gisborne and to country hui.

There's a story about Hēni Materoa I've always loved. Her balcony faced the sea, and although her room was out of bounds some young women couldn't resist taking a peek inside. They saw her talking to a bird, a manu tipua. It was through this bird that she obtained information about what was happening to Māori as well as to the land itself. The human world was not the only one being affected.

Old photographs are also evidence of a time when Māori gentry bred horses; Wī Pere, for instance, had a horse, Māhaki, which won the Wellington Cup. They lived in fine houses or communities like Rātana Pā, Ngāruawāhia or Tūpāroa, and sent their children to the best schools. While East Coast Māori favoured Te Aute and the Māori Agricultural College, dignified Nelson College was also a favourite for Gisborne's

Māori sons — and the Sydney Conservatorium was often a destination for the daughters.

Certainly it's easy to look negatively at these Māori houses and consider them imitative of Pākehā. But look at the early photographs — some of those Māori gentry wear cloaks over their double-breasted suits, and the women have moko. They have not given away their identity as Māori. Far better to think of them, therefore, as footing it with the Pākehā and thereby able to work within Pākehā circles for the advancement of their people.

SOMETHING HAPPENED TO all that energy, that compulsion to equal Pākehā within New Zealand society.

The Māori gentry, while able to foot it, were not able, in my opinion, to obtain a foot*hold*. While some families maintained their illustrious names, within a couple of generations the physical evidence that they had even been there had mostly disappeared.

I'm not the right person to write about this period, but I will try my best to offer what I think occurred. One of the characteristics was that, actually, Pākehā society was not about to accept Māori within their ranks. They administered the blow as if it was a king hit.

In my opinion, this blow occurred right after the First World War. Come back to the Wī Pere memorial on Peel Street with me and I will tell you the story.

Certainly the monument was to honour my ancestor. However, it also served to memorialise the return in 1919 of the local Gisborne Māori boys who had served during the First World War. They were the survivors of the first volunteers from the town; Wī Pere had accompanied them to Napier, on the initial leg of their voyage to Gallipoli, a year before he died. In Wellington, the boys joined the larger band of Māori who comprised the New Zealand Native Contingent.

Not many people are aware of Māori participation during the Great War and that of 103,000 New Zealanders who fought, 2227 were Māori. Don't forget that in 1914 the total population in New Zealand was just over one million; the Māori population was only 50,000, which places the Native Contingent's contribution into extraordinary perspective. Nor should it be forgotten that Māori also enlisted and served in other units.

As far as the contingent is concerned, 518 volunteers were in the first intake, and then the numbers were bolstered by a second draft of 312. The men were limited to serve on training and garrison duties because of an imperial ruling that the native races were not to be involved; to be blunt, the initial idea that natives could take up weapons against white people, even if they were enemy, could not be countenanced. However, persistent petitioning of such Māori MPs as Wī Pere, Te Rangi Hīroa, Āpirana Ngata and Māui Pōmare eventually enabled them to serve on the frontline at Gallipoli, where they fought with valour and distinction; Te Rangi Hīroa volunteered as a medical officer. The rallying call, expressed by Ngata, was that Māori involvement was the price of citizenship.

The Native Contingent's particular and singular achievement at Gallipoli occurred during the attack on Sari Bair, from 6 to 9 August 1915. They set the night ringing with the haka 'Ka mate, ka mate!', to ensure they were all in line (and not ahead of each other) as they advanced on the Turks. Indeed, the contingent's efforts, as well as those by the Gurkhas and other native soldiers, affirm the fact that the Great War was not just a White War.

After Gallipoli, the New Zealand Native Contingent was reconstituted as the Pioneer Battalion; a third draft of 110 increased the numbers. I shouldn't ignore the fact, however, that some Māori did not buy into Ngata's 'price of citizenship' argument. Princess Te Puea was adamant that her grandfather, Tāwhiao, had forbidden Waikato to take up arms. After all, the British Crown had punished her people for rebelling and the 'price' paid for that had been the confiscation of land. When conscription came into force in 1916, 74 Waikato men refused the call. Like Pākehā conscientious objectors, who were treated appallingly for refusing to answer to King and Country, the Māori men were imprisoned and given only bread and water.

The battalion received orders in 1917 to serve on the Western Front with New Zealand, Australian and other Allied forces. Following the recruiting efforts of Māui Pōmare, who made a special trip to Niue, the Māori soldiers were joined by 400 volunteers from that island, plus another 58 from the Cook Islands and the Gilbert and Ellice Islands. The bravery of these barefooted boys defies understanding as they left their island villages for a war on the other side of the world.

And don't forget the native Tahitian troops, and that as many Kanaks as French colonists went from New Caledonia to fight in what *they* called La Grande Guerre. Was their war the same as ours? The Kanaks were a people divided — while Kanak soldiers were in Europe, Kanak rebels were fighting French troops in New Caledonia. To round out the picture, 100 Fijians fought in the war, assigned to Calais to work as cargo handlers. Aboriginal soldiers also served, and that's a story that wasn't engraved on the war memorials of Australia.

Some 18,500 New Zealanders perished in the First World War; some 41,000 were wounded. Of the dead, 336 were men from the New Zealand Native Contingent and the Pioneer Battalion. And 734 members of these units were wounded, making the total casualties 1070, almost half of those who served.

So now we come to the end of the war.

Well . . . from my perspective not much changed for Māori at all. If I were to imagine a conversation with my ancestor Wī Pere on this subject, this is the way it would go:

'E tā, only thirty years before we had been fighting *against* the Pākehā!

'Different circumstances, different times, mokopuna. We had to get past our animosities, which is why, in 1899, I supported the sending of a New Zealand contingent to the Transvaal. If Pākehā had not been willing, I would have taken 100 of my own Māori warriors to do it. And after all, New Zealand in 1907 had become a self-governing dominion of the British Empire. Did it not behove us to go to the assistance of England now that we were all New Zealanders?

'E tā, but why was the Great War our price of citizenship? Hadn't Māori already paid that price during the Land Wars? Hadn't other indigenous peoples? Consider the Kanaks of New Caledonia. They paid the price of citizenship for La Belle France, but it took Jean-Marie Tjibaou in the 1980s to finally achieve some kind of independence for them. In Australia, their government may have raised a monument to commemorate the noble role played by their horses and other animals, but where are the monuments to their indigenous soldiers?

'Mokopuna, could I divine the future? No! I had to act according to the politics of the times. Certainly many of the brown and red peoples had suffered under the hands of England but, now that we were part of the empire, we had to guard lest England's foot should slip and we should follow immediately after. Would the Kaiser's yoke have been preferable? No! Like Ngata and my Māori colleagues in parliament I was of the opinion that Māori had to put aside our enmity and, yes, let us pay that price for New Zealand citizenship. And Waikato were wrong to refuse conscription: they followed Te Puea, well, they had to be punished according to the law. Oh, my Māori people, remove the veil from your faces; open your eyes, so that you may see the world, and the world may see your true and bright faces!'

They came back, those valiant Māori soldiers, to parade at the unveiling of the Wī Pere obelisk. From a personal perspective, it would be so easy for me to go along with the prevailing acclaim that met this brotherhood in war. Once we had fought each other, now shoulder to shoulder we had fought together. At Gallipoli and on the Western Front, Māori and Pākehā inspired a nation — you know the sort of thing. Yes, they had paid the price of citizenship. But did they receive it?

No, I think the country blew the chance. Just as at Gallipoli, where their leaders were Pākehā, Māori were not trusted when they came back.

That was the king hit I alluded to earlier. And then, well, the circumstances of history conspired against any residual chances of equal citizenship that were left. For instance, with the return of those same soldiers came the mate, the sickness, known as the Spanish flu. Geoffrey Rice, in the revised 2005 edition of *Black November*, the Bible on the epidemic in New Zealand, gives the figure for those Pākehā who died as at least 6091. Of Māori deaths he notes: 'Māori mortality was seriously underestimated in the official figures because later registrations in 1919 were not included and no allowance was made for large numbers of unregistered Māori deaths.'

It is now acknowledged that Māori suffered heavily, with an unconfirmed 2160 deaths. Entire kāinga were decimated, and the sorrow must have been staggering.

Throughout Aotearoa, the consequence was a resurgence of interest in charismatic and prophetic leaders. Tahupōtiki Wiremu Rātana was the most famous, creating the Rātana Church. In my whakapapa, Te Kooti was followed by Rua Kēnana and then a proliferation of locally based tohunga.

Two years later, in 1920, New Zealand's population was almost 1,230,000 and the Māori population was approaching 53,000. Despite the loss of men at war, and then of Māori during the flu, we were rallying. But Māori as a race were sliding down a slippery slope and out of the New Zealand consciousness.

How come? Well, most Pākehā were living in cities or boroughs, and it was estimated that 90 per cent of all Māori still lived in the country. Neither did the laudable Māori land development and forestry schemes instigated by Ngata and others impinge on most Pākehā, who considered it was the least that could be done for the natives. Out of sight, out of mind.

Worse, we were getting nowhere with our petitions to get our land back. In 1920 the government had finally set up a Native Lands Commission, which was the first big Māori land grievance inquiry of the twentieth century. Chaired by Robert Noble Jones, Chief Judge of the Native Land Court, the commission, among many diverse matters, considered the vexed problem of Patutahi.

The commission was welcomed in Gisborne by Te Kani Pere and Lady Carroll. At the hearings, Rongowhakaata, Te Aitanga-a-Māhaki and Ngāi Tamanuhiri were represented by Captain William Tutepuaki Pitt; Te Whānau-a-Kai was separately represented by a local solicitor, a Mr Dunlop. Jones did, in fact, recognise the injustice of Patutahi, but could find no way of sorting out the amount of land taken and the process by which it could be revested — and by then Rongowhakaata and Te Aitanga-a-Māhaki were making competing claims. It was a case of divide and conquer, which has existed to this day. In the end, the whole Patutahi affair was sent back to the Native Land Court.

Man oh man, they didn't let go, those ancestors of mine. From July to December 1923 they were back in court, again separately represented, and those who gave evidence on our behalf included Haare Matenga, Ēria Raukura, Haerapō Kahutia, Himiona Kātipa, Taake Kerekere and others. The case was calamitous because the court, in attempting to validate Te Whānau-a-Kai's claim, felt it necessary to define the boundary line laid down in ancient times by Tūī — and deemed that because Rongowhakaata and Te Aitanga-a-Māhaki were clearly involved we did not have a separate case. There were two separate hearings on issues relating to Patutahi in 1929. And then came the worldwide Depression when Wall Street crashed in October.

Pākehā were more concerned with their own plight — and with good reason. Depressions always strike urban dwellers more seriously than those in the country. Wages depend on a cash economy, and exports in New Zealand fell by 45 per cent in two years and the national income by 40 per cent in three years. Not to mention the burden of interest payments to carry on overseas debt.

Easy to assume that Māori could live off the land and fish and hunt, eh. Although it was true that in 1930 the Māori population climbed to 67,000, rural health and welfare deteriorated. Indeed, we were considered too poor even to pay an unemployment tax, which would make us eligible for unemployment relief. Worse, we had no land to till or to run our stock on. The Pākehā now owned the farms; they held the reins. Wī Pere had set up the trust, but even there the control was mainly in Pākehā hands and they made the decisions. Why on earth would we have believed, anyway, that Pākehā would relinquish command in peacetime when they had not been able to do so in war?

When it came to social welfare benefits, Māori did not gain housing, health and employment benefits until the first Labour government, under Michael Joseph Savage, swept into power in 1935. By that time Māori had begun to learn of the power of politics and that they could claim their rights through the vote and political means.

The Māori people tell a parable about those times, and in it that simple tuber, the potato, appears again. My father, Te Haa, was the first to tell me the parable, sometime in the 1970s, so I will phrase it in his voice.

I was asking him why it was that, for Māori, Labour was still the political party of choice.

'Māori have long memories,' Dad said. 'They go all the way back to 1936 when, after the Labour victory, Rātana the Prophet went to see Prime Minister Savage. At that time, Eruera Tirikātene of Rātana held Southern Māori and Rātana gained Western Māori, two of the four Māori seats.

The prophet was in a good bargaining position, and at his meeting with the prime minister he placed four symbolic items on the table in front of him. They were a potato with three huia feathers protruding from it, a broken watch, a jade hei tiki, and a pin with a star and crescent moon.

'"What do these items mean?" Prime Minister Savage asked.

'"The potato represents the ordinary Māori," Rātana began. "He needs his land because how can his staple crop grow without soil?"

'Prime Minister Savage nodded. "And the gold watch?" he asked.

'"It belonged to my grandfather," Rātana explained.

'"But it is broken," Prime Minister Savage observed.

'"Yes," Rātana continued, "because the law which protects Māori land, that too is broken. The Crown, represented by your new government, must repair the broken law."

'Then Rātana turned to the hei tiki, the huia feathers and the decorative pin. "E tā, the tiki stands for the spirit of the Māori people. If you protect them you will earn the right to wear the huia feathers, which is the sign of a chief. And if you promise to do that I will place the allegiance of the Rātana Church, symbolised by the pin, before you."'

Oh, every now and then I have wanted to add a dash of cynicism, something that would act as an antidote to all that Māori hope and expectation that Pākehā would act in an honourable manner. Cynicism, however, does not become a narrative which, for Māori, maintains its grace and optimism.

Although Rātana died in 1939, his Church kept the promise. And when Savage died the following year, it is said that the items from Rātana had had such a profound impact on the prime minister that they were buried with him.

Chapter Thirty

Two Kites Flying

KĀTI, ENOUGH.

I've taken too long already on this narrative and I still haven't managed to get you out to Waituhi. So let's get this whakapapa back on track, hop into the car and go.

Waituhi is eleven miles — eighteen kilometres — from Gisborne, on the outskirts of the farming district where mountain ranges break the blue of sky. Huddled close to the foothills and farms that grow grapes and other fruit crops, it is far from the main arteries pumping commerce to Wellington and Auckland. There's no reason why the village should exist except this: the people of Waituhi live there.

Waituhi has always been our home, and this will always be our land. It is our hearth. Our parents lived here before us, and their parents before them, and so it has always been. We are the tangata whenua, the original settlers.

And there's one thing I need to warn you about the people. If you think my humour is pretty wicked, I am an amateur compared with them; their wit is merciless. For instance, if you ask them, 'Do you know Witi Ihimaera?', they will answer, 'Never heard of him.' In Waituhi, you see, they know me as Tom Smiler's son. Once upon a time they might have referred to me as Teria's grandson, but she and her generation are long gone and so is that history.

Another reason why the villagers might refute me is that it is their way of ensuring that I keep my feet on the ground. They're saying to me, 'You're no better than us.' And they're right. They might be surprised to know that I have always held them in higher regard than I hold myself.

Then again, they might be denying me because they don't like me. After all, I have often been a viper striking at their bosom. Hey, I can accept that.

TO GET TO Waituhi, you head inland, north-west from the city. There's only one highway in or out of Gisborne, unless you take the circuitous road around the East Coast, which is an alternative route north. For Waituhi, you take the highway south to Wellington. Just past Matawhero, you come to a concrete bridge. In the old days there was a red, one-way bridge that always created hilarious confrontations when a vehicle coming from one direction refused to give way to one going the other way. The stand-offs could last for an hour until other drivers, from traffic backed up at the bridge, intervened with threats of fisticuffs and of hurling the offenders into the river.

Once, my mother was driving the car and she was already halfway across when another car came towards her. The male occupant must have thought that a woman would back up for him. He was arrogant enough to tell her to do so. Did she? 'Stupid man,' she said to us. She edged the car forward until it connected with the bumper of his car and then she put her foot down and burned rubber.

On the other side of the bridge is a roundabout with three destinations to choose from. One is the highway south to Wellington, and most traffic takes this route. The second takes you to Tiniroto. The third goes to Ngatapa, and if you follow this road you will reach the place where Māori rebels were murdered by government troops at the siege of their clifftop mountain fortress in 1869.

The third road also takes you to Waituhi. You go to the Patutahi turn-off and hang a left before you get to the pub. You'll see the primary school — the old native school building where I learned all those nursery rhymes that Teria never liked is no longer there — and the war memorial. Yes, even tinpot Patutahi has a war memorial, one of the 500 scattered throughout New Zealand acting as surrogate headstones for all those boys who never came home.

Patutahi looks peaceful in the sun, right? The village holds warm memories for me of dances at the local hall, collecting groceries at the Patutahi general store and, later, trying to inveigle the publican to give me and my mates a crate of beer when the hotel was closed.

You'll come to a small bridge. You wouldn't think, would you, that most of the flat was known as the Patutahi Block and was confiscated from Te Whānau-a-Kai.

Once you're over that small bridge, you know you're nearing Waituhi. I'm looking ahead now for the gateway to the valley. There it is! The silhouette of a powerful-looking hill looms before us. It is called Pukepoto, and it is an ancient fort with serrated edges, crumbling steps that look like a stairway to the sky. Let me fling open the window and shout my ritual huakina hehame, my boyish open sesame:

Ko Ohakuatiu te maunga,
Ko Waipaoa te awa,
Ko Repongaere te roto,
Ko Te Whānau-a-Kai
me Ngā Pōtiki te iwi.

3.

EVERY APPROACH TO Waituhi is a rebirth. This is the womb of my life, and from that womb has come generation after generation of ancestors. Whenever I return, my blood always starts to sing.

Remember earlier I made reference to the movement in Māori from ahau (I) to koe/koutou (you, singular and plural) to rātou (they, others) to tātou (everyone including myself)? This is what made going to Waituhi so special. I was returning from the Pākehā world to the Māori world. Just as important, I was being embraced by a tribal world and childhood memories. You have no idea how much I always longed to be held in Waituhi's arms.

When I was a child, my grandmother's car had no sooner stopped at the homestead than I was out of the door and across the road to help whoever was working in the maize paddock.

'Can I plant my own row? Can I?'

I liked nothing better than to take charge of one of the parallel rows made by the plough as it turned the earth. To have my own sack of plants to push into the dirt and my own watering can to water them with.

In those days, the village was always busy, with people walking along the road. Sometimes there were huge Clydesdales going by, hitched by chains to a heavy sledge and being driven down to the river to fill barrels with water or to the foothills to bring back loads of kānuka firewood. How those horses snorted with exertion, and sometimes the metal sledges would send off sparks like flint.

'Are you going to get water for the fields? Can I hop on? Can I come? Can I?'

I loved the sweat of it, the muscle-straining effort involved. Was I a tourist in the Land of Waituhi? Of course I was. I would have found it difficult to understand that my relatives and my young cousins could not escape from it; I could. After all these years I hope they forgave me for being a child who didn't know.

There was always a time when Teria would call to me, 'E Witsh, time to go to the marae.' This was the way she involved me in the politics of being Māori.

'The boy doesn't understand,' Pera would mutter.

'No, but he listens, he learns. He watches, he remembers. Something goes inside.'

Teria always assumed I would attend with her, whatever the meeting was. Once, however, she asked me, and I said 'No'. I will never forget the look of disappointment that came over her face as she nodded and started to walk down the road. Past Dai Pere and Aunty Hine's place, then Gran Marara, who married an Appleby, past Granny Jack's and then Uncle Te Kani and Aunty Roxie's house. Opposite, Con Harvey's two daughters Noeline and Marjorie were watching; they were the only Pākehā in Waituhi.

Teria had already gone past Nani Paaka Edwards' and Norma's place and was just about at Nani Mana Edwards' before I was able to catch up. I put my hand up for her to hold. I knew the speeches would go on and on and *on*, but I would have to make the best of it.

One night, instead of a meeting at Rongopai, Teria took me to a dance at Tākitimu Hall. Old man Snapper Rangiaho was playing with his three-piece band. I was sitting with my cousin Minnie when I saw Teria looking my way.

'Pera doesn't want to dance with me,' she said, 'but I would love to have a waltz.'

And so we waltzed together. I was concentrating on the rhythm, *one two three, one two three*, and I swear to you that when I first heard 'Va, pensiero', otherwise known as the Chorus of the Hebrew Slaves from Verdi's *Nabucco*, it was the same tune that Snapper squeezed out of the accordion. Somewhere in the 1960s I bought a terribly scratchy long-playing Cetra recording of the opera with Caterina Mancini as Abigaille, and, suddenly, out of the grooves came the chorus. Immediately I was surrounded by the Ringatū men and women of Waituhi, people who believed that they were a tribe of Israel in slavery. The night moths were whirring, the band was playing, and a young boy dipped and swayed in a waltz with his grandmother:

> *Va, pensiero, sull'ali dorate;*
> *Va, ti posa sui clivi, sui colli . . .*
> *Go my thoughts, on golden wings;*
> *Go, alight upon the slopes, the hills,*
> *Where, soft and warm, the sweet breezes*
> *Of our native land are fragrant!*
> *Greet the banks of the Jordan*
> *And Zions razed towers*
> *Oh, my country so lovely*
> *And lost!*

It wasn't just the contemporary tribal world of the valley that embraced me. My mountain, my people's river, my meeting house, my ancestors with all their histories were waiting. Nor should I forget that *other* world.

Teria and I were walking up a hillside in the sparkling sun when she paused and said to me, 'Wait.'

I was impatient and wanted to run to the top.

'E Wit*sh*,' she reprimanded, 'e tū.' Cross, she made me lie down on the slope. 'Ka kite koe, te ao o ngā pungāwerewere?' she asked.

When I was level to the ground I discovered that sparkling light was coming from long glistening spiderwebs, a crystal canopy strung all the way down the slope. I was a young boy who was easily entranced, and some things I saw with childlike eyes. Children do blaze a trail of glory, for, I tell you, there were hundreds of spiders, spinning a billowing world and silver filaments attached from one grass blade to another and shivering in the sun.

'If you are ever cut and bleeding,' Teria said, 'gather spiderwebs and use them as a dressing.' And she began to karakia to the spiders, suggesting they get out of the way of a very clumsy and impatient boy who was climbing up their mauna.

4.

HOW REAL TERIA was and how real our outings were, I just don't know now.

There came a time when our relationship left the physical world and entered the world of my imagination. It's not hard to understand why — she had a presence larger than ordinary people, which stood out. Hēni Materoa, Te Reiri, had her manu tipua; my grandmother had her pungāwerewere tipua, and she spoke to them.

Some people are like that. The way they negotiate their lives, especially if they abut the realm of the fantastic, gives them charisma. Yes, Teria was real, but she was also highly dramatic. By gesture alone could she seize a moment and make it live. A sudden opulence in her voice or a fiery intensity of movement or a smartly articulated turn of phrase would alert me to a kind of many-hued radiance that was both earthy and polemic.

At moments like these my grandmother became another, trans- cendental, being. This was how she began to exist in my work, incarnated as my own Sycorax — on a Shakespearean island, she was its designated and sole ruler. There, within that realm, where she talked to spiders, I wrapped her in all the Māori mysteries: the genealogies, the karakia, the traditions of the Ringatū, with its mix of ancient lore and the Old Testament.

This was her great *preghiera*, her prayer:

'And so I begin your journey, e mokopuna, at the time of your awakening, by pushing you out into the universe. This the people did in Hawaiki when they voyaged to this land. And this is what the mother of Moses did when she placed her sacred son into a tiny woven vessel and consigned him to the royal river Nile so that he would escape the fury of Pharaoh. The child was guided to the daughter of Pharaoh and lived in

Pharaoh's palace and from there he grew into manhood until the time came when he said unto Pharaoh, "E hoa, let my people go."

'In our own country, these were the words said by your ancestors also. By Te Kooti Arikirangi, and by Wī Pere in the parliament of the Pākehā. And these were the words which have come down to me, and which I now pass on to you, "Te Whānau-a-Kai hei panapana mārō. Never retreat. Never."

'E mokopuna, you will need all of the intellect, the spirit, the heart and the memory to guide you on your journey. You will need to be at one with your world, for this is a world made by gods and man, and there are forces of both which may aid you. Learn about them, and understand them, so that when your sails unfurl you will ride with the winds and be supported by the electric currents of the universe. Let no baleful forces prevent you from reaching the unending destination which awaits us all.

'And as you travel the world, let all know that you carry in your hands the sacred kūmara, representing the knowledge of the Māori.

'E mokopuna, I now commit you to the longest journey. For what use is the sacred kūmara if the land is gone and there is no soil to plant it in? Go into the world of the Pākehā. Say to him, as Moses did, "Let my people go." Say to him again, "Take no more of our land, and let us go into our own land of Canaan."'

She was standing at the pillars of the sky. Her face was luminous with grief and anger.

'This is your land,' she said, 'and your task. You have heard the groans of the Māori. Listen to the way in which the land and the people suffer under the Pharaoh. Go now.

'Pass into life.'

Chapter Thirty-one

At the Centre of the Turning Gyre

1.

I HAD BETTER stop the car because, if we go past Pukepoto, I might not get the opportunity to tell you why it is so important to us. This is not just the site of any old hill fort. Here occurred a crucial battle that had a huge consequence for Te Whānau-a-Kai, and the story of that battle was one of the gifts Grandad gave me when I was a boy.

We may have both been in the right place at the right time because I never really thought that Grandad had much interest in me. In my eyes he favoured those male cousins who were physical, whose achievements he could barrack from the sideline of the rugby field. Nevertheless I did share important times with him and this one, in which he told me about a man called Rākaihikuroa and two magic kites, was one of them.

Magic kites? Read on:

'Rākaihikuroa lived right here,' Pera began. 'Here! At Pukepoto. He was a splendid autocrat, who ruled the land by divine right. This was around 1650, and he had a son named Tūpurupuru, who was regarded as the ariki of Tūranga. Now, Rākaihikuroa and Tūpurupuru should have been secure in their dual kingships, but it is true that uneasy lies the head that wears the crown, ne.

'So it proved to be because Rākaihikuroa had a sister named Rongomaitara, who married another warrior chieftain known as Kahutapere, and among their children they had two handsome boys, twins, named Tarakiuta and Tarakitai. So beloved became the twins by everyone that, looking on, Rākaihikuroa and *his* son Tūpurupuru felt a great intensity of jealousy and fear. Out of these emotions came alarm that perhaps the popularity of the twins would be such that they would overturn Rākaihikuroa and Tūpurupuru's rule.

'"We will have to kill your cousins," Rākaihikuroa said to his son.'

'How did they plan to do that?' I asked Pera.

'Wait your patience,' he answered. 'The twins had a particular sport they were good at. It was called potaka, and involved the whipping of spinning tops along a competition track. Competitors lined up at the top of a hill, down which the course would slope and wind to the bottom. The competitors held their spinning tops in one hand and a flax whip in the other and, at the word of the starter, they would place their tops on the ground and begin to whip them, to keep them spinning. In this manner would begin the race, sometimes over an obstacle course of jumps, pits and fences where the competitors had to make their tops leap, soar, pirouette, retreat and veer left or right.

'Rākaihikuroa knew Tarakiuta and Tarakitai would become so absorbed in the race that they would let their defences down.

'"Go tonight to the course," he said to Tūpurupuru, "and right at the bottom build a huge pit. Then make yourself a whero-rua, a double-ended top. When the twins arrive at the pit, their tops will fall in and they will leap in to retrieve them. When that happens, you know what to do."

'That night, Tūpurupuru followed his father's instructions. He dug the pit and made himself a double-ended top. The next morning he went to the course and was on the ground by daylight. Not long after, the twins appeared. Tūpurupuru dropped his top on the ground and began to whip it down the slope. Down and down it spun, a toy of evil weaving its murderous intent and luring the twins to join the competition. They placed their tops on the ground and whipped them into movement and sent them chasing after Tūpurupuru's top.

'Around and over obstacles the rival tops sped and soared and the twins were caught up in the excitement of the chase. They drew nearer and nearer to Tūpurupuru. Suddenly, before them was the pit. It was so wide that not even the boys' tops could have soared over it. Tūpurupuru lashed at his top and it spun into the pit. The twins whipped at their tops which soared, almost reached the other side of the pit, but then teetered and fell into the wide hole also. Laughing, Tūpurupuru asked the two boys, "Can you descend into the pit to retrieve our tops?" They agreed without demur, and Tūpurupuru leapt into the pit after them. He took out his mere and dealt them both the death blow. He jabbed the edge of the mere at their foreheads and levered the club upward — their craniums opened up like lids. Tūpurupuru then buried the twins in the pit and levelled the ground so that no evidence of the murder remained.

'"Is it done?" his father Rākaihikuroa asked.

'"Yes, it is done well," Tūpurupuru answered.

'Now the scene changes to the pā of Kahutapere and his wife Rongomaitara. When the murdered twins did not return home, Rongomaitara became anxious.

'"Where are they?" she asked her husband.

'"I will start a search for them," he answered.

'The search went on for several days, and when it failed to find the boys, Rongomaitara began to grieve because she knew they must be dead. "They have been murdered," she said. "By whom?"

'And so Kahutapere made two kites,' Pera said.

'Kites?' I asked my grandfather. I was getting irritated and couldn't understand how kites could enter the story.

'Why are you always so impatient?' he asked. 'These weren't your normal kites, they were named after the twins. Magic was instilled in them, and they were sent into the sky. Priests chanted incantations, and the kites dipped and swung on the currents of the wind.

'"Show me the place of your murderer," Kahutapere cried.

'The kites therefore rose to a great height, stopped over Pukepoto and, there, they hovered. Slowly they dipped, once, twice, revealing the autocrat as the culprit.

'"Why would a brother kill his sister's children?" Kahutapere wondered. Hoping against hope that the kites had been wrong, he went with his warriors — they included two other sons — to see his brother-in-law. "My two boys, do you know what happened to them?"

'Rākaihikuroa replied obliquely from his royal chair. "Waiho rā kia tū takitahi ana ngā whetū o te rangi. Let there be only one star shining in the sky."

'Rākaihikuroa's warriors attacked Kahutapere. Although he escaped, many of his party and his sons were killed.

'The autocrat must have thought that his and Tūpurupuru's mana in the district was so great that Kahutapere would not dare to oppose it. But Kahutapere and Rongomaitara called for assistance from their close kinsmen. In Rongomaitara's case, she called upon a brother, Rākaipāka (he was also Rākaihikuroa's half-brother); Kahutapere sought aid from his cousins Māhaki and Taururangi.

'The avenging armies advanced on Pukepoto, where Tūpurupuru challenged any of the opposing warriors to meet him in single combat.

'Now,' Pera said, 'are you following carefully?'

'Of course I am,' I answered.

'Are you sure? I know you, and you have a habit of getting things wrong. Well, what Tūpurupuru had done was to make spears of mānuka, and he named them after the warriors he knew would accept his challenge. Therefore he was able to always overcome them because the spears could never be parried. However, although his magic was strong, there was another magic that was stronger and it belonged to Tūmatauenga, the god of war. Let me explain slowly so you understand. One of the warriors was Māhaki's youngest son Whakarau. He arrived late to the battle and had not yet consecrated his first kill to the god of war. Tū always had to be appeased so, when Tūpurupuru threw the spear at Whakarau with his name on it, the god of war waived Tūpurupuru's rights. Instead he approved the rights of Whakarau, who was able to parry it. Whakarau darted at Tūpurupuru and speared him in the head. He was like a fish impaled on a fisherman's hook.

'Tūpurupuru's body was hung by the plaited hair on the end of a swaying kahikatea bough across the stream opposite Pukepoto. The account between Rākaihikuroa and Kahutapere was equalised.

'Sons for sons.

'Rākaihikuroa therefore left the district altogether and, when he left, he dragged his cloak from the lands that he had once possessed. When he did that, lo and behold, was revealed the women descendants of the earlier ancestor, Ruapani.'

WE CAN RESTART the car now and carry on into Waituhi.

Beyond Pukepoto, a sharp corner curves into the foothills and, opening up, is the Waituhi Valley. In fact it's not a valley at all, but that is how I have always described it. Indeed, I once made a remark to a friend of mine from Switzerland, Simone Oettli, who was visiting New Zealand in the 1990s and wanted to go to the village: 'You'll never find it, Waituhi doesn't exist.'

I shocked myself when I said that. What did I mean? Certainly there's the sense that when I began to write about the kāinga in 1970, I was already writing about a Waituhi of twenty years earlier when I had been a boy. I guess I was trying to warn Simone that the village she read about in my work was already four decades in the past. I also wanted to convey to her that fiction sets up emotional resonances that actual places do not.

Most of all, I had to confront myself with the fact that my Waituhi was so inextricably bound up with Teria that when she went, it went.

Nevertheless, I organised for Dad to take Simone out to the village.

'You're wrong, Witi,' she told me after the visit. 'I did find Waituhi. I found it through your father.'

Historically, the valley has always been home to three main marae. The first you come to is Pākōwhai, with a small wooden church nearby, its roof steeply slanted. Taake Kerekere, scribe and priest, used to sit on the verandah of the marae and wave to us children as we went past to go swimming in the river. Mairia Hawea, David's wife, lives there today. She is Taake's oldest living descendant.

Before you reach the second marae, Rongopai, you pass through a settled area of houses, strung mainly along the left side of the road. In the old days people would dry eels on the fences, ready to be packed away until there was a hui. The big eel catches came about when Lake Repongaere overflowed into the nearby paddocks; 200 or 300 eels could often be taken on a single occasion. They must have been descendants of Tangotangorau, the huge man-eating tuna that had been gifted to Te Whānau-a-Kai by Paikea, the whale rider. The giant monster terrorised the valley and it took 100 warriors to kill him.

Slow down here. See that structure just off the road? Once, Pera and Teria's homestead stood there. After they died, my Uncle Puku asked Dad if he could replace the house with a new one, but the building of it ran into troubles of one kind or another. As for the other houses, they belong to whānau who whakapapa from Moanaroa Pere. When I was a boy in the early 1950s I waved to women hanging out washing and played marbles on the road with my cousin Elizabeth.

Water, it was so important. There were times in the summer when Teria would see people walking by and she would say to me, 'E Wit*sh*, it is a hot day. Take some of the cool spring water from the pump to the people.'

I loved to do that. I would run out, give the handle a few pumps, listen to water gurgling up from its underground reservoir and position the ladle underneath. Then carefully I would take the ladle out to the people. They would say: 'Homai te waiora ki ahau. Give to us the healing water of life.'

How could I ever reconcile such people with the prevailing view of them at the time as rebellious, dangerous and even murderers? I could not.

Chapter Thirty-two

A Meeting House Holding Up the Sky

1.

MY HEART IS beating fast.

Here comes the bend, and there is Rongopai. See it? The painted eaves are like an arrowhead thrusting at the sky. The old kāuta, Te Pao, which once stood behind the meeting house, is still there, but its function has now been taken over by the large new dining hall. Named Te Mana-o-Rīria Mauaranui, the hall has become a popular gathering place — a kōhanga operates there, and sometimes you will come across people line dancing to country and western music.

Slow down, slow down! Can somebody go and open the gate? Good, now drive through and park in front of the marae. The concrete ātea and the exterior perimeter fencing, including the elaborate shelter for the local elders, are all recent, dating from 1968. We owe the beauty of the new marae complex to such as Mahanga Horsfall, Martin Baker, Rangi Edwards, Puku Smiler, Nonoikura (Nona) Haronga, Jim Pere, Caesar Pere, Tom Smiler Snr and Puke Peawini among others.

Right-o, let's get out of the car, and I will welcome you onto my tūrangawaewae, the footstool where nobody can contest my right to stand.

And then, would you like to press noses with the meeting house?

'Sacred house, Rongopai, I greet you. As in days of old you still hold up the sky so that all your iwi can stand upright on the bright strand between. I greet you once, for you still stand triumphant. I greet you twice, for you have emerged from troubled histories to become a symbol of resilience and resistance. I greet you a third time, for you have kept alive the millennial dreams of an unconquered iwi. Once, twice, thrice I acclaim you.'

Actually, Simone was right. Dad *was* one through whom you could find Waituhi. And it was arrogant of me to say that the kāinga doesn't exist. Whakapapa, genealogy and storytelling will ensure that the relationships of humankind with land, and people with history, will go on and on.

Indeed, storytelling was the way Dad passed on to me all that I know about the meeting house which stands before us:

'Following the pardoning of Te Kooti in February 1883,' Dad said, 'the prophet settled at Te Tokangamutu, near the present town of Te Kūiti. He devoted his energies to developing the Ringatū faith, fusing Christianity and Māoritanga in a complementary relationship.

'But where would the people worship? The prophet could have built churches but, instead, he said, "Our whare karakia will not have a cross on top, it will have a tekoteko, and our door will not open to rows of pews, instead it will open to the interior of a meeting house. After all, has not the carved meeting house always been our place of gathering?"

'And so Te Whai-a-te-motu was begun in 1870 at Ruatāhuna in the Urewera mountains, and its name enshrines Te Kooti's successful evasion of government forces. Te Tokanganui-a-Noho followed two years later, in 1872. In 1882, Ruataupare was built by Te Kooti at Te Teko as an expression of gratitude to the people in that region for having supported him.

'Then, sometime in 1886, son,' Dad continued, 'something happened that was biblical in its simplicity. I know you have always liked the story of the three magi — Melchior, Caspar and Balthazar — who followed a bright star to Bethlehem. In our case, there were four wise men from Gisborne — a Haronga, a Peneha, a Ruru and a Pere — and they journeyed to see the prophet and asked him to come back to Gisborne.

'He answered the elders, "All right, go home and build the Gospel on charity and love."

'Son, sometimes Te Kooti's utterances were gnomic, runic, and it was left to the four wise men to find the talismanic meanings for themselves and make them manifest in the way they saw fit. What the heck did Te Kooti mean, and what did he want them to do? They were plain and ordinary men — you wouldn't take them for magi — and they wrestled with the words, trying to crack them open and expose the fire inside. Oh, for a long, long time they wrestled!

'"He wants us to build four meeting houses," they decided. "Each one is to be a station on his triumphal return."

'They went home, singing with joy. Thus was Te Whakahau, meaning "To start something up", begun under the supervision of the Haronga family at Rangatira. The construction of Te Ngāwari, meaning "Charity", was supervised by the Peneha family at Mangatū. Te Aroha, meaning "Love" was raised by the Ruru family at Tapuihikitia.

'Here in Waituhi, Moanaroa Pere and Ringatū elder Pā Ruru started to build Te Rongopai, meaning "The Gospel". They chose the site in the lee of a hill where the winds were coolest. A spring was also here, so bountiful that it supplied the whole of Waituhi even during long dry spells when the river was low. The water from the spring had life-giving and medicinal qualities.

'Hark unto the power of the prophet! More than 600 people journeyed to Waituhi to help build the meeting house. The faithful came mostly in family groups from as far away as Tauranga and the East Coast. Some led horses and others drove cattle and pet pigs before them. They carried salted fish, pumpkin, kūmara, kamokamo and honey from their hives. They were very numerous, lean and tall and well shaped. Some had dark eyes, black hair and beards of middling length. Most of the men were tattooed; some of the women had the moko chiselled on their chins. The clothing of both men and women was a mixture of Māori woven cloth and cloak, and Pākehā trousers or bright fabric wrapped around the waist, in the case of the women. They wore hats and smoked pipes. Most were bare-footed.

'The faithful camped out in tents on the hill above the place where Rongopai now stands. Can you imagine what it must have looked like, son? The clear blue sky was scrawled with the smoke from many campfires. In the evenings, the cinders were like fireflies circling above the land.

'And then the people began their great mahi. They started by digging the foundations, oh, they dug and they dug! And once that was done to Moanaroa Pere and Pā Ruru's satisfaction — no theodolite or surveying equipment to help them — the work parties began gathering the logs for the framing of the building. Thus did the men begin to travel far and wide, gathering the tree trunks, chopping them down and trimming them. As they worked, they prayed, chanted and sang all the day and night long.

'The long beam within was made from a kahikatea log, a tall white pine, some distance away in the Waikohu district. A working party was sent to harvest it and, when it was chopped down, it was launched into the river. People in canoes guided the log as it journeyed along the serpentine course. Others arrived on the forest-fringed banks to watch the log's progress and to sing love songs to it. At Pā Whakarau, a wāhi tapu, a sacred site near Pākōwhai marae, the log ended its river odyssey. A hauling party was there, 500 strong, to carry the log to the site at Waituhi.

'Now, the men had been told that the work was tapu and, therefore, they should not sleep with their women. E hika, within about 400 metres of their destination, while still on flat ground, the log suddenly became immoveable! Try as they might, the men could not shift it. Pā Ruru realised the tapu had been broken and asked the transgressors to leave the group. As soon as they did, the kahikatea became as light as a feather. So the lesson is, don't have sex when you are about tapu business, okay? From that moment, the journey of the log to its destination was completed without any further problem.

'Son, in this manner was the meeting house constructed:

'All the logs were fashioned and laid out on the ground — all the wall supports, the two central poles that would carry the roof, and the long beam and rafters of the roof itself. The architects did the calculations the way I do them, by measuring with their eyes, by using rule of thumb, no tape measure, simply by pacing the distances out on the ground. I must get my skills from them, eh.

'Moanaroa Pere and Pā Ruru adjusted and corrected the mathematics so that, when raised, Rongopai would be in perfect balance, with its weight evenly distributed upon the walls and central poutokomanawa. While the men were doing this, the women were plaiting the flax for the tukutuku panels that would be slotted into the walls and roof.

'Auē, Moanaroa Pere and Pā Ruru had a deadline to meet. Rongopai had to be completed in nine months. What good would all the work be if the other three houses were completed and not Te Rongopai? Not only that, but the four wise men had agreed that at Rongopai the prophet would preside over one of the two great annual Ringatū religious masses. Invitations had already gone out for the faithful to come to Rongopai on 1 January 1888.

'What could they do? The men and women were already flat out.

'They decided on something revolutionary. "We'd better get our younger generation onto it," Moanaroa Pere said.

'"They are not carvers," Pā Ruru exclaimed.

'"Let them paint then," Moanaroa Pere said. "Let them paint the panels, daub their dreams, reveal their aspirations, show their histories."

'Son, it was a decision which would bring both controversy and then triumph to all.

'And so came the time to lift the meeting house into place. The pillars were sunk straight into the earth. And Pā Ruru said to everyone, "Pray, pray hard!"

'Up, up, up went the wall supports.

'"Get the roof on now!" said Moanaroa Pere.

'Son, Rongopai wasn't just erected physically, it was also built spiritually, not only out of the muscle and sweat of the people but their karakia too. You don't think that a meeting house can be as much made out of prayer as of timber? Oh, you needed to be there to hear the constant droning of the people to know that the karakia went into the wood, the stories of the Old Testament tightened the timbers to the frame, and the hymnals stopped the cracks and cemented the house so that it would be weatherproof. And verily, it was the reo which provided the nails where there were no nails at all, so that Rongopai would hold, would stand.

'And so Rongopai has prevailed, son, for over 100 years, secured by clever dovetailing of all the timbers and by calculating the distribution of the weight so as to achieve a perfect balance.

'And by karakia.'

COME WITH ME through the gateway.

Of course Rongopai does not look like it did when I was a young boy, but I should stop apologising for that. Rather, I should affirm the fact of the marae's construction under Wī Pere's two sons, the first generation of the House of Halbert. They tend to be obscured in the shadow of the monolith that was their father, but the elder, Hetekia Te Kani, had occasionally accompanied Wī Pere to Auckland on his parliamentary duties and, together with his younger brother Te Moanaroa, he ensured the House of Halbert's continuation by maintaining effective leadership.

They must have been men with the mana to command and organise others. Housing and feeding over 600 people on the ground at Rongopai for nine months, most of them Ringatū followers offering their work for free, must have been quite a logistical feat, let alone a tribute to their faith.

One step, and one step further now.

We are approaching the porch and it is time to take your shoes off before entering the meeting house. In the old days there was a fence with a metre-wide gate which you had to go through. Everything temporal, including money, watches and jewellery, was wrapped in a cloth or handkerchief and left at the gate. In those days nobody stole other people's belongings as it was shameful to pilfer from one another.

Take the time to look at the porch. The words over the lintel of the front window, 'E Nehe Taa', They are the Greatest, could be a tribute to the work of the builders. If you look closely, you'll see that the porch has had a modern extension, bringing it out two metres. A number of carvers worked on the new roof beam, among them Pera Punahāmoa and Moni Taumaunu, and John Taiapa supervised the carving of the two supporting tekoteko.

You can imagine, can't you, the kōrero surrounding how to decorate the new panels of the porch? Artist John Walsh told me he was responsible for the portraits of newer ancestors that feature on them. I've never seen portraits of recent dead painted on a meeting house before — normally their photographs are hung inside — but aren't they a wonderful idea? Most are of the second generation of the House of Halbert and serve to remind us that they did not falter. They continued to support Te Whānau-a-Kai during the 1920s, 1930s and 1940s, and to prosecute the Treaty.

One of the portraits is of Rongowhakaata Halbert. The only surviving child of Hetekia Te Kani, he was sent to Nelson College where he became a prefect, was in the rugby and cricket senior teams and had extensive music training — he played the cello, viola and piano. His two cousins,

Tūruki and Te Kani Te Ua, joined him; the latter had a similar music education, specialising in Chopin.

I wish I had known this mighty spirit, this elder with his piercing intelligence. He was from the tuakana line and he indeed lived up to the expectations of the eldest son of the eldest son when he guided the family through the difficult post-Second World War years. My father Te Haa lived at his home when he was a boy; if I had ever had the opportunity, I would have loved to have spent some time with him, too. He was the intellectual among the Halberts and wrote an astonishing book, *Horouta: The History of the Horouta Canoe, Gisborne and the East Coast*, for which I was asked to write a foreword. I could not do it; by that time I was an adult and had learnt not to be so whakahīhī as to raise myself above my elders.

Along with a number of other prominent rangatira, Rongowhakaata was a member of the Te Tairawhiti Historical Association so, although some people tend to think of Māori culture as not having Māori writers, artists, historians and musicians before the 1950s, we did.

Another of the portraits is that of my grandmother Teria's elder sister, Mana. She was from Te Moanaroa's line, what we call the teina or younger brother line. He had married the striking and regal Rīria Kaihote Wātene, from Wairoa, and, man oh man, were they prolific breeders! Where Hetekia Te Kani had only one son, Moanaroa had Mirianata (Milly), Hani (he died as a baby so I understand), Wheeti Moana Mana (Mana), Tūruki, Teria Moana (Teria), Hiraina, Mahanga and his twin who died at birth, Baden Powell Mafeking (Mafe), Mere Tahatū (Mary), Charles Taare (Charlie), Parakau Bella (Bella), Waiōriwa (Olive) and Te Kani.

Now when Mana's elder sister Mirianata died in 1915, Mana took on the leadership of the teina line with her brother Tūruki and sister Teria. The story I like about Mana concerns the time she crossed swords with one of the greatest Tūhoe and Ringatū leaders, the charismatic Te Pairi Tūterangi. In his youth, Tūterangi had been a close friend and adviser of Te Kooti; in his old age he acquired such a fearsome reputation that even his own family was afraid of him — he upheld the old ways. My colleague Pou Temara tells a story about Tūterangi that I find irresistible. Apparently the old man arrived at the tangi of an old friend:

'At the entrance to the marae he released his horse. He was completely naked except for a chaplet of petipeti leaves on his head; in his hand was his taiaha. He crept and writhed on to the marae like an eel and at intervals he would strike the ground with the blade of his weapon. He continued until he reached the body. There he sat for nine days without taking food. During that time the chaplet began to dry up and wither and Tūterangi seemed to the people to take on the appearance of a ngārara with the passing of each day. Observers were in awe of the spectacle.

As the coffin was being closed he took off his chaplet and cut his hair, placing leaves and hair-clippings in the coffin. The women sitting with the body followed suit.'

Definitely not a person to anger in any way.

From what I have been told, Tūterangi was on a visit to Pākōwhai, some time in the 1940s, when Mana had the temerity to stand up and speak on the marae. Immediately Tūterangi was on his feet, circling her, darting his tongue in and out, hissing and making threatening moves across her head with a mere, as if he was prepared to saw it off. Mana was resolute: no matter what he did, she kept talking until she had had her say. Clearly she was not fazed by Tūterangi's menacing threats to her right to speak; she upheld that right.

Tūterangi must have been impressed with the quality of Te Whānau-a-Kai men and women. Why else would he have had one student and one student only, and that student from Te Whānau-a-Kai? He was Te Kani Te Ua, to whom the old man gave his greenstone earring pendants.

All the children of Te Moanaroa are the reasons why the third generation of the House of Halbert increased in an exponential way. Most had huge broods whereas Rongowhakaata had only six children (did I say *only*?); it must have been nerve-racking for them to watch the ever-burgeoning numbers of cousins — a kind of unbalancing of the numbers by infant-ry.

When it comes to the Wī Pere Trust, the implications are extraordinary, rather like having a company belonging to two directors but the majority of the shareholders on one side. The Te Moanaroa descendants could dominate proceedings, were it not for one important fact: the ownership of the land is split fifty-fifty. Half the shares are in the hands of the small number of descendants of Te Kani; the other half is possessed by the thousands of squabbling, exuberant descendants of Te Moanaroa, who comprise the fifth, sixth, seventh, eighth and possibly ninth generations. No wonder I became adept at negotiation and diplomacy and went into Foreign Affairs. I got my training from all the hugely complex and democratic family decision-making, with its infighting and changing allegiances; I learned from experts.

And look at the House of Halbert now. Leading agriculturalists, government bureaucrats, military commanders, university-trained technocrats and academics, and even a jet pilot all feature in the whakapapa. The current Wī Pere chairman is Rongowhakaata Halbert's grandson, Alan Haronga, who has the position not only by virtue of shareholdings (he owns more shares than anybody else, the advantage in coming from the side of the family with fewer descendants) but also by astute management and directorial sleight-of-hand — watch him dazzle the shareholders at the annual meetings. The deputy chair is another cousin, Kīngi Smiler, who was Agribusiness Person of the Year in 2013 and also happens to have competed in twenty Ironman events. Incidentally, another cousin, Michelle Hippolyte, is the CEO of Te Puni Kōkiri, New Zealand's government agency for Māori people.

Wī Pere would have been proud of them.

3.

NOW, LET ME open the door so that we can go in.

The somewhat imperial bronze bust of Wī Pere was installed as part of his centenary celebrations in 1990, which were attended by some 3000 bloodline descendants. Since then we've had a more recent 120th anniversary in 2010. The bust was cast by Don Smiler, known as Tiger. I think he's living in the United States.

Look through my eyes now, and you will see Rongopai as I used to as a boy: the Māori Garden of Eden.

According to Dad, in the 1950s, when Professor Trevor Lloyd, the curator of the Auckland War Memorial Museum, visited the meeting house, he said, 'The paintings of the flora and other art forms in Rongopai compare favourably with the paintings of the Sistine Chapel in Italy.' He wanted to dismantle the whare in sections, transport it to Auckland and reconstruct it there. The people of the village said 'No'. They were right to keep the meeting place in its papakāinga, where it has become an inspiration to all who visit. However, they've also had to do a lot of work to restore it, with crucial advice from the Gisborne Regional Committee of the New Zealand Historic Places Trust. The installation of protective cladding and a ventilation system reinforced the structure and protected it from dampness and fungicidal erosion. Artists like Cliff Whiting, Buck Nin, Para Matchitt and John Walsh all assisted in the restoration of the paintwork. Recently, Polly Whaitiri led tukutuku conservation and Philip Barry has been in charge of conserving the artwork. They have ensured that the interior retains the magical and strange beauty and whimsical spirit with which it was painted those long years ago.

Look back and up.

Above and to one side of the doorway you have just entered are two sets of eyes, woven and separately painted within the tukutuku panels. The eyes belong to Tarakiuta and Tarakitai, the twin boys who were murdered by Tūpurupuru, and they invoke legendary times involving magic kites.

Follow the line of the ceiling now. The rafters are painted in the typical designs of the kōwhaiwhai, bold red, white and black curvilinear scrolls in the shapes of the unfolding fern, the double spiral, the hammerhead shark, the flower of the kākābeak and the red lips of the ngutukura.

They are infused with a glow that even the years cannot dim.

Now, bring your gaze down the walls and behold the millennial dreams of the iwi.

The carved pillars are like tall trees, elaborately painted in greens, blues and reds; between them are alternating panels of reed work, plaited dragons' teeth, the small triangles known as the little teeth, the double mouth, the armpit weave, the white crosses of the star seeds (purapurawhetū) and roimata, or tears. The pillars are made of pukatea wood and extend on either side like a pathway into an illuminated forest. The healing powers of the house are symbolised in the profusion of painted trees and vines: reds and purples, brilliant flowers and pods pop out from large Victorian vases; oranges and yellow, sunbursting fruits defy botanical reality; the glorious purple of the Scotch thistle, the greens and creams of seeds float upward to the ceiling; the fabulous Tree of Knowledge of Good and Evil sprouts its twelve separate herbal flowers from a central trunk.

Fantastic birds fly through the forest; they could only have been dreamed of in paradise, and swoop and dart amid the painted foliage. Other fabulous creatures also show themselves: monsters of the deep emerald oceans, the manaia and marakihau, the beaked-bird man, the lizard, the seahorse, the semi-human sea monster with the long tubular tongue capable of sucking in both fish and man, all slither within this glittering universe.

And the ancestors are everywhere. They stand, run, climb and fly. Kahungunu is painted on one pillar, handsome and wearing only a waist garment around his thighs to hide the sight of his fabled loins; Kahungunu's daughter, Tauhei, and his grandson, Māhaki, also have places of honour. Other ancestors flourish taiaha and mere, but they are cleverly inflected with European references. A warrior stands with piupiu skirt and tāniko band around his head; in his hair he wears not the traditional royal huia feather but a purple thistle. Hine-hākiri-rangi wears a pretty European dress with a hint of a Victorian bustle, and holds a red rose to her lips. Two men spar in a boxing match; they are a sly reference to the ongoing conflict between the Crown and the iwi. A bushman holds an axe, a reference to the clearing of bush for farmland and the future impact upon the iwi. Delicately daubed horses lift their hooves in a timeless race.

And Wī Pere, yes, there he is, shown in the formal attire of black jacket, grey trousers, hat and spurs on his heels; his mother, a Māori Pallas Athena, is perched on his shoulder like a guardian owl. Do you think he looked like this in real life? No, this is how the artists who painted Rongopai represented him. And if they did that, may I not similarly represent Teria in my work with pearls in her hair — the universal symbol for the tears of God?

Now seek the painting of Adam and Eve in the Garden of Eden. Can you see it? Of all the paintings this one is beyond comparison. To look at it is to weep. Adam and Eve are depicted clothed with cloaks and holding Māori weaponry in their hands. Driven from the garden by the archangel Gabriel, they are already prepared to confront a hostile colonial world.

Rongopai and the painted houses like it are the closest, in my opinion, that Māori ever came to the European tradition of landscape painting. Whenever I looked at such paintings, and the European figures within the powerful landscapes, I often wondered why Māori had never taken it up.

The reasons are many. One of them is that we were already part of the landscape and did not need to paint ourselves in it. We were not outsiders and nor did we view the landscape within a frame as it were; there was no need to miniaturise, to reduce.

Currently Tourism New Zealand has a campaign to go with Sir Peter Jackson's *Hobbit* film trilogy, which brands the country as Middle Earth. Of course that makes sense for Pākehā, because the movies, as well as the phenomenally successful *Lord of the Rings* films, were written by J.R.R. Tolkien and access Western European folklore. But when I was at the Frankfurt Book Fair in 2013, I said that Aotearoa was not Middle Earth but Māori Earth.

My mother had her mountain. I found my place to orient myself from in the Waituhi Valley. It is, was and will ever be Rongopai. Whenever I look at the meeting house I am always conscious of those two bases upon which it was built, muscle and karakia. Out of one has come the Rongopai you see; out of the other has come the Rongopai you *see*.

Whenever I go to Rongopai, I am surrounded by my ancestors. It has become in my mind my own Garden of Eden, a place where I can rest. And once I am rested, Rongopai is the place I can leave and do battle from.

If you want to know what my heart looks like, look to Rongopai.

I WANT TO take a leaf out of Rātana's book.

I ask you to imagine a table, and on it I will place four objects. The first object is a glass of water. I offer the glass to you — the water is from Waituhi. Māori people always say, 'Homai te waiora ki ahau. Give to us the healing waters of life.' I ask you to drink from the glass and know how precious water is.

The second object is a child's kite. If you climb Pukepoto and fly the kite it will show you the lands of Te Whānau-a-Kai. Wherever you look, know that we are the guardians.

The third object is a small wooden box and in it is a skein of spiderwebs. I ask you to remember that we all have a contract to the natural world as well as to our own. Oh, humans are so clumsy, we shred the webs of spiders!

And the fourth is a piece of willow from the trees fringing the Waipaoa. I offer it not as a peace offering. Rather, I want you to take it and draw a line on the ground.

You may have everything you wish on your side of the line. Take the universe. Do what you want with the world. Leave Waituhi to us.

One last memory.

On a visit to Waituhi, Teria said something to me that forever marked my relationship with my grandfather.

Let me set the scene. Rain was falling lightly across the village, like a benediction. My grandmother and I were sitting together in the front of Dad's truck. We were parked at the gateway at the back of the Blue House where Dad was talking to Pera, probably about the stock that he was grazing in the foothills.

From out of nowhere, Teria said, 'Never trust your grandfather.'

When I mentioned it one day to my Uncle Sid, he said, 'Mum would never have said that.' And Pera, in his own hand, writes in his whakapapa book: 'In my married life we were happy. We tried our best to educate our children on[e] of them got the degree of b.a. and m.a. and the other one is [a] teacher.'

So Uncle Sid is right, it would have been out of character for Teria to make a statement like that about Grandad. But I am recalling a particular day, when the sky was grey and it was raining. My grandparents may have had an argument the night before, which triggered her pronouncement. Or maybe sitting there, holding my hands in hers, she recalled something that had never been resolved between them.

I didn't question her. Instead, we continued to sit, silently, watching Dad and my grandfather, and then Pera Punahāmoa gestured towards me and Teria, safely out of the rain, and Dad laughed. They walked to the truck, Teria climbed out, and Dad and I drove away. Yes, the choreography was that specific.

I would rather give my grandmother the richness of saying something inconsistent because people are not always consistent. The point is that she did say it and she said it to me, and I have wrestled with that phrase all my life.

She didn't say 'Don't trust your grandfather'; she said 'Never', which is entirely different. Had she said 'Don't', I think I would have given Grandad the benefit of the doubt in some of our later encounters. Instead, she said 'Never', which implies something specific, an edict that must last a lifetime.

But was she really talking about a matter of distrust between them? My cousins may forgive me this memory if I say to them that I think it had to do with Teria having given me her blessing and Grandad favouring another.

One thing more. My grandmother once told me that she would never die. I believed her.

She should have never said that.

PART FIVE

TE AO
THE WORLD

Chapter Thirty-three

A Post-colonial Town

1.

WHERE HAVE I got to in narrating to you the Māori creation? I mustn't lose the thread of our genesis story because, all my life, it has framed my way of looking at time and the universe, and my place — and, indeed, yours — in it. Remember that long line of ancestors? They are twisted into a giant rope, Te Taura Tangata, The Great Rope of Humankind, and it stretches from the beginning of time to time's end.

To resume the story, after Hinenuitepō became the Great Mother of the Night, her father Tāne returned to the Overworld. Generations came and went, I don't know how many, before the demi-god, Māui, was born. From this point, the narrative turns to Māui and the great cycle of stories involving his travels and exploits. He becomes the person who sets the course of the whakapapa.

Now, I'm going to ask a question and offer some thoughts on it, which might astonish you:

Who was the original Māui?

Most people in Aotearoa consider him to be a Māori, and most depictions of him are as a Māori warrior, but Māui must be more than that; after all, he is known as a demi-god throughout Polynesia, not just Aotearoa.

I think the answer to the question requires following the DNA of the story of Māui to the source. Just as the Genographic Project is predicated on the existence of an original mitochondrial Eve who lived in Tanzania several million years ago (and I have suggested Hinetītama as that woman), is there a chance that one could follow the traces of a story involving a Māuiesque hero also back in time? For instance, some two million years later to, say 3150 BC, in ancient Egypt, where there is a figure named Māui, a personification representing the splendour and light of the sun? Analogues of the Māui cycle have been noted in the ancient lore of India and Babylon, too.

And how about the analogues in Greek mythology? In the 1950s my ancestor, Te Kani Te Ua, considered that although the Māori people might be called a barbaric and savage race, our knowledge and conception of the spirit world showed a high plane of thought similar to the philosophical speculation of the earliest Greek philosophers, Empedocles, Anaximander and others.

Te Kani Te Ua wasn't the only one to think this way. The scholar Agathe

Thornton, in *Maori Oral Literature As Seen by a Classicist* (1988), postulated that the myth of the separation of Rangi and Papa by their offspring was similar to the Greek story of Uranus and Gaea. The god Tūtangāhu cut the sinews that bound Papa and Rangi, and Tānemahuta wrenched them apart and kept them eternally separated; in the Hesiodic fable Cronus separated the heavenly pair by mutilating his oppressive father. No wonder that, with Te Kani Te Ua and Agathe Thornton as scholarly exemplars, I have used Greek mythic parallels in my own work.

The most frequent comparisons of Māui are with Prometheus or Hercules. I find a closer likeness with Perseus who, like Māui, was cast into the sea as a baby, fought with the kraken (fished up New Zealand) and of course faced the Medusa, which paralleled Māui's confrontation with Hinenuitepō in her original incarnation as a malevolent goddess of death.

Five millennia ago, the Māui cycle could have travelled eastward to reside temporarily with the people who possibly lived in the hills of Taiwan. From there, it might have been carried by those voyagers who settled the north Pacific — Samoa, French Polynesia and other island groups — for Māui was known to them variously as Mawi, Mowee, Aitu, Koriro and Tamarangi.

Eventually, from the legendary homeland, Hawaiki, our Polynesian ancestors brought the Māui cycle south to Aotearoa.

2.

BACK TO GROWING up Māori in the 1950s.

Whenever I was in Waituhi I was one boy, but whenever I returned to Gisborne I was another boy. And that same youth, just like any other boy or girl of the time, was growing up in a post-colonial context where one attitude clashed with another.

For instance, in Waituhi I could sit on the marae and listen with Teria to my elders castigating the Crown for the injustices of the Treaty of Waitangi. When I returned to Gisborne, I would join other schoolchildren in lining the streets waving my standard-issue Union Jack as the Queen and Duke of Edinburgh came to New Zealand and visited Gisborne on 6 January 1954. The cavalcade whizzed down Gladstone Road and those same elders welcomed her.

Again, in Waituhi, a week later, I could listen to my Great-uncle Mafeking criticising the Crown. Back in Gisborne a few days later Aunty Billie, who was working as a housemaid at the Masonic Hotel, could wave at Dad and me as we walked by — 'Bring Witi up, Tom' — open the door on the main bedroom suite and say, 'The Queen rested here.'

Although it's simplistic to say this, it's nonetheless true, that while on the surface Gisborne Māori all appeared to function as one group, either for or against Pākehā, you only had to look beneath the surface to see that, actually, we weren't homogeneous and never had been.

The consequences of Pākehā first contact had put paid to that by making some Māori more acculturated to Pākehā than others; this is not a judgement, and not just related to blood quantum. Some tribes were clearly better treated by the government than others. That was to their advantage, and the government's capitalising on it — wouldn't you rather talk to loyalists? — only exacerbated tribal tensions between, say, Ngāti Porou and some of the iwi of the Tūranga, Gisborne, district.

Historical events such as the Te Kooti Wars hadn't made things easier either, with some tribes which were not necessarily pro-Pākehā taking sides against *him*. In the 1950s, as I walked along Gladstone Road with Teria, some people would have sharp words with her. My Aunt Te Nonoikura Haronga told historian Gary Clapperton that the reason why Te Whānau-a-Kai pulled our heads down out of sight was because we were always being blamed for everyone losing their land. No wonder that, as Nona explained, 'For some years we went under the banner of Te Aitanga-a-Māhaki to take attention away from ourselves.'

Our Pere family had a specific cross to bear. I've mentioned earlier the disastrous land losses for which my ancestor Wī Pere Halbert was considered responsible when his and Rees's land company went under in 1892. Whenever the subject came up on the marae and our family was subjected to personal attacks of the 'Your ancestor stole our land' kind, the best strategy was to remain silent, grin and bear it. Somebody must have forgotten to tell my grandmother Teria that, though, as she could give as good as she got.

Following this thread, the churches only exacerbated the divisions. Most of the East Coast was Anglican, Gisborne itself was Anglican or Roman Catholic, and then came the Seventh Day Adventists and Mormons with their chapels in Kaitī, Te Hāpara and Mangapapa; did they ever put all those other white pigeons into a flurry. And some of those Māori Christians could also be seen participating at Ringatū church services — what was that about? Sure, most of the Ringatū services were marae-based and rural, so presumably the otherwise Anglicans could get back in their cars and return to town and their Christian-based lives, where God would excuse them.

Finally, even my mother could often be the subject of scorn from my father's family: 'You're a Ngāti Porou and your people were on the side fighting against us. Why should we listen to you?' Of course Dad copped it in reverse when we went to Tolaga Bay. Although he was well liked by his Keelan in-laws, there were times when some Ngāti Porou were wary of him because he came from the Godforsaken uncivilised tribe that had supported Te Kooti, whereas they had fought on the government (read 'civilised') side against the rebel leader.

Where did all this leave Te Whānau-a-Kai? As Puke Peawini said to me, 'We were out on our sorry arses.'

Despite all this, I have to say that Gisborne was a remarkably bicultural town. While Māori might have muttered imprecations against other Māori in the safety of numbers on their own marae, and against Pākehā too, most of my elders were realistic enough and committed to making Māori–Pākehā relations *work*.

Modern assumptions about the post-war movement of Māori from rural areas to New Zealand cities and towns tend to paint this trend as creating an urban working class who had no other option if they wanted jobs. Not so. In the 1950s, the 1000 Māori who lived in Gisborne chose to be there, and it was their quality and not their quantity that counted. Indeed, when I was growing up, Māori and Pākehā liked to boast that the town was the best example in New Zealand of the two races getting on well together.

'The best race relations in the country,' they said.

3.

A BICULTURAL TOWN, yes, and on the Māori side, one of the main reasons had to do with the fact that Gisborne was what I call a 'company' town. Māori fighting in the First World War might have been lost sight of, but there was no way in which Māori soldiers could be erased from the official histories of New Zealand following their huge and spectacular involvement in the Second World War. Most of them served in 28th (Māori) Battalion, and the headquarters of one of their most illustrious companies, C Company, was Gisborne itself. Thus, when the victorious Māori soldiers came back from the war, they created a framework of *visibility*.

Just as C Company officers and men had fought to represent Māori on the battlefield, you could be as sure as hell that they would lead Māori in peacetime. Affectionately known as 'The Cowboys', they made of Gisborne *the* perfect example of the old military town, a Māori Sandhurst sustained by the military traditions and dignity of the returnees.

And they kept up the bicultural 'look' of Gisborne. The impact of these men, whom you saw in the streets every day and who appeared in their blazers and berets on marae, was inescapable and powerful. They conjured up our greatest warriors — Moana Ngārimu VC, Arapeta Awatere and, of course, my Uncle Rangiora. A roll call would include surnames like Kaa, Tūhura, Ferris, Poutū, Temepara, Reihana, Rangi, Hunia, Hamon, Mulligan, Ranapia, Kīngi, Mackey, Tūhaka, Brown, Nepe,

Milner, Bartlett, Kaua, Kōhere, Delamere, Te Hau and Fox — and their descendants proliferated among my contemporaries as both local and national leaders. They were not broken men; they emerged to maintain leadership. Their military exploits were constantly spoken of, and they infiltrated decision-making within Gisborne institutions. Not only that, they took over from the generation of Māori gentry in representing Māori within the Pākehā community.

A typical battalion couple was my Uncle Pita Kaua and Aunty Mate. In 1964, when Hēnare Ngata became President of the 28th Māori Battalion Association, Pita was secretary.

Uncle Pita had been a sergeant in C Company and looked as though he should be in the movies; after the war, he had a career in Maori Affairs. As for Aunty Mate, she was a very fair, regal and beautiful woman, who began her career as a primary school teacher at Whāngārā and Mangatuna Native School; she was very strict. They had a very handsome son, my cousin Bill. The first time I stayed with Uncle Pita and Aunty Mate was so that they could stop me wetting the bed. Both were disciplinarians and, well, I learned from that visit how to hold my water. Once I had got over my little problem they were very kind to me and, on my second visit, I actually enjoyed myself.

Uncle Pita brought his Māori Battalion persona, namely his discipline, into the home, and in Aunty Mate he had the perfect partner. She became president of the Tūranga Māori Women's Welfare League, a leading member of the Holy Trinity choir, and was several times New Zealand Māori women's golf champion.

Aunty Mate's house was straight out of a home and garden magazine. And of course, there were the pretensions, if not to be better than, then at least to be as good as any Pākehā. On one visit I was fascinated by a particular opera programme that Aunty Mate had, for *Madama Butterfly*. She saw that I was intrigued and acted out the death scene for me. Today I can never go to a performance without seeing Aunty Mate, her face a Kabuki mask, floating down onto the carpet in her high heels, twinset and pearls, holding her red scarf to her throat and chest in simulation of death by hara-kiri.

As for Billy, he was older than I was and didn't like having to occasionally look after me. In every way, however, I idolised him, thinking him to be the regulation product of a regulation army family. Once, however, I spoilt his day on the river with his rowing team, and mid-stream he threatened to throw me overboard. That almost started my bed wetting again, I can tell you.

I like to think of Uncle Pita and Aunty Mate as living the battalion dream. As I grew into a teenager I admired them both. They belonged to all those institutions that came with the assumptions that you had

Made It. They achieved the rare gift of perfect balance within Gisborne's bicultural society. Apart from the Returned Servicemen's Association, Uncle Pita also belonged to the local golf club and was a well-known sportsman; he was probably the most competitive man I knew. For a short time, until I absolutely refused to go out with them again, I would caddy for Dad and Pita. Uncle Pita's stroke was always handicapped by his competitive eagerness. The stroke wasn't fluid and, just as his club hit the ball, he would expel his breath 'Hmmm*nh*', in an effort to give the stroke more energy. The consequence was that the ball would be hooked to the left or to the right, but sometimes it would soar down the fairway — and then he would be happy. If he wasn't he would say to Dad, 'Tell Witi to stand back, he's spoiling my stroke.' I know Uncle Pita didn't intend it, but I took offence easily in those days and would try to hex him with a boyhood spell.

One day when I was in my early teens, for some reason Uncle Pita started to tell me some of his war experiences. To hear a man who was normally so stoic and staunch — after all those years of post-traumatic stress — opening up about what he had seen and experienced was deeply affecting. His moods and the ways he responded to them — his vulnerability — could also have had to do with the fact that Aunty Mate had contracted cancer. She died in November 1961, aged only forty-nine, and Uncle Pita's battalion story continued when he married Peggy Falwasser, née Pitt.

Now there's somebody whose whakapapa was interesting. Her mother, Katherine Rogers, had followed her husband Captain William Tutepuaki Pitt to Egypt during the First World War — this was the same Captain Pitt who, after the war, represented Rongowhakaata, Te Aitanga-a-Māhaki and Ngāi Tamanuhiri at the Māori Land Commission meeting in Gisborne in 1920. He was serving in the First Native Contingent, and Peggy was born in Alexandria; her second name was in fact Alexandria. I understand that Katherine Rogers was the companion of Margaret Buck, wife of Sir Peter Buck, known to Māori as Te Rangi Hīroa.

Buck was a crucial figure in my own career, inspiring me to try to combine a political life with a cultural one. His first career as a minister of the Crown is a matter of record. His second, as an academic, took him to Yale. He published two remarkable books, *The Coming of the Maori* and *Vikings of the Sunrise*, and Professor Joan Stevens considered him one of the finest writers working with the English language. He held academic positions at Yale University and at the Bernice P. Bishop Museum.

In 1985 I flew to Hawaii to talk to the museum and the East–West Center to try to set up a Te Rangi Hīroa Fellowship. On a subsequent visit to the United States I was also able to go to Yale to look at the materials he had bequeathed to the institution.

Te Rangi Hīroa was dying of cancer when he made a final visit to New Zealand. I heard him on radio speaking in his distinctive high and light voice. His death in Honolulu in 1951 was a profound loss to our intellectual world. For me, he came to represent the epitome of a Māori scholar and Renaissance man.

Back to Peggy now. Throughout her life she was always at the centre of Māori society, including battalion reunions. She was a great favourite of Sir Āpirana Ngata and worked on renewing the tukutuku for Te Hau-ki-Tūranga when it was housed in Wellington.

Peggy was a lively, vivacious woman. You can't help but grin at a 1945 photo of her swinging her hips as she dances with a US marine. Her marriage to Henry Falwasser, who died in 1960, was by all accounts warm; he was another ex-Māori Battalion man, having been a lieutenant in D Company. When Henry died, and Uncle Pita and Peggy got together, it was one of those marriages that everyone felt was ideal — within the battalion, as it were. I wasn't surprised when Mum told me they were getting married.

To be frank, I wasn't one of Aunty Peggy's favourites. She and my mother had a cool relationship, but Peggy liked Dad. She always supported me (and Anne Salmond, too) and would never allow me to come back to Gisborne without asking if I would go to see her and Uncle Pita. By then he was not well, but he always made an effort to hide it. When he died, aged eighty, in 1989, he was given a terrific send-off by his band of brothers.

THE BATTALION LEADERS were inspirational. There were also other success stories going on that buoyed up Gisborne's biculturalism. While I can't remember any commercial businesses, shops or firms that were ever owned by Māori, nevertheless Māori were breaking through the glass ceiling. Hēnare Ngata had his own law practice and a number of young legal practitioners like Charles Chauvel were snapping at his heels. Aunty Mate was not the only Māori teacher, and there were a number of Māori doctors and nurses like Aunty Dinah in the medical profession. Bill Parker, Bill Kerekere and Hēnare Te Ua, Te Kani's son, were firmly ensconced in broadcasting.

Indeed, I was born at a propitious time for defying stereotypes.

Culturally, you could go to the Amateur Dramatic Society performances of, say, *South Pacific*, *Rose Marie* or *The Pirates of Penzance* and, like as not, Māori tenor Peter Keiha would be singing the lead. Appearing in recitals was young contralto, Carol Witana, in costume as a Covent Garden fruit seller singing:

Cherry ripe, cherry ripe, ripe I pray
Full and fair ones, come and buy!

Another bright-eyed, ringlet-covered girl with a silver voice was also singing. She would follow an earlier East Coast Māori singer, Princess Te Rangi Pai, and turn from being Tom Te Kanawa's daughter into Dame Kiri Te Kanawa; Dad and Tom sometimes met at the golf course, where I caddied for them.

As for my cultural pursuits, nothing could stop me from rushing to Madge Cole's for my weekly piano lesson. From the day I innocently expressed a wish to learn the piano and Teria finessed me by buying one, I embarked on a discovery of an artform that I pursue to this day. I followed in the footsteps of other whānau pianists such as Te Kani Te Ua, self-taught Bill Kerekere (man, could he vamp) and Huia Chrisp. Madge Cole was wonderful to me, patiently introducing me to Beethoven, Haydn, Mozart and, yes, Chopin — though she would never let me play his music. She kept me at the more mathematical precision of the older masters, and spoke to me of the sonata form, counterpoint and recapitulation; all those early lessons I took to heart.

There came a time when she thought me suitably trained to participate in the Gisborne Amateur Dramatic competitions. We were both relieved, I think, that I didn't do well and clearly needed more training. But I was caught up in the excitement both onstage and backstage with other friends like Fiona Blair, who was one of the best ballet dancers in the business. Her friend Ann Taylor was a close competitor, and I can remember both their mothers, one on either side of the wings, urging them from behind the curtains, 'Smile, smile!'

I had better luck in marae concerts where I could relax and, without Madge Cole knowing, play a Chopin polonaise or Lecuona's flashy 'Malaguena'. And for a time, Johnny Cooper began to hold talent competitions at the Gisborne Opera House, and one competition I actually won. Not that I was all that interested, though the money was good — £5, I think.

I was more fascinated by another juvenile ballet dancer, this time Māori, the beautiful Elizabeth Algie, who performed a variation on Anna Pavlova's famous 'Dance of the Dying Swan'. Dressed in white tutu, she would dance onto the stage, the spotlight following her until *bang* came the loud report of a shotgun going off, frightening the living daylights out of the sleeping aunties. Elizabeth would flip a red cellophane stain on her bodice and spend the rest of the routine pirouetting round and round until, arms flailing, she sank to the ground.

The irony was that there we were, both descendants of Te Kooti Arikirangi, involved in traditional European artforms. But I have a suspicion that he may well have enjoyed our performances as he had not been without sophistication.

What's interesting is that Māori lives were also appearing in the social media of the day. I'm referring particularly to a small glossy magazine that Dad brought home one afternoon and gave to my mother. Unlike the *New Zealand Woman's Weekly* or the *New Zealand Free Lance*, this one, called *Te Ao Hou: The New World*, was published by the Department of Maori Affairs, and it showed Māori out and about and around New Zealand.

At the local level, the *Gisborne Photo News* started up in 1954, offering a fantastic record of events and happenings, and Māori were appearing regularly in its pages. Not only flash Pākehā weddings at Ulverstone Castle but colourful Māori ones — at Ulverstone, too. It wasn't just Pākehā football players who featured in the *News* pages, but also uncles we most often saw coming out of the pub. And aunties we usually saw at housie now looked back at us, smiling, with cakes they had made for the church bazaar. Sheridan Gundry's book, *A Splendid Isolation*, recaptures some of this Gisborne-abilia.

The film *Broken Barrier* had shown ourselves, startlingly, on the cinema screen. But when we began to appear regularly in the magazines, local and national and Māori, we were suddenly everywhere. We were coming out. Disconcerting though the gaze might be, it revealed we were no longer invisible. Not only that, but overseas film-makers were interested in us.

I can still remember the excitement of seeing the poster for the J. Arthur Rank film, *The Seekers*, directed by Ken Annakin and starring Jack Hawkins, Glynis Johns, Īnia Te Wīata and a Javanese German exotic dancer — now her casting should have given off warning signals. I begged to be taken to the film, and Teria agreed. Known for American distribution as *Land of Fury*, its tagline was: 'They Found The Most Exotic Wilderness That Man Has Ever Known!'

Well, 'savage' might have been a better word. 'Exotic' was what you found in French Polynesia or places like Bali in the Far East, where the dancing was prettier.

The Seekers was apparently the first film ever made in colour in New Zealand. The Javanese German exotic dancer was Laya Raki, who was cast as an extremely sultry Māori girl married to a Māori chief. She lusts on first sight for Jack Hawkins and does a dance that has to be seen to be believed. A publicist for the film said, 'Laya has a strong Polynesian cast of feature. We had tested several Māori girls, some of them beautiful, but somehow the cameras didn't take to them. You know how people photograph differently from the way they really look. Well, when we stumbled across Laya Raki and tested her, she photographed ideally for the part. She looks more like a Māori than a Māori.'

The film, from a John Guthrie novel, is escapist entertainment, so you find yourself forgiving the film-makers.

What was important to my growing critical awareness was that the movie showed me what we looked like to outsiders. Actually the films showing Polynesians weren't really about *us*. They were mainly about our being discovered by a handsome white hero who comes to the Pacific, and examples included *Son of Fury*, *Drums of Tahiti*, *Pagan Love Song*, *His Majesty O'Keefe* or *Return to Paradise*.

The Seekers was the New Zealand version. An outsider's camera was trained on us, and what was on film was what it saw. Was it us? Well, no. It was what someone else thought we looked like and how we talked.

What did Teria think? After the movie she waited while I jabbered on about how exciting *The Seekers* had been and how great it was to see Māori in a film at the Regent.

'Māori?' she asked. She looked at the poster of the film, then pulled me through the foyer to a full-length mirror, and made me stand in front of it.

'Titiro, look,' she said. 'That's what a Māori looks like.'

I looked nothing like the cinematic Māori. Not with that kina-head.

 5.

AND THEN THERE were the Māori–Pākehā weddings.

Yes, the amenability of Māori to marrying Pākehā, and vice versa, meant that the racial situation could never be entirely black or white. After all, sexual attraction and love know no boundaries and, if Rōpata and Andrea were in love, or Puti and Kevin, ah well, that wedding cake just better have a Māori doll and a Pākehā doll on top of it. And although there might be, as there often were, huge fights on both sides as relatives came to terms with a Māori in the family or, oh no, another Pākehā in the whakapapa, goodwill usually prevailed, tātou tātou, especially if Puti was pregnant.

The demographic throughout New Zealand was changing, and Gisborne was a good place to see what was happening. The photographs of weddings in the *Photo News* show the stories of blended occasions, bride and groom standing with both families — relaxed or awkward — on either side of them. The Māori families seem to go on forever and, sometimes, tucked into the layout is an oval portrait of the *Monsieur The White* who had started it all.

Intermarriage was more accepted than not. Sometimes tempers got the better of everyone, especially if a best man had drunk too much booze and tried to pick a fight by saying to the groom that he had only married his Pākehā girl because he wanted to go *up*. Or a worried aunt took the girl aside and told her that by marrying a Māori boy she was definitely going down the social register. Families in private chucked off about the other in-laws, with kuia and koro growling that things would have been easier if their mokopuna had married Māori. But the arrival of the first child generally put paid to all the trouble, the raruraru.

Then, of course, there was another difficult row to hoe, that of ensuring that the child did not suffer such taunts as 'You're not a Māori' or 'You're a half-caste'. If my cousin Bill Kaua had ever had to deal with that sort of shit he would have smashed the speaker's head in.

Chapter Thirty-four

Māori Battalion March to Victory

1.

I DISCOVER THAT a memory is forcing me to catch a backward-turning spiral.

It's a recollection of all those old soldiers in their uniforms, sitting on the marae at Poho-o-Rāwiri. One of them, John Tūrei, has waved me over. He and his mates have been shooting the breeze, telling each other stories and jokes, and one of John's mates has been going on about a pretty girl he met in Italy:

> Che bella cosa è na jurnata 'e sole
> N'aria serena doppo na tempesta!

They're still acting like boys, laughing and joshing each other. And then they go silent and give John a look, and he nods and turns to me with a gentle, quizzical smile: 'Don't go so fast. Your uncles and I deserve better. Why not sit for a while with us and enjoy the warm sun?'

With that chastisement ringing in my ears, let me take some time to recall that band of brothers.

Most of them joined up as soon as Sir Āpirana Ngata headed the call for the Māori Battalion. This occurred within a month of England declaring war on Germany in September 1939. The boys were raring to go. Were they happy when the government agreed? Were they *what*. Some of them couldn't wait to get out the front gate, volunteer, leave the farmwork behind and have an adventure. No support role for them; they were to be the frontline 28th (Māori) Battalion of four rifle companies, one of ten battalions comprising the 2nd New Zealand Expeditionary Force — it couldn't get better than that. More satisfactory, the rifle companies were organised along tribal lines, so you would be fighting with your own iwi.

And listen to this: collectively they were given the name of Te Hokowhitu-a-Tū, the seventy twice told warriors of the god of war. Although they were proud to be elevated to such epic stature, they were modest boys and soon took to calling each other's companies the Gumdiggers, the Penny Divers, the Cowboys and the Ngāti Walkabouts. Yeah, that sounded like them. Good old cuzzy Tuini Ngāwai, she was the one who wrote the action song 'Arohaina Mai' when C Company's first soldiers left the East Coast for the war. What a waiata! No wonder they all took it up as the unofficial anthem of the battalion. Still brings tears to the eyes whenever it is sung today, eh boys.

Arohaina mai, e te Kīngi nui
Manaakitia rā ō tamariki e
Horahia mai rā te mārie nui
Ki te Hokowhitu-a-Tū toa.

Stationed initially in Wellington, the battalion went into training to get those farm boys and town lads into shape, hardcase. But they learned quickly, and was that really them, marching *left right left right* up the gangway as if they had been soldiers all their lives? Nah, couldn't be. But there they were, sailing for Europe on the *Aquitania* on 1 May. And as they steamed away, they could hear 'Pō Atarau' being sung from the shore. When would they ever hear that song again?

What was this? Pākehā regulars were still being appointed as the battalion's officers? Āe rā, the first commanding officer was Lieutenant Colonel (later Brigadier) George Dittmer. They had to wait a long time until Lieutenant Colonel Eruera (Tiwi) Love became the battalion's first Māori commander in May 1942. From then on, they were better under their own, like Charlie Bennett, Āreta Keiha and, of course, Arapeta.

2.

I THINK OF those old men, always so impeccably dressed, as if all that spit and polish of military life had never worn off. Whenever I was with them, they always made it clear that having Pākehā appointed over Māori was a sore point.

'We had nobody good enough, that's what they thought, eh boys. Either that or they still didn't trust us. Maybe they thought we might turn on them.'

Their grievance was made all the worse from remarks, after the war, credited by Sir Charles Bennett to Brigadier Dittmer at the battalion's fourth national reunion in Gisborne at Easter, 1964. Close on 2000 people turned up at that shindig, and dignitaries included the said brigadier, who was patron of the Māori Battalion Association, Jack Hunn, Secretary for Defence, and Charles Bennett, who was then Assistant Secretary of the Department of Maori Affairs.

However, Brigadier Dittmer (although a columnist at the event said it was Jack Hunn) made a provocative remark: 'It is a pity that the Māori Battalion has not performed as outstandingly in peacetime as it did in war.'

What? The brigadier was lucky that he wasn't run off the marae with a taiaha sticking out of his bum. Thirty-six years later, still angry myself, I recast the events imaginatively in a scene, slightly amended, in which I envisaged Arapeta Awatere getting up and responding, on behalf of the battalion, to Brigadier Dittmer:

'Our ancestors have always been fighters,' Arapeta began. 'The Māori has never been loath to fight.' He twirled his spear, Tū-whakairi-ora, before the old men in the crowd.

'We were all young,' he said. 'We came from farms, small marae, out of the scrub, and some of us were still learning how to be men. Many of us had never left the marae, but this was a warrior venture and, well, we wanted to be part of it. Ka tuwhera te tāwaha o te riri, kāore e titiro ki te ao mārama. When the gates of war have been flung open, no man takes notice of the light of reason.'

'Ka tika,' the old men called. 'That is true.'

'On 29 November 1940, we were ordered to the Middle East to join the First Echelon. Can you remember? We went via Greece where we had the first taste of battle at Olympus Pass, and had our victory in the sight of the Gods of Greece. We blooded ourselves there, eh.'

Arapeta walked backwards and forwards in front of the old soldiers, pausing before one of them, Hēmi, a local of Poho-o-Rāwiri. Ribboned medals fluttered in the breeze. 'We tasted battle again at Crete, eh Hēmi! You were there! I saw you fighting the Tiamana!'

Hēmi straightened up. 'Āe, that's where we gained our reputation as fearless in the face of battle.'

Arapeta moved on quickly, eyeballing another old soldier, and then he pointed Tū-whakairi-ora at Brigadier Dittmer.

'But it was in the desert campaign in Egypt and Libya that our battalion truly made its mark, wasn't it, boys? I was your officer—'

He caught Brigadier Dittmer's eye. 'I mean no disrespect, sir [Oh, did he not!], but we did not need Pākehā to lead us.'

A murmur of approval ran through the crowd, 'Yes, that's right, Arapeta, stick it to him.'

Brigadier Dittmer remained impassive, though he inclined slightly towards his aide. 'The cheeky bastard.'

'And the spirit of Tūmatauenga, god of war, was with us when we had our trial by fire at El Alamein, and survived,' Arapeta continued. 'He was with us again when we fought at Sidi Maghreb, where the battalion took a total of 1123 prisoners. In February 1942, the 28th Battalion was ordered to Syria. While we were there, Rommel attacked the Eighth Army in Libya, so back we went to help those other fellas out. At Mersa Matruh, while all the good guys were moving out, we were moving in. We saw Rommel's columns of German vehicles approaching us and the 21st Panzer Division encircling us. E hika, we were surrounded. But Tūmatauenga helped us out of that little scrape and we were soon on our feet. You remember Munassib, boys, when Kippenberger decided to send us in? That was in August 1942, and he wanted us to take a pre-emptive strike and thwart an anticipated attack.'

The eyes of the old soldiers were alight with memories. Oh, to fight again! Just one more battle, one more hill to take!

'Then came the battle for Point 209,' Arapeta said.

In the warm sun the old soldiers moaned like a desolate wind.

Arapeta turned to Charles Bennett. 'By then, Charlie,' Arapeta continued, 'you were our commander and you gave the order to attack. We started at 5 o'clock that night. Our mate, Moana Ngārimu, lost his life there, clearing the area of two machine-gun posts. The Germans tried to counter-attack, to push us back. We ran out of grenades and picked up stones and used them instead. By 5 o'clock the next day we had won the point. Moana was awarded, posthumously, the Victoria Cross.'

The marae erupted with calls. 'Āe! Āe! Ka tika tēnā!'

Arapeta proceeded quickly, thrusting into the heart of the memories.

'After that was Takrouna. What a battle that was! Our mate, Lance-Corporal Manahi, should have received a Victoria Cross for his work there, but he didn't. Maybe the authorities thought that having given one Māori a VC, awarding another Māori the same decoration would show the Pākehā up, eh? After that battle, we were sent to Europe to continue the fight at the Sangro River and Monte Cassino.'

Skilled soldier and expert orator, Arapeta paused and looked around Poho-o-Rāwiri. He was accustomed to being listened to, having learnt well how to hold people in the palm of his hand. He did everything with style and with precision and was used to asserting his mana over the likes, yes, even of Brigadier Dittmer.

'The 36th Texas Division lost more than 1500 men on their assault at Cassino but managed to gain a foothold on the mountain. That's when the Māori Battalion was ordered forward to help them out. We were assigned to capture the railway station and from there launch a further assault on Cassino. The Germans threw everything they had at us. Then on 15 February the monastery was bombed. Three days later we attacked. Men began to fall to the fire and the mines. B Company lost 128 men on their charge on the railway station. But on the next attack, we did not fail. We hunted the Germans through the rubble and debris of Cassino until every one of them was down.'

And then Arapeta raised Tū-whakairi-ora and turned and pointed at Brigadier Dittmer. His tongue feathered in and out. 'Sir! We fought for the honour of our tribe!'

'Ka tika! Ka tika tēnā!'

'We fought until there was no enemy left standing! Our strongest enemy, Rommel himself, praised us as the best fighting unit the German troops ever opposed.'

'Yes! Yes, that is what he said!'

'And you, sir, you now opine that the battalion has not performed as spectacularly in peacetime as we did in war? Look to your own people for the reason for that! Look to their own prejudice against Māori! How many Pākehā have ever had a Māori socially in their homes?'

'How many? Tell us!'

Arapeta drew himself up, eclipsing the sun. 'As it was in war, it is in peacetime,' he began. 'If you want us to perform as well in our own country as we did overseas in the war, give us the chance. Because just as it was in wartime, it is still the case in peace. You, Pākehā, still appoint your own over us.'

3.

YES, SO I have imagined the reply to Brigadier Dittmer. And so have I cast Lieutenant Colonel Awatere as our respondent. He always struck awe into all Māori, so great was his mana. Indeed, there's a story the people tell of him that occurred at the end of the war. It befits a man in the mould of Tū-whakairi-ora, the great ancestor chieftain of Ngāti Porou.

They say Awatere walked into Hitler's secret headquarters. Present were other generals of the Allied forces, and they were all surrounded by their staff. Awatere unbuttoned himself and, for want of a better phrase, began to piss on Hitler's carpet.

The generals and their executives were startled. Some staff rushed to Awatere and grabbed him, but he pushed them off.

'I'm not finished yet,' he said.

You can't do that here!' they cried.

'Watch me,' he said.

When Awatere had finished he reminded them that the most absolute form of revenge on any enemy was to eat his head. In the absence of Hitler's upoko, this was the next best way of expressing the sentiments of the Māori Battalion.

It's the kind of story that the legend was made of.

Almost 3600 men served in the Māori Battalion; 649 were killed in action or died in active service, more than 10 per cent of all New Zealanders serving overseas. More than 1700 were wounded. As the New Zealand History website points out, this casualty rate was almost 50 per cent higher than the average for the New Zealand infantry battalions.

If Māori had ever needed to fight for New Zealand as the price of citizenship, as they did in the First World War, they paid the price in the second. Yet still they were denied equality in New Zealand.

But let's not end like this. Those old men, sitting on the marae, would want peace and aroha to prevail. And how they loved to sing the songs of Italy:

Ma n'atu sole,
cchiù bello, oje ne'
O sole mio
sta infronte a te
O sole, o sole mio
sta infronte a te
sta infronte a te!

Chapter Thirty-five

A Childhood at World's End

1.

THE SPIRALS TURN, they ever turn. Some are going forward, others are going back. In between there are the other smaller ones that whisper as they spin: 'You must tell them this, e Witsh, this.'

One of those tiny silver spinning wheels sings this cantilena, a shining aria:

Never did I see my father hit my mother. Nor did he hit us.

If he had, Dad knew Mum would leave him and take us with her.

2.

I MUST ADMIT that I had a happy childhood. When I say that, I offer my homage to those who survived child poverty or an unhappy childhood or, indeed, had no childhood at all. I don't believe that our ancestors would have wanted us to become a nation with one of the worst histories of child abuse in the world. Or, for that matter, for Māori to still inhabit the New Zealand statistics as the most poverty-stricken of all New Zealanders and with the most men in the prison system.

What happened? My sisters, brothers and I had a mother and a father in the house. I have never been able to imagine what it must be like not to have both parents either because one is dead or has left. It shatters me to realise that in Aotearoa in 2014 many households are run by a solo parent. How courageous most of them are, ensuring their kids don't miss out — and some of them may be better off if the absent parent has been violent.

Not only that, but our parents were faithful to each other and brought us up to trust in them. They provided certainty in our lives. We knew that they loved us, and we were protected by their love night and day. We knew that they would be there for us, no matter what.

Sometimes in the mornings at Haig Street my sisters, brother and I would be woken up by Mum and Dad's laughter. We would bang on their bedroom wall and ask, 'What are you two doing in there!'

How wonderful it was to wake up to giggling parents.

One difference in our family's experience was that neither Mum nor Dad drank alcohol; after all, they were Mormon. Ours was not, therefore, a family where there were parties and booze that could lead to arguments and fist fights. Another difference was that my mother would not put up with violence, especially against women and children, and felt that if you witnessed it, your duty was to intervene, even if the fight was between a man and his wife.

This needs some explaining. In those days, the idea of women as chattels who belonged to men still prevailed, and, therefore, whatever happened between a husband and a wife was their business. On one occasion Mum's brother, Brownie, went to help a woman who was being given a hiding, as they called it in the 1950s, by her husband. He was set upon not only by the husband but by the male relatives of the husband *and* the wife, and ended up in hospital. 'It was Brownie's own fault,' my father said, but Mum was proud of him.

'If Tom ever does anything like that to me,' Mum said to Uncle Brownie, who was lying bruised and battered in a hospital bed, 'you give him a good thrashing.'

One evening, when I was eleven, my sisters, brother and I were home at Haig Street with our mother — Dad was scrubcutting — when a woman in Clarence Street began to scream. For a long time nobody went to investigate, and the screams kept cutting the night to ribbons, so my mother looked at me and said, 'Come with me, son. You're the man.'

I really didn't want to go. My mother was always putting herself into situations surrounded by risk, and my father's opinion about men and their wives came fleetingly into my head. But Mum was already making for the door and I wasn't about to let her put herself in harm's way.

My sisters wanted to come with us. 'Lock the door behind us,' my mother told them, 'and don't open it unless it's to me or Witi.'

We walked in the dark to the house where the screaming was. A knot of local men were standing outside and when they saw Mum coming they said to her, 'Don't worry, Julia, we've called the police.'

'The police?' my mother answered. 'Charlotte could be dead by then.'

We went to the door. I don't know why the men hadn't intervened, they were able-bodied enough, or why they didn't accompany Mum and me. I think there was an assumption that because my mother was Tom's wife, the wife of the padrone, that Joe, the man inside, would listen to her when he had ignored them. Perhaps he was a member of Dad's shearing gang.

'When Joe answers the door,' Mum said, 'don't take any notice of what I say to him. Just go past him to the bedroom where the children are and take them out of there and to our home.' She rapped hard on the wood.

'Who the hell are you, Julia, to come into my house?'

Joe's shadow filled the frame. The door opened to the kitchen and behind him I could see Charlotte on the floor. There was blood on her face and her dress.

'It's all right, Julia,' she said. 'I can handle it.'

'You have to stop,' I said to Joe. I was articulating clearly so he could understand. I went past him one way. My mother went to Charlotte.

'Come on, dear, we're getting you and the kids and you'll all come with us.'

'Charlotte isn't going anywhere,' Joe said. He pulled a knife on us.

Did that stop Mum? No, she looked quickly around the kitchen, opened a drawer and took out another knife. 'Now we're even,' she said.

Joe looked at her, surprised. Charlotte and I were shocked, too. Mum's action came out of nowhere and she was lucky that Joe didn't attack her. But her face was raised to the light and, well, my mother was never a woman to back down from any danger. Yes, her move was a provocation and, in those days, you could sometimes get away with it. She took a risk; the outcome could have gone either way.

'Don't try to stop us,' Mum said. 'You know where we live, Joe. Come for your wife and children when you're sober.'

My sisters, brother Derek and I were safe in our house. We had our own bedrooms, one for me (and Derek, when he got older), the other for my sisters. We always had breakfast, a good cut lunch to take to school, and dinner was served at the same time every night, 6 o'clock. Not like today, when some schools now have to provide breakfast and lunch, and those may be the only meals that the child will have for the entire day.

Mind you, Sunday dinners could be a trial, because Mum and Dad always kept an open invitation to anyone who had no family to be with. Mostly these were the young men and women who came to live with us before and after the shearing season. The girls slept inside, where they could be looked after by Mum, and the boys stayed in the small outside sleeping quarters that had been added to the House that Tom Built. Sometimes our young guests were American boys, Mormon elders serving in Gisborne; they called my parents Mum and Dad Smiler. There might also be the uncle or aunty or niece or nephew who had been sent to Mum and Dad so that they could go to work or school in Gisborne. Or they could be other boys kicked out of their own homes or women like Charlotte waiting until their husbands came by, cap in hand, to ask my mother if she would let them take their wives home.

They definitely included any and all of the shepherds or fencers that Dad had met on the road.

What was Mum's response?

'If I have to cook for ten,' she would say, 'I may as well cook for a hundred.'

On those Sundays, my parents, sisters and I would serve everyone else and then ourselves last. Ours wasn't the only family with this tradition either. Whenever we visited other houses for Sunday dinner, we were the ones who were served first and I recognised the quiet hope of the children watching, 'Please leave a piece of cake for us.'

In 1988 Mum and Dad came to stay with me in my thirty-third-floor apartment on Broadway in New York — I was the New Zealand consul — and I knew I was in trouble when, looking out the window, Mum said, 'Oh, Dad, see those poor people sitting out there in the street.' Not only that, but it was snowing.

Actually, I was not surprised when the doorman rang me at the office. 'Mr Ihimaera, sir, would you mind coming to the building? Your parents have some . . . er . . . interesting guests.'

Taxis are difficult to hail when the weather is bad so I ran like heck along Broadway to 67th Street. I had visions of my parents being done over and the apartment being cleaned out. When I got to my building I went quickly past the doorman and took the elevator to my apartment.

Even as the lift ascended I could smell Mum and Dad's boil-up.

'Oh,' Mum said when she opened the door, 'Dad's been cooking fishheads.' Behind her I saw some twenty street people queuing up at the kitchen.

'Good,' I said grumpily, 'so you and Dad are alive then.' I had to laugh, and those street people, well, they were fine. Really.

All their lives Mum and Dad paid tithe — that is, 10 per cent of their monthly earnings — to the Church. Every last Sunday of the month, they would calculate those earnings from Dad's income as a shearer or farmworker, put it in a brown envelope and hand it to the deacon.

I've said before that I have no idea how they did it but, actually, that's not quite true. Here are some clues: 1) work hard; 2) make sure you use the money wisely from your seasonal work to carry you over the winter; 3) complement your food supply by planting crops; 4) run a few cattle and sheep; 5) pay only in cash, and if you can't afford to buy the refrigerator wait till you can; 6) learn as much as you can about engines and become a bush carpenter so that you can fix your own car or truck, lay bricks and use any old timber when building as nobody will know when it's painted; 7) put only as much petrol in the car as you can afford, even if it infuriates your son when the truck runs out right in the middle of Gisborne; 8) never be too proud, a good lesson that your son could have learnt when, sick and tired of all those times the truck went dry, he left you to it (after all, it was Friday night and the whole world was watching); 9) if you are the wife, buy a sewing machine to make the kids' clothes; 10) stop the truck when you see pūwhā or watercress and get the kids out in full sight of Pākehā to go and pick it; 11) and tell your son to *have faith.*

Yes, sometimes we went hungry. Often my sisters looked like they had been replicated as they wore the same patterned dress made out of the same bolt of cloth and went clickety-click down the street in shoes on which Dad had put his own tin toe and heel plates.

But it was a happy childhood.

What went wrong? It is every New Zealand child's right to have a happy childhood or, at the very least, a childhood.

3.

AND SURELY EVERY child has the right to have at least one perfect Christmas. Mine occurred at the end of 1954, when Teria decided the family should all gather for the festivities at the homestead in Waituhi.

My sisters, brother and I woke early in our house at Haig Street that Christmas morning. During the weeks before I had made my parents' life a misery by insisting on a particular present. The reason that I needed the gift was that I would be going to Gisborne Intermediate the next year. My mother, however, was more preoccupied with buying my uniform, and I traipsed gloomily after her in Adair's while she ticked off the list of what was required — shorts, shirt, tie, pullover, cap, black sandals for summer and black shoes for winter. The shorts were three sizes larger than I was; two boys could fit in them with room for a third.

Uniforms were the Education Department's way of ensuring equality among all school students whether we were rich or poor, Māori or Pākehā.

I kept wondering why Mum and Dad were forgetting the more essential purchase. Finally, 'I must have a bike,' I told them with some firmness.

'You don't need a bike,' Dad answered. 'You can walk to school. When I was your age I sometimes had to walk from Waituhi to Gisborne. You can do the same — it's only a mile or two.'

I stood my ground. 'All my friends from Te Hāpara have bikes. I don't want to be the only boy walking. It would be unseemly. If you won't get me a bike, I'll ask my Nani.'

'Unseemly, eh?' Mum smiled, amused. 'The words you use, son. And no, you will not ask Teria.'

Of course Dad caved in. The trouble was he had grand ideas of how tall I was, and he presented me with a second-hand man-sized Raleigh. 'You'll grow into it,' he said.

Yeah, right. When I sat on the seat I couldn't reach the pedals. The only way to ride the bike was stand on the pedals, except there was a problem because a horizontal bar ran from the handlebars to the seat.

Easy, all I had to do was poke my right foot between the bar so that it could reach the pedal on that side. And if I balanced the bike by leaning it one way and my body counterweighting it on the other, pedalling was a done deal.

'Watch out!' I yelled to my sisters as I went on a trial ride down the driveway.

And after all the weather was ideal for Christmas Day.

My sisters, brother and I could hardly contain ourselves as we drove out to Waituhi under a blue sky, with fluffy clouds like sheep scampering before the wind. My mother was looking very pretty in a dark blue suit, and Dad was wearing an open-necked shirt.

'Don't you think you should wear a tie?' Mum asked him. 'And have you brought your hat?'

In those days, people were very formal, and even my sisters and I were dressed in our Sunday best. The boot of the car was filled with Christmas presents. The instruction from Teria was that each family was to buy one family present and, if we wanted to, special presents for the mokopuna. As a result our parents had spent more than usual on gifts for all Dad's brothers and sisters; they had decided Kararaina, Tāwhi, Viki and I could choose which of our cousins to give presents to. I had managed to save some coins and purchased a shiny Woolworths multi-bangle kind of thing, then separated the bangles, one each for my girl cousins, Elizabeth, Hana, Cissie, Minnie, Betty and Josephine.

Our family must have been among the last to arrive because when we parked with the other cars and trucks the homestead was already swarming with uncles, aunts and the children of the clan. Aunty Joey and Aunty Alice were twisting crêpe paper ribbons together, red, black and white, and giving them to my younger uncles to hang along the verandahs.

'E Witsh,' Teria said, 'you're just in time to help finish the decorations.'

My sisters and I couldn't wait to see the tree. The large living room, which was usually somewhat stern to look at, had already been decorated with streamers, and the Christmas tree was right in the middle; my grandparents had a plaster 'His Master's Voice' dog, which looked as if it was cocking its head at the tree rather than at the horn of the wind-up gramophone. The tree was the grandfather of all trees, and there was a goodly pile of gifts beneath it. As I was putting our presents with the others, my cousin Josephine — we called her Jellybeans, to differentiate her, as she shared her name with our aunt — came to peek. Her cherub face glowed when she saw that I'd bought her a present.

Without drawing breath, we raced outside to play in the sun. On the way, another of my aunties, I think it might have been Aunty Girlie, was holding a piece of flowering mānuka over her head.

'I know it's supposed to be mistletoe,' she said, 'but where am I going to find any of that in Waituhi?'

On the way past her, however, our way was blocked by Aunty Mary, who looked as if she was in charge of the sheep race — older children this way, younger children that way. 'Not you girls,' she said to my cousins Elizabeth, Hana and Cissie, 'you're old enough now to help in the kitchen.' Little Minnie was already there, and consoled Hana when she resisted and got a slap from her mother; Minnie was like Cinderella, always cooking or sweeping. Some children never had a childhood, and Minnie was one of them.

Outside, my girl and boy cousins began to play bull rush.

'Pick me! Pick me!' I called to Ivan and Sammy. 'Pick me! Pick me!'

They were the oldest of the boy cousins of my generation. Perhaps this was why, as we were playing, my Uncle Puku called out to them, 'You two boys, you become men today.'

As they walked away, my younger cousin Tom whispered to me, 'They will be killing one of the little piglets.'

'Why?' I asked. 'What for?'

'One of these days it will be our turn.'

As we were playing I heard high squeals of terror as if something was being hurt followed by another series of squeals. And then arose the ecstatic moan as men began cheering.

Christmas lunch was a sit-down occasion at a long table inside the homestead. Teria and Pera Punahāmoa sat at the far end and Dad and the uncles seated themselves in order of seniority by birth. The women and children remained standing while the dishes were brought in from the kitchen and passed from one uncle to another. The plates were absolutely piled up with food, as Teria always believed in feeding her sons. You should have seen what they sometimes had for breakfast: half a dozen eggs, sausages, steak, potatoes, and that was *each*.

For some reason I found this 'Passing of the Plates' very funny, and I began to giggle during the blessing of the food. To stop myself I quickly looked out the window, where a huge clump of flax was clicking in the wind; the flowers looked so radiant and frighteningly alive on their bright yellow stems. Pera had heard me, he always heard me, and he said to Teria, 'Te hōhā tō tamaiti. He laughs, your grandson.'

After lunch, the sharing of the Christmas presents began. I remember it as a warm and beautiful occasion; I never noticed that some of my cousins didn't get many gifts. Indeed, as Josephine tells me today, 'Yours was the only present I got on that Christmas of 1954.'

Late into the evening we offered songs and had a recital. My cousin Betty sang a quasi-Spanish *canción* with her sisters Cissie and Josephine. Uncle Danny played the guitar in a flamenco way, with clever harmonising. Every now and then my aunts would click their fingers, imitating the sounds of castanets:

In her eyes there was moonlight, and a rose in her hair,
In her arms there was no one, so I just put her there!

Watching my cousins singing and smiling was the first time I felt the stirring of something akin to desire. I was not the only one; I could see it in my Uncle Danny's eyes, too. Yes, indeed, as my cousins continued to sing there was no doubt that there was a promise on their lips and a scent from their hair that I would carry throughout my life.

As for my contribution, well, Teria didn't have a piano so I recited a poem called 'The Highwayman' by Alfred Noyes. The ballad was about a highwayman come to visit his love, Bess, the landlord's black-eyed daughter, plaiting a dark red love-knot into her long black hair:

> Watch for me by moonlight,
> I'll come to thee by moonlight, though hell should bar the way.

Later that evening, I couldn't contain the emotions of the day. I went outside, gasping for breath. The sky was a torrent of darkness, and over at the hāngi the wind was flinging the embers high. The moon was a ghostly galleon tossed on the sea of clouds that stormed from horizon to horizon. My heart was full, brimming over. I think it was because, although I wished childhood would go on forever, I knew it wouldn't, that the gilded life of it would soon end. Confused, I wanted it to be impervious to any alteration.

Ah, change! The trouble with growing up was that it brought apprehension that the world wasn't, actually, the way I saw it. At the same time, the knowledge was inevitable, no matter that it was enormous and frightening. One of the most compelling of the mysteries was adolescence, and I felt eager, yes, impatient to embrace it. I had seen in the bodies of my older cousins the powerful moulding of their musculature; one day I would see that reshaping in my own body. In my girl cousins there was a rounding, a softening, a pliability, something to be pushed into.

Meantime, that Christmas marked a point of perfection. So that when my grandmother Teria was farewelling me and she asked, 'Did you enjoy Christmas, e Witsh?', all I could answer was: 'It was lovely, Grandmother, just *lovely*.'

FLASH FORWARD TO 17 April 2014.

I think of that long ago Christmas, sixty years ago, as my sister Kararaina and I sit in Gisborne airport. We are waiting for the announcement for all passengers to board the plane to Auckland. Earlier that week I had flown to Wellington to visit my wife Jane, my daughters Jessica and Olivia, and the grandchildren, before flying to Paris. While I was there I received a text from my sister Gay that Uncle Sid had died. He had been the only one of the Smiler brothers left and, at the news, I felt a huge sense of despair. There was just enough time to squeeze in the visit to his tangihanga before leaving for France.

Auē, so many times in these modern days are we obliged to fit customary obligations into our busy lives. Now, of that generation, only Aunty Alice was left.

And so Kararaina and I sit having coffee and sharing an egg sandwich, and we start talking about all Dad's brothers and sisters.

I say to her, 'They were like gods of Olympus to me.'

My sister looks askance. She is a realist, not as inclined as I am to flights of fancy. After a while she accepts the analogy and we begin to talk about our uncles and aunties.

Within that pantheon, our father was Zeus.

Uncle Win was Poseidon. There came a time when I was doing okay with my studies and therefore didn't have to duck my head, ashamed, whenever I went past his and Aunty Margaret's photograph on Mum's whakapapa wall. He became a Māori inspector in the Department of Education and was the first author in the family when he revised Tā Āpirana's *Maori Grammar and Conversation* in a new edition published in 1964. Every year Naenae College gives the W.K. Smiler Memorial Award for Senior Public Speaking.

Uncle Win and Aunty Margaret had seven children: Pera, Teria, Meri, Kīngi, Ēnoka, Winiata and Hēmi. When uncle died he wasn't brought home to Waituhi, preferring to be buried next to a baby son in Wellington.

'Which marae was it?' I ask Kararaina.

'I think it was the one in Petone,' she answers.

'Not in Naenae?'

'No, I remember Uncle's tangi. The meeting house was Tatau-i-te-Pō on one side of the road and the karanga came from the wharenui side while we waited on the other. Remember? They had to dig the hāngi in the asphalt.' My sister pierces me with a glance. 'When Uncle died, you should have paid more attention to Aunty Margaret. You should have kept the contact between her and her children and the family.'

I had tried. One afternoon in the 1970s, after I had come back from working as a New Zealand diplomat in Australia, I went to Naenae and parked outside her house.

'Why have you come to see me?' Aunty Margaret asked.

Families, especially extended families, have old sorrows. There had been one such matter which my father should have resolved, but didn't. Aunty had sought his help and not received it.

'You don't want to be forgiven do you?' she asked.

'No.'

'Then what do you want?'

Uncle Mike was Apollo. He married Aunty Waina née Green. Both

Waina and Mum were closely related, being from Ngāti Porou; her and Mike's children were my cousins Cissie, Sam, Minnie, Betty, Josephine (aka Jellybeans), Louise, Frances, Gillen, Vance and Winiata. In the 1940s Uncle Mike had a terrible accident when a large boulder smashed his back, but he didn't know it was broken until two years later. I can remember once looking at him and his laughing brothers together and thinking, 'This family has always depended on its physical strength.' Of all the brothers, Mike stayed in Waituhi the longest. The rest of the family scattered to Wellington or Gisborne. When he and Aunty Waina finally left for Hastings in the 1990s, it was the end of an era.

'Which god of Olympus will Aunty Mary be?' Kararaina asks, her eyes twinkling.

Aunty Mary, the next sibling and first daughter, married one of my favourite uncles, Hape Rauna, from Nūhaka. Hape had a merry laugh and teasing humour and adored his wife; they had my rebellious cousin Hana, her whirlwind brother Tiopira and sisters Okeroa and Arihia.

'She shall be Demeter,' I answer, 'the goddess of agriculture, grain and bread, the prime sustenance of humankind.' Indeed, Aunty Mary was the one to whom all the brothers and sisters deferred, the Big Sister.

'That sounds like Aunty,' Kararaina grins, sipping her hot water. 'Remember when we went with her to Hastings to go tomato picking?'

Did I remember? Did I *what*. The acidic tomato juice went into the cracks of our hands and, by the second day, the cracks had opened, oozing blood. I took to wrapping rags around mine and Kararaina's hands, but Aunty told me to take them off and let the cracks harden and heal.

We were all bedded down in her VW Kombi and I must have been whimpering in my sleep and scratching the deep wounds. She put some grease on them, whispering just like Teria, 'E Wit*sh*, hush, boy, hush.'

Next was Uncle Puku, Dionysus. Oh, I had such a conflicted relationship with this uncle! Another of the brothers with killer film-star looks, he was a cross between 1940s actors Tyrone Power and Cesar Romero. He married the gentle and loving aunt, Betty, who was a Kerekere. They started a large brood beginning with Bison, Pop, Elizabeth, Mīni, Kiki, Rangi, Tom, Kathleen, Charlie and Yo.

Uncle Puku was always patient with me — well, tolerant more like it. His smile was winning, and most of our encounters were jousting and competitive. He should have slapped me around to put me in my place, but he didn't. Like the titular god I have invoked to represent him, Uncle had a huge appetite for life. Indeed, there came a time when this lust took him beyond the bounds of customary behaviour and that set us against each other. No normal chains could hold him.

Aunty Joey was Aphrodite. She married the handsome Joe Ferris, couldn't have children, so adopted my cousin Anthony, but that wasn't enough for Joe, who hopped on his motorcycle and was off and away. Aunty Joey is remembered forever in a photograph that appeared on the cover of the *New Zealand Listener* in 1964. There she is, along with other Māori women of Ngāti Poneke Māori Club, having welcomed the Beatles to Wellington.

My sister and I are trading stories of those fabulous uncles and aunts, but as we tell them a sense of panic invades us. Are our memories correct? Have we got the facts right?

Among the other uncles were Danny and Mafe — let me dub him Hermes. I was supposed to be the pageboy at his wedding to Aunty Girlie, something I had never wanted to do from the very beginning. On the day I made my body all lumpy and refused to get into the black suit and red tie.

'That boy is never obedient,' Pera said.

After the ceremony I watched as my debonair Uncle Mafe and Aunty Girlie walked from the church beneath a rain of white petals.

And then there was Uncle Hani, he was like Hephaestus, god of fire; I think he would like that. He married Aunty Lena. What year did they go to Hawaii? Again, you can see Aunty Lena in the last shots of the film *Blue Hawaii*, twirling her poi for all they're worth. In the foreground, Elvis Presley is singing a love song to his beautiful co-star, Joan Blackman, as their canoe travels the canals of the Mormon Polynesian Center at Laie, just outside Waikiki.

Uncle Hani died in Hamilton while teaching at the Mormon College. I can remember Aunty Mary sitting at the graveside, black-garbed, watching and organising the burial in the high, hot sun. Her fury mounted when we discovered the hole was too small and we had to wait during the bizarre attempts by a mechanised digger to make it larger for the casket. Apart from Uncle Win and Uncle Hani, all the uncles and aunties are buried in the family graveyard at Waituhi.

As they began to die, Dad became the one to go up to the family graveyard to prepare the ground for them. He was also the gravedigger for many of his beloved uncles and aunties. Once, I climbed the hill with him and saw again all those billowing spider threads, silver lines going all the way to the fence.

I felt so sorry for Dad. The burden.

'Better for me to dig the hole for my brothers and sisters than some stranger,' he said.

I watched him with his shovel in his hand and wondered, 'What do you do when the gravedigger himself dies?' The thought was inconceivable.

5.

THE BOARDING CALL is made for my flight to Auckland. From there I shall travel to France, to the other side of the world, but memory is anchoring me here, now, in the present that is the past, which is also the future.

Where did Teria and Pera live before they built the Blue House? Now that Uncle Sid has died, who will look after the papakāinga land? For a moment Kararaina and I both panic. *We must remember. We must.* Our world is crumbling. Uncle Sid was the last of the god brothers. Aunty Alice remains in Dad's family, and in Mum's there are only two aunts, Dinah and Violet.

With that world will go a childhood of such joys, for what my parents and all those uncles and aunties have given us is the gift of an enormous canvas. Never have I breathed so deeply. Never have I gasped with such ecstasy. Their huge passions and appetites constructed a world of such immense breadth and depth, of such moral force, that I could never go weakling into it. They forced me to stand: 'All this is yours.'

Of course there came a time when I discovered that divinity was not always theirs. There were choices they made and acts they perpetrated on others, yes, even within their own family and upon their own children, that made me realise they were, unspeakably, human.

But after all, were not the gods of Olympus as capricious and wilful? Take, for instance, Zeus, the shape-shifter, coupling with goddesses and mortals, changing himself into bull or swan to do so. And Poseidon, who changed into a horse and coupled with Demeter; he also coupled with the gorgon Medusa. And what about Dionysus, who had an affair with Aphrodite? Hera cursed her, and she bore a disfigured child, Priapus.

Acts of bestiality, rape, incest, murder and revenge were rife within Greek mythology, attesting to the dual nature of those we considered divine. Should I not, therefore, allow my family pantheon the same immunity as that given to the gods?

The boarding call is made and Kararaina walks me to the gate. She smiles at me, and in her bearing is such power. 'It will be all right,' she says. 'It will be all right, brother.'

We are the ones who must remember. If we don't, who will?

Chapter Thirty-six

A Place in the World

1.

LET ME TELL you about the demi-god Māui. Assuredly his story is one to thrill the imagination, with as much resonance as any tale from the ancient classical world.

Māui's mother was Taranga and, at parturition, she thought she had given birth to a dead child. She cut off her long black hair, wrapped the foetus in it and threw him into the stormy sea. These circumstances are remembered in his name, Māui-tikitiki-a-Taranga — Māui, who was wrapped in Taranga's hair. Māui might have been alive when he was born, in which case Taranga committed infanticide. But some texts refer to his being disfigured, with one eye that was like an eel and another that was like greenstone, and these defects alone would have been reason enough to submit him to the ocean's mercy.

The ancient texts say that Māui was washed ashore, entangled in seaweed. If he was dead, he revived. Seagulls hovered over him, slashing at his flesh and feeding on his mother's rich afterbirth. Flies also swarmed around his body, and some planted their white maggots in him. Then came the rescue that turns his story into a spellbinder.

Some say the great god, Rangi, the sky father, was in the shape-shifter form of the wanderer of all epic stories, walking along the seashore, when he noticed the nest of seaweed and the scavenging birds above. Others tell of Rangi looking down from his kingdom in the skies, seeing the child thrashing helplessly amid the kelp. Jellyfish had come at his cries to form a protective cocoon around him.

Rangi intervened, setting off the next great transformation in the story of the Māori. He took Māui up into the sky, where he was nursed back to life and spent his childhood. I like a variation that tells how Rangi commanded the gods and goddesses of the oceans, clouds, waves and tides to raise Māui and to bring him up to boyhood.

Once this was done, Māui set out on his first quest. We are not told of his state of mind, but we do know the intention. Like every lost, orphaned or forsaken son, he wants to find the mother who had abandoned him.

2.

FOLLOWING THAT PERFECT Christmas, 1955 unfolded like a dream. The year began with a train trip to Dunedin for the Māori Lawn Tennis

Championships at Te Huna Park. Originally Mum and Dad had planned to go without us, but my sisters and I, recalling the Empire Games, were not about to let them do that again.

'Oh, all right then,' Mum said to me, exasperated. 'After all, you start at Gisborne Intermediate in February, and this will probably be the only trip we can take as a family, so we'd better do it now rather than later.'

My sisters and I were so excited. Māori tennis was in its heyday and a tiny woman by the name of Ruia Morrison was achieving national renown.

The East Coast–Poverty Bay contingent was eighty-six strong, including such Māori tennis greats as Mose Harvey, Lorna Ngata, Joe Pere and Dad, of course, and rising stars like Lewis Moeau, Mackie Herewini and David Goldsmith. The ope, travelling group, included families and supporters and, therefore, two special carriages were added to the train. At the station there was a huge throng to see us off, and then, just as the train was leaving, some of those well-wishers decided to come with us.

'What the heck, we'll get a ticket on the train,' they said, 'and borrow clothes from you lot.'

The trip took the entire day and, while the adults played cards or sang along to a guitar, my sisters and I and the other children played tag from one end of the train to the other. This required us to open and close the doors, and thrillingly bridge the gap between the carriages; young couples were standing out there, taking the opportunity to kiss and be with one another. Ooh, gross.

The best times came when somebody would yell, 'Tunnel coming up!' We'd run outside and stand with the lovers. *Whump.* The train would enter the tunnel, and the dark would fill with smoke and glowing cinders. *Whoosh.* Out the other end. Alas, we hadn't turned black from the ash.

One lesson I learned. Never eat oysters and bananas . . . together . . . at the same time. They don't like it.

We arrived at Wellington in the early evening, and there wasn't much time to waste. The express was running late and the inter-island ferry to Lyttelton, the *Maori III*, was waiting especially for us.

'Come on, children!' Mum laughed as, along the carriages, doors opened and shut and people were running across the wharf and up the gangway of the boat. I have a vague recollection of harassed porters, trundling our luggage after us. Mum was looking vivacious in her warm woollen coat and cloche hat.

As for the ferry, it was so huge. After all, we were travelling *overseas.* Our family had a four-berth cabin somewhere near the waterline. When I looked out the porthole I kept thinking, 'Just as well the ferry wasn't settling further into the sea otherwise, glug glug glug all the water would spill through the porthole and down we would go to Davy Jones's locker.'

The ferry sounded its farewell to Wellington and off we went, sailing into a brisk wind and out between the heads. The ocean swell was as high as mountains. The next morning, a steward woke us up with a cup of tea and a biscuit. My sisters and I watched the South Island going past to starboard.

I don't know what time we landed at Lyttelton, but we were soon on the train again, bound for Dunedin. When we arrived I couldn't believe how different the city was from Wellington. I thought I was in a foreign country. And where were the Māori? Dunedin citizens welcomed us with great warmth, and we were invited to visit places like the Botanic Gardens, Larnach Castle and the Otago Museum.

The players couldn't be let off their tight match schedules, so, while they fought their games out on the courts, Peggy Falwasser organised some of the supporters to accept the invitations. She selected Mum, Kohi Rangiuia and Pani Whatuira to go along to the museum and, at the last minute, Bill Kaua was able to join us. Peggy could sometimes be imperious with her lilting but commanding voice: 'Julia, why don't you take Witi with you.'

My mother put on her coat against the cold, and I put on my school uniform, and off we went.

Clearly the museum was expecting a higher-level delegation because we were met on arrival by Dr H.D. Skinner, museum director and Pacific anthropologist. As soon as he began our tour I was totally entranced. I had never been to a museum before and, like every other youngster, I was stunned by the exhibit suspended in the atrium — the gigantic skeleton of what was then advertised as a juvenile blue whale (it was a fin whale), 53 feet 6 inches in length. I had recently been told the story of Paikea, the whale rider, and I asked Dr Skinner if I could take a closer look, 'Can I, sir, can I?' I ran up the stairway to the Animal Attic, where I could observe the whale at eye-level. Transfixed, I wondered to myself, 'Did you or your ancestors ever swim with the same whale that brought my ancestor to Aotearoa?'

I could have remained at my post all day, swept up in fantasies of whale pods in proud procession through the Pacific Ocean and storming after krill in Antarctic seas, except that my mother called to me, 'Come down, a photographer has arrived.'

A photographer? We were to have our picture taken?

Reluctantly, I dawdled down the stairway. I wasn't looking at where I going, the museum was crowded, where was Mum? All of a sudden there was a gap in the crowd. I went through it.

'This will be ideal,' the photographer said.

Looming in front of me was the magnificent, imposing and intricately carved wonder of the Mātaatua meeting house and, among the main figures, were two sets of twins. One set was Tarakiuta and Tarakitai, the boys whose histories are so closely connected with Waituhi.

This is how it occurs sometimes. It can happen so quickly, being in one reality and then suddenly being given that vigorous shake to your soul. I had experienced it only once before, and over the course of my life I have known that dizziness and disorientation many times. I've told you of one of those occasions — the time I was photographed in front of Te Hau-ki-Tūranga in Wellington.

So, Ihimaera, tēnā koe, e te mokopuna.

Eyes looking up from beneath the water / Teria asking me, 'E Witsh, so what great wisdom did the Pākehā teach you today?'

Wasn't this a museum? A collection of dead things? Then what was a meeting house doing here? We weren't dead yet.

I didn't want to have my photograph taken, but what was new about that. But there I am, dutifully watching as Dr Skinner points out a detail on a poupou of the meeting house. The next morning, there we were on the front page of the *Evening Star* under the headline: 'Maori Visitors in Dunedin.'

'If I had known you would all be in the newspaper,' Peggy exclaimed, 'I would have jolly well come with you.'

Later in my life I came across the history of the wharenui. I like the way in which Professor Sir Hirini Moko Mead refers to it as having been a 'captive museum exhibit'.

Mātaatua was built in 1875 by a tribe, Ngāti Awa, that was already reeling from land confiscations and illness. The whare was generously dedicated as a house for Queen Victoria, should she come to New Zealand. Against the tribe's wishes, in 1879 Mātaatua was dismantled and sent to the Sydney International Exhibition, and to Melbourne and then on to Britain. In Australia when the meeting house was reassembled something horrific occurred — the carpenters thought the walls with their carvings and tukutuku were supposed to be on the outside, and the consequent display constituted a disembowelment.

Mātaatua was then shipped to London, where it was erected in the grounds of the South Kensington Museum. Then the meeting house was stored in the cellar of the Victoria and Albert Museum for over forty years; it came to light in 1924 for the British Empire Exhibition at Wembley, where King George V and Queen Mary visited it, as did Māori guide Maggie Papakura, who cried to see it standing there, alone, without its iwi.

In 1925 Mātaatua returned to New Zealand to feature at the South Seas Exhibition in Dunedin. There it stayed, a permanent exhibit at the Otago Museum for some seventy years. Not until 1996 was Mātaatua finally returned to Whakatāne as part of Ngāti Awa's treaty settlement.

After careful restoration, it was reopened in 2011.

Let me turn to a happier memory of that Dunedin trip.

On our last night we went to a concert by The Ink Spots, who were touring New Zealand. An black American four-man vocal group, they were famous as exponents of doo-wop. The Mills Brothers, The Ames Brothers, The Platters and many others have taken their whakapapa from The Ink Spots. Seldom absent from the pop charts, they were a favourite among Māori. While in New Zealand they unveiled their latest 45, 'Melody of Love', on Parlophone. Some critics say that doo-wop ushered in rock'n'roll.

At the very end of their show, The Ink Spots asked for a young boy to go up and sing with them, always a crowd pleaser. Nothing could stop little kina-head.

'What song do you know, kid?' Deek Watson asked.

'What song do *you* know?' I countered.

Oh, the audience loved that! And so did The Ink Spots. 'You better do something nice and simple so that we can follow along,' Charlie Fuqua said.

And so I began 'I Saw Mommy Kissing Santa Claus', and The Ink Spots came in with their snapping fingers and a capella doo-wop-a-doo-wee-doo-wee and bom-bom-bom and shang-a-lang and doomph-doomph:

> *Oh, what a laugh it would have been*
> *If Daddy had only seen*
> *Mommy kissing Santa Claus last night!*

No boy ever had a better backing group. A doo-wop-a-doomph-doomph, shang-a-lang-*bang*.

 3.

ON OUR RETURN from Dunedin I began my first year at Gisborne Intermediate. By the day school started I had mastered riding my bike, leaning one way, the bike the other, but I hadn't learnt how to stop it. I swerved into a fence or a conveniently open gateway where I could jump off before I hit the rose bushes. Definitely not cool.

Mum watched as I put my schoolbag over my shoulders, pulled my cap down, poked my left leg through the triangle of the bike's frame and wobbled my way out the front gate.

'Don't kill anybody,' she yelled.

When I met up with my friends, I no doubt looked like an accident waiting to happen. They were talking at the corner of Gladstone and Lytton roads and when they saw me coming, they scattered.

'If you're riding with us,' Tripoli Tuau said, 'you stay well clear or way at the back.'

My feelings weren't hurt. *I* would get as far away from me as possible too, rather than end up crashing in a tangled heap.

Whenever Mum wanted me to wind the hanks of wool she used for all her beautiful cable-stitched Argyle-pattern jerseys, I would jump on my bike to escape her. You would have too, as she liked to do the work in the front garden where my friends could see and, well, how embarrassing was that?

As for Tripoli, Ray and the others, well, they learned their lesson. One of them, it may have been Athol Hjorring, said that he had heard the *Gisborne Herald* was looking for a boy to deliver the paper on the run that included my neighbourhood. 'I'm going down there to check it out,' Athol said.

My mates all hopped on their bikes because the first one to get to the *Herald* office would no doubt get the job, and I was left in the dust. Even so, I wobbled after them and arrived at the office where they were waiting for the dispatcher to arrive.

'What are you doing here?' Tripoli laughed. 'You can't even ride a bike properly.'

He didn't know that the dispatcher was watching and listening in.

'Are all these boys picking on you?' he asked. He must have had a tender heart and, well, I could be beguiling when I wanted to. 'All you other boys clear off,' he said. And he gave me the job.

I made 14 shillings a week. On the first Saturday morning when I went to collect the money from the householders, some of them gave me more money than they needed to, and wouldn't take the change. They said the extra money was a tip, but I was stupid and didn't know what that was.

I handed all the money in at the office and tried to explain why there was so much extra. I wanted to give it all back.

'You're a strange lad,' the dispatcher said.

As for my friends, well, they did get compensated. What with after-school music lessons on Tuesdays, Boys' Brigade on Wednesdays and hockey practice on Thursdays, I had to set up a system whereby they could cover my run, and you could say I got into the franchise business. At first Ray, David, Rangi and others were happy to work for me, but when they discovered the pittance I was paying compared with the wage I was getting, they went on strike and I had to increase their salary. It was not easy playing King Rat.

4.

I MENTIONED HOW busy I was, with all this energy. Even Teria complained when she came into Gisborne to pick me up and I wasn't at Haig

Street: 'Auē te hōhā o te tamaiti nei. Where have you been! Don't you love your Nani any more?'

'I've been playing with my friends.'

'Your Nani comes first, though?'

'Yes, you come first.'

Perhaps if I had been around I would have noticed how short of breath she was and that her thrilling voice was growing softer. She simply turned up all her inner resources to ensure her āhua, her appearance, was always, to my eyes, glorious. Less oil in the lamp only made the flame brighter.

And finally, I found the way to pay for the piano. Ever since Teria had bought it for me I had been determined to honour her gift. I purchased a small notebook and I gave it to her with 10 shillings from my wage as a paperboy.

'What's this for?' she asked.

'It's my first payment for the piano. Could you ask Grandad to sign it as having been received? I'll pay him 10 shillings every month.'

'But *I* bought it for you, it was a gift.'

Before we knew it, we were arguing with each other and, to be honest, I'd seen a toy submarine that submerged and came up to the surface that I wouldn't have minded buying. I don't think we had ever argued before, but I had to be firm with Teria — and myself.

'My mind is made up,' I told her. 'I won't change it, I just won't.'

She stared at me and then she smiled. 'Kei te pai, e Wit*sh*, okay.'

When I saw Pera Punahāmoa a few days later he said, 'You think I don't know what you're doing, do you?'

There are two important memories associated with those *moments musicaux*, and they have to do with Madge Cole's student piano recitals. She was one of those piano teachers who surrounded any event with glamour. She hired a hall and decorated it with flowers, and she sometimes sat on the stage turning the pages for us, whispering and guiding our playing.

'Accelerando here — no, not too much! A touch of the pedal — no, not too much! Ppp, no — not too much! Pay attention to the composer's markings, agitato — no, not too much!'

Her earrings sparkled and she loved wearing silver fox furs.

The first memory was about something that happened following a recital when the parents and students were mingling in the hall eating cake and drinking tea or juice. Mrs Cole shepherded me through the crowd when we came across the end of a conversation: 'Oh, that Māori boy,' someone said. 'Why does Mrs Cole persevere with him? A guitar would be a more appropriate instrument.'

Mrs Cole went white in the face. She knew I had heard the comment. In a loud voice she called, 'Mr Cole? Mr Cole! Would you kindly escort these people off the premises immediately.'

And then she said to me, 'I won't have that kind of comment, Witi, I simply won't.'

The second memory has to do with Teria, and it's not something that I witnessed myself. My grandmother would sometimes be driven to the recitals by one of my uncles or aunts, who would then have to sit and wait until I came on. Aunty Joey didn't seem to mind, but to some of my younger uncles, well, it must have been bor-*ing*. It was Uncle Mafe who some years later told me about one such occasion. He was talking with Teria in a jocular, teasing way and said to her that I would be just like any other boy. Shake a pound note in front of my face and I would take it.

She answered, 'No, son, you will never be able to do that, for I have made e Wit*sh* into a likeness as unto me.' And then she told him about the piano money.

It was the cadence, the biblical way of saying it, which intrigued me. Why would she say that? What kind of likeness was I? Did she say it in a triumphant, unseemly way? Did I want to be manipulated, fashioned by the desire to please her? Even more worrying, would I live up to it?

And yes, I am in her likeness.

Chapter Thirty-seven

Before the Fall

INTERMEDIATE SCHOOL WAS a revelation.

The two years there, according to best education theory, provided all students with the required academic and social skills to transition from the primary school system to secondary school. In my case, those years also created the opportunity for my political and cultural growth. It wasn't so much a question of developing identity but, rather, of a young Māori boy's growing sensibility of his place in the world — which is an entirely different matter.

I had kept my friends from Te Hāpara and I was glad to be reunited with those I knew from my old school, Kaitī. Other children came from all over Gisborne — Central, Mangapapa and other suburbs as well.

I was a keen joiner of clubs. Already a member of Boys' Brigade, which I had graduated to from Life Boys, I also joined the choir. You could not fault my enthusiasm. At the first public recital, when I appeared in the front row with dirty shoes, the headmaster Mr Grono reprimanded me; I'd been so excited I had forgotten to polish them.

I was in Mr Green's room. I enjoyed my friendships with classmates David Burns, Ray Sheldrake, Joan Robinson, Vanessa Rare, Lottie Pōhatu, Dallas Atkins, Beverly Beal, Lyn Angell and Spud Arthur; Vanessa, Lottie and I may have been the only Māori in the class.

On my eleventh birthday, Mum and Dad gave me a watch. The timing was fortuitous, because Mr Grono was looking for a bell-ringer and I looked responsible enough — yeah right. The job was an easy one: to ring the bell at the end of each period so that pupils could go to their next class. Some of the other boys would whisper to me, 'Ring the bell early at the end of our arithmetic period!' Or, 'Don't ring the bell when we're at sports.'

Most times, their wishes coincided with my own. I hated sums and, no matter the extra tuition Dad gave me at home, was never good at it. Conversely, I loved sports, especially when we had sports days. Gisborne Intermediate was divided into four houses — from recollection they were Rata, Kowhai, Kauri and Rimu, but I could be wrong — and we paraded on the sports ground before playing against each other.

When I made the school hockey team, well, I had my own reasons for letting school out early. The sooner I could get to practice the better. The consequence was that my bell-ringing was all up the boohai.

'Where is that bell-ringer boy!' Mr Green would roar.

2.

ONE DAY I arrived home from intermediate to discover new neighbours moving into the empty house at No. 9. They were Archibald Gordon Waugh, though we called him Gordon, his wife, Jeanne, and their two platinum-blond curly-haired tots, David and Janet; another daughter, Annette, came later. They looked for all the world as if they had stepped out of the pages of *John Bull*, a popular British magazine of the times.

I don't know who poked out tongues first — probably us at No. 11. Was it my sisters and I who also began the long I-can-stare-you-out contests that took place across the fence before Jeanne called out, 'Come indoors, children'? Let me admit that the pūkana probably comes more naturally to Māori tongues than to Pākehā.

I do know that not long after began a conflict which mirrored in microcosm the clash that was happening around New Zealand when new English migrants rubbed up against old established New Zealanders, including Māori.

New Zealand wanted to increase its population growth, which had dropped in the 1920s and 1930s. A Dominion Population Committee, set up at the end of December 1945, reported back several months later that immigration was not perhaps the right answer — and in fact the dramatic post-war 'baby boom' caused a big increase. But the country needed labour, and many British people were keen to leave behind their war-torn memories. Accordingly, assisted immigration was introduced in July 1947, and in the next two decades a huge surge of 77,000 men, women and children arrived. Although most of the old established New Zealanders, of the Pākehā variety, were from Britain themselves, not all of them welcomed the immigrants. They also forgot that quite a few of their ancestors had come to New Zealand under subsidised arrangements.

Gordon and Jeanne Waugh were what were known as 'assisted migrants'. Gordon's father, Archibald Freebairn Nesbit Waugh, was actually a New Zealander who volunteered for military service when New Zealand entered the Great War. At sixteen going on seventeen he was a first-aid medic at Gallipoli, laid explosives at Messines, and fought at Passchendaele and the First Battle of the Somme. He was wounded in the Second Battle of the Somme and sent to England to recover and recuperate, where he met Gladys Sheppard, an ambulance driver, and they married in 1918. One interesting sidelight is that his best man was a New Zealander named Rua Tāwhai. Rua carved a Māori-designed table with a pocketknife for the newly married pair, who settled in Boscombe, halfway between Broadhurst and Bournemouth.

He was a big, burly man, was Gordon, who looked as if he could take care of himself in any fist fight. During the Second World War he joined the Royal Engineers and, stationed at Doncaster, he was taught how to weld underwater dressed in a big rubber suit and a diving mask. Next he knew, he was being shipped out to the Suez Canal to 'keep it open for shipping needed for the war front'; he acquired a nickname, Killer. At the end of the war he met Jeanne, who was the sister of one of the friends of his brother Ian — you know how these things sometimes go. She was petite and pert, and there was always a sparky, teasing humour between her and Gordon. That must have been one of the attractions when they married three months later on 15 February 1947. And then in the mid-1950s, the idea of getting away from England for ten quid, either as a single person (preferred) or a family with two children, appealed to their sense of adventure and fun, and they came out to New Zealand on the SS *Captain Cook*.

Australians called the new migrants the 'Ten Pound Poms', as did New Zealanders, but we also labelled them 'Bloody Poms', and Pom-bashing became a national game like rugby. Gordon took up a job at the Gisborne wharf as a diver, but, after a near-miss accident, he gave up the profession. As for Jeanne, she traded on her experience as a nurse, did a few relieving jobs at nursing homes and then went to work for Dr Bowker. For extra income they became beekeepers, with sixty hives on farms at Hexton; farmers liked hives on their farms as the bees ensured healthy grasslands. The Waughs also replaced Joan Wilson's old house with a brand-spanking-new one and put in a fowl run at the back. Jeanne went into breeding goldfish too, and, much to the envy of other breeders in Gisborne, managed to create a beautiful specimen of a purple-rose colour.

In the end Gordon and Jeanne became Mummy and Daddy Waugh. My sisters and I think of David, Janet and Annette as our brother and sisters. For a short while, Kararaina actually lived with the Waughs, and it was most odd to see David, Janet and Annette treating her as their sister and not ours. Mummy Waugh became the leader of the Brownies and Kararaina joined her troop: tu-wit-tu-woo.

Gordon's parents, Archibald and Gladys, came out for a visit, the first time he had returned to New Zealand since he left for war in 1915. Dad arranged to do a haka of welcome, and both David and I remember the look on Archibald's face. David remembers surprise and delight, I remember horror.

When I began writing in the late 1960s Gordon challenged me — he was always provoking me, as if I should do better. He said it was easy for me to write my Māori stories and that I should write something from a non-Māori perspective. I took up his rākau and wrote a story for Gordon called 'The Other Side of the Fence'. The invitation was fair enough, but I think the reasons for it were wrong. After all, I wasn't planning to write about Pākehā at all in my career. The story is therefore one of the very few written from that perspective, and it isn't very good. I turned it into a metaphor of what was happening in New Zealand between Māori and Pākehā and, in the process, leaned on it too hard.

For a time, Gordon became a constable on the beat. His mates and comrades in England nearly died laughing at the news. When I got a few years older I was always wary of Gordon, because if he saw me in Gladstone Road he would point his baton at me and say, 'I'll have you, sonny boy' and then proceed to interrogate and pat me down as if I was carrying a concealed weapon. No matter how much I told my friends that Daddy Waugh was only playing with me, they took to their heels.

The Waughs were as shocked as we were when, near the end of the 1960s, they decided to leave Gisborne. Jeanne had always had a love of dogs and the family bought the Meeanee Boarding Kennels in Napier. Mummy Waugh died of cancer in February 1990 and Daddy Waugh didn't remarry. As for David, he met and married Lyn and became a much-loved art teacher at Hastings Boys' High. Janet also married well, and she and her husband went into the orchard industry, auditing imports and exports of fruit products. Annette was about six when I read the story to her that I had called 'The Child'. Today she raises a breed of big quarter horses known as settanne — an anagram of Annette's. Quite a turnaround from the little girl who became frightened when Dad first put her on one of his horses at Waituhi.

David told me that when his family first arrived at No. 9, the reason why he and his two sisters always looked out the window at us was because they used to hang on the *life* that was happening next door at No. 11.

I had to laugh at that, because my sisters and I found these strange new neighbours just as fascinating.

3.

THE POMMIE INVASION was only the beginning of the assisted migrant phenomenon.

In 1950 Bert Bockett, the marvellously named man in charge, extended the scheme to The Netherlands and some other European countries, such as Austria, Germany, Denmark, Switzerland and Greece. Today we forget how long it took for post-war Europe to get back on its feet. There were continuing political and economic troubles, such as the Hungarian uprising and the Suez crisis. One of the largest diasporas of the period, that of Jewish men and women, dispersed to many countries, including New Zealand. Here at the end of the world they hoped to find haven and to build a new life. I hope they were able to escape the experiences of the Holocaust that took away their families, but I suspect that the *memory* always haunts even when the horror is over.

I like to think that all those other European migrants, transplanted cuttings from Europe, far from home like the Northern Hemisphere trees at Eastwoodhill, improved the life and culture of our town. Sure, we had always been guaranteed the sight of the dragon at Chinese New Year, weaving its way along Gladstone Road. Every now and then we could go down to Gisborne Harbour and watch the Italian community blessing the boats, invoking Poseidon here, in our southern waters. We could also go to the Caledonian Club or watch the Highland fling or Scotsmen tossing the caber. Or watch the Irish or Welsh dancers at the A&P show.

These new 1950s migrants, however, brought a special glamour and beauty to the otherwise angular and ugly Anglicised and Anglophone culture that threatened to keep New Zealand drab and dour. They introduced a different aesthetic and a new kind of intellectualism. They *talked* about where they had come from, and they argued about things that seemed to matter. In their company I felt an affinity because they were like Māori, they liked to kōrero.

Apart from friendship, my new European mates at intermediate, and their families, opened me up to the possibilities of a life of the mind. They brought to it different histories.

Ola, who was Finnish, was one of the most beautiful girls I had ever seen. Her looks were remarkable — platinum hair, a face that was white and gleaming like the moon, and I swear that her eyes were violet. One day she invited a group of classmates to her house because we were working on a school project. Her mother, anxious to please, made us lovely sweet cakes, the taste of which I have never forgotten.

Then her father, who worked at the port, arrived in great excitement. He yelled to Ola's mother, 'We have guests, Mother, from Finland!' He had two young men with him, Finnish sailors who had just arrived on a trawler and were staying only a few hours. I remember the flurry of excitement, and I asked Ola if I could stay after our school friends had left. She was very patient, translating for me everything her parents and the visitors were saying. They were talking about a history of which I had no knowledge. Of a culture that I had never before comprehended. At the end of the visit, the occasion turned into tears and farewells that I felt privileged to witness.

My greatest friendship, however, was with a young Dutch boy named Maarten van Dijk. This statement may come as a surprise to him, as over the years we have lost touch, but in those days he lived at 720 Aberdeen Road and we were constantly in each other's houses.

Maarten was about my size, thin and wiry. The moment when we became friends escapes me but he may have had a paper run, like me. For a time we were inseparable. Maarten was so much fun, and I think, because of him, I decided that for the rest of my life I would surround myself only with people who were fun. We went to movies together, and afterwards Maarten would proceed to critique the films we had seen. I discovered my own critical voice on those Saturdays when we were bicycling home, arguing. His argumentative nature seemed to reflect his keen mind. He even argued with his parents, Anton (Anthonie) and Ada (Alexandrie), in ways that astonished me.

After Sunday lunch at Haig Street I sometimes raced around to Maarten's because his parents followed the Dutch custom of having other Dutch people to socialise in the afternoon. Alexandrie was small and bustling, and Anthonie was tall and bald. Their house on Sundays was always filled with arguing voices and drama, with people gesticulating and speaking loudly in a language I couldn't understand. Maarten made dramatic exits whenever he was disagreed with: maybe he was practising for the Shakespearean plays he and his sister Eushje (Eugenie) took up when Maarten went to Victoria University and Eugenie appeared in at Gisborne's local Unity Theatre. Maarten adored his sister and would often say to her, 'You are too beautiful, Eugenie, you are a little minx', and he would tickle her and refuse to stop even when she asked him to.

Whenever I needed to take a break from the Sunday socialising at the Van Dijk house, I would go to the front room and read a Dutch comic or, rather, look at the illustrations. And then Maarten would come to me and say, 'Let's go to your house, it's quieter there!' or 'Oh, let's get away from here and go to the beach!' Once, an exasperated Mrs van Dijk joined us, and said, 'I will come too.'

In 1964, the Dutch government awarded Bert Bockett the Oliver Van Noort medallion for services to The Netherlands. The following year Maarten graduated BA from Victoria University; among other Gisborne locals to graduate were regal Suzie Kwak and Hans Everts — that European vine was bearing welcome fruit. Maarten went on to a brilliant career as an academic in theatre and wrote a book on Bertholt Brecht. Incidentally, another Gisborne boy, Jack Richards, became the most famous of us all, as the creator of education materials for high schools in China; bookman Graham Beattie and literature maven Murray Gray are not far behind.

Maarten's mother, Alexandrie, died in 1999 — Anthonie had died a year earlier — but I didn't hear about it. Around 2007 Maarten wrote me a letter to thank me for sending my father to his mother's funeral service. When I asked Dad why he had gone to Mrs van Dijk's tangi, he told me that he saw a notice in the *Gisborne Herald* and, remembering my boyhood friendship, wanted to represent me at her farewell. Dad was always doing things like that.

The question that was always on my mind whenever I met migrants who had come to New Zealand was: 'Why New Zealand?'

We were lucky that, for whatever reason — searching for a new life, escaping from an old one, tempted by the image of New Zealand as a lucky country where God lived, or having thrown a dart at a board — they arrived. I hope they felt the sacrifice was worth it. I shall always be grateful for the friendships they graced me with when I was a young Māori boy.

And now the tika.

Oh, it would be so easy to end on this upward trajectory. If you had seen the photographs of me in my mother's album during my first year at intermediate, you could have witnessed for yourself how glossy, smiling (not oversmiling), relaxed and self-assured I am.

But then my wairua was sucked out.

Indeed, when my headmaster, Mr Grono, met me on the street the following year, he asked me, 'Witi, what's happened to you?' I can still remember the alarm in his eyes, but I wasn't about to tell him anything.

Nothing at the beginning of the year presaged the two traumatic events that happened at the end. The first took away all the protection that had kept me safe and, when that happened, the second event was able to sneak in and utterly destroy my boyhood.

Chapter Thirty-eight

Paradise Lost

1.

I REMEMBER MY baptism at the Te Hāpara chapel.

The Mormon Church's practices had become streamlined since Dad's day; no going to the river. My proud parents were witnesses, along with other church members. Dressed entirely in white, I stepped down into the baptismal font where Brother Mohi, I think it was, was waiting to receive me. I was among a number of young adults being baptised that day.

The room was intensely bright. The music was muted and playing softly. Brother Mohi asked me to cross my arms in front of my chest. He asked me if I was ready to receive the Holy Ghost.

'Yes,' I said.

Gently he tipped me so that I was lying horizontal on the surface of the water, supporting me with his left arm. He raised his right hand and blessed me, received me into the Church and firmly pressed me down to achieve full immersion.

I didn't close my eyes. I could see Brother Mohi through the shivering surface of the water and, on all sides, people watching.

I don't know how long it was after my baptism that I felt a sense of great loss, a perception that I still experience from time to time. Although I am still a Mormon, the feeling of grief is so profound, and associated with the residual swirlings of that first dawn when my mother told me, 'Don't be afraid, son, it is only the old people and they are saying their prayers.'

I don't blame my grandfather at all for turning the entire Ihimaera family to Mormonism. I have often found myself in tears because of it, and I know that it has something to do with losing one pathway, the Ringatū, for another.

A paradise expected had also led to a paradise lost.

2.

ONE DAY, 22 November 1955 to be exact, near the end of my first year at Gisborne Intermediate School, my father arrived to pick me up from class.

He came in the early afternoon. I had my head down, I must have been writing something in my exercise book, when Mr Green called to me. When I looked up and saw Dad standing at the doorway of the classroom, he had taken off his hat. I felt important as Mr Green waved me over and told me I was excused from class.

As we walked away, Dad said, 'Your grandmother has died.'

For some strange reason I didn't think the news was real at first, that is, until I saw the sadness in Dad's face. I hope I can be forgiven for my first rather callous thought, 'Hurrah, I won't have to go to school for three days.' I knew the tangihanga would take at least that long. In my defence, although I had heard Dad's words clearly, I just didn't believe him. Perhaps that's also the reason why, when I walked with him to the truck, I didn't tell him how sorry I was that he had lost his mother.

Now most New Zealanders will know, but others won't, that the tangihanga, or period of mourning, is one of Māoridom's most important ceremonies. During the ritually conducted series of encounters between whānau and mourners, the deceased is remembered with affection and aroha. Tribal memory is shared and blood ties are reinforced in a passionate and impassioned letting go of the emotions.

The rites provide catharsis. They also affirm, in the constant reiteration of history both personal and tribal over the three days of mourning, that great binding force: whakapapa.

I was silent in the car. Perhaps Dad mistook my silence for grief. 'I know you loved your grandmother,' he said as he drove us to Haig Street.

I nodded but I was puzzled by his use of the past tense. Why was he doing that?

When we arrived at the house Mum was packing our suitcases with belongings, and baby food for Derek. Dad said he would go and get the car filled with petrol, and Mum told him we would be ready by the time he returned.

'You get into your good clothes, son,' she said to me, 'and help your sisters get ready, too.' Kararaina, Tāwhi and Viki were looking distressed, and I felt ashamed that they were feeling so emotional and I wasn't.

Of course I should have known that we would be staying out at Waituhi for the duration of the funeral. Sometimes people assumed that I understood when I didn't. I combed my hair, looking at myself in the mirror. Mum came in and adjusted my tie. 'Are you ready?'

I nodded. I wanted to look my best. You would have thought I was going to a wedding.

Dad returned, but we couldn't go right away because Mum said he should wash, change his shirt and put on his coat and hat.

On the drive out to Waituhi, I sat with my sisters in the back seat. Mum and Dad were talking about the arrangements, particularly who was going to do the catering and where everyone would sleep. From my recollection, Rongopai was still tapu and I don't think anybody slept there; they must have been hosted by the two marae at Tākitimu and Pākōwhai. Not only that, but the old kāuta would not have been big enough to cope with feeding of all the people; where was the dining room to seat them in?

It was a hot day and I was feeling scratchy from the heat. We sped past Pukepoto into the Waituhi Valley and everything looked the same, everything in its place, and there on the left was the Blue House where Nani lived. As soon as we turned into the gateway to the homestead, Dad saw Uncle Mike and Aunty Waina on the verandah.

'Mum's not here yet, Science,' Uncle Mike shouted. 'There was a hold-up with her death certificate at the undertakers in Gisborne, but Dad must be on the way with her by now.'

My Nani not here yet? Had she been on a holiday without telling me?

I jumped out of the car. Mum and Dad went into the homestead where some of my other uncles and aunties, including Aunty Mary, were preparing the house just as they had done for Christmas. I heard Aunty Mary's sharp orders cracking through the air. My cousins were all red-eyed and hastening to obey her instructions — sweep the courtyard, dust the front room, put flowers in the sitting room — but, as was my habit, I went to the pump to have a drink of water.

I had my face fully under the pump, the water splashing all over me, when I heard a yell and saw that the people on the verandah were looking up the road. Above, the sky was filled with clouds and, every now and then, a patch of bright blue.

Travelling slowly along the road, its headlights on, was a big black car. Dust was drifting in its wake. 'Open the gate, son,' Dad shouted.

I ran to the latch and managed to swing the gate open just as the hearse approached. As the car passed by I looked through the windows and, inside, was a dark shiny casket, a coffin. Aunty Mary came onto the verandah, and as soon as she saw the car she collapsed onto her knees, moaning.

I don't know which uncles helped the undertakers to take the coffin into the homestead. I stayed at the gate, watching people from Waituhi walking along the road and going into the house. Every time they did that, a burst of wailing and crying would resound, 'Auē e te kuia nei, kua ngaro i te Pō', a plaintive sound for such a beautiful day.

After a while, my father came to look for me. 'What are you doing out here?' he asked. 'You should be inside with everybody else. Your grandmother's ready, and Dad wants us to have karakia.'

I went with Dad into the house. It was warm but it smelt different. I thought I would find Nani in her bedroom, but Dad said, 'Not there.' He led me, instead, into another room. I don't know which one it was, but the sun was just declining in the sky and coming through the curtains.

Nani Teria was lying there with her daughters and other women around her. The coffin was laid on woven flax mats. My grandmother's long hair was like sable, unpinned, thick and curling down one side of her face into her cupped hands. She was dressed in white, and draped over her was a huge cloak of red and brown feathers. A slight wind from an open window made the cloak ripple and glisten like the wings of a giant moth.

I walked up to Teria and looked down at her beautiful face. Oh good, she was just asleep and would wake soon.

3.

YOU MAY THINK that my attitude was extraordinary.

I guess it was; after all, I had seen death before when he had come to take other nannies, uncles and aunties away with him, and in all cases I was sad and respectful. Indeed, one of the great gifts of a Māori childhood was that you were always, in life, in the presence of death.

Death was constant, both in the human and the natural world. He sent his harbingers — the disturbing dream, the owl hooting a name, or a moth or a bird flying into the house — to announce his coming. My mother, upon seeing such a portent, would simply say, 'Thank you for your message', and then wait for the telephone call or the visitor to the house to confirm it.

If you look at the statistics for the period, they are alarming. In 1955 there were significant differences in the life expectancy of Māori and non-Māori. A Māori man could expect to live to fifty-four and a Māori woman to fifty-eight, whereas a Pākehā man could expect to live to sixty-nine and a Pākehā woman to seventy-four. Look at the gravestones in the Māori cemetery on Tāmaki Drive in Auckland and you will see that the ages average out to death somewhere in their thirties. As far as infant mortality was concerned, Māori babies died at the rate of fifty-four per 1000, whereas non-Māori babies died at the rate of only twenty in the same number.

Even in those days the most common causes of Māori deaths were motor vehicle accidents and homicide. So-called natural causes for death were attributable mainly to rheumatic heart disease, high blood pressure, diabetes, stomach cancer or cancer of the cervix, and respiratory diseases such as influenza, pneumonia and bronchitis. The statistics are so stark you can't avoid shivering. With large extended Māori families and tribal clans, going to a tangi sometimes seemed like the main customary duty of our lives.

In other words, death and its associated rituals was a normal event, and travelling to see a relative who was dying either in the hospital or at home, or else to the tangi itself, was something we did almost every month. We tried to get there before sundown; nobody arrived at a marae at night. Sometimes we stopped by the side of the road, sleeping in the car until the dawn came and we could continue our journey.

Depending on what day we arrived, we either visited the whānau pani, the grieving family, in their own home or went onto the marae where their loved one had been taken. At the gateway, we joined others waiting to be called on by the old women, some black-gowned, their heads wreathed in green leaves. While we waited, a discussion would take place on who would speak and in what order, and which waiata we would sing. As well, a small envelope circulated so that everyone could slip some money into it to help with the funeral expenses.

Our tribal women washed and clothed our dead before they were laid in their coffin; the public viewing of the dead relative was expected. So, too, the formal accolades and tributes paid as he or she lay in state on the marae. That's an appropriate way to describe the event, *in state*, because the dead man or woman was always accorded the highest status, no matter if they were pauper or murderer. On the final day came the ritual hongi ki te tūpāpaku, the pressing of noses with the dead relative, before they began their journey from our world to the one that awaited them.

The strong young men went to the family graveyard to dig the hard, compact clay, to open it up to receive the coffin as it was lowered into the ground.

Why then, knowing about the tangihanga, did I not *let go* of Teria and proceed through the catharsis that marks the grieving process? I guess I can only reply with other questions: 'Let go? But where was my Nani going?'

And after all she had told me she would never die, and I believed her.

Mum, Dad, my sisters, brother and I slept with other relatives from Gisborne at the homestead that evening. The next day Aunty Mary said, 'Everybody up, it will be time to take Mum to Rongopai soon.' We had breakfast, got dressed and, very shortly, the hearse arrived at the house. As Nani was taken out to the shiny black car, Dad said, 'Mum will never come back again.'

Why was she not coming back? I wondered.

At Rongopai the locals had already prepared the marae for Teria's tangi. They had put up a small tent to one side of the meeting house and they welcomed us on with ringing karanga: 'Haere mai, e te whānau pani nei e, nau mai, haere mai ki tō marae.'

The lid was taken off the coffin, the feather cloak was draped over Nani Teria again, and a selection of large framed photographs and beautiful flower wreaths was spread around her. And then we all waited to receive the first group of mourners.

There was immediate tension as the protocol was sorted out. Although

Pera Punahāmoa would have liked the Mormon elders to be in charge of the karakia, Rongopai had always been regarded as a Pere marae; it was also a Ringatū marae. Teria's brothers and sisters therefore wanted a say in how the funeral would be conducted, and so did the local Ringatū priests. In the end, the Mormon elders were invited to be part of the proceedings, but they took the back seat as the kawa of the marae took over. Here, the locals were the bosses.

By the afternoon, the marae was crowded with groups coming on and paying their respects to Teria. To this day I am amazed that people would hear the news, 'Auē, kua mate a Teria', drop what they were doing and come.

How did they find out? That was another mystery. I think that people would stop their cars when they saw another car with Māori in it. Before you knew it, the news had gone the length and breadth of Aotearoa. When death came and took one of us away, the loss resonated through the tribal whakapapa and further to other tribes, and everybody felt it.

Late in the afternoon, Dad told me he was going into Gisborne to pick up Uncle Win, who was arriving from Wellington at the railway station. 'Would you like to come with me?' he asked.

We arrived with time to spare. The large eye of the train burst through the dark. The temperature must have been cold because Uncle Win was wearing a coat and scarf, and his breath steamed when he cried out, 'Brother!' They embraced, and Uncle Win didn't want to let go of Dad. Uncle's face was red, as if he had been crying for years and years.

We got into the car, drove to Haig Street to pick up some extra blankets, and then went back out to Waituhi. All the while, Dad and Uncle Win talked about Teria. Every time a car would approach, it would illumine Uncle Win's face.

As we approached Waituhi I saw a glow of light in the dark sky.

'The people know you're coming,' Dad said to Uncle Win. Indeed, as we arrived, I saw that every house on both sides of the road had their lights on and people were crying out to Uncle Win as we drove through Waituhi.

Rongopai was ablaze with a different kind of light, firelight, and when the car went through the gate I saw shadows walking around with torches. Where Teria was lying, tilley lamps had been hung around her.

At the sight of Uncle Win, a threnody of passion and yelling arose from the women seated around Teria. 'Titiro, Teria, look! Winiata is here.'

Uncle walked towards the tent in a corona of bright whirring insects.

BY THE SECOND day it was clear that Nani Teria's tangihanga would be huge. Mourners were arriving by car and bus, and whenever they walked onto the marae would arise a loud burst of wailing, inescapable, jagged and raw.

Come, sit with me and watch the mourners as they come onto Rongopai marae.

Who are these people coming out of the sun?

The kuia of Waituhi are stirring again, unfolding, to peer into the sunlight. They look into the red haze of the day and another welcoming. A black-veiled group is approaching Rongopai. From out of the sun they are coming.

One of the Waituhi women asks, 'Are we ready, ladies? Time to call the mourners on.'

Is that the karanga again? Haere mai ki ō tātou mate e, haere mai, haere mai, haere mai.

The sound pierces the sun as the mourners step through the gateway. The Waituhi elders who sit on the paepae, the place of speakers, try to identify the leaders, the male chiefs who follow with dignity behind their women. 'Do any of you boys know these people?'

Boys? Most of them are fifty, if they are a day. It's always a relief when the visitors are identified because then the appropriate links by whakapapa can be made, so the paepae can relax.

One of the visiting elders comes forward to stand, head bowed, in front of the tent where Teria lies. From the corner of an eye he sees Pera.

'Auē, Pera.' He gestures to Nani Teria. 'Tō hoa wahine, te wahine ātaahua, your beautiful wife.'

The mourners take seats on forms set at an angle to the meeting house. After a moment's silence, the speechmaking begins.

Ka tangi te tītī! Ka tangi te kākā! Ka tangi hoki ahau! Tihei mauri mate. The mutton bird weeps, the kākā weeps, and I weep also. Alas, it is death.

A large group is approaching, walking towards Rongopai. They stir the dust with their feet, the dust swirling like angels in the clear sky. Already, even though they are not in sight of the marae, their women are calling, karanga pealing through the air.

They appear before us. As they come to a halt, the dust swirls over them. And when they catch their first glimpse of Rongopai, they start to howl and moan, and some of the women kneel in the dust and throw handfuls in the air.

'Why are they doing that?' I ask Dad.

His voice is hushed. 'They are Ringatū. We heard that they were coming, and they are reacting to the dread, the mana, of Rongopai.

Probably some have never seen it before, but all know of its importance in the history of the prophet Te Kooti.'

The Ringatū make their procession onto the marae. They seem to have come out of some cyclonic eye of time. Striking, proud, polished ebony by the sun, their impact is stunning.

'Their history joins ours,' Dad says. 'That's why they have come to honour your grandmother. It's all to do with whakapapa, son.'

Goodness, all this noise, I would have expected Nani to be woken by it. I look at her. What is that? A small trickle of blood is coming from one of her nostrils. 'Nani's got a bloody nose,' I tell Dad.

For a while there is consternation. Such things, small though they are, are taken as signs of something, but I am too young to understand the meanings.

And then a car arrives, and when the door opens I can see Uncle Danny. He is sitting there, reaching for his crutches, his right leg in plaster, and he is calling, 'Mum! Mum!' And the women are wailing and people are crying because Uncle Danny is crying and I have to put my hands to my ears.

Make it stop. Make it *stop*.

 5.

MEMORIES RISE IN the still air like smoke from many fires. Is this the same place, this place of ashes? Yet the stream still runs and the sun rides over the sky. The mountains are always there. A bitter wind blows dust and ashes from the south. I can no longer see the streams, the sun, the mountains.

The third, last, day of the tangihanga arrived.

In the early morning, as dawn was rising, the Ringatū and Mormon elders offered their aroha to the family. One by one they said their personal farewells to my Nani and bent to press noses with her.

My mother pushed me forward but I didn't join the others. 'Sometimes I don't know what gets into you,' Mum said.

The day was hot, I could feel the sweat running in rivulets down my back. My mother told me to take off my jacket and school cap if I wanted to. I kept them on.

Uncle Win stood beside Pera. 'Kua pai, Dad? Are you ready?'

'Yes,' Pera answered. And with that, the undertakers came forward with the lid and placed it over my Nani. I can't remember if they had screws to affix the lid or nails, I wasn't watching. I wanted to tell them: *Stop*.

'Kua tae mai te wā,' Uncle Win said. 'The time has come to take Mum to the graveyard.' He always had such a beautiful, resonant voice, and he thanked everyone on the marae for coming; they must have numbered over 300. 'What are we if we do not support each other?' he asked. 'Are we not whānau?'

The hearse left the marae. The rest of the cortège followed.

When we reached the bottom of the graveyard, the day suddenly turned dark and cold. By the time the pallbearers took Nani out of the hearse, the sky over the graveyard was grey and rain was falling. 'It always rains when a chief dies,' I heard someone say.

The ground was muddy underfoot as we followed the coffin up the hill. Some of the older women were so overcome with grief that they waved everybody else onward. They cried out to Nani, 'Haere rā, Teria, ki Hawaiki, go sister, to your people who await you.'

I heard my Nani rolling around inside the coffin, and by the time we were halfway up I couldn't help thinking, 'They're not going to bury Nani, are they?'

It was then that I went into shock and terror. I stopped where I was. My mouth was dry, I was gasping, I couldn't speak, couldn't say to Mum and Dad and my sisters, 'No, wait.'

And when it began to rain everyone was in a hurry to get up to the graveyard because they flowed around me, buffeting me this way and that as they went through the gateway. I could see them all, and I was alone. Even the spiders had gone to join them.

One of the old women had paused on the hillside. Thinking that I had decided to stay with her, she wrapped me in her arms. I pushed her aside and stumbled up the hill. By that time, the Ringatū minister and the Mormon elder were taking the service. The mourners were pressed tight against each other. It was difficult to get through.

All of a sudden I was at the lip of the hole that Nani was to be lowered into. It was so deep and the black earth at the top gave way to yellow clay. On all sides were flower wreaths and photographs and suitcases and mats. What were they doing there?

Nani's coffin was swaying gently on ropes, above the hole. When my father and his strong brothers began to ease the ropes so as to allow the casket to go down to its rest, Uncle Danny flung his crutches to one side. He wanted to go with it.

The suitcases and photographs and mats and flowers were thrown in. The glass of the photographs broke, the frames splintered. My Nani was going away after all, and all her earthly belongings were to go with her. I remember the feather cloak going into the hole like the wings of a beautiful bird.

Nani was leaving me and she was never coming back.

The diggers began to shovel dirt onto the coffin.

Uncle Mike started a haka, 'Ka mate, ka mate, ka ora, ka ora!'

I was feeling so hot, so awfully hot. My throat was dry, perspiration sprang suddenly on my brow and I took off my cap to wipe the beads of sweat away. The world was spinning and my heart was pounding as I finally found my voice. I pulled Dad's arm, hard.

'You mustn't put Nani in the ground,' I said, but he didn't hear me. I raised my voice, looking at everybody, 'Do you hear me? I forbid it.'

I tried to speak again to someone, everyone, anyone. Nobody could hear me, they were too busy crying and wailing or else trying to shelter from the rain. But I had to try once more: 'Please don't. Don't. Don't.'

I looked at my mother. 'How will Teria get out when she wakes up?' I yelled. 'It will be so black in there and how will she be able to breathe? And all that earth on top of her, she'll never make it, Mum, never.'

And then I passed out.

Chapter Thirty-nine

What Came Next

1.

FOR WEEKS AFTER Teria's funeral, I had terrible nightmares. My mother told me that I would scream and yell, and when she went in to me she would find me standing on the bed, speaking in tongues and with my arms flailing the air.

'My Nani's going to wake up at any moment and she will find herself all alone in the dark. We have to go and dig her up before it's too late.'

I had to have the light on all night and it must have been the only one that burned in Haig Street until dawn. I felt responsible that Nani had been buried and I hadn't stopped it. Every time I tried to tell Mum or Dad, I couldn't get the words out, I couldn't give reo to my guilt.

I was fortunate that the tangi had taken place near the end of the school year, so Mum kept me at home where I managed a semblance of recovery. I know she took me to Dr Bowker because later he told me that I was very, very sick. Today, I guess I would have been put under the care of a child psychologist. I was left to find the resources to heal myself.

Why didn't my mother take me to a tohunga or medicine woman? I don't know. Maybe she did, I can't remember and nobody can confirm it. 'There was nothing we could do,' Mum said.

Yes, there was.

Mum and Dad, you should have hauled me to the cemetery and left me there at the graveyard so that I could finally come to grips with the inevitability of the whole process of mourning and letting go. No matter how hard I fought, you should have tied me to a post and given me charge of a reed, as happens with some African tribes, which joins the body to the surface of the earth. You should have left me to keep vigil at the side of Teria's grave, to realise the cruel physical consequences of death, and to wait until the first maggot appeared, glistening, on the surface, after its long crawl up the reed. How beautiful that custom seems to me today, surrounded by a society that does not wish to come to terms with its mortality.

Then and only then would I have understood that my Nani was not coming back and that I would never see her again. Never.

I suspect that my behaviour back then is the reason why, as I grew older, my parents never told me when somebody died, unless it was an immediate relative; usually, I found out later. Although the deaths of family and friends still affect me terribly, I have realised that tangihanga is a ritual beyond compare when it comes to achieving catharsis.

It's loss, rather than death, that affects me. In the case of Teria, there was something in my own personal psychology, that unconscious holding up my hand for her as if it was the most natural thing in the world, that established a certain emotional connection. From now on, she would never be there to take it.

Actually, I am not afraid of death. The only thing I fear in my own life is not death at all but my judgement before God.

I HAVE TO get this over with.

I mentioned that a first event took away all my protection: that was Teria's death. I also said that when that happened a second event was able to sneak in and destroy my boyhood.

You may have thought that my 'special' status as a loved grandson of Teria would protect me from all the ills and spites of the world. After her death, however, I was the subject of a sexual attack. Children are vulnerable and, oh, it's so easy for this to occur when boys share beds with their male cousins and sexual experimentation is going on.

But what happened to me, anal rape, was without my consent, and the relative who performed it was much, much older than me. My parents, family and I were out shearing and I was sleeping with my cousins in one of the quarters. Halfway through the night my relative woke me up and, putting a finger to my lips, beckoned me to go to another, empty, hut with him.

I was trusting. I followed him and he made me lie down on a bed and wanted me to stroke him. I didn't realise he had another purpose because, after a while, he said, 'Time to break your arse, cousin.'

Before I knew it, he had chopped my windpipe and pushed me into the mattress. He knew what he was doing and why he was doing it. I struggled, gasping for breath as he turned me onto my front, took down my pyjama trousers and entered me. I had never felt such pain.

I don't know how long the rape took. After it was over my relative smiled at me, and then walked me back to my cousins' quarters. I was still in shock as I rejoined them; I was glad that it was dark. I was bleeding; I felt like I had been ripped to pieces.

Deeply ashamed, I never told anybody — I took the sin upon myself. Whenever I saw my relative around Waituhi, I would put my head down, I would feel listless, almost in a trance, and my whole body would go limp. Although I don't know what it's like to suffer the consequence of long-term abuse, sexual or otherwise, as some of my girl cousins did, I felt loss of self-esteem and self-worth, and understood the impulse to obedience and compliance. You feel defenceless and caught in the coils of something that will never let you go.

I had a friend in New York, gorgeous Emma, who kept in her apartment a pet boa constrictor called Elvis who needed to be fed every two weeks. Elvis was very fastidious, and to please him Emma would buy a rabbit. Once she got back into the apartment she would let the rabbit out of the cage and it would hip-hop around the apartment until it saw the boa. Then it would freeze.

The rabbit never tried to escape; it knew it was only a matter of time. Sometimes Elvis showed no initial interest, but eventually hunger would gnaw at him and he would make a quick strike.

If my relative had wanted to rape me again, I would have let him do it. If he had said, 'Come', I would have gone to him. If he had said, 'Sit', I would have sat.

I grew older and able to protect myself. I worried for a long time about any internal scars or damage: the thought really did my head in. Eventually, when I convinced myself I had healed, I still had to mentally get over what had been done to me. I was strong enough in my brain to do that. I suspect my relative had been stalking me for some time, waiting for the opportunity to take me unawares. I don't think the rape was born out of desire. No, it was more sinister than that, premeditated, deliberate, an attempt to take away my tapu, sacredness. Was I getting too whakahīhī and had to be taught a lesson? The predatory nature of the act still makes me shiver.

When something like rape occurs, everything that happens becomes more important. I know that I began to deeply question life. I learned that there were no guarantees. I vowed that I would never let anybody or anything take me to the depths of such abject degradation, helplessness or humiliation again.

As for my relative, oh, he lived to be a middle-aged man with children and grandchildren who loved him. I had to wait until I was taller than he was and stronger before I was able to confront him. I did a bad job of it; I was still afraid. When he died I went to his tangi just to make sure he was dead and in his coffin.

AFTER TERIA'S DEATH and the sexual attack, there's no doubt that I became a different boy.

Even today, friends have told me that sometimes they think I'm observing my life as if there's a third person in the room. It's not me but it looks like me, and I'm thinking out that if it does this, then *this* will happen, and if it does that, then *that* will happen. There is an element of working out my life while I am living it so that I am not surprised by it. I'm so directive that sometimes I think that I am actually forcing my life to go the way it is going; I cannot allow it to go that way simply by itself. I observe, make the choice, and then dictate my path.

Can you blame me for that? Oh, I do a very good job of creating the semblance of spontaneity, but I am the least spontaneous person I know; I am very constructed. I became the boy and then the man who never cried. If I had ever felt like a child, I never felt like that again.

One day I arrived home after delivering newspapers and Dad said, 'Your grandfather's been round. He's left you a present.'

A present? I wondered what it was. What could Grandad possibly have left for me?

The gift was a top. Grandad had whittled it himself. He always liked to have a piece of wood and a pocketknife in his hands. The top came with a piece of flax, which he had also woven.

My father took me outside and showed me how to use it. He actually got more fun out of it than I did. 'See how it can jump!' he exclaimed. 'This is an excellent kaitaka.' And then Dad asked me gently, 'Can't you try harder with your grandfather?'

I couldn't tell Dad I blamed Grandad for Teria's death. Later, Pera turned up and my father and I walked out to meet him. 'How are you?' he asked.

My grandfather was reaching out to me. I am ashamed to say that during the entire time of Teria's funeral I had not even thought to reach out to him.

'Say thank you for the kaitaka,' Dad ordered.

'Thank you,' I said.

PART SIX

MATAKITE
FORESIGHT

Chapter Forty

The Man Who Rode a Whale

1.

WE'RE NOT SURE what age the boy, Māui, was when he left the sky father and set out to search for his mother. What we do know is that he was a magic child and, like all such children, he had been given great powers by Rangi. With these gifts, he would continue the creation of a world for its human inheritors, the Māori.

He began his search at the very place Taranga had thrown him into the waves. From there he went from village to village along the shore asking, 'Do you know me? Do I look familiar to you?' Some of the people he asked were preparing to go to a famous kāinga where a great festival of kapa haka was about to be held. Eventually Māui came upon that settlement. Already the dancing had started and people were feasting, and there Māui saw Taranga.

How did he know she was his mother? A son always knows.

Māui's joy mounted when he saw her waving to four boys, older than he was. Were they his brothers? The drums were beating out an intoxicating rhythm as the boys presented themselves to Taranga so that she could prepare them for the dancing. The scene is the classic set-piece of all ancient cultures — the arrival of the exiled prince at the royal court while the festivities are at their height.

Māui slipped in beside the four boys. Astonished, Taranga asked, 'Who are you?'

'I am your fifth son, Māuipōtiki, Māui the youngest.'

Taranga did not recognise him and, thinking him an interloper, commanded him to leave.

Māui, however, reminded her and his brothers of the circumstances of his birth. 'You are not to blame, Mother, that you considered me disfigured, wrapped me in your hair and cast me into the sea. And you, my brothers, I know of you because our mother would say your names lovingly while I was in her womb. I present this whakapapa, this knowledge, as my proof. You are Māuitaha, Māuiroto, Māuipae and Māuiwaho.'

It is said that the debate over accepting Māui continued late into the night. At long last, however, came the great recognition scene when mother reconciled with long-lost son and his brothers accepted him. Nevertheless, while the dancing and feasting resumed, the brothers were already plotting to kill him. After all, he could usurp their birthrights as elder children.

2.

THERE CAME A time, after the death of Teria and the sexual attack, when the world righted itself. Children are resilient, and I was able to rise from my grief.

One Saturday morning, during the summer of 1956, after collecting the money from the neighbourhood for the paper run and taking it to the office, the refrain of a well-known action song popped into my head:

> *Uia mai koia whakahuatia ake, ko wai te whare nei e?*
> *Whitireia, Whitireia! Ko wai te tekoteko kei runga?*
> *Ko Paikea, ko Paikea!*

The song woke up the ancestors in that room behind my eyes, having caught them sleeping on the job. This was too good an opportunity to lose, and they sent a message to me and I received it: 'I think I'll go to see the whale rider,' I said to myself.

I went around to Maarten's place and asked him if he wanted to come with me.

'Where is this whale rider?' he asked, mystified.

'At Whāngārā,' I answered. I didn't tell Maarten that the village was about twenty miles away. His mother gave us some bread and cheese and water, and away from Gisborne we went.

As we pedalled, I told Maarten the story:

'Once upon a time in faraway Hawaiki, there lived a boy prince by the name of Kahutiaterangi, son of a paramount chief named Uenuku. Actually the village they lived in was the original Whāngārā.

'Kahutiaterangi had a half-brother, older than he was and of less chiefly rank, by the name of Ruatapu, who had long plotted to kill his brother as well as the other chiefly sons of Hawaiki; he was like Tūpurupuru, the Waituhi chieftain, and wanted to be the only star in the sky. Another reason was that Kahutiaterangi was very handsome, the most comely boy in all the land, and Ruatapu was jealous of his looks.'

'Is that really in the story?' Maarten asked sceptically as he noted my attempts to show him my own somewhat comely profile. He also knew my penchant for gilding stories a little.

'Aren't princes supposed to be handsome?' I asked, offended.

'The opportunity came when Ruatapu, Kahutiaterangi and the other chiefly sons were due to travel on a large ocean-going waka. Ruatapu took a seat at the rear of the canoe where the remu, the drain plug, was; he also took with him a hand-held bone club.

'Out at sea Ruatapu took his heel from the remu and the waka began to sink. He drew his weapon and, moving swiftly among those on board, killed them. Some of the chiefly sons had dived overboard, and Ruatapu went in pursuit, swimming from boy to boy and clubbing them to death too. The sea was soon stained red with blood.

'But Kahutiaterangi escaped death. One of his kaitiaki was a whale and he called for its assistance. A huge tohorā surfaced beside him, Kahutiaterangi mounted it and then sent it plunging away from the murderous Ruatapu. This enraged Kahutiaterangi's half-brother because, after all, Kahutia had been the main object of the murder spree.

'Ruatapu was not without supernatural powers either. He caused a great tidal wave to pursue Kahutiaterangi and then followed his quarry himself. Kahutiaterangi decided to seek refuge in a far-off land, Aotearoa.

'Now some people say that Kahutiaterangi didn't ride a whale at all and that, instead, he used transformative powers to *become* a whale. Ruatapu was also a shape-shifter and, for the pursuit, turned himself into a speedy taniwha.'

Maarten was looking sceptical again, but before he opened his mouth I headed him off at the pass — the shape-shifting was really in the story.

'And when Ruatapu realised Kahutiaterangi was getting away he sent twelve waves ahead of him to try to catch the—'

'Comely?' Maarten suggested helpfully.

'—prince and swamp him. But Kahutiaterangi managed to stay ahead of the waves and land at Ahuahu before the twelfth wave caught up. Ruatapu set up a huge defeated roar to the heavens.'

'Definitely not in the story,' Maarten said.

To celebrate his safe arrival, Kahutiaterangi took another name, Paikea. He may also have wanted to do this to evade any future attempts by Ruatapu to kill him. He made his way south to Te Kautuku, where he met his wife, Huturangi. But his yearning was to find a place like the Whāngārā he had left in Hawaiki, and he did not rest until he found that bay 'being reached by the rays of the sun'. There, he arrived in the *new* Whāngārā, at dawn, just as the star Poutūterangi appeared over Hikurangi mountain. He became the founding ancestor of the people of Ngāti Porou.

Ah yes, Hikurangi again, exerting its extraordinary power. And that Bethlehem star creates a great scene, doesn't it? The voyager, heading to the horizon and over, arriving at his destination as a new day is dawning.

Maarten and I were pedalling fast. By the time we reached Wainui Beach, where we stopped for lunch, I could tell that he was getting suspicious that maybe the bike ride would be longer than he had expected it to be. 'How much further do we go?' he asked.

When I waved vaguely towards the north-east he decided to bail out and turn back to Gisborne. I kept riding, having set my mind on getting to Whāngārā to see the figure of Paikea riding his whale, on top of the meeting house, Whitireia.

All in all, the bike ride took me the whole afternoon to get there, and when I arrived at the seaside village darkness was falling. I sat cross-legged on the marae in the last rays of the sunlight, eating one of Mrs van Dijk's yummy sandwiches and squinting up at the tekoteko of Paikea. He looked so imposing on the whale, silhouetted against the crimson-streaked sky. The waves were thundering and the sea was opalescent and pearly as I asked my boyish questions: 'How did you know where to come? When the whale dived, how did you stay on? The whale doesn't have a mane to hold onto. How did you breathe when you were underwater? And how did you tell the whale where to come unless, unless . . .'

In a moment's insight I grasped what the answer to my last question was.

At that moment, old man Moni Taumaunu saw me on the marae and yelled out, 'What are you doing out here?'

I turned and went running across the grass to him. 'Moni! Moni! If Paikea was able to tell his whale where to come, whales must speak Māori!'

Moni took me to his house near the marae and rang Dad up on what passed, in those days, for a telephone — a handset attached to the wall with a handle you turned to connect to an operator. I heard him say, 'Hello, Tom. Are you looking for Witi? He's out here at Whāngārā.'

'What is he doing there?'

Moni calmed him down. 'Don't worry. No good his going back tonight — he hasn't got a lamp on his bike. He can sleep out here with us and somebody will bring him back to town tomorrow.'

Once I'd begun, I couldn't stop biking out to Whāngārā.

And so also started the, well, I'll call it the legend that the people of Whāngārā later liked to recall when I wrote *The Whale Rider*. They made my bike rides sound epic, but the truth is that I doubt I made the journey more than four times, five at most, and they were not as heroic as might first appear. I was picked up for most of the trips, as there was always good traffic on State Highway 35 going to Tolaga Bay or Tokomaru Bay and I would pretend to be out of breath. I was known to many of Dad's shearers or to other shearing gangs, and they would pull up beside me. 'Going to Whāngārā again, Witi? Put your bike in the back and we'll take you to the turn-off.'

After a while, it seemed only natural to stay the night. Indeed, Roger Robinson, an academic colleague at Victoria University of Wellington (and a world-ranked runner to boot), spoke with Hone Taumaunu, Moni's son, and Hone remembered those days when I would fetch up at his father's house and sleep over.

And whenever I went to the McCrae Baths with my friends and they wondered where I was, who was that sitting on the bottom? Oh, just Witi, trying to see how long he can stay underwater without taking a breath.

'Did I beat my record that time?' I would ask them. 'How long? Only two minutes?'

Not. Good. Enough. Under I would go again.

3.

NOW THE TIKA. So where does Paikea, the whale rider, fit in my childhood? Without him I would not have begun my lifelong interest in cetaceans and in the relationship between the human and the whale worlds. This relationship was set down in mythological times after earth and sky had been separated and the god children divided between themselves the various kingdoms. Tangaroa took the kingdom of the ocean, and Tāne, father of humankind, took the kingdom of the forests. Then Tangaroa appointed the triad of Kiwa, Rona and Kaukau to assist his sovereign rule — Kiwa to be guardian of the southern ocean, Rona to help control the tides, and Kaukau to aid the welfare of the sea's many citizens.

To the triad, two guardians from the kingdom of the land, Takaaho and Te Pūwhakahara, brought a special suit — their offspring had been given lakes to live in, but they preferred to roam the freedom of the sea. The suit was accepted, and thus sharks and whales were granted habitation of the ocean. From the very beginning the whale was grateful for this release, and this was why the whale family became known as the helpers of men lost at sea.

'Whenever you are in trouble in the ocean,' Moni told me, 'call for help in the name of Paikea. After all,' he added, his eyes twinkling, 'you already know their language, don't you, boy?'

Through Moni I began to understand how close Māori people were to the whale iwi.

My good friend, author Philip Hoare, wrote that Māori actually followed whale roads in the sea, what their Anglo-Saxon seafaring comrades would call *hwaelweg*, the whale's ways. 'To ally oneself to a whale,' he said, 'is not so strange. Throughout history, humans have celebrated their animal affiliations.

'When Māori arrived in Aotearoa, a land that lacked native mammals, they responded to cetaceans, seeing them as tribal in the same way that they were tribal. Whale tribes had honorific titles: Tutarakauika, Te Kauika Tangaroa, Wehengakauki.

'Māori often expressed situations in their lives in cetacean imagery. Te kāhui paraoa meant not only a gathering of sperm whales, but also a meeting of a group of chiefs. He paenga pakake or beached whales indicated fallen warriors on a battlefield, while men assumed the guise of whales in their warfare. The Ngāti Kurī tribe created a Trojan whale from dog skins in which were hidden one hundred warriors; when their besieged enemy came out to feast on its meat, they were killed.'

For Māori, Philip went on to say, there was no demarcation between the life of the land and that of the ocean; such distinctions made no sense. Trees and whales were as one. The god, Te Hāpuku, was god of both whales and tree ferns, and thus whales were known as fish of the forest. The Māori saw the sperm whale in the kauri tree. When the tohorā asked the kauri to accompany him on his return to the ocean, the tree preferred to stay on the land; they do share, in appearance, the same skins.

Most recently, when a pod of pilot whales stranded on the South Island, a Māori elder arrived with his sleeping bag to spend the night with them in order that they should not die alone. In one famous incident in 1970, fifty-nine stranded sperm whales were declared to be tangata, human.

Auē, the world grew older, and humankind, in its arrogance, has driven a wedge through the original oneness of the natural world with the human world. At risk are now those species that we once shared this world with. Among them are the last fifty-five (at the time of writing) Māui's dolphins. I have for many years been a trustee of the South Pacific Whaling Research Consortium, and in 2014 I launched the petition to save Māui's dolphins.

Back to Whāngārā.

My father liked very much the idea that I was being motivated to go out to the village. It was he who put the thought into my head that Paikea had what he called a 'manifest destiny', an idea that people don't like these days.

Dad believed that Māori, too, had such a destiny, and that we looked as if we were failing to achieve it. 'Your ancestor Paikea didn't come all this way to Aotearoa,' he would tell me, 'just to see us sitting on a beach smoking dope and drinking beer. No! His journey may have been an ending for him, but it was just a beginning for us. The Māori journey will not be over until we reach the stars.'

Little was I to know that those bike rides would lead, some thirty years later, to the incident that brought back all those childhood memories of Whangara and the vast inventory of whale mythology: the arrival of a whale through the neck of New York Harbour and up the Hudson River almost to Pier 86 at 12th Avenue and West 46th Street.

I was living in New York at the time and became aware of the whale when helicopters began to buzz up and down the river. I went to the window, looked out and took a deep, grateful breath. The Māori world does not stop at the borders of the Pacific Ocean.

I wrote the first draft of *The Whale Rider* in six weeks. It was a novel about a contemporary Paikea, a young girl, because my elder daughter Jessica made a remark to me about the lack of stories in which young girls were heroes. Fifteen years later the book became the feature film *Whale Rider* in 2002. Produced by John Barnett and directed by Niki Caro, it was a breakout international success, and people began to call me the Prince of Whales. When Keisha Castle-Hughes, the actress who played Pai, became the youngest woman to be ever nominated in the Best Actress category of the Academy Awards, she was christened Moby Chick.

We cut to Rarotonga in 2003.

I went there for the Cook Island premiere of *The Whale Rider*. I was treated like royalty and greatly enjoyed the hilarity of the night. The film was shown in two theatres, but we only had one copy. The audience in Theatre No. 1 would watch the first reel while the audience in Theatre No. 2 would wait, singing and dancing in the aisles. At the end of the second reel in Theatre No. 1, some of that audience rushed into Theatre No. 2 to take a second look — somehow we all squeezed in.

The local people have a story about Paikea, only he isn't the stuff of fantasy. They tell of his arrival from Raiatea and his marriage to a local woman. One day she saw him leave to go fishing. He disappeared into a storm, and in fact her bones were discovered just before I arrived for the premiere, at the place where she watched him depart. They say she pined away for love — women did that in those days.

I looked up at the stars strewn across the night sky and I thought of my Dad's dream for Māori.

Of a day when a great whale of a starship, let's call it *Paikea 2*, will carry a new generation of Māori to the universe. Artificial intelligence will have replaced computer technology and distance and time will be defined in light years and parsecs, but bearings will still be taken as of old, as the original Paikea would have done when he crossed his sea. Only this time the sea will be celestial, not oceanic.

From Mount Hikurangi the starship will float on beautiful light-wings; its sails will catch subatomic particles generated by the ultra-energetic jets spat out of black holes, particularly supermassive Kerr black holes, in the centres of active galaxies. The passage of *Paikea 2* will be set to the Magellanic Clouds by way of Matariki, 50 kiloparsecs at the far edge of Earth's galactic disc; then across the Milky Way, 130 kiloparsecs to the Great Square of Pegasus and the Palomar 13 global cluster buried beneath it. From there the ship will jump 670 kiloparsecs to the Magellanic Stream and the Andromeda Spiral Galaxy.

Ascending to the Local Group, 1000 kiloparsecs out, the starship will make a quick jump to the Triangulum/M33 and onward through the multifaceted spectacle of the Virgo and Como clusters. Dancing along the black holes in the centres of the galaxies of the Great Wall, and gaining vast energies at each encounter, the ship will shoot off toward the Hubble Ultra Deep Field that marks the outer perimeter of the known universe.

Of course the captain of *Paikea 2* will be a young woman and she will stand with our descendants on the threshold of another beginning, another beach. How I wish I could be there to see them take their rightful inheritance.

There is no Plan(et) B. Saving the planet has become crucial. And if we can't save it, let us hope that we will have given our children the time to get *off* it.

After all, they are the seeds sown in Raiatea.

1.

IN 1957 DAD decided we would shift out to Te Karaka to start farming. Te Karaka was a rural township, about an hour and a half's drive north from Gisborne on State Highway 2, and the largest settlement before you reached Ōpōtiki in the Bay of Plenty. Our farm was further north of Te Karaka, say another hour's drive. While SH2 continued to the Waioeka Gorge, to get to our place you took a dusty road off the highway, which took you eastward, and in the distance was a mountain known as Arowhana.

We were one of the remote farms on the isolated Whakarau Road. Apart from the farm families and a roadman, Henry Williams, his wife, Myra, and daughter, Polly, the only people you would see were the occasional drovers, council workers and possum hunters. It really was the back of beyond.

This is how our shift came about.

During the late 1940s, Teria had asked Dad to purchase what was left of a ninety-nine-year lease on Māori land; Grandad was one of the owners. From memory, the lease had some sixty-seven years to run. Dad was successful in bidding for it and we had taken earlier trips out there, staying in a flea-ridden hut that left us all badly bitten. Mum ordered us to take everything out of the whare, to put creosote on the floors, walls and ceilings and to spread the bedding outside. There, she splashed kerosene over the bedding and put a torch to it. Burning fleas tried to jump from the flames. 'Fry, fleas, fry!' we yelled.

There was no access from the Whakarau Road and we either walked in and across the river to the leasehold by way of a paper road that existed on Fred Beer's farm or by way of Hallidays' farm.

When Fred Beer died, his estate contacted Dad to see if he wanted to purchase the property and, by doing so, ensure access to our land. Dad said yes, and that was the catalyst for the move. We kept Haig Street, but Mum and Dad shifted us out to the farm.

'It's not flash,' Dad said, 'but we're lucky to own it.'

We didn't go out alone. Dad's brother, Puku, agreed to bring his family and join us on the farm later.

Dad combined the Beer farm and the leasehold under the name Maera Station. By thrift and careful financial management, he had managed to come all the way from seasonal worker to shearing contractor to owner of his own farm. It was quite an achievement: Māori may have been managers of Māori land incorporations, but very few owned their own farms.

To some degree it would be true to say that my life had, to that point, had a strong forward momentum. I had been fortunate to have had such a vigorous Gisborne childhood. There had been people like Mr Grono, Madge Cole and Barbara Hossack, whom I can think of only as people gathered at a christening, planting kisses on my head as they passed me from one to another. When I left Gisborne, they had to let me go. They must have wondered if I would survive.

Our arrival had a sinister overture. The duck season was under way and hunters had grown accustomed to coming onto the farm because, presumably, Mr Beer had allowed it.

Not any longer. Dad never liked guns, and when he saw three hunters sauntering onto the property, rifles in their hands, he went up to them and told them that the farm was out of bounds. They laughed and asked to speak to Mr Beer. Dad told them that he had bought the farm. The duck shooters didn't believe him. And then one of them said, deliberately, in coon English: 'So the Māori buy the Pākehā farm, eh. He think he better than us, can order us around, eh.'

At the time, Uncle Puku and his family had yet to join us. I ran up to the farmhouse and told Mum.

'Stay inside and keep your sisters safe,' she said, and then she went down to join Dad.

I decided to go to the wardrobe where Dad kept his rifle; I couldn't find any bullets, though. I knew he would be angry, but I thought if the hunters saw that I had a rifle they would think seriously about backing off. Certainly the act was provocative; in that I was like my mother.

This may sound strange but, although I am writing about childhood, in many ways I was always an adult. I told my sisters to wait in their bedroom and then I watched from the window.

The stand-off was getting dangerous. The air was filled with raised, angry voices.

Suddenly there was another man, someone my family had never seen before. His name was Bulla, and he was a grizzled, hardened itinerant Māori worker who wandered around the farms getting work. His arrival, on a horse loaded with sacks that contained his belongings, interrupted the argument. Bulla must have been known to the hunters because he spoke sharply to them. They shook their heads angrily, then laughed and headed back to the main road. As they unlatched the gate and went out, one of them turned to Dad, raised his rifle and mimed a shot. *Bang, you're dead, Hori.*

The message was clear. As long as Māori stayed where we were supposed to, we were tolerated, but any indication that we were as good as our masters and could issue orders to Pākehā was met with anger.

2.

LET ME TELL you a little more about Te Karaka and the surrounding rural region in 1957.

The demographic was at least four-fifths Māori. The main tribe was Te Whānau-a-Taupara of Te Aitanga-a-Māhaki. The tribe's main marae had originally been Te Poho-o-Pikihoro, which stood from 1888 until 1940. However they began to build a new marae, Tākipū, on the outskirts of Te Karaka, which was opened in March 1958. Tākipū was a beautiful complex, and in it was an effigy in wood of Sir Āpirana Ngata who, together with his successor, Pāhau Milner, was one of the prime instigators of the complex.

What's inspiring about Tākipū was that it was created as a memorial to Māori servicemen and -women who fought in the Second World War. It joined the earlier First World War Pākehā memorial in the township, a crowned lion standing on a plinth and holding a pennant. On the plinth are the words 'Soyes Ferme', Stand Firm.

As for the township itself, Te Karaka was the hub of a prosperous farming hinterland. Among its most illustrious families were the Holdsworths, whose matriarch had given over the running of the farm to her son Jim. The railway was still operating, and kids from Matawai came to school in Te Karaka by train and left by train every day; the Hāmis and Hollises still lived in the railway houses. The town had the usual smattering of public services such as a post office (Sam Bartlett did the rural delivery runs three times a week if he could get across our culvert), a telephone exchange, a volunteer fire service, a doctor's surgery and a library. There was a butcher's shop, Graham Motors, John Robinson Electrical, Bill Aitken had a general store, the Bensons had a bakery, and the Hardacres sold haberdashery. The town benefited from the local industries, mainly sheep and cattle farming; drovers regularly drove their herds and flocks down the main street. At the same time, there was a growing interest in forestry, attracting a labour force to prepare for the planting of trees over almost 30,000 acres of what later became the Mangatū Forest. The Road Service bus made a regular stop at the corner goods store, and people could get a pie and drink at a number of other small-town eateries.

Like most rural towns, Te Karaka had its range of festivities. The region prided itself on its sense of community and there were calf days, bring and buys and sports days. Everybody turned up to cheer the barefooted boys who, whether they wanted to or not, had to run an annual marathon from school along Main Road to Tākipū, then up the range and parallel to the town below and back through Te Karaka to school again. I know how hard it was; I did it three times.

Fridays were busy days for the Rangatira Hotel, and people preferred to see movies on Wednesdays, Fridays and Saturdays at the Krause Hall, Te Karaka, rather than go into 'town', as they called Gisborne. The cinema showed double features, usually a Technicolor Western like Ronald Reagan and Rhonda Fleming in *The Last Outpost*, and a comedy film in glorious black and white like *Abbott and Costello Go to Mars*. The lack of high-quality cinema fare is definitely responsible for my taste for 1950s B movies. Once, quite by accident, my schoolmate Willie Wilson and I were passing by the picture theatre when the projectionist came out and threw some old posters into the rubbish bin. When I expressed an interest in them he invited us in to select even older memorabilia. In bad movie heaven, I forgot the time, and when Willie and I got back to school we were caned for playing hookey.

On the corner of Main Road and the Kanakanaia Road was Te Karaka Primary School alongside its co-educational secondary equivalent, Te Karaka District High. You could go all the way from Primer One to Form Two at the primary school and then do high school from Form Three to Form Five. Prosperous farmers chose to bypass the high school and send their sons and daughters to board at Gisborne Boys' or Woodford House in Havelock North.

Most of us were bussed into school, either on the sleek red bus service or local transport from small surrounding villages like Ormond, Waihīrere, Whātātutu, Kanakanaia, Mangatū, Ōtoko and Matawai. In the case of the Whakarau Road kids, we travelled on the somewhat rattly antique model driven by Hamie Brown.

He must have been surprised that day. As well as the three Wright children and Polly Williams, the roadman's daughter, waiting at the roundabout was a new group of nine Māori children from two families, all recently arrived at the old Beer farm. We had walked over five miles to the roundabout to meet Mr Brown, and we did that every morning. During winter the culvert between our farm and the roundabout overflowed and we piggybacked the younger children across. Not until a few years later, when the Halliday farm was taken over by the Harding family, did the Education Department consider there were enough children to warrant the bus coming further.

These are some of the images I associate with the daily school bus trip.

Sitting in the back seat while my sisters chatted with Polly Williams near the front; clouds of dust from trucks in front of us, making Keith Wright, the bus monitor, run from window to window closing them; a possum hunter on his horse with dead and bloodied animals in saddle sacks; dogs chained at the hydatids strip at the bottom of our hill and vomiting; cattle milling across the road; a harrier hawk feasting on road kill — maybe a rabbit — startled by the bus and carrying its prey into the clear blue sky. Over the next few years, I often felt like that rabbit.

One week, as the bus descended the hill parallel to the Wright farm, a Fletcher topdressing aircraft with its familiar bent wing configuration, was preparing to take off. The strip was short and I watched with my heart in my mouth as the plane sped down the incline, dropped over the edge and finally lurched skyward.

Other memories?

I went crazy over Frankie Lymon and *Why Do Fools Fall in Love?* As well, after a Saturday hockey match in Gisborne, my older cousins managed to get me into *Rock Around the Clock* with them at the Regent Theatre. Those were the days when dangerous movies, i.e. any that encouraged delinquency, were prefaced by the appearance of the duty manager to declare nervously, 'No rowdiness during the film, dancing in the aisles or the throwing of any offensive substances at the screen will be tolerated.' During his remarks there were jeers and catcalls and he was pelted with jellybeans and Jaffas. When the lights went down, ushers patrolled the back seats with their torches to ensure no serious necking was happening. Any movement of hands below a girl's waist and through her voluminous petticoats qualified.

I sang 'Rock Around the Clock' on the school bus for a whole week after seeing the film, until Keith Wright threatened to throw me off while the vehicle was still moving.

Then there were the running races that my cousins and I began in the afternoons when Hamie Brown took us back to the farm. I was exhilarated by the competitions with Mīni, Rangi and Charlie, as we ran neck and neck from the roundabout along the dusty road, down into the bend where the culvert was and then up to our rural delivery box.

3.

I WAS THIRTEEN now, a teenager. If you were passing the school bus and happened to look up at one of the rear side windows you would have seen me looking back.

A very skinny boy, approaching his adult height of 5 feet 7 inches (1.7 metres). He had a habit of walking with a bit of a limp, mainly because his left leg was shorter than his right; it took many years for him to perfect a way of walking that disguised this impediment.

The boy had never thought of himself as good-looking and, well, comely. He never had that royal House of Halbert tilt to the head or languid look of disdain whenever he was in a state of repose. He was glad that there was only one small mirror in the farmhouse, above the washbasin in the bathroom, which showed his face and nothing else. If he wanted to look at all of himself, the only place was down at the river, in the water. He was not in love with his reflection. He would look into it, hoping to see another hair on his chin as he desperately wanted to start shaving.

The boy never understood why girls at school or the sports grounds and church were attracted to him. His father made jokes about this girl or that girl who came around to Haig Street during the weekend to ask him out to the pictures or to join friends at the beach or to a church social function — American elders, nostalgic for home, organised hay rides and hoedowns. His piano playing had made him popular, too, and girls knew who he was.

Already the boy has begun to exhibit what he calls his 'Ihimaera Smile', a way of cocking his head and looking sideways at the world and people. On first appearance it was charming, but it was a version of the smile of the people of Anatolia, which is now part of the modern ethnic mess that is Turkey. Those upturned lips hid more than they showed and, by that age, he was beginning to suspect he would have a lot to hide. The smile conveyed his history; it was the same smile that Teria had. In her case, it masked anger, resentment, and frustration at Pākehā refusal to recognise the land rights of Te Whānau-a-Kai, and he inherited it.

Director Elia Kazan, who made a film called *The Anatolian Smile*, said it was a stigmata; it was a mark written on the faces of all the Mediterranean minorities such as Greeks and Jews. In the boy's case, the smile was that of his ancestors sitting in the room behind his eyes. However, it also hid some personal insecurity, some secret.

Whatever the case, the Ihimaera Smile has become one of the boy's greatest assets; he uses it with charm and seeming sincerity to get what he wants. The boy, however, is not sincere or sensitive and tender. Even at his age, he can plot, scheme and organise his way through the world without anybody knowing.

I DON'T KNOW how long Fred Beer had been living on the farm, but there was a small hut near the house stacked with publications like *Town & Country* and *Tatler* from the First World War years. On rainy days the hut became a haven where I loved to read the magazines. They were filled with fascinating pictures of the débutantes at the London Season or what was on in the Drury Lane theatres of the day — *Charley's Aunt* and *Chu Chin Chow*. Fans of the television series *Downton Abbey* would have been in nostalgia heaven. The magazine collection continued through the Second World War and then petered out, but I read every one of them.

I wasn't the only one to find sanctuary in the small hut. I had a run-in with a feral cat who, full-bellied pregnant, took possession while waiting for her litter of kittens to be born. We shared a short residency, and I was very quiet, but, spitting and scowling, she finally picked each kitten up by the scruff of the neck and took them mewling to some other haven where I could not disturb them.

By the time Mr Beer died the farm was seriously rundown or had been let to run down. I'm not sure, but I think he was an old man living on his own and his children had moved either to the South Island or maybe to Australia or South Africa. Everywhere, in the sagging fences, dilapidated farm buildings, shearing shed with outdated press and steam-driven shearing machinery, unkempt sheep and cattleyards, were the classical signs not of the rural dream but the rural nightmare; of a man who had held on through the Depression and then the war. Indeed, I can never read the stories of Frank Sargeson or Fiona Kidman's classic collection, *The Trouble With Fire*, without thinking of Mr Beer. He had tried to keep his head above water but, by the time he died, he was beginning to sink beneath mounting debts. And then, of course, the farm's isolation also told heavily against its financial prospects.

When our family arrived, the house had been taken over by bees. They had created a huge hive in the roof space: how long it had been developing there, Lord only knows. Dad tried to get rid of the bees by poking smoking embers into the cavity but almost burned the house down and so, for a time, we learned to live with them; they dropped through gaps in the ceiling and crawled into our bedding. Then Dad recruited Daddy Waugh, with his beekeeping knowledge, and he came in a protective suit to get rid of them. I don't know what he did, but the bees came swarming after him as he fled for the trees. They ended up building a new hive near our stream.

My father was forty-two, strong and healthy, just the type of man you would think could turn a farm around. He also had his brother, Puku, to help him and he enlisted Bulla, the itinerant worker, as an extra farmhand. And, of course, he had a growing son.

I'm not sure why, but it seems to me, looking back, that life became harder. I think there must come a time when parents look at children and say, 'Our son is becoming a man, time to teach him discipline, about pulling his weight in a man's world.'

My father began to depend on me to do the simple chores like getting up at 5.30 a.m. to light the kitchen range for breakfast in the mornings. He showed me how to milk our two cows (I alternated with my cousins) — just the once, no 'Will you show me again?' — and then left me to it. He gave me the task of chopping the wood and, as usual, I had the responsibility of getting my sisters to school. In the afternoons, on return from Te Karaka, I was to light the kitchen range, chop up the meat for tea while my sisters set the table, go down to help Dad and Uncle at the shed, and then milk the cows again before it was dark. While I did this, Dad and Uncle and Bulla would concentrate on bringing the farm from the brink of collapse into production.

During the weekends, those chores were absorbed into a longer working day. My sisters and I were full on, joining Mum and Dad in scrubcutting or fencing or helping to shift the sheep from the farmland on the other side of the river to the shed, and back again.

There was no way to fail at this, but, in the beginning, I did not take to farming as to the manner born. Nor did Dad make things easier for me by saying things like, 'When I was your age I was already shearing, I was already skinning sheep, I was cutting scrub.' Sometimes he got so exasperated with me that he would lose his patience, and Bulla would intervene: 'I'll show the young fulla.'

For instance, Bulla could see that Dad didn't understand that I was left-handed. When Dad tried to teach me how to shear a sheep I had to do it with my right hand, and I was clumsy. In fact, most of Dad's instructions were for right-handed boys and I would stand on the wrong (left) side of him. And a right-handed man handles the skinning of a sheep differently from a left-handed boy. Sometimes, when some of my cousins were around, Dad would point out how fluidly and easily they were doing any work and say, 'See? Your cousins can do it easy. Why can't you?'

The best building on the farm was the big owner's house on a slope close to the road. The roof and weatherboards were rusty and rotted and badly in need of paint; the wind whistled through the rot, and the rain came through the rust during a downpour. However, you could imagine what the house must have looked like in its heyday with its high ceilings, four bedrooms, huge sitting room and large farm kitchen. My sisters slept in the front bedroom, I slept in the smaller one in the middle and Mum and Dad along the hallway in the third bedroom. The fourth bedroom was for baby Derek.

In the sitting room was a very big fireplace, and on the wall an antiquated telephone; we were on a party line that we shared with other farmers in the district and connected via telephone exchange operator in nearby Te Karaka. When the piano came up to the farm, that was put into the sitting room too, along with a sofa and armchairs. In winter the uninsulated house was freezing, so during that season Mum and Dad shifted their big bed into the sitting room and Mum would sometimes bring in a chicken coop to ensure that her hens and their newly hatched chicks would be warm.

From the very beginning the farm was without electricity. For lighting at night, we had tilley lamps in the kitchen and sitting room, and kerosene lamps for the bedrooms. Kerosene was rationed out very carefully, and my sisters were given lamps with only enough fuel in them to last, perhaps, around an hour after total darkness.

In a moment of enthusiasm, Dad tried out an electric generator and in his usual DIY way wired some of the rooms with electric light bulbs. Although we gave a loud hurrah when the generator sputtered into life, we didn't much like the loud racket that went on until bedtime. Not only that, but the harsh glare *invaded* the sitting room and kitchen, showing up every corner, broken plaster, rain-spattered wallpaper and cobweb. Much better to sit as a family by the light of the wood fire or the lamps.

Of course, without radios or refrigerator or anything to be set ticking or humming or vibrating, the whole house was totally silent. The only noises came from the morepork hooting in the trees or the weka calling through the night, or the victorious squeal of a stoat as it pounced on its prey. The noises reminded us that while we were going to sleep the natural world was coming to wakefulness.

And the farmhouse came with *grounds*. Outside there was still a lovely grapevine; when the grapes were purple-sweet, the bees soared all over the place in drunken delight. There was also an orchard of apple, pear, quince, loquat and fig trees and, fringing the lawn tennis court, citrus. However, sheep and cattle had trampled the grass surface, and one of the first tasks to bring the court back to life was to pull a heavy roller back and forth to tamp the surface down.

Behind the farmhouse was an uneven brick courtyard with a woodshed, the washhouse and Dad's toolshed. Mum washed the clothes by hand in the copper and, until Dad built a bathroom on the back verandah, we bathed ourselves in the washhouse, too. An overgrown path took you to the cowbail — on the slope were Queenie and Bess, the two most disobedient cows known to man. At the bottom of the slope was a huge spreading walnut tree and a wire-netting enclosure which Mr Beer must have used for his hens and chickens; Mum renovated it and, because she loved Muscovy ducks, we soon had a large covey of them quacking every morning and afternoon to be fed, as well as pullet chickens.

A long lane with two series of gates led to the shearing shed, which was the worst building on the farm. Dad and Uncle Puku had planned from the outset to pull it down, replace it, and ready it for electricity, which was still some years away from reaching us. Close to the shearing shed was the paddock where Dad kept a small number of farm horses and his useless sheepdogs. Among the horses were two called Bluey, an ex-thoroughbred whose real name was Blue Mist, and Stupid; the latter named because he had a habit of turning his head and biting you if he was cross. My father and Uncle Puku and my cousins never liked riding Stupid. Consequently I had him to myself and cured him of his biting habit by letting him know, in no uncertain terms, that if he bit me he got no crabapple treat. We became good companions, and one of my favourite pastimes was to saddle him and ride him to a place where nobody could find us.

Across a small dip was a smaller farmhouse, where perhaps a farm manager had resided. That became the house where Uncle Puku and his family lived when they joined us. I never questioned that the house was smaller than ours, even though Uncle Puku had the bigger family — my cousins Elizabeth, Ivan, Mīni, Kiki, Tom, Rangi, Kathleen, Charlie and Yo. In later years my cousin Charlie brought this up with me, clearly it had bruised his childhood years. Behind his anger smouldered a larger fire, which was the assumption that our two fathers had gone into the farm as equal partners.

Everywhere were possums, snarling and fighting, *rack a cack cack*.

AS I HAVE mentioned, Dad purchased the farm in order to have access to the Māori leasehold, where he planned to run cattle and sheep for the wool and meat market. We were on one side of the Waihuka River and the leasehold was on the other, with a steep valley between and a rickety swingbridge across the river.

One of my early memories of the farm is of a grader widening a path for the stock, and an attempt to dynamite the riverbed so that the stock could be swum across rather than use the time-consuming swingbridge for the task. When a draught horse, carrying small bales of wool, fell and rolled off the track, Dad realised he needed the causeway between the farm and the leasehold, to enable him to efficiently herd newly bought stock onto the good pasture. Once they were fattened, he would round them up and drive them back across the river to waiting trucks that would take them to market. As well, we were constantly moving sheep back and forth to be shorn, dosed and dipped.

We called the leasehold land 'The Other Side'. It took at least an hour to go by horse to the leasehold, and often two or three hours to return, if we had stock to bring back. Whenever the lambing season came, Dad and Uncle Puku would stay *on the other side*: otherwise we might lose too many newborns if their mothers needed help birthing them. Sometimes when I came home after school Mum would have left a message: 'Look after your sisters and give them their kai. Have gone to help Dad on the other side.'

And always, the sky over on the leasehold was wreathed with smoke because, as well as helping Dad, Mum was always burning scrub to increase the land marked out for grazing.

I think I developed a solitary nature on the farm. I became perfectly happy with my own company. Sometimes, after school, if Mum was home, I would make myself a sandwich and take a hook and a bottle of cordial, saddle Stupid and ride across the river. There I would hitch the horse to a tree, wrapping the reins tightly, because one time he got loose and I had to walk the whole way back.

I liked to work on the scrub that Mum had begun cutting down, slashing away with the hook. As I hacked away, and with the clouds scudding across the sky, my thoughts would lead me to wonder: 'If I kill myself, will Mum and Dad miss me?'

I didn't know then about what had happened to my grandmother Flowers, and my mother had not yet told me about her time on Whiro's farm, otherwise I would have cynically concluded, 'Why should I dodge the bullet?'

There were a few times when, in a fury, I would mount Stupid and dig my heels in and ride hell for leather across the hills. I didn't care that I endangered his life or mine. Once, when I returned to the farm, Dad asked me, 'What have you done to your horse?'

I thought, Great, my father is more concerned about Stupid than he is about me.

And there were always times when a deep loneliness would invade my soul and I would think of mine own Sycorax, Teria.

This is how I expressed that sadness:

The clouds swirled across the sky, casting strange patterns like fleeting kōwhaiwhai designs over the earth. My heart was thundering with longing for Teria. I wanted her to be there with me again, taking my hand and filling my life with splendour.

'Where is the mana?' I asked. 'Where is the tapu? Grandmother, you said you would live forever.'

Trembling with sorrow, I sank to my knees. The clouds were swirling. It was so difficult to think of life without her.

And suddenly, the clouds *changed*. I was walking on a long ago day with Teria. We were looking across the greenstone land. The kōwhaiwhai in the sky swirled a pattern of calm, such calm.

'Kia kaha,' Teria whispered. 'Kia manawanui.'

Her voice struck the reverberating drum of the land. Her face, veiled, was mysterious. Her beauty shone out of her with a gleaming light that you could almost touch and feel. It vibrated and electrified the air.

'Haven't you understood anything?' Teria asked. 'The mana and the tapu are not things that wax and wane at birth and death and birth again. They are passed from generation to generation through whakapapa, and I have already passed them to you. Open your eyes, child. People may try to take the mana from you, but that I will never allow them to do.'

That was when it happened, and I felt it happen. One moment I was looking at the hills and bush and then I blinked and looked again and the world had undergone a transformation. I saw into the essence of things. I saw the gleaming sap of the trees and I saw the blood coursing through my veins, and both were one and the same. I saw the geological formations of the earth, and the interlocking structures were one and the same with the gleaming cellular composition of my body. The movement of the light and wind and cloud were the same as my own life forces. The heartbeat of the Earth was no different from the rhythm of my own beating heart.

Then I looked up into the heavens and saw worlds being created beyond this Earth, and the creation of new suns and nebulae were the same as the worlds in my blood. I was in the universe and the universe was in me.

Suddenly, I felt myself being lifted into the universe and I began to be afraid and wanted to cry out. I was spiralling back through the many changes of day, into Te Pō and the many changes of night. The light began to diminish, ever diminish, until all was utter and complete blackness. So black it was that I felt as if I had no form or shape at all. The blackness was me and I was the blackness. With the blackness came ice, cold and the sense of dread, and I knew that I had reached Te Kore, The Void. The Nothingness.

'Kia kaha, kia manawanui,' Teria said again. She was a voice a million aeons away.

I don't know how long I was in The Void. I thought I was going to die. Perhaps I did die because I lost all sense of existing. I could not cry because I had no tears to weep. I could not reach out because I had no form.

Voices began chanting in the dark. Where were they coming from? At first I feared them and then I realised that they were only the old people across the hills and that they were at their prayers. The voices reached out to me, a karakia creating a cocoon of sound, and I felt that I was being lifted out of The Void. From out of Te Kore I came, journeying back through the changing of the night.

The chanting grew stronger and louder. And suddenly, I saw the dawn.

I heard a karanga and I saw that it was Teria. She was calling me to return. From one generation of the tribes of man to the next I returned, generation upon generation. The light grew brighter and brighter as I spiralled through the many changes of day.

And then Teria spoke to me again.

The clouds were swirling in the sky, casting strange patterns across the hills.

'E mokopuna, listen,' Teria said. Her voice was not unkind. 'The mana and the tapu remain. They are not something that can be seen with the eye but with the heart, soul and intellect.'

The clouds ever, ever swirling.

Chapter Forty-two

Te Karaka District High

1.

MĀUI WAS NOT a god and nor was he human. He was a demi-god, less than a god but more than a man. Such beings occupied a special place in the evolution of humankind and, in Māui's case, there was no doubt that his godly qualities were required to continue the great work of making a world for us to live in. Who else but Māui could ever have tamed the sun?

He must have achieved maturity when he led his troublesome brothers in this daring undertaking. In those days, Tamanuiterā, or Rā as the sun was sometimes called, did not take as long to move across the space between night and day as he does in our modern times. His traverse was so swift that the tribes of Māui's homeland barely had time to tend the gardens and gather food than Rā was already setting.

'Why should we be slaves to the Rā?' Māui asked.

He resolved to capture Rā and cause him to move more slowly. But he needed his brothers and the iwi to help him. This is what they did — under Māui's instruction they made flax ropes, it took five days, and Māui uttered a sacred karakia when the work was completed: 'Taura nui, taura roa, taura kaha, taura here i a Tamanuiterā, whakamaua kia mau kia uta.'

His karakia was designed to make the ropes strong and resistant to the flames of the sun.

Māui began the venture by hoisting the ropes. Once that was done he led his brothers east to where the sun rose every morning. They took calabashes of water with them, and hid under trees and bushes during the day so that Rā would not know they were coming.

On the twelfth night they arrived at the huge red-hot pit from which the sun mounted the sky. Inside, Rā was sleeping. The brothers were terrified because they felt they would surely perish when he awoke. However, Māui pacified his siblings and gave instructions to build a wall around the pit that would shelter them. He spread the flax ropes into a noose. He splashed himself and his brothers with the water, both as blessing and as protection.

Hurrah, just in time, he finished before dawn. Rā began to rise from the pit. His head went through the noose and then his shoulders. 'Pull on the ropes!' Māui cried.

There's an evocative black and white wood engraving, drawn by E. Mervyn Taylor in 1949, which expressively depicts the battle Māui had with Rā. Māui stands, weapon upraised, silhouetted in the brilliant rays of the sun. For me, the drawing became a metaphor — no matter the odds, they could sometimes be triumphed over.

Fighting off the intense heat, Māui battled the sun. The weapon he raised was a magic jawbone given to him by the great god Rangi. The sky father was more powerful than Rā, and therefore the jawbone could overpower him.

Māui soon had Rā pleading for mercy.

'From now on,' Māui said, 'you will travel slowly across the sky and never again will the length of the day be dictated by you.'

So did Māui enable the daily tasks of humankind.

I HAD TO have a uniform before I began school at Te Karaka District High. Grey shirt, black shorts, knee-high black socks, black shoes and a cap — misery.

On my first day, after I had enrolled my sisters in Te Karaka Primary, I sauntered over to join the high-school students where they were assembling on the basketball quadrangle. The students were a mix of young girls and boys, and as soon as I saw the boys my first thought was, 'Witi, you're a goner.'

They were mostly Māori, and they looked like every tekoteko I had ever seen in every meeting house come to life — among them were Crete Hāmi, Rāwhiti Brown, Star Rūtene, Henry Ruru and Mac Peneha. Even my sister Kararaina commented, 'Oh, the classroom is dark', but what she really meant was that there were not enough Pākehā to shine a light.

Years of conditioning as farmers' sons had given the boys the physiques of mature men; some of them were built like brick shithouses. I saw a couple of guys who looked as though they wouldn't eat me, Barney Tautau and Willie Wilson, stood beside them, nodded, 'Hey.'

They appraised me, giving me the stare, and then they nodded back, 'Hey.'

I couldn't help my astonishment. 'It can't be this easy,' I thought.

However, as Jack Allen, first principal, cast a horrified look upon the student body for the new year and shouted at us, 'Pay attention to your teachers and keep your socks up at all times', I realised I had natural protective colouring: I was Māori like them and, actually, they were more interested in bullying the white boys like Hans Schmidt, who was mercilessly called The Hun (I regret this even today). Some of those Pākehā boys, though, like the Wright and Thompson brothers and Roy Orlovsky, could fight back.

There was a larger foe, the teachers, not one of them a hori; the only brown man in sight was the groundsman, Uncle Kume Kīngi. Yup, my fellow Māori students were more concerned with our unity as a Band of Māori Brothers against *them* (being the teachers). Especially Jack Allen.

So my fear of bullying? Didn't happen. Even so, it took me a while to get over the feeling that I had crash-landed on another planet. Some of the girls were pretty, like Venus Robin, Lena Kīngi, Blanche Hāmi and cute Carol Lamont, but I wasn't about to risk approaching any of them yet as they might already be taken — and the boys, well, they were like a haka team and I could get stomped on. Indeed, I thought I would have another problem when the Māori guys saw that, although I was one of them, I was heading for another paddock.

Let me explain. At intermediate, most of my friends had been Pākehā and my interests had always been academic. At Te Karaka District High, I calculated that most of my friends were definitely going to have to be Māori — you can tell I was already thinking out a survival strategy — but what would they think when they saw me standing out academically?

In those days, selection for what you would become in your life began at high school. Although Te Karaka District High was smaller than most, there was still a process that all students went through, rather as if we were sheep going down a race and being divided into three yards in preparation for shearing: 3A (for Professional), 3B (for Commercial) and 3C (for General Studies).

Ahead, in control of the gate, was Mr Allen — this Māori boy this way, that Pākehā girl that way, this Māori girl this way, that Māori boy that way.

Yes, I'm being unfair to Jack Allen. When I got to know him better I appreciated his dedication to his job, and he had a wonderful unselfconscious way of laughing. But most of the Pākehā boys (and brainy Pākehā girls) went into 3A; all remaining girls went into 3B where they could be taught commercial typing and shorthand by Mrs Bradley, just in case they didn't get married and became spinsters. Woe betide if you were a boy, Māori or Pākehā, and got mistakenly drafted into 3B. And 3C was for those below the educational Plimsoll line — the boys did horticulture and the girls dressmaking and home economics.

What happened to me? I was the black sheep who, as I approached the gate, caused Mr Allen a moment of indecision, 'Baa baa, black sheep, so what kind of wool do you have?' He must have seen from my intermediate school reports that I had promise. A moment of indecision occurred before he made a dramatic gesture and opened the gate and there I was, skipping and gambolling with those white-woolled sheep.

To be frank, I couldn't have been happier, but, for the sake of survival, I put on a mournful face and assumed a protective colouration. 'I'm in 3A,' I told my new Māori mates.

Wonder of wonders, Barney Tautau was also selected for genetic engineering and drafted to 3A. 'Me, too,' he said.

His Māori mates gave him the stare, 'Hey.' And they included me in their sympathy, phew.

I owe Barney my *life*. 3A really only had three teachers: Jack Allen who took us for maths, John Tarrant for general science and Bernie Graham who took us for everything else (primarily geography and English). And then there was Mrs Bradley who took us for library period.

From memory, there were only seven of us in 3A, so we were pretty exposed to clips over the head and being shouted at, 'Are you stupid, boy?' Although I was the stupid one of us two Māori boys in 3A, Barney copped most of Mr Allen's wrath. At the same time, Barney was also a local and well liked, and, when I first arrived, and at lunchtimes, he would go to join the wrong crowd rather than the white crowd. I tagged along with him. I knew I was 'in' when a group of us Māori boys were kicking the football around during lunchtime and I was with them, and the ball went sailing through Mr Allen's window. He lined us all up and asked, 'Which one of you boys was responsible?' I think he was surprised that I was among the likely suspects. None of us spoke up and he told us to bend over his desk and gave us six of the best across our sorry arses. They were the most fortunate straps I had ever received.

'Hey,' my band of brothers said to each other afterwards.

3.

I NEED TO qualify my days at Te Karaka District High. Reconsidering them, I see that I did not make much investment in myself. How could I? Hamie Brown's school bus arrived at 8.30 a.m., right before the beginning of school; my sisters and cousins and I had to be on the school bus at 2.50 p.m. before school was out as there was an Education Department ruling that all children under the control of the school system should be back with their families by 4 p.m.

The school didn't give me the opportunity to shine in the way that I had at Gisborne Intermediate — there was no hockey team, for instance. And although the school had students who had acquitted themselves well academically, like Alan Ward who later became one of New Zealand's foremost historians, and Haare Williams, the Māori broadcaster, its offerings didn't advantage me at all. Because the roll at Te Karaka District High was small, the school provided only a minimal four courses in the A stream: mathematics, general science, geography and English. That was all a student needed to sit for School Certificate in the Fifth Form year. And although I played the classical piano, would I have let that little achievement be known? In that company, you would have to be kidding.

Nor did my sisters, brother and I become much involved in weekend activities of the school — no Boys' Brigade, no Brownies, no stamp club. This meant that the friends I made at Te Karaka District High were those I was able to fraternise with only during school hours. Most of my mates were still those in Gisborne, where Mum and Dad continued to take us for sports on Saturdays and church on Sundays. Not to mention all my cousins on papakāinga land at Waituhi.

There was, however, one school trip in which I surpassed myself — yeah, right.

Te Karaka District High arranged, under the guise of vocational guidance, a visit to Gisborne factories, businesses and government offices. You didn't have a choice of which venue you would go to, that was up to the teachers, but most of my Māori friends hoped they'd be picked for D.J. Barry's, because you would be given a free bottle of fizzy drink when you left. The place that nobody wanted to be selected for was the Gisborne courthouse.

You guessed it. When I consulted the list I saw my name down for the courthouse. I wrote a fictionalised version of the occasion, which is pretty much the way it happened:

From the moment I boarded the school bus I was kidded mercilessly.

'Why tempt fate?' Willie Wilson asked.

'And I'm the only Māori with the group going there,' I groaned.

Crete Hāmi winked. 'Shit happens.'

Mr Allen was a stickler for being on time. We dropped the other classes off on the way to the courthouse, the bus getting whiter and whiter, and at five to ten we were pulling up outside. There, Mrs Bradley gave us our orders: 'Should you be addressed by the judge, you must refer to him as Your Honour,' she said. 'This is the title by which he is known. Everyone else may be addressed as either sir or madam. Our guide while we are at the courthouse is Clerk Simpson and he may be addressed as sir.' On she went, blah blah blah yackety yack.

She paused and then gave me the stare. 'No Māori is to be spoken.'

Jeez, can't a guy even breathe?

'I am very pleased to welcome you,' Clerk Simpson said as we stepped off the bus. 'Court is in session right now, but there is so much else to see. I think we'll start in the chambers, shall we?'

We followed him dutifully around the side of the building. Two policemen came out with a young man handcuffed between them. He was about nineteen, and Māori. Our eyes connected. I knew him immediately. He had gone around with one of my girl cousins.

'Oh dear,' Clerk Simpson said. 'I'm sorry about that, girls and boys.'

I watched as the handcuffed boy was pushed across the front lawn. I heard Mrs Bradley clucking away when Clerk Simpson told her, 'The boy has just been sentenced to jail for assault. He swore at his employer.'

As the police van sped away, the young man's mother came running from the courthouse screaming his name, 'Mihaere! Mihaere!'

The chambers were cool and comfortable, gentlemanly and tastefully decorated. Photographs, diplomas and plaques adorned the walls. The judge came away from the courtroom to greet us.

'Judge Forbes,' Mrs Bradley explained to us, 'has a short break before the court reconvenes. We are very lucky to have him say hello to us. Please thank him for taking the time.'

Thank you Judge Forbes Judge Forbes Forbes orbes orbes es.

His eyes twinkled. 'Well, ladies and gentlemen,' he said, 'thank you for coming to see me on the *right* side of the bench.'

Ho ho ho, what a funny fellow.

Judge Forbes proceeded to tell us how important he was, why justice was important and why the judicial system in New Zealand was the best in the world. 'Does anybody know why?' he asked.

'Because it is based on the Westminster system,' said Andrew Clark. 'The Westminster system is used throughout the Commonwealth.'

'Very good,' Judge Forbes answered. He beamed at Mrs Bradley. 'We may have the makings of a fine lawyer here, what?'

Haw haw haw, jolly boating weather and all that.

Just to show how busy and important he was, Judge Forbes asked Clerk Simpson to show us the schedule of cases he had dealt with during the month. 'Well,' he ended, 'I must read up on the next case. I understand you will be sitting in my court?'

'Yes, Your Honour,' Mrs Bradley answered. 'But we will be quiet, won't we, boys and girls?'

Yes Mrs Bradley adley badley.

The judge swept out of the lobby. He gave Mrs Bradley the eye and she bobbed as he went past. Clerk Simpson guided us to Judge Forbes's schedule. One by one we filed past and oohed and aahed at the number of cases on his plate today and ones he had dealt with in the past:

JUDGE FORBES
Presiding Judge
9 a.m.
White v. Hakopa
10.30 a.m.
Crown v. Wharepapa
1 p.m.
Crown v. Karaitiana
2 p.m.
Williamson v. Heke

On and on and on. Page after page of cases involving being drunk and disorderly, murder, intent to obstruct justice, manslaughter, casting offensive matter in public, grievous assault, car stealing, domestic dispute, indecent behaviour, theft, petty larceny, land dispute, attempt to defraud, and so on.

Mrs Bradley looked at me reprovingly. 'Don't take up all the time. Let someone else look.'

I stepped to one side. The rest of the class had their turn. When we had become suitably impressed, Clerk Simpson said, 'Well, then, let's take our seats in the public gallery, shall we?'

We filed into Courtroom No. 1.

This was the place of judgment. Here in this large quiet room, panelled with polished wood and hushed with the weight of legal process, people were put on display, like deer antlers, their future determined with a stroke of the gavel. Over there, higher than anybody else, was where the judge sat. In front of him sat the recording clerk. To the right and left were the prosecuting lawyer and the lawyer for the defence. At right a small corridor led to the room where the defendant waited to be called to trial. In front were the seats for the public.

'Not a word,' Mrs Bradley said.

The public gallery was packed. With some surprise I realised that I knew some of the people there. Was that Nani Caroline from Anaura Bay and, if so, was one of my cousins on trial today? And was that Nani George Tūpara from Waituhi and had he come to support one of my own whānau? All of them stared straight ahead, down a narrow funnel of vision, as if afraid to see who was sitting left and right. That suited me fine. I hunched down, hoping I wouldn't be seen either. I felt as if I was on the wrong side.

The session that morning seemed to be one where the defendants had already pleaded guilty and were being processed for sentencing.

'How do you plead?'

'The defendant pleads guilty Your Honour.'

'Fined £100.' The judge lifted his gavel and *bang*. A pair of antlers on the wall.

Next case. 'How do you plead?'

'The defendant pleads guilty, Your Honour.'

Bang, the gavel again. Another pair of antlers.

'How do you plead?'

'The defendant pleads guilty, Your Honour.'

This time the judge paused and looked gravely down at the defendant. 'Your crime is a heinous one in our society, young man. Assault on another person with intention to commit grievous harm must carry with it the maximum penalty available to the law. You have brought shame on your family.'

Bang. More antlers on the wall.

At each sentencing the defendant bowed his head and nodded as if all this was to be expected. His family group did the same. They were passive in their acceptance of the Pākehā law. The Pākehā was the punisher and the Māori's place was to be punished. There was a sense of implacability about the process, as if the Pākehā was always right and the Māori were always wrong.

Why didn't we fight back? We didn't know how.

Bang bang bangbangbang an gang.

By the end of the court session my whole world had been shattered. And then Mrs Bradley made it worse by asking me to give the speech of thanks to Judge Forbes. Here in the courtroom, in public with my relatives looking on? For yes, that was Nani George Tūpara and over there was, indeed, Nani Caroline, and with her was her daughter Kuikui.

I shook my head. 'No.'

'Just do it,' Mrs Bradley commanded. The judge was still in his chair waiting.

Do it do it ititit It.

'We're waiting,' Mrs Bradley hissed.

I wasn't angry really. Just lost and bewildered. I looked at the judge in his ridiculous wig and: 'Sir,' I began, 'I mean no disrespect. All my life my parents have taught me what is right and what is wrong and I have appreciated their advice. My mother has told me to say "No" if I do not believe what is happening is right. To say "Yes" if I believe it is right, even if other people are telling me don't do it. This is why, Your Honour, while I thank you for allowing our class to visit I cannot thank you for what we have seen today.'

By this time Mrs Bradley was trying to get me to shut up.

'There is something wrong, Your Honour, with a place like this, if the majority of cases that come before you are Māori and are placed by Pākehā against Māori. I cannot thank you for being part of a court that enables this to happen, I cannot.'

Someone in the court began to sob. Was it Nani Caroline? And then I heard Nani George say 'Kia ora, boy' and Kuikui called out 'We love you, cousin'. What did they mean, they loved me? I loved *them*.

'How can I thank you for all the Māori people you have jailed or sentenced for one crime or another? All those names in your book, do you know I am related to all of them? Or that I know them? Sir, what is more, I know them as good people, not as names that you bang your hammer at or put in prison or make pay huge fines. That boy we met when we were just coming in, he was my cousin's boyfriend. And what was his crime? That he swore at his employer? You call that assault? Are you telling me that he should be sent to jail for that? If I thank you, what am I saying to all my relations in court today? My aunts, uncles and cousins? That our relations deserved it? They didn't.'

I was almost done.

'Therefore, Your Honour, I will *not* thank you.'

Of course Mrs Bradley couldn't wait to tell Mr Allen when we returned to Te Karaka.

I expected the usual punishment, but he looked at me thoughtfully and surprised her when she requested I be caned. 'No, Mrs Bradley,' he said. 'The boy is entitled to his opinion.'

This Māori boy this way, that Māori boy that way, this Māori boy this way, that Māori boy that way.

As I walked from Mr Allen's office, I could not help but think his fair opinion mitigated what I felt about the education system. Nevertheless, by privileging Pākehā education, that system overall was just as flawed as the legal system.

Bang.

More antlers on the wall.

Chapter Forty-three

Man and Wife

1.

I DON'T WANT to leave you with a romantic impression of the farm. I know now, but didn't then, that Mum and Dad took a huge financial risk in deciding to go farming. In his ledger book, Dad outlines the way it all came about:

'In 1951 my parents wanted me to go farming. We acquired the lease on the Waikohu 1B land. I raised finance from the firms & Maori Affairs etc. I had a freehold property in 11 Haig St I had bought it in 1940 300 Pounds and rented it to Arthur Muir for one pound a week. He left & I moved in 1947 free home.

'So I raised a loan on it & was only able to buy 200 ewes & I started farming my 200 sheep at Whakarau Waikohu–Matawai 1B. No home on the block. I bought a tent I lived in it on & off but operating from 11 Haig St Gisborne. The block was run down. 1300 acres 2/3 of it in scrub, fences in disrepair, Boundary fences were almost nil.

'I got grazing cattle to keep grass down. It wasn't much but it was a help. I worked hard shearing crutching fencing part time looking after my sheep. Now I think about it I was never discouraged. I just kept going — Now children were coming. By 1951 we had five children. It was a daunting task. I had two young boys with me staying. Patrick Huhu & Fred Cassidy from Northland and they were a great help to me. They were just like sons & I believe they really loved living with me. They have both passed on. Moe mai e aku hoa pumau. You were both wonderful companions & a help. Julia and I will remember you always with love.

'After 5 years my flock had increased to 500 sheep. My firm was Dalgety's. I was operating on cash somehow. Dalgety's were paying my rent & supplying me with the necessities like sheep drenches etc. My first two years I bought a crutching plant & shore my sheep on the property packed the wool down a steep gully across the Waikohu River onto my 6 wheeler truck baled it at Tangihanga Station & then to Dalgety's. I built a little hut on the property. I packed all the timber a mile and a half onto the block. I was lucky. I am a bush carpenter. So this was the story of my life. Mum used to come & camp with me & the kids do the wool work and back to Haig Street for the kids school.

'By 1956 I had worked a good relationship with Dalgety's. They said I needed cattle. I said I have no money. They bought 100 cows for me. My a/c jumped up to about 20,000 pounds at the time. No mortgages or anything between me & Dalgetys. We operated on trust alone. Nothing signed. I guess they trusted me. I sent all my wool in to them. Sheep [and] cattle sold by them.'

WE OPERATED ON trust alone.

From the beginning my father had no capital. He was living on the tick from Dalgety's. He and Uncle Puku still went shearing every summer, and our families went with them, and Dad would sink his earnings into Maera Station. I don't know what arrangement he had with his brother, but I presume that he was paying Uncle a wage as well as Bulla and anybody else who came to work for him.

Dad's main worker, however, was Mum. He used to say that she was as good as any man. Although he did not ask it of her, as soon as she had sent us off to school she would join him in fencing, cutting thistles, burning scrub, shifting sheep and cattle, and dosing them. My sisters and I became accustomed to her notes when we returned home — 'Helping Dad, start the tea' or 'On the other side, back later'.

The life was hard and we could have been defeated by it. It was also physical and repetitive, and there were times when it was routine and numbing. The determination to make a success of Maera Station forced us as a family to rely on each other. One of the surprising outcomes was that my sisters and I became closer. While we were in Gisborne I had had so many after-school pursuits that I hardly paid any attention to Kararaina, Tāwhi and Viki; now isolation threw us together. Most afternoons Mum was helping Dad, so, after returning from school, we were alone with one another. We had our own chores and did those quickly — chop and stack wood, feed the Muscovy ducks and hens, wash and peg out the clothes and bed linen. We had to be intuitive about doing other work. We took sugarbags into a pine plantation and collected cones for the fire. Sometimes we worked in Mum's vegetable garden. If Dad had killed a sheep, my sisters and I quartered it and sectioned it.

We ate alone and afterwards we would make tea for ourselves, following Mum's cooking instructions, do the dishes and take a bath and get ready for bed. As darkness fell, we would light two kerosene lamps, one for me to take to my bedroom and the other for my sisters to take to theirs, and I would do my homework. We soon learned that, instead of measuring the kerosene for two lamps, the light would last longer if we put our two measures in one lamp. That way, we could wait up for Mum and Dad and, as well, they would come home to a lighted house.

'We just have to make the best of it,' I said.

I came to depend on my sisters. Ever since those days, when the going has got rough in my life, I turn naturally to them for support or advice. The simple wisdoms that we grew up with on Maera Station are still the ones that animate our decisions.

Actually, knowing our mother was with Dad was a relief in many ways. They were a hard-working team and we knew that if anything happened to him, she would be there and would bring him home to us. She was always looking out for him.

This is how I wrote about her:

Hers has always been a handsome face. The features are sculpted of warm earth, the chiselled planes softened by wind, rain and sun. It is a face that has seen the passing of the seasons and understands that all things decay and fall of their own accord. A calm face, which understands the inevitable rhythms of life, that the sun rises and sets, that night follows day, and that winter is always followed by spring.

The face belongs to a woman who has always cleaved to her husband. Once, she looked out the window and saw the hills streaming with rain. Her husband and son were still out there somewhere and she realised they must be running behind schedule; they hadn't come back to the farm to pick up the next lot of battens and take them across the river.

She attended to Kararaina, Tāwhi and Viki, telling them to mind Derek, and then put on her gumboots and a raincoat. She went down to the shearing shed where the battens were stacked and loaded them onto the packhorse, saddled another horse and rode down the track toward the river. The rain was bucketing down. Right at the moment she reached the river, her husband and son arrived on the opposite side. Her husband saw what she intended to do, and that nothing would stop her.

'No Julia, stay there. It's too dangerous.'

She had no intention of staying anywhere. She rode down to the river.

'Go back, Julia, go back.' The river was swollen and thick with silt. It roared with the voice of thunder. Every now and then an uprooted tree would leap past on the heaving water. 'Woman, are you deaf? Go back.'

Did she listen? No. Her husband's words went in one ear and out the other.

Her horse whinnied and backed away from the rushing water. She screamed at it, 'Hup! Hup!' She put her spurs into its side, urging it into the river. She pulled the packhorse after her. Her husband blanched, wondering if she was going to make it. Her son watched with pride, knowing that she would. But it was touch and go as the horse battled against the current. She held on tightly while the water pounded down on her. The horse wanted to turn back. She pulled its head round again, towards the bank where her husband and son waited. The packhorse was faltering.

'Let the packhorse go,' her husband yelled.

Was she going to do that and waste all that energy and effort getting it across the river? What must her husband be thinking!

'Bloody stubborn woman.' He rushed down to the bank and waded out to help her. When he reached her, he lifted her from her horse. 'You shouldn't have done that,' he said.

No time to be sentimental. She was already handing him the reins to the packhorse. 'Don't stay out too late,' she said. 'Our son has homework.'

Before he could stop her, she turned her horse back into the river. After all, she had to get back to her daughter's younger son at home.

> *My mother was the earth, my father was the sky.*
> *They were Ranginui and Papatūānuku, the first parents,*
> *who clasped each other so tightly that there was no day.*
> *Their children were born into darkness.*
> *They lived among the shadows of their mother's breasts and thighs*
> *and groped in blindness among the long black strands of her hair*
> *until the time of separation and the dawning of the first day.*

And if, whenever our mother returned home, and my sisters and I had not done what she had instructed us to do, should I blame her that she lost her temper with us, sometimes beat us and threw us down the back stairs? Should I blame her that, with pressure on money and living a life of worry with our father, wondering how they were going to manage to pull the farm through, she turned on us because we were there? Or that sometimes she remembered being a six-year-old girl blowing on embers and found us, in the comparison, wanting?

No, I will not do that, I will not blame her, I will *not*.

Instead, I will join my sisters on those mornings when we stood at the foot of her and Dad's bed, waiting for them to wake up. Together, we watched our mother's circling feet, moving under the coverlet, as if she was swimming. And Tāwhi, as ever, would ask: 'If ever we were lost in Te Pō, would Mum be able to find us?'

'Yes,' I would answer, 'even if we were lost in Te Pō, the great darkness at the other side of the universe. She will take her bearings from sacred Hikurangi Mountain and begin her search. No matter how long it takes, she will come for us. She will say, "Put your arms around my neck, children." Our mother has always loved us. Always.'

 3.

THE FOLLOWING YEAR there was a terrible drought; some old-time farmers may remember it. The hills were bleached and yellow, very little feed on them for the cattle and sheep and, from memory, Dad sold his sheep early — better that than have them die on the hoof.

As the drought deepened, Dad tried to buy in as much feed as he could afford, and we watered the stock at the river. Soon we took to putting the cattle out onto the road where the roadside grass could feed them. My sisters and I would arrive home from school and take over from Mum and Dad. Whenever trucks came along we moved the stock out of the way so they could get through. Morning and night we did this, hoping for rain to break the drought.

One day, when Dad had just finished his breakfast, there was a knock on the door. The man who stood there was a Pākehā neighbour, old Henry Devine, whose farm backed onto ours. He was tall, thin, a lean face with bushy eyebrows, and he said to Mum, 'Good morning, Mrs Smiler.' Then he turned to Dad. 'Tom, I want you to take down the fence between your property and mine. I've got good grass and your cattle need it.'

Dad didn't want to take advantage of Mr Devine's offer. If the drought went on for too long, Mr Devine's own cattle might suffer for want of feed. However, the next day when he went to move his cattle, he saw that Mr Devine had taken down the fence himself and our cattle were feeding with his on his grass.

Dad never forgot what Henry Devine did for a neighbour. From that action came a covenant between our whānau and the Devine family. I wouldn't recognise them at all today, but my sisters and I want them to know that whenever they need help we will give it.

We survived the drought and other hardships. And no matter what they were, there were always moments, shafts of illumination, when our parents would show us that they had not forgotten that we were children and that children liked to play.

Once, my sisters and I arrived home from school to find Mum making ginger beer. 'What's the occasion?' I asked her. Our mother only made the fizzy drink for special times.

'We are going to have a sports day,' she said.

Dad had constructed a high jump and a small sandy area for the hop, step and jump. He had also marked out the grounds for sprints and put up the net so that we could play competition tennis on the court. All of a sudden Bulla, Uncle Puku and Aunty Betty and our cousins arrived. Not long after that, there was a shout from the road as Mr and Mrs Williams, the roadman and his wife, came with their daughter, Polly. 'Anybody home?' Mr Williams teased. The Devines and Hallidays may have come; I'm not sure.

We had so much fun as we competed against each other. Even Mum and Mrs Williams entered into the spirit of it, partnering the kids in the two-legged race and taking opposite sides in the bull rush. In the sprints from the house to the shearing shed and back, Dad and Uncle Puku ran with hobnail boots on. Dad told us, 'When Uncle and I were in training, Pera Punahāmoa would make us run like this because, according to him, when we took the boots off, our feet would feel so light we would fly on the wings of eagles.'

The day was darkening when Mum said, 'We have just time enough for a few games of tennis before we have tea and then can play cards.' Mum loved to play cards with Mr and Mrs Williams. She was really good at five hundred, pretending to have cards that she didn't.

Suddenly, as we were playing doubles tennis, a morepork came flashing from the citrus trees.

'It's after the ball!' Dad laughed. 'Quick, Kararaina, hit the ball back to me!'

Back and forth we hit that ball, with the morepork swooping after it, trying to take this new prey home to its chicks.

And then there were the evenings when there was no kerosene left in any of the lamps. Lying in bed, I would hear my father call out to me, 'Will you play the piano for your mother and me, son?'

I had become accustomed to playing music in darkness. I felt for the keys with my fingers. 'Clair de Lune' and 'La Maja y el Ruiseñor' were my parents' favourite pieces. I developed a very sure, strong and deft touch, caressing the keys first before firmly sounding them.

'Play that one about the nightingale, son,' Dad would ask. 'You know how your mother likes that one.'

On those nights when owls were about and the moon was caught within the arms of cabbage trees, I loved nothing better than to be asked to play for Mum and Dad.

AND NOW THE TIKA.

At Te Karaka District High, I eventually settled in and got down to my studies. I wished that I could have got to know my classmates better. I suspect that, if the truth were told, I probably remember more about them and some of the events of our schooldays than they do about me and my part in them. My sisters, I think, had more of a relationship with school than I did. They were able to begin in Te Karaka Primary, whereas I started in high school where relationships were already fully formed.

I absolutely loathed maths, with its complex algebra and logarithms; nor did it help my ego that Dad, remembering his own schooldays, could do my homework faster than me, but, after all, he was always good at everything. I didn't mind general science and I quite enjoyed geography. Were it not for teacher Bernie Graham, I doubt that I would have got through to the Fifth Form. He saw something in me that wasn't coming out in my schoolwork, and always took my side when I needed it.

Of all the subjects, however, I loved English. The problem was the textbook we were learning from. To invoke a parallel, another gatekeeping process was taking place — English literature this way, Māori literature that way. Except that in the case of Māori literature it was non-existent. Instead, for three years we had *Plain Sailing*.

Ugh, in that title such a lack of imagination.

I have already written that I was not born in a ponga hut and I was not raised on a marae. My world had long been compromised. From the time that I was born, there were many disconnections from the traditional umbilical of the old Māori world and new connections with the wider Pākehā world that surrounded me. Like all people born in Aotearoa New Zealand, my life has been negotiated primarily through one frame of reference, Māori or Pākehā, not both.

At school, the frame of reference was exclusively Pākehā, and *Plain Sailing* was part of that frame. Some years later, when I was asked to write for *Education* about the book that had the most effect on me as a young adult, I wrote about *Plain Sailing*:

'When I was first invited to do this article, I declined because the only book I could write about was *Plain Sailing*, the school text we studied in third, fourth and fifth form English.

'At that time, *Plain Sailing* was the only book to introduce me to the wide world of literature. I have a love-hate memory about it because, although it had extracts in it from real books written by authors like Katherine Mansfield, Mark Twain, Charles Dickens, Somerset Maugham and James Thurber, it was in many ways a rotten book because it turned literature into comprehension exercises.

'Until *Plain Sailing*, my childhood had been relatively bookless. That's hard to understand in these literate times, but I don't think my own experience was different from that of other Māori kids. For one thing, our families were too busy trying to live, to actually read about life. For another, books were the things that other people had, not us. They were Pākehā things set in a landscape other kids were accustomed to, the same landscape that was such a nightmare for us. And thirdly, for us books represented education, not enjoyment.

'At the time, the books that we did read, like *Plain Sailing*, were an inseparable part of school. They were part of the process of learning and that was a serious business. We learned spelling, reading and grammar from them. At high school, the set texts we studied had one function only: to get us through exams. We got enough of books at school and sure didn't want to read them out of school. They weren't fun.

'In our own way, though, we read: comics, magazines like the *Weekly News*, *Pix*, and of course Dad had his *Best Bets*.

'Yes, we did have library periods at school but, boy, the books recommended only reinforced our opinion that books were lousy. Most of them were at least twenty-five years old and were supposed to be children's classics. Perhaps they were, for the kids who had a tradition of reading for pleasure; but for us they were things you propped up and yawned behind. Anyway, we were never allowed to take books from the library, even if we had wanted to. They were too valuable, you see. They were not to be taken for granted.

'But at least we had *Plain Sailing* and could even take it home. It was unavoidable, compulsory, my staple literature both at school and at home. It taught me what literature was and wasn't. I read it, learned from it, sweated doing homework from it and, most important, survived it. It accompanied me through those grey years when life was not a case of *Plain Sailing* at all. In a way, I and many of my friends made up the *Plain Sailing* generation. If the book has now fallen from grace, then that perhaps represents a sufficient indictment of education of the time, explaining why many of my mates are still relatively ignorant of books. If I hadn't known Pākehā families in the same social class as ours was, I would harbour a sneaking suspicion that this was a case of institutional racism.'

Ah well, perhaps it was better to be absent from the canon than to be written into it.

This I was soon to discover when Mrs Bradley set us an assignment to read 'The Whare' during library period. Written by Douglas Stewart in 1944 and included in *New Zealand Short Stories*, edited by Dan Davin (Oxford University Press, 1953), the story is set in the Depression. As Bill Pearson describes it in *Fretful Sleepers*, 'It concerns a young man . . . who drifts into a Māori settlement near the Kaipara Harbour. He is offered permanent hospitality with an old couple who live in a flea-infested whare, who talk vaguely of him perhaps marrying a Māori girl.'

I had the same attitude to the story that the Nigerian novelist Chinua Achebe had when he read Joyce Cary's novel, *Mister Johnston*: 'It began to dawn on me that although fiction was undoubtedly fictitious, it could also be true or false.'

What was Mrs Bradley thinking? Was she trying to rub our noses in our own pathetic lives? I found the story poisonous, the setting demonic and the Māori characters demeaning. As my Māori schoolmates ducked for cover I was incensed enough to ask Mrs Bradley, 'Why have you made us read this story?' Despite her protestations that *New Zealand Short Stories* represented the best of our writers, I threw the book out the window. Quite rightly, she hauled me before Mr Allen and he gave me six of the best.

My ambition to be a writer was voiced that day. I said to myself that I was going to write a book about Māori people, not just because it had to be done but because I needed to unpoison the stories already written about Māori; and it would be taught in every school in New Zealand, whether they wanted it or not.

Witi Ihimaera, circa 1957: On the way to
developing my Ihimaera Smile, a way of
cocking my head and looking sideways at the
world and people.

Portrait of Thomas Halbert, my
English *Messieur*, circa 1840s:
'Ancestor, look at *you*, look
at *you*, look at *them*, your
children.'

Exterior porch
paintings, Rongopai, Waituhi.
Peter Coates

Rongopai meeting
house, Waituhi, circa late 1950s:
'Sacred house, Rongopai, I greet
you. As in days of old you still
hold up the sky so that all your
iwi can stand upright on the
bright strand between.'
Peter Coates

TOP Interior ceiling, Rongopai, Waituhi.
Peter Coates

BOTTOM Interior corner walls, Rongopai, Waituhi.
Peter Coates

Wī Pere Halbert, parliamentarian, circa 1912.

LEFT Te Moanaroa Pere, my grandmother Teria's father as a young man; circa 1880s.

BELOW Rīria Kaihote Wātene, Te Moanaroa's wife.

ABOVE 'She called me e
Witsh.' Teria Pere (left,
standing) with her relative
Kairangatira Te Raumiria
(Lardelli). The two young
women had just won an
indoor roller-skating
championship in Gisborne,
1910. Even at this age,
Teria appears self-aware,
and there is no doubting
her intellect. But I wish
you could have heard her
voice. It had a singular
beauty.

LEFT Teria's sister,
Mirianata Pere (right)
with her cousin Putiputi
Halbert.

Te Moanaroa Pere (left) and his older brother Hetekia Te Kani Pere with taonga of the Wi Pere family, circa 1919 or 1920.

ABOVE Teria and
Pera Punahāmoa with their
sons and daughters: Dad
is on the left of the
back row.

LEFT Winiata K. Smiler,
the first writer in the
family.

OPPOSITE TOP Teria
(centre, back row) and
Pera Punahāmoa (extreme
left) with the Waituhi
Men's Hockey Team.

BELOW Champion Haka Team at Tūrangawaewae or Te Puea
Memorial Marae in Ngāruawāhia, from left: Thomas
Smiler, Belgium Collins, Danny Smiler, Charlie Pere,
Puku Smiler and Mike Smiler. 'The gods of Olympus
. . . Their huge passions and appetites constructed a
world of such immense breadth and depth, and such moral
force, that I could never go weakling into it.'

Pera Punahāmoa Smiler (centre, holding the infant) with his tribe of 'fair and delightsome' grandchildren, 1956 or 1957. Witi Ihimaera, back row, third from left, showing the Ihimaera Smile. Puke Peawini, Witi's brother, first left.

LEFT Dad (right) with George Tūpara — champion hockey players.

BELOW Dad (right) with Mike (left), along with Raymond Gear (centre) and Witi Teka (front), winners of the Hui Tau 400 metres relay, Mormon Church, 1935–1938.

Witi Ihimaera (back row, left), Te Karaka
District High School, 1959.

THE BOY IN HIS CHRYSALIS OF
AFTERNOON LIGHT, HALFWAY
THROUGH RE-INVENTING HIMSELF.

Witi Ihimaera, aged 16.

Chapter Forty-four

Of Sex and Dreams

1.

TWO DIGRESSIONS IN my memoir now, and they both involve dreams. I know they interrupt the narrative but, as I warned you earlier, digression is a part of the method of Māori storytelling.

At least a third of our lives is spent sleeping. It stands to reason, therefore, that our dream world plays an important part of our lives. To give you an idea of the enormity of sleep, if you have a lifespan of eighty years, and slept eight hours a night, you would have spent more than twenty-six years sleeping. This may surprise you, but only two hours of sleep a night is spent dreaming. However, physical time is not the same as dream time, which can span eternity. The laws of physics don't apply in dreams.

2.

THE FIRST DIGRESSION concerns the fact that, during my thirteenth year, I came to puberty and I was plagued by erotic dreams.

When my first nocturnal emissions, as they were called in those days, began, I was distraught rather than excited. I didn't know what they were and thought that the rape, no matter that it had occurred a year ago, had damaged me in some way. I was alarmed by the uncontrollable nature of my urges and I wanted them to stop.

I couldn't ask Dad for fear that I would have to disclose the sexual attack to him. Nor could I ask any of the men from the Mormon Church as they would mention it to Dad. And I felt I couldn't ask my friends at school because, well, as far as sex was concerned, that would be like the blind leading the blind.

I turned to the most unlikely person of all, Bulla. One afternoon when I was helping him strain a fence, I asked him straight out: 'Some white stuff is coming out of my cock.'

Well, it was more a statement than a question, and Bulla just about dropped the wire strainer in shock. For one thing, he wasn't accustomed to my asking him anything and, for another, what a question. Not only that, but had I said the word *cock*? What other word could I have used! Bulla would never have understood phallus or penis.

He staggered away from the fence, sat down on a mound of grass and started to roll himself a cigarette; he seemed to take years. He wet the paper with his spit, spread tobacco with shaky fingers, sealed the cigarette and lit it. And then, finally, he answered, 'Not to worry, boy. You're making spunk for babies.'

I thought about that for a moment, so it had nothing to do with the other *thing*. Instead, hey, my brain began to flip with excitement. 'Is that why my cock is getting bigger?'

Poor Bulla wriggled on my hook. I didn't have the heart to tell him that, regardless of my anxieties, I had sneaked the tape measure out of his tool box and had been using it to measure circumference and length. All he did was take a draw, expel smoke, offer a croak and a cough, and nod his head.

I shook his hand, man to man. 'Thank you,' I said, 'I really appreciate it.'

Well, that was a relief. I wasn't going to be a eunuch then.

I didn't dare ask him a third question: Why was I dreaming as much about boys as I was about girls? No doubt that one would work itself out. There were other questions too but, well, I understood Bulla could take me far but not as far as I wanted to go, and that I should try to obtain some appropriate sex information.

Risking Mrs Bradley's eagle eye, I was able to consult a medical compendium during library period. I wasn't sex-mad but, rather, inquisitive. When I finally did have sex, I wanted to be good at it. The alarming diagrams did nothing for me and the manual was amazingly coy. I can still remember one phrase: 'When erect, the phallus of all men approximates the median.'

I would have to find out about sex by practical experience.

3.

THE SECOND DIGRESSION is larger and involves a world not often talked about when writing a life. I can't see how I can avoid it in this synoptic view of New Zealand boyhood.

It has to do with another kind of dream and the Māori world of moemoeā. And there's no doubt that this kind of dream played an important part in my writing of the Māori Imaginary. Let me ask a question: Do you think Māori dream different dreams to Pākehā?

While I have no neuroscientific proof of it, my view is that we do. We have the same range of dreams as all people have — dreams that relate to our families, dreams of desire and sexual arousal, and nightmares that resolve the stress and tension of our lives — but they are coloured by different cultural memories, myths and histories.

My dreams come from a different realm, a different inventory. I suspect that I drew the energy for them from my mother's powerful attachment to Ngā Iwi o te Ao Kōhatu, Mount Hikurangi and Te Rāwheoro, the great

House of Learning. I know some tohunga would disagree with me about the last-named source. All I needed was the bravery or foolishness to step over the paepae, the Māori threshold, to access it. I know now that I took a grave risk in doing this and that there are others who could go deeper and wider into that dimension because of the strength of their knowledge of tikanga, practice, of karakia, prayer, and of genealogy, whakapapa. As seers and revelators, this is their realm, not mine.

I can quite understand why, when depicting the dream state, artists and photographers choose to render it as a huge, mesmerising, swelling sea within which we can breathe and where we move in slow motion. After all, in sleep and dreams we naturally surrender to a state of suspension and suspended animation, and our core body temperature drops to the lowest of our daytime and evening lives.

But ours is not the same sea. The papakāinga, the world of it, is constructed from a different ihi, wehi and mana, a different energy, dread and strength. It has a different tapu.

One evening I fell asleep. A dawn blossomed around me, like the dawn that I had seen when I was a boy. I heard chanting in the dark: 'Don't be afraid son, it is only the old people and they are at their prayers.'

I found myself in a limbic zone of myth and surreality.

You must remember that at the time I was undergoing tremendous emotional pain and stress. This might explain why my first encounter with moemoeā was so interlaced with the symbols and signs of the Māori darker myths; a maelstrom of activity burst around me, terrorising and alarming, and I was at the centre of it.

I later re-enacted that first dream in a fictional narrative. I have shorn the narrative of its fictional underpinnings so that it is closer to the original:

I opened my eyes. I was standing at the edge of a tall cliff. Far below, my very own Sea of Dreams was waiting.

I was falling.

The sky was blood red. The wall of the cliff was sheer, black. A thousand miles below, the sea was swirling, opalescent, luminous and as deep as a constellation.

An updraught caught me and I was tumbling over and over. Disoriented, I saw the surface of the sea rushing up at me. Just in time, I snapped my arms against my sides and knifed cleanly through the surface and

I was falling.

The impact took my breath away. I cried out in pain and, with fear, found that my headlong moment was taking me further into the depths. Terror overcame me. I was holding my breath. Soon, however, I ran out of air and, moaning, opened my mouth. The air belched out, but instead of drowning I found myself breathing the sea.

In. Out. In. Out. My heartbeat steadied, no longer pounding in my ears.

The sea was the colour of pounamu, of greenstone, stretching to the end of the universe, reaching higher than the highest heavens and lower than Rūaumoko's domain. I was alone. Totally alone. Terror again possessed me. I would never be able to find my way out. I was trapped forever unless . . . I set my face with determination, began to kick through that swelling sea and burst through the membrane of it and

I was falling.

As I was tumbling down the sheer cliff I saw birds coming out of a blood-red sun, thousands of birds. When they came closer I saw that they were half-men, half-avian, winged ponaturi with clawed hands and wings jagged like a bat's. The ponaturi plummeted after me.

Other people were tumbling in the infinite air. We were a tangled mass of falling men and women, soundlessly screaming. I watched, afraid, as ponaturi caught my companions by their ankles and soared with them to some eyrie to feed their young. Three ponaturi, wings folded, pursued me, and with mounting terror I felt their ravenous beaks flailing at my feet. One of them nipped my left ankle and I screamed.

I must have battled with the ponaturi for 3000 years, 1000 years for each level of descent until I wrested myself free and

I was falling.

With a sob of relief, I found myself in a universe of utter blackness, studded with tekoteko. They had pāua eyes staring out of the dark. I fell another 1000 years and the mass of falling men and women fell with me. The ponaturi still pursued us.

Below, something began to sparkle.

It was a huge brine pit. Perhaps there I could escape the ponaturi. However, as I fell towards the surface of the pit I could see a mass of men and women beneath it, looking up with fearful eyes. When they could no longer hold their breaths, they broke through the surface. There, other ponaturi were hovering, picking them up by their throats. A sharp shake to snap their necks and they were carried limp upward into the blood-red sun. The sea was blood red with the sun, blood red with blood.

I crashed through the surface of the brine pit, bulleting among the men and women below and

I was falling.

The water was thick with men, women and children, holding their breaths, looking up through the surface at the hovering, glittering ponaturi.

In. Out. In. Out. The blood was pounding in my ears, splitting my skull.

There was no way to go except to descend. I propelled myself downwards, blindly swimming this way and that, trying to find an escape. I found myself in a maze of caverns and channels. This way? No, it was a cul-de-sac. That way? Another blind alley.

Rising through the maze came schools of mermen ponaturi. Certain death was above, death was also below. The eyes of the ponaturi were red and their teeth were razor sharp, and I closed my eyes and something nipped my ankles and I screamed and

I was falling.

All around me ponaturi were chittering and chattering, and landing on ledges in the walls. Pulling the carcasses of their victims in. The air was filled with thick clouds of ponaturi, wings clacking, wheeling in the blood-red sky and one of them was above me, looking down, ready to rend me open and eat my heart. I began to fight the ponaturi, no, no no, and ...

4.

THE MOST FEARFUL anxiety was not actually the dream itself but whether I would get out of it. My heart was hammering and the sheets were sweat-soaked. My mother heard me groaning and grinding my teeth, speaking in tongues. She thought I had relapsed into the nightmares I had when Teria died and came to shake me awake: 'Son, wake up, come back.'

Since that first dream I have been able to manage my moemoeā better. I will not allow them to take me to the dread heart of that swirling sea. I know my limits; I have never reached the point of no return.

On the other hand, I sometimes delight in my dreams, for they are not always nightmares. Sometimes my companions and I swim through beautiful undersea gardens. When that happens, I am the one in the meeting house who, late at night, you can hear laughing.

Rubin Naiman speaks for me when he writes: 'Dreaming is a natural neurological art. The dream gathers dark, splintered, disparate emotions and experiences. It collects unresolved pain, confusion, grief and fear. And it rearranges all this bad stuff into a good form. It creates a collage. It produces pithy vignettes, writes good short stories or, on occasion, great epic tales. It creatively transforms our dark stuff into something cohesive, presentable and imaginative, even if mysterious. Even if we cannot discern the dream's exact meaning, we are almost always left with a clear intuitive sense that the dream is indeed meaningful.'

These days I never think of waking and dreaming in the usual binary fashion — conscious and unconscious, real and unreal, voluntary and involuntary and so on. I like to think of the two states as worlds that balance each other. One is an ordinary world and the other, by virtue of its amazing dimensionality, is the extraordinary world.

I cannot imagine a life where I am deprived of one or the other.

Chapter Forty-five

The Third Telling

1.

I WAS FOURTEEN when, one day, I came home from Te Karaka District High, did my chores and walked down to the shearing shed. I saw Dad and Uncle Puku across the sunlight and waved to them.

I asked Dad, 'Where's Mum?'

He said, 'Can you see the fire?' He pointed to the other side of the river where I saw smoke curling into the sky. 'She's over there, burning scrub. You'd better go and tell her it's time to come home. She'll listen to you.'

I thought he was referring to the fact that our mother never arrived home until a job was finished. Sometimes that meant she was still working when it was very dark.

I saddled my horse and went across the river. As I was riding away I heard Uncle Puku say, 'He had to find out, sooner or later.'

It took me an hour to reach Mum and, as I approached, I could tell that she was breaking apart. She was cutting the scrub in a savage way and building the fire higher and higher. I jumped from the horse and pulled some of the branches from the flames. 'What are you doing? The fire could spread, Mum.'

She didn't seem to care whether it did or not. 'Your father never told me,' she said. 'When we were married, I didn't know.'

Know? Didn't know *what*?

The next morning, the day was sunny, the rays slanting through the trees. Uncle Puku, Aunty Betty and my cousins left Maera Station early to go into Gisborne, honking the horn and waving. Getting out of the way. Letting Tom get on with it.

Dad went down to the shearing shed and I went to help him. I knew something was happening but, in all that time, Dad never said anything to me. Meanwhile, Mum and my sisters started to bake and tidy up, as if we were expecting visitors.

Around eleven Dad said, 'It's time we got back to the house.' When I arrived the table was set for lunch and there was an extra place setting.

Not long after that, my sisters and I heard a motorbike coming along the road. Sometimes, especially in the valley where the culvert was, the sound amplified and ricocheted across the hills. The motorbike sounded like a rifle, bang, bang, *bang*.

'I'll go and open the gate,' I said. I arrived just in time to see a young man, about six years older than me, whom I recognised. 'Hello Puke,' I yelled.

His name was Puke Peawini and I grinned as I opened the gate and let him through. He wore a black leather jacket and trousers, and black glasses, and he came out of the sun like a film star. By the time I got back to the house he had dismounted and was saying hello to Mum and Dad.

'Can we have a ride?' my sisters were asking. 'Will you take us for a ride on your bike?'

'After lunch,' Mum said, and then she turned to my father. 'Well, Tom, are you going to tell Witi and his sisters now?'

'Puke is your brother,' he said.

As my sisters whooped with joy and my father took Puke into the house, I looked at my mother and asked her a question. Oh, it came with all the assumptions of a son afraid for his birthright, wanting to protect his position in his whakapapa, and I know that my mother understood how imperiled I felt: 'Am I not the eldest then?'

MY BROTHER PUKE was part of the story my father never told my mother when he married her.

It's the story of siblings who were born to different mothers. I was one of those brothers, born to my mother; Puke was my half-brother, born in Ōpōtiki on 2 April 1938 and christened Pukepuke Alfred Thomas Smiler-Peawini. His mother was a sweet woman named Emalina Tūhou. When I occasionally met her as a child, not knowing about my father's relationship with her, I called her Aunty Annie.

My father, while courting my mother, never told her about Emalina and his other son. Nor did he tell her that he was expected to marry Emalina. The reason he suggested — when Mum agreed to marry him — that they go to the Mormon Easter hui in 1943 was because he didn't want Teria and Pera to know he was courting Mum.

In one version of the event, Dad said his parents had also decided to go to the Mormon conference in Hastings, but I had always been puzzled over that: why had they not been at the wedding at the registry office?

They were never in Hastings. When Mum and Dad returned to Gisborne as a married couple, they returned alone. The story that when they arrived and Dad went to see his parents and Mum hers, to tell them that they were married, was also a fabrication. What I believe happened was that they went to the small property at 165 Crawford Road, Kaitī, to begin their married life and, while they were there, Dad received a visit from Teria and Pera.

'What's that young girl doing here?' they asked.

'She's my wife,' Dad said.

During this time of my father's confession somebody told my mother about Emalina and her son Puke.

You will know by now that I'm very good at hiding how I feel. To be frank, when I thought about it, I realised I shouldn't have been so surprised that Dad had a son before I was born; I would not have expected him to have had no sex life before he married my mother. The more I pondered it, however, the more I felt angry that Dad had not told me and my sisters before. All this time the people at Waituhi had let me wander among them and they had known? I felt humiliated.

During lunch I hid most of my feelings. I watched as Puke took my sisters for rides on his motorbike. He asked me if I wanted to ride the bike. I said no.

When he left, Mum said to him, 'Come back and see us.' Once Puke was gone, she turned to Dad. 'So, it's done then? Good.'

Sometimes my father's way of dealing with difficult situations was to walk away from them. I had some questions I wanted to ask him, my sisters did, too, but he brushed us aside and went down to the shearing shed. I wasn't about to let him off that easily and stalked after him.

He saw me coming, and when I was standing squarely in front of him I asked him, 'Why, Dad?'

Again, sometimes my father didn't answer square on. Instead he responded in an oblique way, 'You know, son, if I hadn't met and married your mother I would have met somebody else and married her.'

What could I say? All my life I had believed in the huge love between my parents. I threw him a look of disgust and walked away. That night, however, my memory kept on going back to his words, and I found myself getting angrier and angrier. The next morning, Sunday, he knew I was in a mood.

'So Dad,' I began, 'are you saying that you didn't love my mother at all? And if you hadn't married her, I wouldn't have been born? Is that what you're saying?'

On and on I went, around and around in circles and he tried to embrace me, to stop me.

'It's not that simple, Dad,' I said to him.

'You think too much,' he sighed.

I had one more question: 'Is Puke coming to stay with us?'

'I haven't decided yet,' he answered.

Later that night, I heard Dad say to Mum, 'Thank you, Julia.'

I was still awake in my bedroom when Mum came in and sat down on my bed. 'Had I known about Puke,' she said to me, 'I would never have married your father.'

No, she would not have married him, even if he was Tom Smiler. My father knew this, which was why he didn't tell her, even after they had arrived back from Hastings. Once she was told, however, it was too late for her. All her life Mum had lived according to a simple moral code of conduct. Among its precepts — you were always obedient to your parents, you were always obliged to your iwi. It was the same with marriage. The vows you made, to love, honour and obey your husband until death parted you, were to be kept, no matter what you subsequently discovered about him.

Mum believed that if somebody loved you, you were supposed to believe them, and that they would love you for the rest of their lives, which Dad in fact did; he never forgave himself for, as he would tell me, 'what I did to your mother'. Nevertheless, she had tried to leave Dad. She went to Tolaga Bay with no intention of returning to him. My Grandfather Kereama told me, 'Tom came up many times to plead with her to go back with him, but she said she wouldn't.'

What made her change her mind? She discovered she was pregnant with me.

At some point, however, I think Mum would have returned to Dad, pregnant or not. Why? She had already been fatally disarmed by love. It had rendered her defenceless. She *was* in love with him, and her view of love was somewhat implacable. She was the kind of person who could die of love.

My mother attempted to be reasonable about Puke. She encouraged Dad to maintain the relationship and to bring Puke more regularly into our lives. It never happened, and the only times I ever saw him were at iwi functions or, sometimes, at the hockey grounds.

Puke has a different story about Mum's efforts to attempt a lasting reconciliation. Just before he died, some four years ago, I asked him why he hadn't taken up Mum's invitations. I don't want you to think I was being noble about this; I had never personally made any approaches to him throughout our lives.

'That's not what I heard,' Puke answered. 'After I first met you and your sisters up at the farm, Dad told me not to come again because your mother didn't want it.'

'She did,' I answered.

Tears welled in Puke's eyes. Although we both loved our father, we realised intuitively that it was him all along who had preferred not to have Puke around, possibly out of respect and love for the woman whom he almost lost because of his indiscretion.

Neither of us bore our father any ill will for his decision.

However, there may have been another reason for Dad not encouraging Puke to visit. He may have told Puke that Mum didn't want it; he would have known that *I* didn't want it.

Of course there was more to the story of brothers born to different women. At the time I thought it was the story of two brothers. Instead, it was a story of three, but I was not to know that until I had left childhood far behind.

THIS WILL MAKE no sense to you, it still scarcely makes sense to me, but over the following weeks I continued to brood over my father's comment that if he had not married my mother, he would have married someone else. He was right — sometimes I thought too much.

One weekend, not long after Puke's visit up at the farm, Mum and Dad brought my sisters and me to stay the weekend at Haig Street. On Friday night, I went to the 5 o'clock pictures with Maarten van Dijk. After the movie, I was standing at the corner of Gladstone Road and Peel Street waiting for Dad to pick me up. He was often late — oh, sometimes on the way to Gisborne he irritated us by stopping to talk to anybody on the road, a stockman, a farmer, a shepherd — it didn't matter who it was.

Ponaturi were wheeling in a blood-red sky and I was falling from a tall cliff as I thought about Dad. My mind was whirling and it pushed me into self-pity. I wouldn't have wanted Dad to have married anybody else but my mother, but he did deserve a better son.

Right on 8 o'clock I saw Dad driving the truck on Gladstone Road and parking opposite; good, so it had petrol in it. He had come from a coaching appointment for some sport or other, probably rugby or hockey, but it could also have been indoor basketball. Dad was always good at any sport.

I was just about to cross over the street when I saw that some boys a little older than me had seen him. They yelled out, 'Hey, Tom!'

People were always doing that, calling him by his first name. As he got out of the truck they started to talk to him. He looked at me, smiled, but took the time with them.

I heard them say, 'Thanks, Tom.'

'Sorry, son,' he said as he came up to me. 'I've been teaching those boys how to shear. They wanted to check on some of the moves.'

I remember how handsome my father was. So handsome in his coat and hat. His heart was always so open anybody could have walked into him and stolen it. And those boys, they had been handsome and masculine. No matter how much I prayed, no matter how much I wrestled with my masculinity, I would never find absolution. How could I possibly have thought I could escape what had happened to me those few years earlier when I had been sexually attacked?

I often had wondered, when Dad met my mother at that dance at Poho-o-Rāwiri in 1943, whether I would have liked him or not. I thought of the tennis tournament where we won the father-and-son game — I would have done anything for my father. Oh yes, in the future, as I grew into manhood, I would manage to forgive myself and to let my father *in*. I made myself vulnerable enough to allow and to believe in his fatherhood and that he truly loved me. Eventually he would become my best friend as well as my father.

Meantime, he was a man's man, a man among men, whereas I had been unmanned. I should have fought for breath and then found the strength to fight off my relative's sexual attack, but I was a weakling. I thought to myself: Dad, you deserve better.

My father is dancing with my mother. I tap him on the shoulder and look at him. He doesn't know who I am. Just a skinny boy with a kina head and lopsided grin. But, oh, I am monstrous.

'Yes?'

I say to him: 'I'm so sorry, Dad, that I am your son.'

 4.

THERE'S MORE.

You may recall that, when mentioning a photograph of myself as a baby, I said it was one of very few that survive. This is why.

I was still falling, and within the sea ponaturi were rising after me. When our family returned from our weekend in Gisborne to the farm, and while Mum and Dad were working on the other side, I went into their room and took out the two family photograph albums.

I opened Mum's sewing kit and took out her scissors. I must have hated myself very much. I was calm and controlled as I cut myself up, the scissors slicing through my head, decapitating me, dismembering me, disembowelling me. I was halfway through the album when my mother, returning earlier than I expected, came into the room.

'What are you *doing*, son?'

Surely she, who upheld whakapapa, would not have needed to ask.

I put down the scissors and walked out.

1.

THERE WAS A photograph that survived.

It's the Te Karaka school classroom shot where I am in the back row. I look at this photo and I can't recognise myself at all. The boy with the disarming grin is supposed to be me, but he is casual, too attractive in his chrysalis of afternoon light. I do not like him. There is too much calculation in his pose. But, after all, he is halfway through re-inventing himself.

And so I was still shape-shifting and looking to become another person when, at fifteen, at the end of 1959, I sat the School Certificate examination. Once the exam was over, I joined my parents out shearing at Tangihanga Station. I did not expect to get School C, but I scraped through with the bare 200 marks required.

In those days the results were published in the newspaper, often before you obtained the official results separately in the post. Whether you liked it or not, you were scrutinised by your entire community, and the telephone would ring with people either offering you congratulations or commiserations. The first news I had that I had been successful was from Sally, one my fellow Fifth Formers, who rang me up to congratulate me.

When my mother opened the *Gisborne Herald* and looked for my name in the list, she could not find it.

'Look under "I" for Ihimaera,' I said.

'What did you want to do that for?' Dad asked, astonished.

I did it for many reasons, but the one I gave Mum and Dad was that I wanted to honour my Ringatū ancestor, Ihimaera the Honey Gatherer. At the time nobody in the entire Smiler clan used the name publicly. The School Certificate examination was an appropriate occasion to reclaim the name and, from that moment, I would always use it.

Mum and Dad were cross. 'Nobody will know it's you.'

To placate them, I added that I wanted to begin a new whakapapa for myself all the way back to the original Ihimaera, son of Hakara from whom the Arabs were descended. He had become a wanderer in the desert; I thought the imagery was appropriate. But the truth was that I had decided to give myself a new history, a new place to start from. A new name was part of my new identity and I would leave the old one behind. Maybe nobody would know it was me but, one day, they would.

I thought that Pera Punahāmoa would be as cross with me as Mum and

Dad. However, when Dad told him about it he looked at me, amazed, as if seeing me in a different light. He was bemused, and then proud and delighted.

'Ka pai koe, grandson,' he smiled. 'Good on you to take that old name of ours.'

I was glad that, for once, I had pleased him.

2.

NOT LONG AFTER I received my marks, I was at a hui at Pākōwhai, one of the marae in the Waituhi Valley. I think the occasion was the blessing of the church; a new roof had been erected.

The marae was crowded and I was talking to the priest when my cousin Sammy came to collect me. 'Uncle Puku wants you,' he said.

'Okay,' I answered. 'I'll just tell Dad.'

'No, you must come alone,' Sammy continued. As we walked through the crowd I was aware of glances being exchanged. 'This will be good,' Sammy said, 'you will enjoy it.'

I thought we would stop at the hāngi pit but we walked on past, through the mist and steam of it, to a small animal enclosure. There were only men there, Uncle Puku, Uncle Mafeking and Uncle Danny, and others from Waituhi. In the enclosure were some hogs and sows and a few piglets. There was a chopping block and I saw that a piglet had already been slaughtered by my cousin Tommy, who was a bit younger than me. Uncle Puku was slapping him on the back.

'So here he is,' Uncle Puku said, smiling, as I approached. 'We should have got you to do this a few years ago, but you were never around.'

He handed me an axe and twisted the handle in my hands so that the blunt head was facing downwards; I saw blood on it. Uncle's fingers pressed mine into a firm grip.

He pushed me forward to a chopping block. The slaughtered piglet had been replaced by another, which had been tied to the wood with its head on the block.

'Take good aim,' Uncle Puku said. 'Aim for the snout.'

I felt the blood rush from my heart. I was in the company of men and I had no option but to go along with the ceremony. I closed my eyes and swung the axe and brought it down on the piglet.

The blow glanced off the piglet's face. It squealed.

Uncle Puku laughed and looked at the other men. 'That's not the way he should do it, eh boys. Open your eyes, nephew. Make your next blow a clean one.'

The men nodded among themselves and offered me encouragement. 'You can do it.'

I swung again. This time I kept my eyes open but I had pulled back on the swing and the blow may have smashed the piglet's snout but it was not a killing blow.

Uncle Puku looked at me closely. I could see him searching for the boy who was a man. His face was firm. 'You need to put that piglet out of its misery.'

The other men waited in silence for my strength to return. Then a voice said, 'I'll do it for him, he's not like us.'

It was Puke, my half-brother, and of all the men there he was probably the most appropriate person to act on my behalf. And I knew what he meant about not being like them; after all, they had lived all their lives in Waituhi and I hadn't.

I shook my head. 'No, I'll do it.'

I raised the axe again and I doubt if there had ever been as useless a job done in killing a pig as mine. I kept on hitting it and hitting it.

Please stop squealing. Stop squealing. Stop. Please stop. The sooner you stop the sooner it will be all over.

After I had finished the job I looked at the men. They were all staring at me and then one of them broke the tension by saying, 'Man oh man, that poor little pig.'

They started to laugh, and then Uncle Puku slapped me on the back and a cousin offered me a beer. I realised the men meant to be kind but I could have raised the hammer and smashed their snouts in with it.

It was the end of my childhood.

Chapter Forty-seven

Mount Hikurangi

1.

I HAVE OFTEN pondered the magnificence of the demi-god Māui.

Having claimed his birthright and tamed the sun, he set about drawing up land from the depths of the ocean for humankind to live on. He must have had a waka of supernatural dimension, sanctified by karakia. The canoe would have been double-hulled and driven by holy spells. Incantations would have enabled the prow to cleave the waves apart, and holy songs would have set the sails spinning. He launched his waka upon the titanic sea and he took his troublesome brothers with him.

What an accomplishment he performed! His fish hook was the same grandparent's jawbone he had used to belabour the sun into submission. Having no bait, however, he gashed his nose and smeared his own blood on the jawbone as a lure. And then he began fishing.

Lo, he fished up Tonga. Lo, he fished up the Cook Islands. Lo, he fished up Hawaii. Lo, he fished up Manihiki. Lo, he fished up Mangareva. All the islands of Polynesia did Māui bring up from the bottom of the sea.

By 'fished up', can we conjecture the word 'discovered'? For isn't fishing merely a metaphor for discovery? If so, Māui must surely have been one of the greatest sea-voyaging navigators the world has ever known.

And then Māui set sail with his brothers southward, his sacred waka bounding full across the waves. When the water turned lustrous green, the colour of pounamu, he let down his jawbone hook. There was a mountain underneath the waves. As Māui's canoe sailed over it, the trailing hook was caught in a crevice of the mountain. Māui felt the line grow taut. His eyes gleamed and he laughed with joy.

He began to pull, 'Hikurangi rises!' The morning light shone full upon the mountain.

Lo, he fished up Aotearoa.

2.

AND SO HIKURANGI exerts its centrality again. No matter how wide the spiral of childhood has taken this narrative, no matter how deep, it always returns to the mountain. It brings me back to the story of a valley where there was once a young girl of six who went to look after two weavers.

In 1990 I returned to New Zealand after resigning from my position as

Counsellor Public Affairs at the New Zealand Embassy, Washington. For the previous fourteen years, I had tried to balance a diplomatic career with a writing life, but I had reached the point where I had to make a choice: either commit myself to diplomacy or to a life as a writer. The 150th anniversary of the signing of the Treaty of Waitangi marked my decision.

The following year, I was living in Auckland, but went back to the East Coast, to Tokomaru Bay, with my mother. I can't remember what the occasion was, but, when we were returning to Gisborne, Mum said to me, 'Would you mind, son? I would like to go to that valley where I lived with those two old weavers.'

So we travelled to a rendezvous with the past. The landscape was changed from the time Mum had stayed in the valley: good roads, farmland and most of the bush was gone. Throughout her life, she had clearly visited the nearby marae and other whānau places; however, I am not sure whether she had ever returned to that small patch of land itself. I didn't ask her, so I could be wrong in assuming not.

I purposely stayed in the car while Mum got out, opened the gate and walked across a paddock towards the base of the hills. I think my being with her had given her the courage to return. When I finally joined her, I put my arms around her and hugged her tight.

'This is where the whare was,' she told me. 'Over there was where the kitchen stood.'

I knew she was grieving and trying to make peace with herself. I didn't let her know that I had been told two stories of what had happened to Hauwaho and Kaingākau. In the first story, some people said that a young girl had been looking after them. They said that when she ran away the two old ladies couldn't keep the fire going or feed themselves, so were taken to live with relatives. In the second story, one of the weavers was found in front of a cold fire in the kāuta, dead. I don't know what happened to the other old lady.

'You can't blame yourself for being a six-year-old girl,' I said to Mum.

And then my mother, who never cried, began to weep, huge shuddering sobs. I couldn't stop her. Oh, she was racked with pain. At the time I thought she was crying for the child she had once been, but recently I have found something she had written in one of her whakapapa books.

'I'm sorry tūpunas,' she writes. 'I should have stayed and taken care of you.'

No matter that she had been six, she was the keeper of the fire. How was she to know that those old people would become so feeble that they wouldn't be able to blow on the embers to keep themselves warm?

Tama o Hikurahi Son of Sycorax

Chapter Forty-eight

Oseburg, Norway, June 2014

1.

FLASH FORWARD TO Oseburg, a small town on the outskirts of Oslo.

I am here to give a keynote paper at the New Zealand Studies Conference on the Pacific Ocean. This is the final day and I have taken the opportunity to visit the Viking ship museum on the peninsula. The museum is crowded with three busloads of French, Japanese and German tourists.

And I am standing here on a platform looking at the huge Viking ship from AD 800, around the same time that Māori were voyaging across the Pacific from Raiatea in French Polynesia to Aotearoa.

Discovered in 1904, the Viking craft has a psychic presence, despite the crowds. As huge as an ocean-going waka, it was originally an active warship, with a large sail and oar placements for thirty men. When unearthed from its mound, however, it was clear to the archaeologist discoverers that it had become a burial ship. The surprise was that within the wooden burial wharenui on the deck were not the skeletal remains of some Viking king but, rather, the bones of two women. Nobody knows who they were, but clearly they were of high rank, either royal or of the priesthood. One of the women was in her seventies or eighties; her smaller companion was in her fifties.

The museum's text suggests that the remains may have been those of a high-born noblewoman and a slave buried with her; or, perhaps, some priestess and her adviser. Whoever they were, they must have been highly revered or, conversely, feared; nobody knows who was the more important. Thirteen horses, four oxen and two dogs accompanied them on their journey to the spirit world. Although grave robbers had plundered the mound of most of its gold and silver, enough treasure remained to reveal that, in the Viking age, had existed two remarkable women.

On this ship, with its elaborately carved prow and stern, topped by rearing koru looking back and looking ahead, the women set sail for the setting sun.

2.

I BEGAN THIS memoir of childhood with my mother.

On this day that I ponder the mystery of a Viking funeral ship, my thoughts return to the other side of the world where the sun is rising, to a boy on the cusp of adulthood and an image of Mount Hikurangi sparkling in the sun's first rays. 'Ah, ko Hikurangi, there and *mark*.'

They also return to a woman known as Julia.

Let me ask you a question: if you were lost and drowning on a dark sea at midnight, and you had one person you could call to come to rescue you, who would that person be?

I suspect most people of faith would call for God. Others would call for a husband or wife or favourite son or daughter. In my case I seriously pondered my dad, and then remembered that he couldn't swim. Once, in London, when I asked the audience the question, a young boy exclaimed, 'You should call for your whale!'

If you evaluate the question long enough, however, you realise that you wouldn't call the people you love the most because you would place them most at risk. Who would want to do that?

With Teria gone, there was only one other person in my life and her commitment to me was unconditional. There was something about her love that was more binding than chains, and a certainty bordering on arrogance in my expectation of it. She would come whether I called or not; all her life she had thrown water over me, blessing me. Even if I was in hell, she would not leave me there.

Of course, I am now mature enough to know that, once the terror has gone, and you have been treading water beyond the time when hope of rescue fails you, you find within yourself the courage to take your salvation into your own hands. You don't need to call anybody.

This is what I found for myself. Indeed, I am now the eldest brother not just of Kararaina, Tāwhi, Viki and Derek, but also of Gay and Neil who came quite a few years after. I am also the father of Jessica and Olivia, and grandfather of James, Ben and Aria. I have become somebody others can call and, if they need me, if you need me, I will come.

Life is not about waiting for someone to come and rescue you, but about finding instead the courage to strike out for that distant shore, wherever it is.

A PLACE OF loss is a place to write from.

My mother became my muse, that old-fashioned idea which enshrines someone, usually female, who becomes your inspiration. My muse, however, was not really my mother. Just as Mum had given herself her own birthdate and created her own origin story, so did I create my muse.

I called her Tiana, and she was entirely an original creation. Given that I have offered you an insight into my imaginative process and the making of a whakapapa, a universe, a creative cosmos, this should not come as a surprise. She was a woman who in her sleep could enter her dreams and swim through them; she was the dream swimmer, born out of my family history, who chanted powerful karakia as she swam. I remember the first time she appeared. I was at the farm. I had turned off the lamp even though there was a little kerosene left, and drifted off to sleep.

I saw a figure swimming through a luminous sea, shafted with sunlight stretching to the end of forever. She was wearing a white gown, her hair was unpinned and flowing around her. Her qualities were sacerdotal; she was anointed by the dawn. Her courage was fashioned from the ancestral women figures of myth and twined from the memory of her struggles against the man from Maori Affairs. I had given her a butcher's knife as a symbolic weapon.

She was not alone. Another woman, or rather, a taniwha companion, the merwoman named Hine Te Ariki, was with her to carry her from one side of the world to the other if ever such a journey was required. Hine Te Ariki was twenty feet tall, with eyes that flashed like pāua and gills and giant flukes, which churned the water.

Surrounded by the sound of swelling, triumphal karakia and tumultuous sea, I heard the dream swimmer say to me: 'When you were born you were the first thing I had ever truly owned.'

I woke up then and lit the wick of the lamp with a match. The light flickered across the walls of my bedroom. I know now that I started to write on that wall as I was waking up, reaching in a daze for the pencil and writing automatically while I remembered what I had dreamt.

My scribblings represented the hieroglyphs of my dream life. Sometimes I could never remember completely what I had dreamt, and often the narrative was disconnected and fragmentary. The words scrawled and swam, going forward and returning, and nobody but myself could ever have deciphered them.

The dream scribblings were my earliest cave drawings. They were like the diminutive figures that can be found at Wadi Sura in the mountainous Gilf Kebir plateau of the Sahara, in south-west Egypt near the Libyan border. The paintings, estimated to have been created during the Neolithic Age, 8000 BC to 800 BC, exist in a cavern long hidden in a valley known as the Cave of Swimmers.

I turned the wick high. The light danced around the room. There was never a curtain on the window; beetles and bats may well have been attracted by the light to look in.

They would have seen a young boy pick up a pencil. His head was filled with stories, with whakapapa, a royal inheritance. The stories brimmed and spilled over as he remembered all the qualities of a history, a life, a stone woman, a honey gatherer, a Monsieur, a whale rider, a Pommie neighbour, a farmer who let our cattle feed from his grass.

Right at the centre of those spiralling stories was a place called Waituhi, where he was his own king, having fresh springs, brine-pits, barren places and fertile.

A painted meeting house, Rongopai, held up the sky.

And then came a thrilling low sibylline voice, belonging to a beloved grandmother questioning a simple nursery rhyme: 'What a silly girl to be afraid of a spider! Why didn't she say kia ora to it?'

The dark room behind his eyes was a universe exploding with stars.

Slowly, he began to write the story of the spider.

Acknowledgements

I WANT TO thank historian Judith Binney, who was one of the inspirations of my life.

There were other historians who maintained a strong commitment to Gisborne and East Coast history. Among them were Jim Holdsworth, Rongowhakaata Halbert, Hetekia Te Kani Te Ua, Te Ao Mamaaka Jones and Kiki Smiler. Alan Ward and my dear friend Anne Salmond are contemporary historians of whom Gisborne and New Zealand can be proud. Of other historians, I also honour Michael King as a close colleague and friend.

The writing of the memoir, a work of creative non-fiction, began while I was teaching at the Manukau Institute of Technology. I had to spend a bit of time at my own archive, and I thank Sue Hurst, Chrissie Tetley and Tracy White of the J.C. Beaglehole Room at Victoria University of Wellington for their assistance as I trolled through my papers. I spent two months at this work, courtesy of Copyright Licensing Ltd and the New Zealand Society of Authors, who awarded me a short-term $5000 research grant associated with the Stout Centre, Victoria University of Wellington. With that I was able to rent a studio, thanks to Te Waimihia Wātene and Kelvin Taylor. The Stout Centre provided an office for the period. For good company, thanks to my longstanding friend Lydia Wevers and other research fellows, including Brad Patterson, Simon Nathan, Richard Hill, Rachel Barrowman and Matt Basso. I also spent time in London writing the memoir and thank the Grange Hotel group for accommodation.

I had a moment of despair when something happened to my iPad. Thank the stars for iCloud and automatic back-up, and to Alicia Rameka, of Yoobee in Manners Street, for recovery of data. My old mate in Gisborne, Ray Sheldrake, helped me with local information.

As always, my grateful thanks to Harriet Allan: it's been a tussle. And, as ever, to Anna Rogers for her usual superb editing eye. You two never let me get away with anything. I should note that the edited draft was passed through a program that picks up inadvertent research duplication; I take full responsibility for any that may have been missed.

Jane McRae provided excellent advice with regard to Māori aspects, particularly relating to the reo. At Jane's recommendation, macrons have been used throughout, according to Te Taura Whiri (the Māori Language Commission) standard.

My thanks to my sisters and brothers for being, well, my sisters and brothers. Thanks also to the great Smiler and Keelan families who have inspired me throughout my life. Please forgive me for any errors or attitudes I have taken in this memoir that you might disagree with. I have done my best.

My cousins Tiopira and Josephine assisted with Smiler family photographs. The ones given by Tiopira came with the following family narrative: 'Nanny Tolo (Pera Punahāmoa) picked up part of the collection after Uncle Win died in 1963 and left it with Aunty Joey (Josephine) in Wellington. When Aunty Joey died in 1975, Mum (Aunty Mary) told Aunty Alice to pick them up, and they arrived in Gisborne at Mum's house, and combined with her collection.' Today the photographs are an identity trail going back to those wonderful families who inhabited all our lives. The other photographs are from Mum's albums.

Finally, to Jane, Jessica, Olivia, the sons-in-law and the grandchildren. And to the dream swimmer, I thought you had gone forever.

WITI IHIMAERA WAS the first Māori to publish both a book of short stories and a novel, and since then has published many notable novels and collections of short stories. *Metro* magazine has described him as 'part oracle, part memoralist; Ihimaera is an inspired voice, weaving many stories together'. He has also written for stage and screen, edited books on the arts and culture, as well as published various works for children. Ihimaera's first book, *Pounamu Pounamu* (1972), has not been out of print in the over forty years since publication. His best-known novel is *The Whale Rider* (1987), which in 2002 was made into a hugely successful film. Witi Ihimaera has also had careers in diplomacy, teaching, theatre, opera, film and television. He has received numerous awards, including the Wattie Book of the Year Award and the Montana Book Award, the inaugural Star of Oceania Award 2009 presented by the University of Hawaii, a laureate award in 2009 from the New Zealand Arts Foundation, the Toi Maori Maui Tiketike Award 2011, and the Premio Ostana International Award, presented to him in Italy in 2010. In 2004 he became a Distinguished Companion of the Order of New Zealand.

Published and Other Works

Short Story Collections

Pounamu Pounamu, 1972 (rewritten 2003)
The New Net Goes Fishing, 1977
Dear Miss Mansfield, 1989
Kingfisher Come Home, 1995
Ihimaera: His Best Stories, 2003
Ask the Posts of the House, 2008
The Thrill of Falling, 2012

Novels and Novella

Tangi, 1973 (expanded as *The Rope of Man*, 2005)
Whanau, 1974 (rewritten as *Whanau II*, 2004)
The Matriarch, 1986 (rewritten 2009)
The Whale Rider, 1987 (rewritten 2002)
Bulibasha, King of the Gypsies, 1994
Nights in the Gardens of Spain, 1995
The Dream Swimmer, 1997
The Uncle's Story, 2000
Sky Dancer, 2003
The Trowenna Sea, 2009
The Parihaka Woman, 2011
White Lies (novella, with film script by Dana Rotberg), 2013

Film Adaptations

Whale Rider (John Barnett, South Pacific Pictures), Associate Producer, 2002
Kawa (Christina Milligan and Nicole Hoey, Cinco Cine Film Productions), adapted from *Nights in the Gardens of Spain*, 2010
White Lies (John Barnett, South Pacific Pictures), adapted from *Medicine Woman*, 2013

Children's Illustrated Books

The Little Kowhai Tree, text, 2002
Whale Rider Picture Book (with Bruce Potter), 2002
The Amazing Adventures of Razza the Rat, text, 2006

Selected Non-fiction Works

Maori, contemporary history, 1975
Into the World of Light, editor (with D.S. Long), 1982
Vision Aotearoa, editor (with Roz Capper), 1994
Te Ao Marama 5-volume Maori Writing, editor (with Haare Williams and Irihapeti Ramsden), 1992–1996
Mataora, The Living Face, editor (with Robert Jahnke, Sandy Adsett and Derek Lardelli), 1997
Land, Sea, Sky (with photographer Holger Leue), 1998
On Top/Down Under (with photographer Sally Tagg), 1998
Growing Up Maori, editor, 1998
Where's Waari?, editor, 2000
Get on the Waka, editor, 2007

Selected Libretti and Texts for Theatre and Television

Waituhi: The Life of the Village, opera libretto, composer Ross Harris, 1984
The Clio Legacy, cantata libretto, composer Dorothy Buchanan, 1991
Tanz Der Schwane, opera libretto, composer Ross Harris, 1993
The Two Taniwha, play, producers Vapi Kupenga and Miriama Evans, 1994
Symphonic Legends, composer Peter Scholes, 1996
Woman Far Walking, play script, 2000
Galileo, opera libretto, composer John Rimmer, 2002
The Wedding, ballet scenario, choreographer Mark Baldwin, composer Gareth Farr, 2006
Whale Rider on Stage, adaptation, Logan Brewer Productions, 2008
Whero's New Net, play, adapted by Albert Belz, 2008
Kaitiaki, orchestral libretto, composer Gareth Farr, 2011
Ihimaera, stage production, producer Charlotte Yates, 2011 (available on CD and DVD)
What Really Happened at Waitangi?, TV documentary, story consultant, producer Robin Scholes, 2011
Sky Dancer, composer Gareth Farr, 2013
Waiata Aroha, song cycle, composer Rod Biss, 2013
His First Ball, adaptation, director Ruth Dudding, 2014
The Whale Rider Puppet Show, adaptation, Tim Bray Productions, 2014